FLEXIBLE BAYESIAN REGRESSION MODELLING

FLEXIBLE BAYESIAN REGRESSION MODELLING

Edited by

YANAN FAN

DAVID NOTT

MICHAEL S. SMITH

JEAN-LUC DORTET-BERNADET

ELSEVIER

ACADEMIC PRESS

An imprint of Elsevier

Academic Press is an imprint of Elsevier
125 London Wall, London EC2Y 5AS, United Kingdom
525 B Street, Suite 1650, San Diego, CA 92101, United States
50 Hampshire Street, 5th Floor, Cambridge, MA 02139, United States
The Boulevard, Langford Lane, Kidlington, Oxford OX5 1GB, United Kingdom

Notices

Knowledge and best practice in this field are constantly changing. As new research and experience broaden our understanding, changes in research methods, professional practices, or medical treatment may become necessary.

Practitioners and researchers must always rely on their own experience and knowledge in evaluating and using any information, methods, compounds, or experiments described herein. In using such information or methods they should be mindful of their own safety and the safety of others, including parties for whom they have a professional responsibility.

To the fullest extent of the law, neither the Publisher nor the authors, contributors, or editors, assume any liability for any injury and/or damage to persons or property as a matter of products liability, negligence or otherwise, or from any use or operation of any methods, products, instructions, or ideas contained in the material herein.

Library of Congress Cataloging-in-Publication Data
A catalog record for this book is available from the Library of Congress

British Library Cataloguing-in-Publication Data
A catalogue record for this book is available from the British Library

ISBN: 978-0-12-815862-3

Publisher: Candice Janco
Acquisition Editor: Candice Janco
Editorial Project Manager: Susan Ikeda
Production Project Manager: Omer Mukthar
Designer: Christian Bilbow

Typeset by VTeX

Contents

Contributors

Taeryon Choi
Korea University, Department of Statistics, Seoul, Republic of Korea

James S. Clark
Duke University, Durham, NC, United States

Erika Cunningham
Duke University, Durham, NC, United States

Maria DeYoreo
The RAND Corporation, 1776 Main St., Santa Monica, CA 90401, United States

J.-L. Dortet-Bernadet
Institut de Recherche Mathématique Avancée, UMR 7501 CNRS, Université de Strasbourg, Strasbourg, France

Y. Fan
School of Mathematics and Statistics, University of New South Wales, Sydney, NSW, Australia

Michele Guindani
University of California, Irvine, Department of Statistics, Brent Hall 2241, Irvine, CA 92697, United States

Maria Kalli
University of Kent, School of Mathematics, Statistics & Actuarial Science, Sibson Building, Parkwood Road, Canterbury, CT2 7FS, United Kingdom

Nadja Klein
Humboldt Universität zu Berlin, School of Business and Economics, Unter den Linden 6, 10099 Berlin, Germany

Thomas Kneib
Georg-August-Universität Göttingen, Faculty of Business and Economic Sciences, Humboldtallee 3, 37073 Göttingen, Germany

Jeong Hwan Kook
Rice University, Department of Statistics, 6100 Main St, Houston, TX 77005, United States

Athanasios Kottas

University of California, Santa Cruz, Department of Statistics, 1156 High Street, Santa Cruz, CA 95064, United States

Peter J. Lenk

University of Michigan, Stephen M. Ross School of Business, Ann Arbor, MI, United States

Yadong Lu

University of California, Irvine, Department of Statistics, Brent Hall 2241, Irvine, CA 92697, United States

Andrew A. Manderson

The University of Western Australia, Department of Mathematics and Statistics, 35 Stirling Highway, Crawley, WA 6009, Australia

Giampiero Marra

University College London, Department of Statistical Science, Gower Street, London WC1E 6BT, United Kingdom

Yinsen Miao

Rice University, Department of Statistics, 6100 Main St, Houston, TX 77005, United States

Kevin Murray

The University of Western Australia, School of Population and Global Health, 35 Stirling Highway, Crawley, WA 6009, Australia

John T. Ormerod

School of Mathematics and Statistics, University of Sydney, Sydney, NSW 2006, Australia

ARC Centre of Excellence for Mathematical & Statistical Frontiers, University of Melbourne, Parkville, VIC 3010, Australia

Rosalba Radice

Cass Business School, City University of London, Faculty of Actuarial Science and Insurance, 106 Bunhill Row, London EC1Y 8TZ, United Kingdom

T. Rodrigues

Departamento de Estatistica, Universidade de Brasilia, Brasília, Brazil

Surya T. Tokdar

Duke University, Durham, NC, United States

Berwin A. Turlach

The University of Western Australia, Department of Mathematics and Statistics, 35 Stirling Highway, Crawley, WA 6009, Australia

Marina Vannucci

Rice University, Department of Statistics, 6100 Main St, Houston, TX 77005, United States

Preface

The 2000s and 2010s have seen huge growth in Bayesian modelling, which now finds application in fields as diverse as engineering, law, medicine, psychology, astronomy, climate science and philosophy. Much of the increase in popularity is due to advances in Bayesian computation, most notably Markov chain Monte Carlo methods. The availability of general and easily applicable simulation-based computational algorithms has made it easier to build more realistic models, involving greater complexity and high dimensionality.

Introductory textbook accounts of Bayesian regression inference often focus on rather inflexible parametric models. When planning this book, we wanted to bring together, in a single volume, a discussion of Bayesian regression methods allowing three types of flexibility: flexibility in the response location, flexibility in the response-covariate relationship, and flexibility in the error distributions. The aim is to produce a collection of works accessible to practitioners, while at the same time detailed enough for interested researchers in Bayesian methods. Software implementing the methods in the book is also available.

Chapters 1 and 2 cover quantile regression. These are methods where inferential interest may lie away from the mean, in noncentral parts of the distribution. Quantile methods do not specify an error model, and are therefore challenging to implement in the Bayesian setting. Chapters 3 and 4 cover regression using Dirichlet process (DP) mixtures to flexibly capture the unknown error distribution. In Chapter 3, DP mixtures are considered in an ordinal regression setting, where the relationship between the covariates and response is modelled flexibly via density regression. In Chapter 4, DP mixtures are used for time series. Chapter 5 extends to regression with multivariate response, using the copula approach to handle mixed binary-continuous responses. Chapters 6 and 7 cover scalable Bayesian modelling using variational Bayesian inference: in Chapter 6, variational inference is described in detail for various spline-based models to flexibly model the covariate-response relationship in the mean. Chapter 7 develops a variational algorithm for count response data, in the presence of variable selection. Finally, Chapters 8 and 9 showcase some of the flexibility of the Bayesian methods when models incorporate shape constraints. The chapters of the book often deal with quite specialised and complex models and data types, but some general themes emerge from the discussion. The reader will obtain an understanding of the basic modelling and computational building blocks which are fundamental to successful new applications of modern and flexible Bayesian regression methods.

Each of the chapters is written in an easy to follow, tutorial style, with the aim to encourage practitioners to take advantage of powerful Bayesian regression methodology. Computer codes are available for each chapter at the website

https://www.elsevier.com/books/flexible-bayesian-regression-modelling/fan/978-0-12-815862-3

Wherever appropriate, the chapters contain instructions on how to use the codes.

We are proud to be able to bring together a book containing the latest developments in flexible Bayesian methods. We warmly thank all the contributors to this project.

Yanan Fan
David Nott
Michael S. Smith
Jean-Luc Dortet-Bernadet

CHAPTER 1

Bayesian quantile regression with the asymmetric Laplace distribution

J.-L. Dortet-Bernadet[a], Y. Fan[b], T. Rodrigues[c]
[a]Institut de Recherche Mathématique Avancée, UMR 7501 CNRS, Université de Strasbourg, Strasbourg, France
[b]School of Mathematics and Statistics, University of New South Wales, Sydney, NSW, Australia
[c]Departamento de Estatistica, Universidade de Brasilia, Brasília, Brazil

Contents

1.1 Introduction

Following the seminal work by Koenker and Bassett [15] quantile regression has been recognised in recent years as a robust statistical procedure that offers a powerful alternative to ordinary mean regression. This type of regression has proven its interest and its effectiveness in many fields where the data contain large outliers or when the response variable has a skewed or multimodal conditional distribution. It has been also successfully applied to regression problems where the interest lies in the noncentral parts of the response distribution, often found in the environmental sciences, medicine, engineering and economics.

Let τ, $0 < \tau < 1$, be a probability value and, for an integer $d \geq 1$, let $\mathcal{X}$ be a bounded subspace of $\mathbb{R}^d$. Let X be a d-dimensional vector of covariates taking values in $\mathcal{X}$. The linear τth quantile regression model specifies the conditional distribution of a real response variable Y given the value $X = \mathbf{x}$

Flexible Bayesian Regression Modelling
https://doi.org/10.1016/B978-0-12-815862-3.00007-X

as

$$Y|\mathbf{x} \sim \beta_\tau^0 + \mathbf{x}'\beta_\tau + \epsilon, \tag{1.1}$$

for some unknown coefficients $\beta_\tau^0 \in \mathbb{R}$ and $\beta_\tau \in \mathbb{R}^d$, and for a noise variable ϵ whose τth conditional quantile is 0, i.e. $\mathbb{P}(\epsilon \leq 0|X = \mathbf{x}) = \tau$. Equivalently, we can write the τth quantile of the conditional distribution of Y given $X = \mathbf{x}$ as $Q_Y(\tau|\mathbf{x}) = \beta_\tau^0 + \mathbf{x}'\beta_\tau$. In the case of a single real covariate x, this linear model (1.1) encompasses the model of the τth quantile regression curve

$$Y|x \sim f_\tau(x) + \epsilon \tag{1.2}$$

when the curve $f_\tau(x)$ is modelled with spline functions of a given degree $P \geq 1$, so that

$$f_\tau(x) = \alpha_0 + \sum_{j=1}^{P} \alpha_j x^j + \sum_{k=1}^{K} \eta_k (x - \gamma_k)_+^P, \tag{1.3}$$

where $z_+ = \max(0, z)$ and γ_k, $k = 1, \ldots, K$, represent the locations of K knot points (see Hastie and Tibshirani [12]). Typically, the degree P is set to 3 here since using cubic splines gives a curve that looks sufficiently smooth to the human eye.

Let $\{(y_i, \mathbf{x_i})\}_{i=1,\ldots,n}$ be n observed values of $(Y, \mathbf{x})$. If the distribution of the noise variable ϵ is left unspecified, then the point estimation of the coefficients β_τ^0 and β_τ, hence the curve $f_\tau(x)$ in the case of model (1.2), is typically carried out by solving the minimisation problem

$$(\hat{\beta}_\tau^0, \hat{\beta}_\tau) = \arg\min_{(\beta_\tau^0, \beta_\tau)} \sum_{i=1}^{n} \rho_\tau(y_i - \beta_\tau^0 - \mathbf{x}_i'\beta_\tau), \tag{1.4}$$

where the function $\rho_\tau(\cdot)$ is given by $\rho_\tau(\epsilon) = \tau\epsilon$, if $\epsilon \geq 0$, and $\rho_\tau(\epsilon) = (\tau - 1)\epsilon$ otherwise (see Koenker and Bassett [15]). This so-called 'check function' $\rho_\tau(\cdot)$ replaces the traditional quadratic loss used for mean regression. In this frequentist semiparametric setting, test procedures are usually based on asymptotic arguments or resampling techniques; see Koenker [14] for details and properties of the approach. Bayesian treatment of quantile regression has long appeared as a challenging task, mainly owing to the need to specify a likelihood. In the 2000s and 2010s, the asymmetric Laplace (AL) error model has emerged as a popular solution to this problem, largely due to its flexibility and simplicity, and the fact that the corresponding maximum likelihood estimate is the solution of the minimisation problem (1.4).

In this chapter, we give an overview of the use of the AL distribution for Bayesian quantile regression. More precisely, we start by briefly presenting this distribution in Section 1.2, and we describe the estimation of the regression parameters with the help of a simple Gibbs sampler, as proposed in Kozumi and Kobayashi [17] or Reed and Yu [23]. Then we focus in some more detail on the quantile curve fitting problem and describe a possible extension of the sampler that allows random knots and knot selection. We illustrate all these points on several examples by using R functions that are publicly available.

In the following sections we discuss two potential problems that arise with the use of the AL error model. Firstly we present the problem of the coverage probabilities that has been tackled recently, for example in Yang et al. [36]. Secondly, since the quantile curves corresponding to several τ levels are fitted separately, they may cross, violating the definition of quantiles. We describe how this problem can be overcome using a simple postprocessing procedure. Note that we do not consider here the use of a likelihood that is capable of simultaneously fitting several quantile curves; this approach is covered by Chapter 2 of this book. Finally we conclude with a short discussion.

1.2 The asymmetric Laplace distribution for quantile regression

The centred AL distribution with scale parameter σ, hereafter denoted $\mathrm{AL}_\tau(0,\sigma)$, has density

$$d_{AL_\tau(0,\sigma)}(\epsilon) \quad = \quad \frac{\tau(1-\tau)}{\sigma}\exp\left\{-\frac{1}{\sigma}\rho_\tau(\epsilon)\right\}, \qquad (1.5)$$

where $\rho_\tau(\cdot)$ is the check-function used in the minimisation problem (1.4). Clearly, for any σ, if we use this AL distribution to model the error ϵ in model (1.1), then the maximum likelihood estimator corresponds to the solution of the minimisation problem (1.4). This motivated for example Yu and Moyeed [38] to use the corresponding likelihood in a Bayesian setting and to estimate the regression parameters $(\beta_\tau^0, \beta_\tau)$ via a random walk Metropolis–Hastings algorithm. They noticed that, on simulations, the resulting estimation is satisfactory even when the data do not arise from the

AL distribution. The good behaviour of this Bayes estimate is studied more theoretically in Sriram et al. [31], who established posterior consistency for the linear quantile regression estimates and gave the rate of convergence in the case of AL distribution misspecification.

1.2.1 A simple and efficient sampler

A desirable feature of the AL distribution is that it can be decomposed as a scale mixture of Normals (Kotz et al. [16]). Let

$$\epsilon \quad = \quad \sigma\frac{1-2\tau}{1-\tau}V+\sigma\sqrt{\frac{2V}{\tau(1-\tau)}}U, \tag{1.6}$$

where V and U are independent, $V\sim\mathcal{E}xp(1)$ and $U\sim\mathcal{N}(0,1)$. Then ϵ follows the $\text{AL}_\tau(0,\sigma)$ distribution. Here $\mathcal{E}xp(\lambda)$ denotes the exponential distribution with mean λ^{-1} and $\mathcal{N}(\mu,\sigma^2)$ denotes the normal distribution with mean μ and variance σ^2. Based on this representation, Kozumi and Kobayashi [17] or Reed and Yu [23] proposed a simple and efficient Gibbs sampler.

In short, the sampler uses data augmentation by introducing a random variable $V_i\sim\mathcal{E}xp(1)$ for each observation $i=1,\ldots,n$, where $V_1,\ldots,V_n$ are independent. If the proper prior $\pi(\beta_\tau^0,\beta_\tau,\sigma)$ is such that

$$\pi(\beta_\tau^0,\beta_\tau,\sigma)=\pi(\beta_\tau^0,\beta_\tau)\pi(\sigma),$$

with $\pi(\beta_\tau^0,\beta_\tau)$ taken as a normal distribution and $\pi(\sigma)$ an inverse-gamma distribution, then the full conditional posterior distributions are known distributions easy to sample from: the full conditional distribution of $(\beta_\tau^0,\beta_\tau)$ is normal, the full conditional distribution of each V_i is generalised inverse Gaussian and the full conditional distribution of σ is inverse gamma. See Kozumi and Kobayashi [17] for more details on these conditional distributions and the corresponding Gibbs sampler. They also provide an extension of the work using double-exponential priors on the regression parameters and to the analysis of Tobit quantile regression. Other extensions of the sampler include quantile binary regression (Benoit and Van den Poel [5]), ordinal quantile regression (Rahman [21] or Alhamzawi [1]) and lasso quantile regression (Alhamzawi et al. [4] or Li et al. [18]). Note also that Tsionas [33] gives an alternative version of the Gibbs sampler, less appealing in practice since each component of the regression vector is updated separately.

The Gibbs sampler described in Kozumi and Kobayashi [17] or Reed and Yu [23] is implemented in several publicly available R packages. We can quote the package Brq (Alhamzawi [2]) or the package bayesQR described in Benoit and Van den Poel [6], along with an overview of the AL distribution for quantile regression. As a first example, we use the package bayesQR here on the famous Immunoglobulin-G data set. This data set, studied in for example Yu and Moyeed [38], contains the serum concentration of immunoglobulin-G (IgG) measured in $n = 298$ preschool children and has been used to search for reference ranges to help diagnose immunodeficiency in infants (Isaacs et al. [13]). More precisely, we consider IgG as the response variable and the age of the children as the predictor. Following previous studies, a quadratic model is used to fit the data due to the expected smooth change of IgG with age. If the data are in the file 'igg.dta', we can proceed as follows to fit the quadratic model for each decile, using chains of length 2000 and a burn-in period of 500, fitting nine equally spaced quantiles from 0.1 to 0.9:

```
> library(bayesQR) # for Bayesian quantile regression with ALD
> library(foreign) # to read .dta files
> IGGdata<-read.dta("igg.dta")
> y<-IGGdata[,1]
> x<-IGGdata[,2]
> out <- bayesQR(y~cbind(x,x^2), quantile=seq(0.1,0.9,by=0.1),
              ndraw=2000, normal.approx=F)
> su<-summary(out, burnin=500)
> su
```

We have used the default, noninformative prior here; this quantity can be specified using the prior function in bayesQR. The summary command produces posterior mean and 95% credible interval estimates for the regression parameters β_τ, for each level $\tau = 0.1, \ldots, 0.9$, and for σ^2. We show below the output for $\tau = 0.1$.

```
#Type of dependent variable: continuous
#Lasso variable selection: no
#Normal approximation of posterior: no
#Estimated quantile:  0.1
#Lower credible bound:  0.025
#Upper credible bound:  0.975
```

```
#Number of burnin draws:  500
#Number of retained draws:  1500

#Summary of the estimated beta:
#                    Bayes Estimate  lower upper
#(Intercept)                  0.898  0.568  1.238
#cbind(x, x^2)x               1.393  1.062  1.680
#cbind(x, x^2)               -0.167 -0.219 -0.107

#Summary of the estimated sigma:
#                    Bayes Estimate  lower upper
#sigma                        0.224  0.205  0.246
#*************************************
```

The raw Markov chain Monte Carlo (MCMC) samples are contained in the output of bayesQR, and typing

```
> out[[1]]$betadraw
> out[[1]]$sigmadraw
```

produces the MCMC sample from the first quantile level $\tau = 0.1$, with the following output in R:

```
> out[[1]]$betadraw
#               [,1]       [,2]        [,3]
#    [1,] 0.03953925 0.9024486 -0.17204285
#    [2,] 0.86363783 0.4834613 -0.07419609
#    [3,] 0.71404299 0.8667774 -0.11435549
#    [4,] 0.62527738 1.2187158 -0.16876779
#    ...


> out[[1]]$sigmadraw
#    [1] 0.2277762 0.2177013 0.2185341 0.2294405 0.2134314  ...
```

These MCMC draws, for instance, are useful for checking MCMC convergence, choosing burn-in period and calculating credible bounds for other quantities of interest. To plot the data and the nine estimated quantile curves we can use

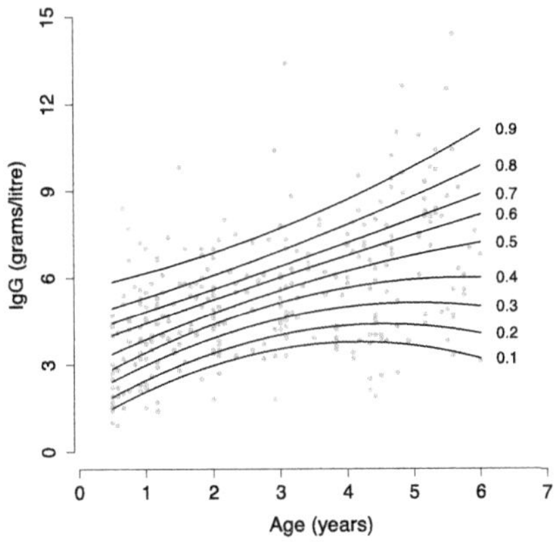

Figure 1.1 Growth chart of serum concentration of immunoglobulin-G for young children. Quantile regression using a quadratic model and bayesQR for $\tau = 0.1, \ldots, 0.9$.

```
> plot(x,y,pch=20,xlab="Age (years)",ylab="IgG")
> for (i in 1:9){
    + beta0<-su[[i]]$betadraw[1]
    + beta1<-su[[i]]$betadraw[2]
    + beta2<-su[[i]]$betadraw[3]
    + estimated<-beta0+beta1*x+beta2*x^2
    + lines(x,estimated)}
```

where the resulting plot is given in Fig. 1.1.

On the whole, for these intermediate τ levels, the quantile lines resulting from this fitted quadratic model appear satisfactory. Nevertheless we will see later that some problems arise when we fit the quantile lines at many levels and at more extreme τ levels.

1.2.2 Quantile curve fitting

As noted in the introduction, the quantile regression curve model (1.2) with spline functions (1.3) can be handled under the framework of linear quantile regression. It is thus tempting to use in this setting the AL error model and to fit the quantile regression curve with the help of the previous Gibbs sampler. Nevertheless, in the curve fitting setting, one also has to consider the appropriate specifications of parameters such as the number and position of the knots.

Chen and Yu [8] provide a Bayesian inference on this model, where the number of knots and their location are automatically selected. Their method relies on a reversible jump Markov chain Monte Carlo (RJMCMC) algorithm which, under the prior specifications they use, needs to compute an approximation of the ratio of marginal likelihoods. For a Bayesian inference using natural cubic splines see Thompson et al. [32]. We present here an alternative method for quantile curve fitting that allows for both random knots and knot selection with a strategy that avoids the use of RJMCMC.

Under the representation (1.3), fitting the curve consists of estimating the number of knots K, the knot locations γ_k, $k=1,\ldots,K$, the corresponding splines coefficients η_k, $k=1,\ldots,K$, and the regression coefficients α_j, $j=0,\ldots,P$. Let K_{max} represent the (known) maximum number of potential knots and let γ_k, $k=1,\ldots,K_{max}$, represent the corresponding knots. The quantile regression curve model (1.2) can be written as the linear model

$$Y = X_\gamma \beta + \varepsilon, \tag{1.7}$$

where $Y=(y_1,\ldots,y_n)'$, $\beta=(\alpha_0,\alpha_1,\ldots,\alpha_P,\eta_1,\ldots,\eta_{K_{max}})'$ and $\varepsilon=(\epsilon_1,\ldots,\epsilon_n)'$. The design matrix X_γ is defined by

$$X_\gamma \quad = \quad (\mathbf{1}_n, \mathbf{x}, \ldots, \mathbf{x}^P, (\mathbf{x}-\mathbf{1}_n\gamma_1)_+^P, \ldots, (\mathbf{x}-\mathbf{1}_n\gamma_{K_{max}})_+^P), \tag{1.8}$$

where $\mathbf{x}=(x_1,\ldots,x_n)'$ and where $\mathbf{1}_n=(1,\ldots,1)'$ denotes the unit vector of size n. Following Fan et al. [10] we adopt an auxiliary variable approach for the spline regression model: we consider $I_1,\ldots,I_{K_{max}}$ some nonoverlapping intervals that are defined on the range of the x_i's, and then we introduce some binary indicator variables z_k, $k=1,\ldots,K_{max}$, such that

$$z_k = \begin{cases} 1, & \text{if there is a knot point } \gamma_k \text{ in the interval } I_k \text{ and } \eta_k \neq 0, \\ 0, & \text{if there is no knot point in the interval } I_k \text{ and } \eta_k = 0. \end{cases}$$

Each interval I_k contains at most one knot with unknown location γ_k. In practice, such intervals can be defined by either using prior information on regions where a knot is suspected or, in the absence of such prior information, an equal partition of the range may be adopted.

We denote by γ the vector $(\gamma_1,\ldots,\gamma_{K_{max}})'$ and by z the vector $(z_1,\ldots,z_{K_{max}})'$. We consider as prior distribution on γ the product of uniform distributions on the intervals I_k, $k=1,\ldots,K_{max}$. Each possible value for γ gives a model of the form (1.7). Let $X_{z,\gamma}$ denote the matrix constructed with the columns of X_γ corresponding to nonzero entries in z, and let $\beta_{z,\gamma}$ denote the vector of corresponding regression coefficients. If we use the scale mixture of normals decomposition (1.6) of the AL distribution, for each $w_i = \sigma V_i$, $i = 1, \dots, n$, if W is the diagonal matrix with entries w_i, then the conditional distribution of Y given W is multivariate normal

$$f(Y|X_{z,\gamma}, \beta_{z,\gamma}, z, \sigma, \gamma, W) = \mathcal{N}\left(X_{z,\gamma}\beta_{z,\gamma} + \frac{(1-2\tau)}{\tau(1-\tau)} W\mathbf{1}_n, \frac{2\sigma}{\tau(1-\tau)} W\right). \tag{1.9}$$

Conditionally on W, we use the following decomposition of the joint prior distribution of the unknown parameters:

$$\pi(\beta_{z,\gamma}, z, \sigma, \gamma | W) = \pi_{\beta_{z,\gamma}}(\beta_{z,\gamma}|z, \sigma, \gamma, W)\pi_\sigma(\sigma)\pi_z(z)\pi_\gamma(\gamma),$$

where we set

$$\pi_{\beta_{z,\gamma}}(\beta_{z,\gamma}|z, \sigma, \gamma, W) = \mathcal{N}\left(0, \frac{2\sigma}{\tau(1-\tau)} c(X'_{z,\gamma} W^{-1} X_{z,\gamma})^{-1}\right). \tag{1.10}$$

This conditional prior for $\beta_{z,\gamma}$, related to g-priors (Zellner [40]), has the advantage of conjugacy in the case of normal errors, in which case the regression and variance parameters can be analytically integrated out. It has been used in the context of variable selection for quantile linear regression in Alhamzawi and Yu [3]. We can use a diffuse hyperprior for the parameter c

$$\pi(c) \propto c^{-2}\exp\{-2n/c\},$$

and use the standard uninformative prior $\pi_\sigma(\sigma) \propto 1/\sigma$ for the variance parameter. Finally, to define the prior distribution for z, we consider the decomposition of this prior given by

$$\pi_z(z) = \pi(z \mid |z|)\pi(|z|),$$

where $|z| = \sum_{k=1}^{K_{max}} z_k$ is the number of nonzero entries in z, i.e. the number of knots that are used in the corresponding model. We use for this term a Poisson distribution with mean λ that is right-truncated at a specified maximum value, L. We assume also that, given this quantity, all possible configurations for z have equal probabilities, so that

$$\pi_z(z) \propto \frac{\lambda^{|z|}}{|z|!} I_{\{|z| \le L\}}.$$

Importantly, under these specifications, the parameters $\beta_{z,\gamma}$ and σ can be integrated out of the full joint posterior distribution $\pi(\beta_{z,\gamma}, z, \sigma, \gamma, W, c|Y)$ and we get

$$\pi(z, \gamma, W, c|Y) \propto \frac{\pi(c)\pi_z(z)\pi_\gamma(\gamma)}{\sqrt{\prod_{i=1}^{n} w_i}(c+1)^{(|z|+P+1)/2}} \times \left\{\frac{\tau(1-\tau)}{4} S_{z,\gamma,W,c}(Y) + \sum_{i=1}^{n} w_i\right\}^{-3n/2}, \quad (1.11)$$

where

$$S_{z,\gamma,W,c}(Y) = Y'_{(W)} W^{-1} Y_{(W)} - \frac{c}{c+1} Y'_{(W)} W^{-1} X_{z,\gamma}(X'_{z,\gamma} W^{-1} X_{z,\gamma})^{-1} X'_{z,\gamma} W^{-1} Y_{(W)}$$

and where

$$Y_{(W)} = Y - \frac{(1-2\tau)}{\tau(1-\tau)} W \mathbf{1}_n.$$

A Gaussian random walk Metropolis–Hastings sampler can be used to study this marginal posterior distribution $\pi(z, \gamma, W, c|Y)$, as detailed in Dortet-Bernadet and Fan [9]. Once MCMC samples $\{(z^{(t)}, \gamma^{(t)}, W^{(t)}, c^{(t)})\}_{t=1,\ldots,T}$ are obtained, it is possible to estimate the curve $f_p(x)$ by a Bayesian model averaging approach. The posterior expectation for β given z, γ, W and c being

$$\mathbb{E}(\beta_{z,\gamma}|z, \gamma, W, Y, c) = \frac{c}{c+1}(X'_{z,\gamma} W^{-1} X_{z,\gamma})^{-1} X'_{z,\gamma} W^{-1} Y_{(W)}, \quad (1.12)$$

an estimate for $f_\tau(x)$ can be obtained by

$$\hat{f}_\tau^{BMA}(x) = \frac{1}{T}\sum_{t=1}^{T} X_{z^t,\gamma^t} \frac{c^{(t)}}{c^{(t)}+1}(X'_{z^t,\gamma^t}(W^t)^{-1} X_{z^t,\gamma^t})^{-1} X'_{z^t,\gamma^t}(W^t)^{-1} Y_{(W^t)}.$$

This method for quantile curve fitting using splines and random knots is implemented as a function called rkquant available at the website accompanying the book,

https://www.elsevier.com/books/
flexible-bayesian-regression-modelling/fan/978-0-12-815862-3

As an example, we use it now on the Global Mean Sea Level Variation data set studied in Nerem et al. [19]. This data set consists of 762 observations of ΔMSL, defined as 'the area-weighted mean of all the sea surface height anomalies measured by the altimeter in a single, 10-day satellite track repeat cycle', dating from 1992 to 2014. We can proceed as follows to fit cubic splines ($P = 3$) for $\tau = 0.5$ using a chain of length 2000 plus 200 of burn-in:

```
> source("codeRKquant.R")  # source the code
> data <- read.table("sl_ns_global.txt", header=T) # read data
> x <- data[,1];y <- data[,2]
> quant05<-rkquant(y,x,tau=0.5,ngibbs=2000,nburnin=200,P=3)
```

Note that it may take some time to run these simulations under the default settings, and to gain speed one can run a much shorter chain with this type of data set and the default settings of the algorithm (for each iteration of the Gibbs sampler many moves for $z^{(t)}$ are done; this can be easily changed by the user). Several other default settings for the algorithm, such as the maximum number of knots or the number of intervals, can also be easily changed in the code. The function stores some output files with the simulated values from the MCMC algorithm. It returns as a list several features of the MCMC output draws. For example, the component $postmean gives the posterior mean of the quantile curve and the components $CIboundInf and $CIboundSup give the lower and upper bounds of the credible intervals, respectively (by default these bounds contain 95% of the posterior mass on the quantile curves, this can also be changed by the user). To plot the estimate of the quantile curve corresponding to $\tau = 0.5$ we can proceed as follows:

```
> plot(x, y, pch=20, bg="gray", col='gray', cex.lab=1.5,
     xlab='Year', ylab=expression(paste(Delta,'MSL (mm)','')))
> lines(quant05$x.sorted,quant05$postmean)
```

To plot the bounds of the credible intervals (we use the sorted values of the covariate given by quant05$x.sorted) we simply add

```
> lines(quant05$x.sorted,quant05$CIboundInf,lty=2)
> lines(quant05$x.sorted,quant05$CIboundSup,lty=2)
```

The resulting plot is given in Fig. 1.2, along with the plot of the three fitted quartile curves corresponding to $\tau = 0.25$, $\tau = 0.5$ and $\tau = 0.75$. Note

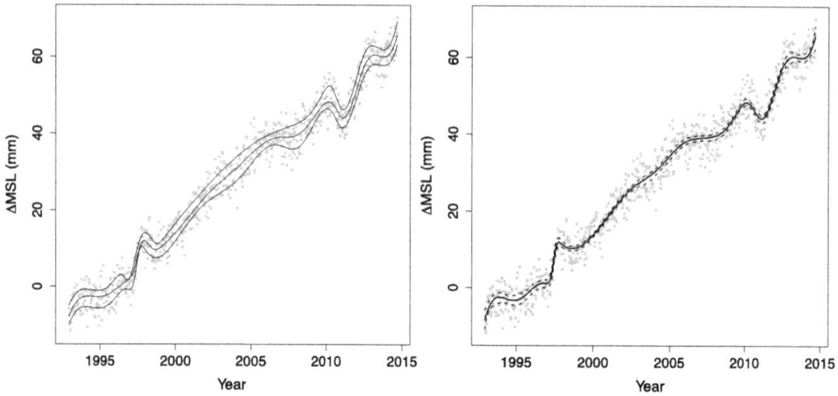

Figure 1.2 Global mean sea level variation. Quantile curve fitting for $\tau = 0.25, 0.5, 0.75$ (left) and quantile curve fitting for $\tau = 0.5$ with confidence intervals (right).

that the period around the years 1997–1998 looks problematic since these curves nearly merge; we will come back to this problem later. Generally, problems with crossing curves manifest when there are fewer data points. Finally note that this code for quantile curve fitting can be easily adapted to the problem of quantile regression with variable selection as in Chen et al. [7]; in this case the terms γ_k do not appear in the standard regression with variable selection.

1.2.3 Additive models

When several potential predictors for the response variable are available, a possible solution to the 'curse of dimensionality' is to use an additive model (Hastie and Tibshirani [12]). In the context of quantile regression, if X is a d-valued vector of covariates and if $\mathbf{x} = (x^1, \ldots, x^d)$, the additive model comes down to model the τth quantile of the conditional distribution of Y given $X = \mathbf{x}$ as the sum

$$f_\tau(\mathbf{x}) = \sum_{j=1}^{d} f_\tau^j(x^j), \tag{1.13}$$

where $f_\tau^1(x^1), \ldots, f_\tau^d(x^d)$ are univariate functions. Several references that study this additive quantile regression model are available, including Yu and Lu [37] which uses a kernel-weighted local linear fitting or Yue and Rue [39] that describes a Bayesian inference either with an MCMC algorithm or using INLA (Rue et al. [30]).

If we use spline functions to model the different curves $f_\tau^1(x^1), \ldots, f_\tau^d(x^d)$, it is still possible to use a linear model of the form (1.7). The only adjustment to make is to now use a design matrix X_γ made up of the columns of the individual design matrices corresponding to (1.8) with a single common intercept term for identifiability. Thus inference on the additive quantile regression model can be performed via the same methodology and algorithm described previously for the single quantile curve fitting problem. This method is implemented as a function called **rkquantAdditive** available at the website of the book.

As an example of real data set that involves additive quantile regression, we revisit the so-called Boston house price data available in the R package MASS. This data set has been originally studied in Harrison and Rubinfeld [11]. The full data set consists of the median value of owner-occupied homes in 506 census tracts in the Boston Standard Metropolitan Statistical Area in 1970 along with 13 sociodemographic variables. This data set has been analysed in many statistical papers, including Opsomer and Ruppert [20], who used an additive model for mean regression, and Yu and Lu [37]. Following these two references, we consider the median values of the owner-occupied homes (in \$1000s) as the dependent variable and four covariates given by

RM = average number of rooms per house in the area,
TAX = full property tax rate (\$/\$10,000),
PTRATIO = pupil/teacher ratio by town school district,
LSTAT = percentage of the population having lower economic status in the area.

As noted in Yu and Lu [37], these data are suitable for a quantile regression analysis since the response is a median price in a given area and the variables RM and LSTAT are highly skewed. More precisely, we consider the additive model where the τth quantile of the conditional distribution of the response is given by

$$\begin{aligned} f_\tau(\mathbf{x}) &= \alpha_0 + f_\tau^1(\mathrm{RM}) + f_\tau^2(\log(\mathrm{TAX})) + f_\tau^3(\mathrm{PTRATIO}) \\ &\quad + f_\tau^4(\log(\mathrm{LSTAT})). \end{aligned}$$

We can proceed as follows to fit cubic splines ($P = 3$) for $\tau = 0.5$ using a chain of length 2000 plus 200 of burn-in:

```
> source("codeRKquantAdd.R") # source the code
> data<-read.table("bostonDat")
> y<-data[,1];X<-data[,2:5]  # X matrix n*d
> quant05<-rkquantAdditive(y,X,0.5,2000,200,3)
```

The default prior settings correspond to $\lambda = 5$ and $L = 8$ for the truncated Poisson prior. For each predictor we set the intervals I_k to be 10 equally sized partition sets over the range of the variable. Excluding the possibility of knots in the first and the last intervals, we get $K_{max} = 8$ for each variable. All these settings can be easily changed in the code. Again, it returns a list of different features of the MCMC simulations. For example, to plot the curve corresponding to the posterior mean for the covariate RM, similar to the function described in the previous subsection we use the component $postmean, now a matrix where each column corresponds to a covariate. We can proceed as follows:

```
> ord<-sort.list(X[,1])  # need to sort the covariate values
> plot(X[ord,1],quant05$postmean[ord,1],type="l",
                              + xlab="RM",ylab="value")
```

To plot the posterior credible intervals we use again the components $CIboundInf and $CIboundSup, now matrices where each column corresponds to a covariate. We can proceed as follows:

```
> lines(X[ord,1],quant05$CIboundInf[ord,1],lty=2)
> lines(X[ord,1],quant05$CIboundSup[ord,1],lty=2)
```

Other quantities of interest are the component $consttermResult, which returns the simulated values for the constant term, and $consttermpost, which returns the corresponding posterior mean. We present in Fig. 1.3 the different estimated curves, along with the posterior credible intervals, for $\tau = 0.05, 0.5, 0.95$ (we do not show here the curves corresponding to $\tau = 0.25$ and $\tau = 0.75$ since they look very similar to the median curves $\tau = 0.5$). Each curve is represented with some data points corresponding to the original data minus the effect of all the other variables and the constant term (so we do not plot on the same graph the curves corresponding to different values of τ). The fact that the values of log(TAX) are not well dispersed over their range and the presence of a few outliers in the data set did not seem to be a problem for this method.

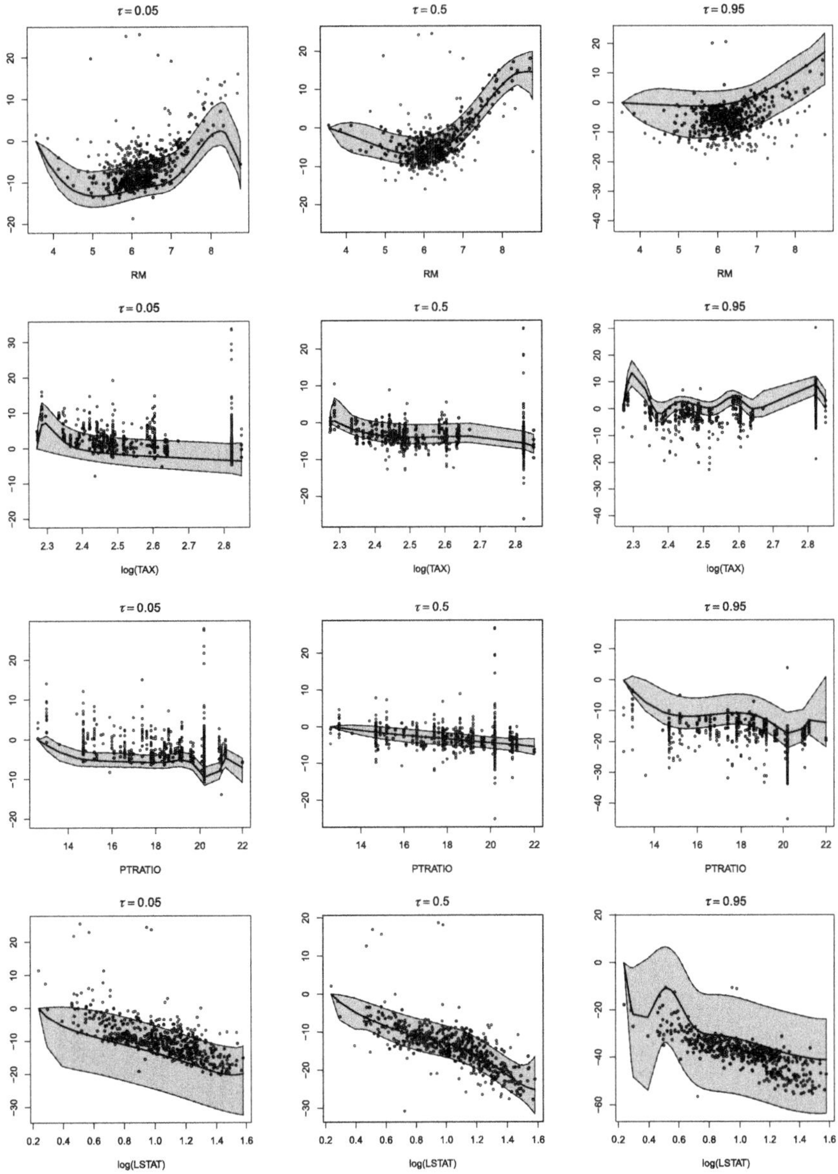

Figure 1.3 Boston housing data set; fitted quantile curves (central solid lines) with 95% posterior credible intervals shaded in grey for $\tau = 0.05, 0.5, 0.95$, $P = 3$, for the four variables that have been considered. On each figure, the data points correspond to the original data minus the effect of all the other variables and the constant term.

The results appear consistent with the results provided in previous analyses cited above. Briefly, by looking at the range of the plotted functions, the variables RM and LSTAT appear as the most important covariates. If the contribution of LSTAT looks similar for the three represented quantiles levels, the contribution of RM looks slightly more important for $\tau = 0.5$ and for $\tau = 0.95$ than for $\tau = 0.05$.

1.3 On coverage probabilities

Several authors have noted that the AL working likelihood provides good parameter estimates even when it is misspecified. Sriram et al. [31] established sufficient conditions for posterior consistency under this likelihood. However, the results do not extend to the validity of the interval estimates given by the posterior. Therefore, while it is fairly common to see the use of posterior intervals obtained from MCMC in the literature, these estimates generally do not provide a good frequentist notion of coverage and often underestimate the variance.

Yang et al. [36] proposed an adjustment to the posterior variance-covariance based on some asymptotic arguments. Let β_τ denote the vector of regression coefficients for the τth quantile level regression and let β_τ^* denote the true value of β_τ. Then, assuming σ is known and a flat prior for β_τ, the posterior density is approximately normal with mean $\hat{\beta}_\tau$ and covariance $\hat{\Sigma} = \sigma D_1^{-1}/n$, where

$$D_1 = \lim_{n\to\infty} \frac{1}{n} \sum_{i=1}^{n} d_{AL_\tau}(x_i^T \beta_\tau^* | x_i) x_i x_i^T.$$

We note that the asymptotic covariance of $n^{1/2}\hat{\beta}_\tau$ is known to be $\tau(1-\tau)D_1^{-1}D_0D_1^{-1}$ (see Koenker [14]). Yang et al. [36] suggest an adjusted posterior variance given by

$$\hat{\Sigma}_{adj} = \tau(1-\tau)\hat{\Sigma}\left(\sum_{i=1}^{n} x_i x_i^T\right)\hat{\Sigma}/\sigma^2. \tag{1.14}$$

Yang et al. [36] acknowledged that the asymptotic theory does not address models with high-dimensional covariates or broader classes of models. Nevertheless, their simulation studies showed that in the partially linear model where the nonlinear component was modelled by B-spline functions, the adjustment remained useful for the parametric coefficients, while for the nonparametric component further investigation is required.

These results suggest that, if we are fitting a standard AL distribution model of Section 1.2.1 under a flat prior for regression coefficient, we can obtain the estimate of $\hat{\Sigma}$, the variance-covariance matrix based on MCMC sample output, and use the adjusted covariance matrix (1.14) for inference, and use an estimate of σ when this is unknown. However, for the models described in Sections 1.2.2 and 1.2.3, these corrections may not be sufficient.

The correction in (1.14) is implemented via bayesQR by calling the normal.approx argument when this is set to be T (default). Recalling the Immunoglobulin example of Section 1.2.1,

```
> library(bayesQR) # for Bayesian quantile regression with ALD
> library(foreign) # to read .dta files
> IGGdata<-read.dta("igg.dta")
> y<-IGGdata[,1]
> x<-IGGdata[,2]
> out <- bayesQR(y~cbind(x,x^2), quantile=seq(0.1,0.9,by=0.1),
              ndraw=2000, normal.approx=T)
> su<-summary(out, burnin=500)
> su
```

Again, the output for $\tau = 0.1$ is shown below, with the adjusted 95% credible interval shown in the columns corresponding to adj.lower and adj.upper.

```
#Type of dependent variable: continuous
#Lasso variable selection: no
#Normal approximation of posterior: yes
#Estimated quantile:  0.1
#Lower credible bound:  0.025
#Upper credible bound:  0.975
#Number of burnin draws:  500
#Number of retained draws:  1500

#Summary of the estimated beta:
               Bayes Estimate   lower   upper adj.lower adj.upper
#(Intercept)            0.875  0.0602  1.5930    -1.098     2.847
#cbind(x, x^2)x         1.346  0.6289  2.0582    -0.915     3.607
#cbind(x, x^2)         -0.157 -0.2822 -0.0306    -0.613     0.299
#*****************************************************
```

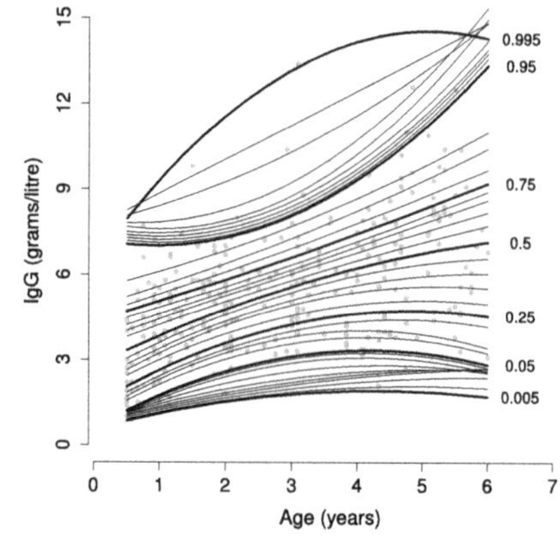

Figure 1.4 Growth chart of serum concentration of immunoglobulin-G for young children. Quantile regression using a quadratic model and bayesQR for several values of τ.

1.4 Postprocessing for multiple fittings

Consider for example Fig. 1.4, which gives the results from the fitting at many quantile levels $\tau = 0.005, 0.01, \ldots, 0.995$. For ease of visualisation, fewer levels are plotted from $\tau = 0.05$ to $\tau = 0.95$ (step size equals 0.05). The quantile lines resulting from this quadratic model appear satisfactory for intermediate τ levels, but they are problematic at more extreme levels: for closely spaced values of τ, the estimated curves can be seen to be very different, which is not realistic, and this leads in some cases to the quantiles crossings, which violates the definition of quantiles. Again, the crossing phenomenon is more severe in the tails of the distribution where data are scarce.

Rodrigues and Fan [29] proposed a strategy to postprocess MCMC samples obtained using a standard AL likelihood, as those described in the previous sections, to correct crossings. Suppose we have obtained posterior estimates via MCMC for quantile levels $\tau_j, j = 1, \ldots, J$, using the AL distributed error (1.5) in the regression models of the form of either (1.1) or (1.3). For the τ_jth conditional quantile under the AL model $d_{AL_{\tau_j}}$, let $Q^{(t)}(\tau_j|x, d_{AL_{\tau_j}})$, or in short $Q^{(t)}(\tau_j|x, \tau = \tau_j), t = 1, ..., T$, denote the tth posterior sample of the quantile estimate given by MCMC. Thus, the τ_jth quantile point estimate for a given value of x is given by $\widehat{Q}_s(\tau_j|x) = \frac{1}{T}\sum_{t=1}^{T} Q^{(t)}(\tau_j|x, \tau = \tau_j)$, where the index s denotes the standard estimate from fitting the AL model at τ_j.

For each quantile fitted using $d_{AL_{\tau_j}}$, we can also find induced quantiles at any other value $\tau \neq \tau_j$, where the τth quantile can be obtained directly from the quantile function of the fitted model at τ_j,

$$Q^{(t)}(\tau|x, \tau = \tau_j) = \begin{cases} \mu^{(t)} + \dfrac{\sigma^{(t)}}{1-\tau_j} \log\left(\dfrac{\tau}{\tau_j}\right), & \text{if } 0 \leq \tau \leq \tau_j, \\ \mu^{(t)} - \dfrac{\sigma^{(t)}}{\tau_j} \log\left(\dfrac{1-\tau}{1-\tau_j}\right), & \text{if } \tau_j \leq \tau \leq 1, \end{cases} \tag{1.15}$$

where $\mu^{(t)}$ and $\sigma^{(t)}$ denote the tth MCMC estimate of the mean and σ parameters. Thus, for each quantile level of interest $\tau_j = 1, \ldots, J$, we can obtain $(J-1) \times T$ additional posterior samples.

A smoother noncrossing quantile estimate can then be obtained by borrowing strength from these induced samples using Gaussian process regression on all $J \times T$ MCMC posterior samples [22],

$$Q^{(t)}(\tau_j|x, \tau = \tau_1, \ldots \tau_J) = g(\tau) + \epsilon, \text{ with } g(\tau) \sim \mathcal{GP}(0, K), \ \epsilon \sim \mathcal{N}(0, \Sigma), \tag{1.16}$$

where Σ is a $J \times T, J \times T$ diagonal covariance matrix whose diagonal entries are the posterior variances of the corresponding $Q^{(t)}(\tau|x, \tau')$. For the kernel K of the same dimension, we use the squared exponential kernel, and covariance matrix entries between induced quantiles from any two auxiliary models are given by

$$k(\tau, \tau') = \sigma_k^2 \exp\left\{-\frac{1}{2b^2}(\tau - \tau')^2\right\}, \tag{1.17}$$

where b is the bandwidth and σ_k^2 is a variance hyperparameter of the prior set to be around $\sigma_k^2 = 100$.

The final τth quantile estimate takes the form of an adjusted posterior mean from the standard, and it is given by

$$\widehat{Q}_a(\tau|x) = \sum_{j=1}^{J} \sum_{t=1}^{T} w_j Q^{(t)}(\tau|x, \tau_j),$$

where w_j is an element of the row vector of weights $W = K(\cdot, \tau)^{\top}(K + \Sigma)^{-1}$ and $K(\cdot, \tau)$ is the τ column of the covariance matrix. Therefore the adjusted quantiles are just a weighted sum of the induced quantiles and can be guaranteed to be noncrossing if the weights are equal or $b \to \infty$.

Table 1.1 Postprocessing procedure to estimate quantiles at $\tau = \tau_1, \ldots, \tau_J$.

1. Fit J separate standard models d_{AL_τ}, $\tau = \tau_1, \ldots, \tau_J$ (Eq. (1.1) or (1.3)).
2. Calculate induced quantile posterior means $\widehat{Q}_s(\tau|x, \tau')$ for all x and $\tau = \tau_1, \ldots, \tau_J$ (Eq. (1.18)).
3. Initialise $b \approx 0$ and while quantile estimates cross, increase b and calculate regression-adjusted quantile estimates (Eq. (1.19)) for every x and $\tau = \tau_1, \ldots, \tau_J$.

It was further noted that working directly with the posterior means of the induced quantiles,

$$\widehat{Q}_s(\tau|x, \tau') = \frac{1}{T}\sum_{t=1}^{T} Q^{(t)}(\tau|x, \tau'), \tag{1.18}$$

rather than with the T MCMC samples, would simplify calculation, resulting in the adjusted quantile estimate of the form

$$\widehat{Q}_a(\tau|x) = \sum_{j=1}^{J} w'_j \widehat{Q}_s(\tau|x, \tau_j), \tag{1.19}$$

where $W' = K'(\cdot, \tau)^{\top}(K' + \Sigma')^{-1}$, with W' and K' now of dimension $J \times J$.

The variance of the adjusted quantiles is given by

$$\sigma_*^2 = \sigma'^2 + \sigma^2(\tau|x, \tau),$$

where $\sigma'^2 = k'(\tau, \tau) - W'K'(\cdot, \tau)$, and vanishes to zero with rate $1/T$. This means that the variance of the adjusted estimator is the same as the variance of the standard estimator as T increases. The postprocessing procedure described above is summarised in Table 1.1.

We return to the serum concentration of immunoglobulin-G (IgG) data, fitted with quadratic quantile regression with the bayesQR package in Section 1.2. Recall the data are in the file 'igg.dta'. The R source file GPreg.R (also available at the website accompanying the book) can be used to fit the two-stage procedure. In the first stage, the function gpqr calls bayesQR to fit a quadratic model for a sequence of quantiles, and in the second stage gpqr postprocess the output from bayesQR. We use chains of length 5000 and a burn-in period of 500, 197 quantiles from 0.01 to 0.99 by 0.005:

```
> source("GPreg.R") # source the code
> library(foreign) # to read .dta files
> IGGdata<-read.dta("igg.dta")
> y<-IGGdata[,1]
> x<-IGGdata[,2]
> x.data <- as.data.frame(cbind((x), (x^2)))

> nmc=5000 # length of MCMC chain
> burn=500 # discard burn in
> keep=1   # every kth iteration to keep
> gridtau=seq(0.01, 0.99, by=0.005)
> prior=prior(y~x+I(x^2), beta0=rep(0, 3), V0=diag(3)*10e8)

> out=gpqr(t(y), t(x.data), gridtau, nmcmc=nmc,
              burnmcmc=burn, keep=keep, prior)
```

The gpqr function requires input data y and covariates in a data frame format. Also required is the grid of quantile levels, MCMC specification, the prior distribution. By default, the program works for nonlinear regression. In the case of linear regression, an approximation is used (see Rodrigues and Fan [29]) and we need to set the linear=T argument. The function outputs quantile and regression coefficients estimates before and after post-processing, as well as the corresponding confidence interval estimates.

The left panel of Fig. 1.5 is plotted using the output from gpqr. The rows of the output initial.quant correspond to separate quantile levels, and the columns correspond to the estimated quantile at each value of the covariate.

```
> print(out$initial.quant[1:5,], digits=3)
#      [,1]    [,2]    [,3]    [,4]    [,5]    [,6]    [,7]   ...
#[1,] -0.0619 -0.0619 -0.0619 -0.0619 -0.0619 -0.0619 -0.0619 ...
#[2,]  0.4583  0.4583  0.4583  0.4583  0.4583  0.4583  0.4583 ...
#[3,]  0.6275  0.6275  0.6275  0.6275  0.6275  0.6275  0.6275 ...
#[4,]  0.7916  0.7916  0.7916  0.7916  0.7916  0.7916  0.7916 ...
#[5,]  0.9126  0.9126  0.9126  0.9126  0.9126  0.9126  0.9126 ...
```

Similarly, the right panel of Fig. 1.5 is plotted using the output quant.final.mean, shown below:

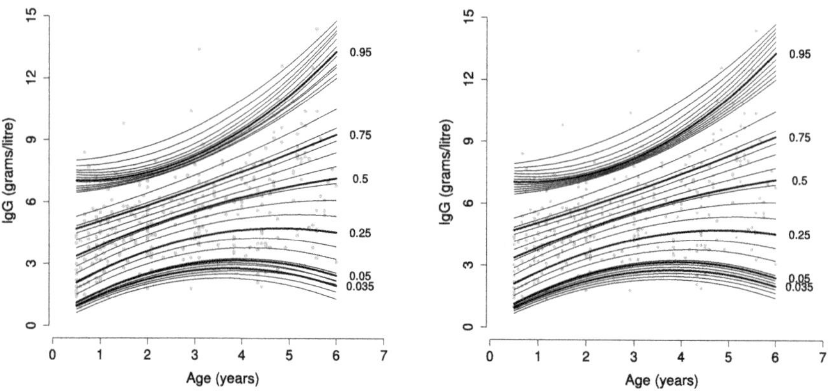

Figure 1.5 Growth chart of serum concentration of immunoglobulin-G for young children, using bayesQR for the initial quantile estimates (left) and gpqr for postprocessing (right).

```
> print(out$quant.final.mean[1:5,], digits=3)
#       [,1]    [,2]    [,3]    [,4]    [,5]    [,6]    [,7]   ...
#[1,] -0.0216 -0.0216 -0.0216 -0.0216 -0.0216 -0.0216 -0.0216  ...
#[2,]  0.4261  0.4261  0.4261  0.4261  0.4261  0.4261  0.4261  ...
#[3,]  0.6678  0.6678  0.6678  0.6678  0.6678  0.6678  0.6678  ...
#[4,]  0.7948  0.7948  0.7948  0.7948  0.7948  0.7948  0.7948  ...
#[5,]  0.8784  0.8784  0.8784  0.8784  0.8784  0.8784  0.8784  ...
```

The figure in the left panel of Fig. 1.5 demonstrates how the quantiles can cross; this is particularly evident in the higher and lower quantiles. Crossing also appears to be more severe where curves change more drastically; see for instance around age 2. The right panel of Fig. 1.5 shows the adjusted quantiles, which constrains the neighbouring quantiles to be similar and produces fitted quantiles which changes more gradually as a function of the quantile level. In other words, postprocessing quantiles have the effect of producing more smoothly changing quantiles, which is more desirable.

1.5 Final remarks and conclusion

In this chapter, we have provided a detailed description of fitting Bayesian quantile regression using the AL distribution as the error distribution. We have highlighted some potential pitfalls with the use of this 'misspecified' error distribution, and provided some solutions. While these are not perfect, the AL working likelihood remains attractive due to its simplicity and computational efficiency, while still providing reasonable estimates. More advanced Bayesian methods fit multiple quantiles simultaneously, which can provide more efficient estimation due to the borrowing of information between neighbouring quantiles; see for example Reich et al. [25], Reich and Smith [26] and Yang and Tokdar [35], who directly model the quantile coefficients as a function of τ; Yang and He [34], who used an empirical likelihood approach as a working likelihood; Rodrigues et al. [27] and Rodrigues et al. [28], who used a Bayesian nonparametric model for the error distribution; and finally in the frequentist setting, Reich et al. [24], who provided noncrossing fittings of multiple quantiles, using an asymptotic argument to derive the confidence intervals.

References

[1] R. Alhamzawi, Bayesian model selection in ordinal quantile regression, Computational Statistics and Data Analysis 103 (C) (2016) 68–78, https://doi.org/10.1016/j.csda.2016.04.014.

[2] R. Alhamzawi, Brq: An R Package for Bayesian Quantile Regression, Working Paper, 2018.

[3] R. Alhamzawi, K. Yu, Conjugate priors and variable selection for Bayesian quantile regression, Computational Statistics and Data Analysis 64 (2013) 209–219, http://www.sciencedirect.com/science/article/pii/S0167947312000345.

[4] R. Alhamzawi, K. Yu, D.F. Benoit, Bayesian adaptive Lasso quantile regression, Statistical Modelling 12 (3) (2012) 279–297, https://doi.org/10.1177/1471082X1101200304.

[5] D.F. Benoit, D. Van den Poel, Binary quantile regression: a Bayesian approach based on the asymmetric Laplace distribution, Journal of Applied Econometrics 27 (7) (2012) 1174–1188, https://onlinelibrary.wiley.com/doi/abs/10.1002/jae.1216.

[6] D.F. Benoit, D. Van den Poel, bayesQR: a Bayesian approach to quantile regression, Journal of Statistical Software 76 (7) (2017) 1–32.

[7] C.W.S. Chen, D.B. Dunson, C. Reed, K. Yu, Bayesian variable selection in quantile regression, Statistics and its Interface 6 (2) (2013) 261–274.

[8] C. Chen, K. Yu, Automatic Bayesian quantile regression curve fitting, Statistics and Computing 19 (2009) 271–281, https://doi.org/10.1007/s11222-008-9091-x.

[9] J.-L. Dortet-Bernadet, Y. Fan, On Bayesian quantile regression curve fitting via auxiliary variables, arXiv:1202.5883v1 [stat.ME], 2012.

[10] Y. Fan, J.-L. Dortet-Bernadet, S.A. Sisson, On Bayesian curve fitting via auxiliary variables, Journal of Computational and Graphical Statistics 19 (3) (2010) 626–644, https://doi.org/10.1198/jcgs.2010.08178.

[11] D.J. Harrison, D.L. Rubinfeld, Hedonic housing prices and the demand for clean air, Journal of Environmental Economics and Management 5 (1) (1978) 81–102.

[12] T.J. Hastie, R.J. Tibshirani, Generalised Additive Models, Chapman and Hall, London, 1990.

[13] D. Isaacs, D.G. Altman, C.E. Tidmarsh, H.B. Valman, A.D.B. Webster, Serum immunoglobulin concentration in preschool children measured by laser nephelometry: reference ranges for IgG, IgA, IgM, Journal of Clinical Pathology 36 (1983) 1193–1196.
[14] R. Koenker, Quantile Regression, Econometric Society Monographs, vol. 38, Cambridge University Press, Cambridge, 2005.
[15] R. Koenker, Gilbert J. Bassett, Regression quantiles, Econometrica 46 (1) (1978) 33–50, http://www.jstor.org/stable/1913643.
[16] S. Kotz, T. Kozubowski, K. Podgorski, The Laplace Distribution and Generalizations, 2001.
[17] H. Kozumi, G. Kobayashi, Gibbs sampling methods for Bayesian quantile regression, Journal of Statistical Computation and Simulation 81 (11) (2011) 1565–1578.
[18] Q. Li, R. Xi, N. Lin, Bayesian regularized quantile regression, Bayesian Analysis 5 (3) (2010) 533–556, https://doi.org/10.1214/10-BA521.
[19] R.S. Nerem, D.P. Chambers, C. Choe, G.T. Mitchum, Estimating mean sea level change from the TOPEX and Jason altimeter missions, Marine Geodesy 33 (S1) (2010) 435–446.
[20] J.D. Opsomer, D. Ruppert, A fully automated bandwidth selection method for fitting additive models, Journal of the American Statistical Association 93 (442) (1998) 605–619.
[21] M.A. Rahman, Bayesian quantile regression for ordinal models, Bayesian Analysis 11 (2016) 1–24.
[22] C.E. Rasmussen, C.K.I. Williams, Gaussian Processes for Machine Learning, MIT Press, 2006.
[23] C. Reed, K. Yu, An Efficient Gibbs Sampler for Bayesian Quantile Regression, Technical report, Department of Mathematical Sciences, Brunel University, 2009.
[24] B.J. Reich, H.D. Bondell, H.J. Wang, Flexible Bayesian quantile regression for independent and clustered data, Biostatistics 11 (2008) 337–352.
[25] B.J. Reich, M. Fuentes, D.B. Dunson, Bayesian spatial quantile regression, Journal of the American Statistical Association 106 (493) (2011) 6–20.
[26] B.J. Reich, L.B. Smith, Bayesian quantile regression for censored data, Biometrics 69 (2013) 651–660.
[27] T. Rodrigues, J.-L. Dortet-Bernadet, Y. Fan, Pyramid quantile regression, Journal of Computational and Graphical Statistics (2019), https://doi.org/10.1080/10618600.2019.1575225.
[28] T. Rodrigues, J.-L. Dortet-Bernadet, Y. Fan, Simultaneous fitting of Bayesian penalised quantile splines, Computational Statistics and Data Analysis 134 (2019) 93–109.
[29] T. Rodrigues, Y. Fan, Regression adjustment for noncrossing Bayesian quantile regression, Journal of Computational and Graphical Statistics 26 (2) (2017) 275–284.
[30] H. Rue, S. Martino, N. Chopin, Approximate Bayesian inference for latent Gaussian models by using integrated nested Laplace approximations, Journal of the Royal Statistical Society, Series B 71 (2009) 319–392.
[31] K. Sriram, R. Ramamoorthi, P. Ghosh, Posterior consistency of Bayesian quantile regression based on the misspecified asymmetric Laplace density, Bayesian Analysis 8 (2) (2013) 479–504, https://doi.org/10.1214/13-BA817.
[32] P. Thompson, Y. Cai, R. Moyeed, D. Reeve, J. Stander, Bayesian nonparametric quantile regression using splines, Computational Statistics and Data Analysis 54 (4) (2010) 1138–1150.

[33] E. Tsionas, Bayesian quantile inference, Journal of Statistical Computation and Simulation 73 (2003) 659–674.
[34] Y. Yang, X. He, Bayesian empirical likelihood for quantile regression, Annals of Statistics 40 (2) (2012) 1102–1131.
[35] Y. Yang, S. Tokdar, Joint estimation of quantile planes over arbitrary predictor spaces, Journal of the American Statistical Association 112 (519) (2017) 1101–1120.
[36] Y. Yang, H.J. Wang, X. He, Posterior inference in Bayesian quantile regression with asymmetric Laplace likelihood, International Statistical Review 84 (3) (2016) 327–344, https://onlinelibrary.wiley.com/doi/abs/10.1111/insr.12114.
[37] K. Yu, Z. Lu, Local linear additive quantile regression, Scandinavian Journal of Statistics 31 (3) (2004) 333–346.
[38] K. Yu, R.A. Moyeed, Bayesian quantile regression, Statistics and Probability Letters 54 (4) (2001) 437–447, https://doi.org/10.1016/S0167-7152(01)00124-9.
[39] Y.R. Yue, H. Rue, Bayesian inference for additive mixed quantile regression models, Computational Statistics and Data Analysis 55 (1) (2011) 84–96, http://www.sciencedirect.com/science/article/B6V8V-504BSVR-2/2/6a3cc16d399b3bbc4097f1a1e3413b13.
[40] A. Zellner, On assessing prior distributions and Bayesian regression analysis with g-prior distributions, in: Bayesian Inference and Decision Techniques, in: Stud. Bayesian Econometrics Statist., vol. 6, North-Holland, Amsterdam, 1986, pp. 233–243.

CHAPTER 2

A vignette on model-based quantile regression: analysing excess zero response

Erika Cunningham, Surya T. Tokdar, James S. Clark
Duke University, Durham, NC, United States

Contents

Flexible Bayesian Regression Modelling
https://doi.org/10.1016/B978-0-12-815862-3.00008-1

2.1 Introduction

At the end of the 1970s, Roger Koenker and Gib Bassett showed how to formalise statistical inference using quantile regression [11]. Today quantile regression is widely recognised as a fundamental statistical tool for analysing complex predictor–response relationships, with a growing list of applications in ecology, economics, education, public health, climatology, and so on [5,8,6,1]. In quantile regression, one replaces the standard regression equation of the mean $E[Y \mid X] = \beta_0 + X^T\beta$ with an equation for a quantile $Q_Y(\tau \mid X) = \beta_{0\tau} + X^T\beta_\tau$, where $\tau \in (0, 1)$ is a quantile level of interest and $Q(\tau)$ denotes the 100τth percentile. A choice of $\tau = 0.5$ results in the familiar median regression, a robust alternative to mean regression when one suspects the response distribution to be heavy-tailed. But the real strength of quantile regression lies in the possibility of analysing any quantile level of interest and, perhaps more importantly, contrasting many such analyses against each other with fascinating consequences.

This strength of quantile regression has also been its liability. Most modern scientific applications of quantile regression involve a synthesis of estimates obtained at several quantile levels. Estimates and P-values are pooled together to build a composite picture of how predictors influence the response and to analyse how this influence varies from the centre of the response distribution to its tails. But such a synthesis is flawed! The composite picture is not based on a single statistical model of the data. Instead, for each single quantile level in the ensemble, a new model has been fitted, without sharing any information with models fitted at the other τ-values. It is entirely possible that the quantile lines estimated at different quantile levels cross each other, thus violating basic laws of probability. Additionally, due to a lack of information borrowing, estimated standard errors and P-values may fluctuate wildly as functions of τ [17]. This, at best, creates confusion and, at worst, may encourage selective reporting!

A composite quantile regression analysis can be formalised with the simultaneous equation

$$Q_Y(\tau \mid X) = \beta_0(\tau) + X^T\beta(\tau), \quad \tau \in (0, 1), \tag{2.1}$$

where $\beta_0(\tau)$ and $\beta(\tau) = (\beta_1(\tau), \ldots, \beta_p(\tau))^T$ are unknown intercept and slope curves. Because quantiles are linearly ordered in their levels, estimation of β_0 and β must be carried out under the 'noncrossing' constraint, i.e., $\beta_0(\tau_1) + x^T\beta(\tau_1) < \beta_0(\tau_2) + x^T\beta(\tau_2)$ for every $0 < \tau_1 < \tau_2 < 1$ and every $x \in \mathcal{X}$, where $\mathcal{X}$ is the domain of the predictor vector X. A largely under-appreciated, simple observation is that the simultaneous quantile regression equations and the noncrossing constraint together offer a fully generative probability model for the response

$$Y = \beta_0(U) + X^T\beta(U), \quad U \mid X \sim Unif(0, 1), \tag{2.2}$$

opening up the possibility of obtaining proper statistical inference on the intercept and slope curves by means of a joint analysis.

Yang and Tokdar [18] offer an estimation framework for the joint quantile regression model (2.2), subject to the noncrossing constraint, by introducing a bijective map of the intercept and slope curves to a new parameter ensemble consisting of scalars, vectors and curves, all but one of which are constraint-free. The likelihood score, as a function of the new parameter ensemble, can be efficiently computed through numerical approximation methods. Parameter estimation can then proceed according to either a penalised likelihood or a Bayesian approach. An instance of the latter, where curve-valued parameters are assigned Gaussian process priors, is further investigated by Yang and Tokdar [18], who establish that the resulting estimation method is consistent and robust to moderate amounts of model misspecification.

To the best of our knowledge, Yang and Tokdar [18] provide the only estimation framework that supports quantile regression as a model-based inference and prediction technique in its full generality. Their reparameterisation technique applies to any predictor dimension and to any arbitrarily shaped predictor domain $\mathcal{X}$ that is convex and bounded. Both issues have proven major vexing points to the earlier attempts at a joint quantile regression analysis, e.g. [10,7,4,14,17,9].

In this chapter we demonstrate that the joint quantile regression method of Yang and Tokdar [18], as implemented in the R package[1] `qrjoint`, offers a comprehensive, model-based regression analysis toolbox. We demonstrate how to fit models, interpret their coefficients, improve and compare models and obtain predictions under the joint quantile regression setup. Taking this modelling one step further, we show how utilising the censored-data options built into the `qrjoint` package can yield an interpretable yet distributionally flexible model for nonnegative, continuous data with excess zeroes. This latter extension fully exploits the generative model interpretation (2.2) of joint quantile regression.

[1] https://CRAN.R-project.org/package=qrjoint.

2.2 Excess zero regression analysis

Zero inflation, or the frequent occurrence of zeroes, is common in ecological data. For instance, when counting the number of species in a region, some regions may not have any of the target species, resulting in 'zero' records. Another example, one that will serve as case study here, involves measuring the basal area of trees within a site. When trees are present, basal area is measured as a continuous, positive number, but when trees are not present, a zero is recorded.

Tobit regression [15] is commonly used to model censored data but can also be used to model data with excess boundary zeroes. To do so, it uses a latent construct, namely, $y_i^* = \beta_0 + \beta x_i + \epsilon_i$, $\epsilon_i \sim N(0, \sigma^2)$, with observables $y_i = max\left\{y_i^*, 0\right\}$. Under this assumption of normality, the mean $\beta_0 + X\beta$ and variance σ^2 fully specify the response distribution. If the latent Tobit model is framed in terms of a joint quantile regression it would be written as $Q_{Y*}(\tau|X) = \beta_0(\tau) + X\beta$, where $\beta_0(\tau) = \sigma\Phi^{-1}(\tau)$. That is, the normality is captured in the τ-functional intercept by the normal inverse CDF, and all remaining variability in the response quantiles is explained by τ-constant slopes and the design matrix X.

Joint quantile regression is also capable of both capturing the probability of atomic zero-measurements and modelling the remaining positive, continuous response distribution. Like the Tobit model, it captures the zeroes via a censored-data or latent-truth construct; however, unlike Tobit, it is not limited by an assumption of normality. In fact, it makes no assumption about the distributional form of the response distribution and has only two other modelling assumptions: (1) data can be explained as linear combinations of covariates expressed in the design matrix X, which incorporates any desired interactions or nonlinearities (e.g. via splines); and (2) observations are independent of each other.

Other quantile regression methods [13,12] are capable of distribution-free estimation in the presence of excess zeroes; however, these other methods estimate regression quantiles independently and, lacking a comprehensive model specification to capture dependence between regression quantiles, they only make adjustments for and do not actually model the probability of atomic zero.

We demonstrate how to use the `qrjoint` package on tree basal area data from the U.S. Forest Service. Tobit regression models are included, both as a stepping stone to understanding censored joint quantile regression and as a foil to the more flexible joint quantile regression.

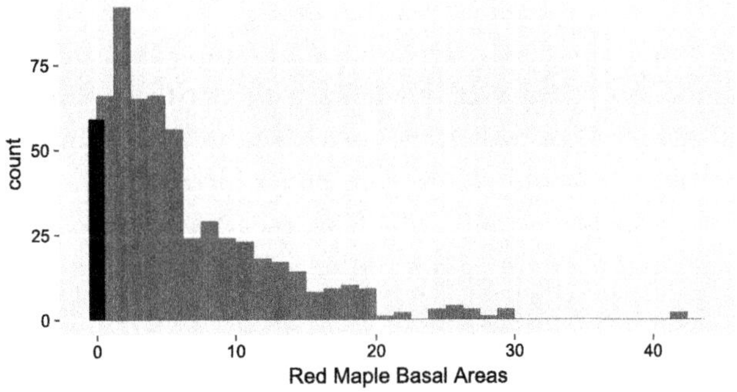

Figure 2.1 Red maple basal areas for 608 sites in Massachusetts, Connecticut and Rhode Island. Those with no red maple trees, i.e. baRedMaple of zero, are displayed in black.

2.3 Case study data and objective

The U.S. Forest Service tracks the biomass of hundreds of species of trees on thousands of plots of land throughout the United States. We consider a subset of data from the Forest Inventory Analysis composed of 608 unmanaged and forested sites in Massachusetts, Connecticut and Rhode Island.[2]

```
library(qrjoint)   # For joint quantile regression fitting
library(ggplot2)   # For plotting results
library(gridExtra) # For arranging side-by-side plots
data(redmaple)
dat <- redmaple
```

While tree counts and cumulative basal area (ft^2/acre) are recorded on hundreds of species, we focus on basal area for a single species, the red maple tree (*Acer rubrum*). Red maple is common among the 608 sites with 59 sites (9.7%) having no red maple trees (i.e. basal area equals zero) and the remaining sites having a median basal area of 4.7 ft^2/acre. A histogram of all basal areas from the sample is shown in Fig. 2.1.

In addition to basal area, several covariates are available for each site:

- `elev`. Elevation of site, measured in feet.
- `slope`. Slope of site, measured in degrees.
- `aspect`. Aspect of site, measured in degrees proceeding from North clockwise around a compass. For sites with zero or near-zero slopes, aspect is recorded as 0. North is recorded as 360.

[2] http://apps.fs.fed.us/fiadb-downloads/datamart.html.

- `region`. EPA Level-III geographical region.

The first three covariates are continuous measures, and the fourth, `region`, is categorical. We desire to build a model to understand the relationships between these explanatory variables and red maple basal areas. More specifically, we would like to gain direct inference not only on how the predictors affect the mean or median response but also on how they affect the upper and lower quantiles of the response distribution.

2.4 Fitting single covariate basal area models

For pedagogical reasons, we start with a model that uses a single covariate, elevation (`elev`), to predict red maple basal area and compare to the more widely recognised Tobit model. R's `AER` package is used to obtain maximum likelihood estimates for the Tobit model. Note that this `tobit` function sets the left limit of the censored dependent variable to zero by default.

```
library(AER)        # for Tobit regression fit
fit.tbl <- tobit(baRedMaple ~ elev, data = dat)
summary(fit.tbl)
#>
#> Call:
#> tobit(formula = baRedMaple ~ elev, data = dat)
#>
#> Observations:
#>          Total  Left-censored     Uncensored Right-censored
#>            608             59            549              0
#>
#> Coefficients:
#>              Estimate Std. Error z value Pr(>|z|)
#> (Intercept)  6.321077   0.462592  13.664   <2e-16 ***
#> elev        -0.003316   0.001864  -1.779   0.0752 .
#> Log(scale)   1.911352   0.030748  62.162   <2e-16 ***
#> ---
#> Signif. codes:  0 '***' 0.001 '**' 0.01 '*' 0.05 '.' 0.1 ' ' 1
#>
#> Scale: 6.762
#>
#> Gaussian distribution
#> Number of Newton-Raphson Iterations: 2
```

```
#> Log-likelihood: -1889 on 3 Df
#> Wald-statistic: 3.165 on 1 Df, p-value: 0.075246
```

2.4.1 Joint quantile regression call

The `qrjoint` package contains an eponymous function which performs a Bayesian parameter estimation of the generative model (2.2). Posterior computation is done with the help of Markov chain Monte Carlo (MCMC) over an unconstrained parameter space that offers a complete reparameterisation of the original model. Likelihood score calculation is done by discretising the quantile levels to a finite, dense grid of τ-values. The function-valued parameters of the model, which are assigned independent Gaussian process priors, are approximated by closely related finite-rank predictive processes [16,3]. See [18] for more technical details.

The `qrjoint` function uses a data-formula specification similar to the `lm` function from the `stats` package to build the design matrix X. The function performs all necessary data centering so that inference may proceed anywhere within the convex hull of the data predictor space. The default `incr=0.01` provides estimates over a τ-grid at 0.01 resolution, i.e. 0.01, 0.02, 0.03, ..., 0.98, 0.99, with slightly more dense grids in the tails; the same grid is used in likelihood score computation. This resolution is sufficient for our needs. Also sufficient is the default `nknots=6`, which dictates the number of knots used in the finite-rank predictive process approximation. One may consider increasing `nknots` to allow for more waviness or multimodality of the response distribution. While the likelihood computation scales well in `nknots`, the overall MCMC may take much longer to mix when a larger `nknots` is used. The total number of parameters (after reparameterisation and discretisation) is `(p+1)*(nknots+1) + 3`, where `p` is the number of predictors (excluding intercept).

Several nondefault options are employed in the code that follows for the basal area model. We explain our use of them here:

- *Excess Zero as Censoring.* We repurpose the censoring argument to identify observations that are truncated at zero. Within the vector, `cens=2` indicates left censoring or left truncation and `cens=0` indicates uncensored observations.
- *MCMC Initialisation.* The `par="RQ"` option allows us to initialise our regression coefficients in the MCMC chain to be close to the traditional (τ independently estimated) quantile regression estimates.

- *'Base' Distribution.* The `fbase` argument specifies a prior guess for the shape of the distribution at the centre of the covariate space. That prior guess will be deformed to match the actual shape of the distribution; however, the estimated tails are designed to retain the decay behaviour of the prior guess. The options when modelling on the full real line, albeit truncated to the nonnegative reals, are `"logistic"` or `"t"`. We use the `"logistic"` option because (1) we are primarily concerned with estimation in the distribution's bulk and do not desire to guarantee t-like, power decay in the tails and (2) because it runs slightly faster than the 't' option.
- *MCMC Sampling and Thinning.* The `nsamp` argument tells us how many total samples to retain, while `thin` designates how often to retain the MCMC sample. As the output objects can get large and the MCMC chains can exhibit some autocorrelation, we choose to retain every 20th sample. After running `nsamp` * `thin` = 500 * 20 = 10000 total iterations, of which only 500 will be retained and displayed, we pause to assess the state of the MCMC chain.

  Even this simple model may take a minute or two to run.

```
set.seed(11111)
fit.qrj1 <- qrjoint(baRedMaple ~ elev, data=dat,
            cens=ifelse(dat$baRedMaple==0,2,0),
            par="RQ", fbase="logistic", nsamp = 500, thin = 20)
#> Initial lp = -3226.81
#> iter = 1000, lp = -1783.68 acpt = 0.21 0.12 0.16 0.16 0.07
#> iter = 2000, lp = -1784.07 acpt = 0.13 0.24 0.14 0.11 0.28
#> iter = 3000, lp = -1782.49 acpt = 0.13 0.15 0.16 0.18 0.22
#> iter = 4000, lp = -1782.23 acpt = 0.12 0.13 0.13 0.11 0.19
#> iter = 5000, lp = -1778.64 acpt = 0.11 0.14 0.16 0.13 0.14
#> iter = 6000, lp = -1778.55 acpt = 0.17 0.15 0.13 0.19 0.16
#> iter = 7000, lp = -1784.54 acpt = 0.16 0.17 0.13 0.12 0.16
#> iter = 8000, lp = -1784.02 acpt = 0.12 0.15 0.16 0.11 0.15
#> iter = 9000, lp = -1781.3 acpt = 0.13 0.14 0.15 0.16 0.13
#> iter = 10000, lp = -1782.77 acpt = 0.16 0.12 0.15 0.15 0.17
#> elapsed time: 49 seconds
```

2.4.2 MCMC progress and convergence assessment

The output prints, on the fly, the log posterior value at initialisation and subsequently prints updates to the log posterior after each 10% of total iterations completed. The MCMC calculation utilises a blocked adaptive Metropolis sampler [2] that places the model parameters into `p+4` overlapping groups. At each update, acceptance rates for each block of the adaptive metropolis sampler are also printed. Having not changed the default `acpt.target` option, we are looking for each block to approach the default acceptance target of 0.15, which they are beginning to. The final line of output gives the total run-time.

The `summary` function provides insight into the convergence of the MCMC sampler. The `more.details=TRUE` option gives additional diagnostic plots. The suite of plots created by the `summary` call are shown in Fig. 2.2.

```
summary(fit.qrj1, more.details=TRUE)
#> WAIC.1 = 3550.2 , WAIC.2 = 3550.29
```

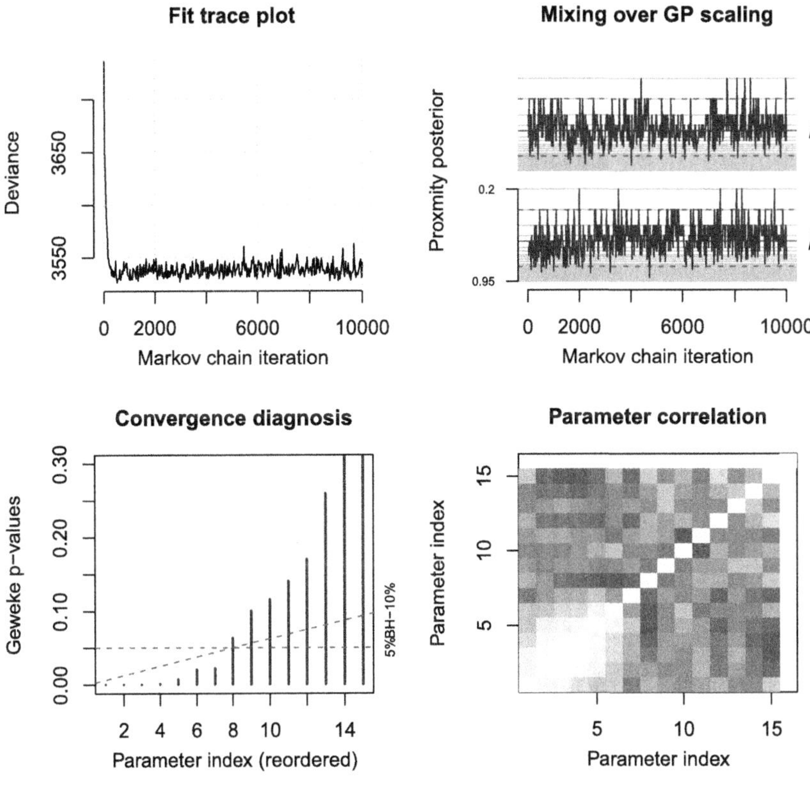

Figure 2.2 MCMC diagnostics for `qrjoint` model fit.

In Fig. 2.2, the 'Fit trace plot' shows that the chain has moved away from its initial values and may be coming closer to a stable state. Here and in the subplot labelled 'Mixing over GP scaling', we are looking for 'fuzzy caterpillar' plots indicating good mixing, as is typical in evaluating MCMC trace plots. The GP scaling plot shows, for each β_j curve, how much correlation exists between its values at quantile levels 0.1 apart. These proximity parameters are sampled from a discrete set of values over a fixed range, so if we see posterior mass building at either an upper or a lower boundary we may need to adjust the `hyper` parameters for `lam` to cover a better range of values. The horizontal red (mid grey in print version) dashed lines show prior 95% credible intervals on the proximity parameters.

The 'Convergence diagnosis' subplot displays P-values from Geweke tests for convergence. The diagonal dashed line represents a Benjamini–Hochberg adjustment for multiple testing across parameters (controlling false discovery rate at 10%). Seeing parameters with P-values below the diagonal line, as we do here, is one indication that the MCMC chain needs to run longer. The 'Parameter correlation' subplot gives a heat map of the correlation among model parameters.

We use the `update` function to add an additional 500 draws to our sample. The sampler maintains the thinning rate (every 20th observation) specified in the original `qrjoint` call.

```
fit.qrj1 <- update(fit.qrj1, nadd=500)
```

```
summary(fit.qrj1, more.details=TRUE)
#> WAIC.1 = 3550.71 , WAIC.2 = 3550.75
```

The MCMC diagnostic plots run on the extended chain, shown in Fig. 2.3, look better. The summary function prints two versions of the Watanabe Akaike Information Criterion, which can be used to compare models (lower WAIC indicates a better fit).

It is possible to run multiple MCMC chains and assess convergence with associated multichain diagnostics, e.g. Gelman and Rubin, although we do not do so here. In the `qrjoint` call, setting `par` equal to a numeric vector of length equal to the total number of model parameters can override `par`'s supported options and directly specify desired MCMC starting values.

To recap, 20000 total MCMC iterations have been run using the `qrjoint` and `update` functions, and 1000 of those samples have been retained.

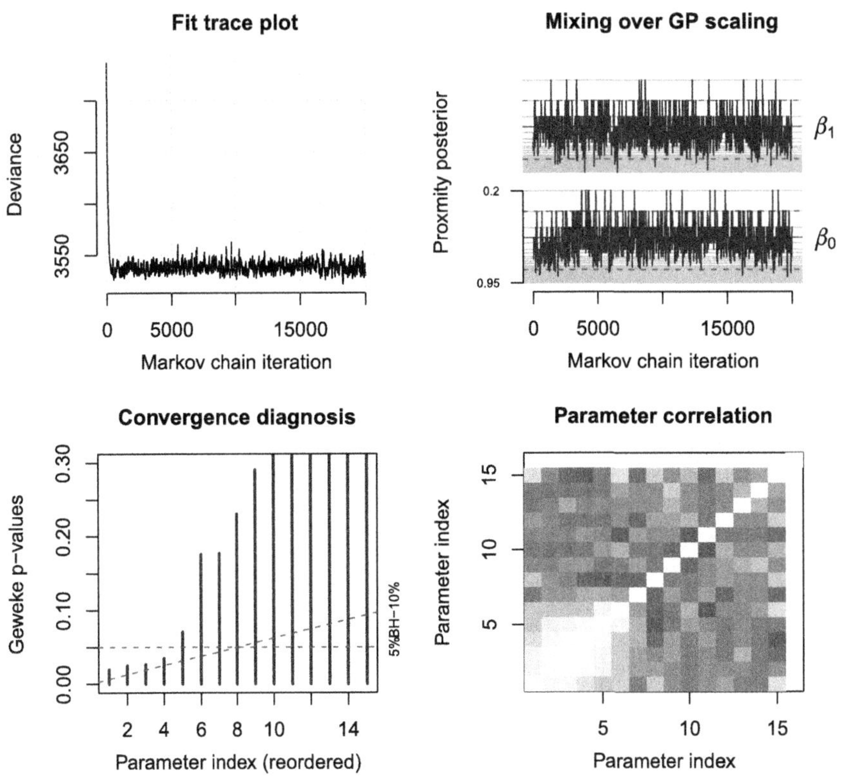

Figure 2.3 Updated MCMC diagnostics for `qrjoint` model fit.

We will use the auxiliary functions' default burn-in rates of `burn.perc=0.5` to obtain posterior summaries (medians, 95% credible intervals, etc.) from the second set of 500 retained samples.

2.5 Interpreting quantile regressions

2.5.1 Coefficient plots

The `coef` function returns posterior samples for intercept and slope parameters at all quantile levels matching the τ-grid used in model fitting. It also returns, as estimates, posterior medians and the end points of the 95% posterior credible intervals of those parameters. By default, the `coef` function also plots the regression coefficients across τ. We suppress plotting in favour of constructing our own plots that also contain the estimated Tobit parameters (Fig. 2.4).

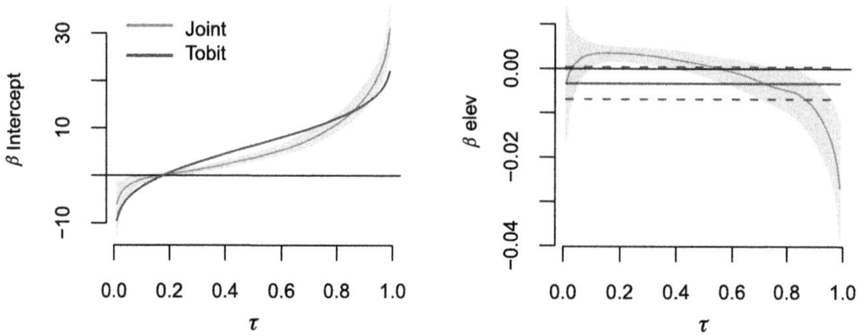

Figure 2.4 Coefficient estimates and 95% intervals across quantile levels for simple basal area model.

```
tau <- round(fit.qrj1$tau.g[fit.qrj1$reg.ix],2)
coef.qrj1 <- coef(fit.qrj1, nmc = 500, plot = FALSE)
beta.qrj1 <- coef.qrj1$beta.est
finite <- !(tau%in%c(0,1))
p <- dim(beta.qrj1)[2]


beta.tb1 <- array(NA, dim(beta.qrj1), dimnames=dimnames(beta.qrj1))
beta.tb1[,"Intercept","b.med"] <- qnorm(tau, fit.tb1$coef[1],
                                    fit.tb1$scale)
for (i in 2:p){
  beta.tb1[,i,"b.lo"]  <- confint(fit.tb1)[i,"2.5 %"]
  beta.tb1[,i,"b.med"] <- fit.tb1$coef[i]
  beta.tb1[,i,"b.hi"]  <- confint(fit.tb1)[i,"97.5 %"]
}


varname <- dimnames(coef.qrj1$beta.samp)$beta
par(mfrow=c(1,2))
for(i in 1:p){
  getBands(coef.qrj1$beta.samp[,i,], xlab=bquote(tau),
          ylab=bquote(beta~.(varname[i])), bty='n')
  abline(h=0)
  matlines(tau[finite], beta.tb1[finite,i,], col="blue",
          lty=c(2,1,2), lwd=1.5)
  if(i==1) legend("topleft", c("Joint","Tobit"),
                  col=c("red","blue"), lty=1, lwd=2, bty='n')
```

```
}
par(mfrow=c(1,1))
```

The estimates and intervals at $\tau = 0.5$ correspond to median regressions, whereas those at $\tau = 0.8$ correspond to the 80th percentile regression, and so on. When looking at these plots, three types of comparisons are useful. We illustrate by interpreting the `elev` plot.

Comparisons to zero. Tobit's slope estimates are constant for all parts of the response distribution. Because the 95% confidence interval bands contain zero, the Tobit regression might lead us to conclude that `elev` is not linearly related to `baRedMaple`. The 95% intervals from the `qrjoint` fit, however, *do* have nonzero coefficients. The positive bands in the τ-region of (0.1, 0.4) means that an increase in elevation is associated with increased basal areas, but only for those low-to-mid quantile levels. When we consider the upper quantiles, i.e. $\tau > 0.8$, an increase in elevation is actually associated with a decrease in red maple basal areas. These interpretations are similar to traditional interpretations of a regression model; however, here we are able to make inferential claims for all parts of the response distribution and not just for the mean or median.

Comparisons between quantile levels, τ. The increasingly negative slopes for `elev` across τ in the joint quantile regressions illustrate a differential effect of elevation on basal area at different places in the response distribution. The lower quantile levels have positive slopes, whereas the upper quantile levels have negative slopes. This likely reflects a fanning of the data with larger variance at small `elev` values and smaller variance at large `elev` values. In this way, quantile regression can capture heterogeneity of variance. Tobit, with its flat slopes across τ, is not capable of capturing heterogeneity of variance or other types of differential effects.

Comparisons between methods. Finally, a visual comparison of interval estimates between methods at any given τ shows overlap or concordance between the joint quantile regression and the Tobit regression in parts of the lowest decile and for τ in (0.4, 0.95).

2.5.2 Quantile line plots

It may be instructive in this single variate case to plot the regression lines for a few τ values.

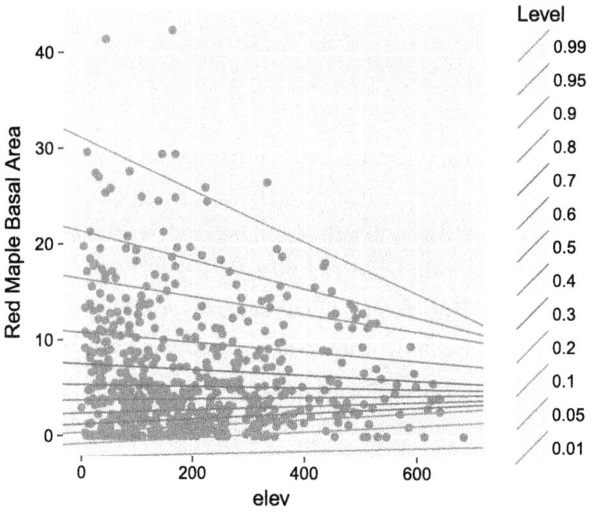

Figure 2.5 Quantile regression lines.

```
# Retrieve subset of tau-fitted lines
tau.use <- round(c(0.01, 0.05, seq(0.1,0.9,by=.1), 0.95,0.99),2)
tau.factor <- factor(tau.use, levels=rev(tau.use))
beta1 <- beta.qrj1[which(tau %in%tau.use),,"b.med"]
beta1 <- data.frame(Level=factor(rownames(beta1),
                    levels=levels(tau.factor)), beta1)

# Use quantile-fitted coefficients to add ablines to scatterplot
of data
p.dat <- ggplot() + geom_point(data=dat, aes(x=elev, y=baRedMaple),
      col="#999999") + ylab("Red Maple Basal Area")
p.dat + geom_abline(data=beta1, aes(slope=elev, intercept=
                                          Intercept, col=Level))
```

Fig. 2.5 shows that approximately 1% of the observations lie above the 0.99 quantile line, about 50% of the observations lie above the 0.5 line, etc. Note that the regression lines do not cross within the range of the `elev` covariate, i.e. they obey the monotonicity constraint. Here the heterogeneity of variance across `elev` is visible, and it makes sense that regression slopes generally progress from positive to negative slopes as τ, the quantile level, is increased. Some lines extend below zero because the plotted lines are estimates for the latent or nontruncated model.

The above comparisons were made for didactic purposes. Prior to interpreting coefficients, an assessment of the model assumptions is warranted.

2.6 Assessing model assumptions and making improvements

After the assumption of independence, joint quantile regression has only one other assumption: all effects can be explained as linear combinations of the design matrix X. The Tobit model additionally assumes that the latent responses are normally distributed with constant variance across all observations. A first instinct may be to turn to 'residual' diagnostics for evaluation of these model assumptions, where residuals are traditionally defined as the difference between an observed value and its predicted mean. Diagnostics based on residuals may be sufficient when the (assumed) response distribution can be summarised by its mean, as in the case of the Tobit model; however, they are insufficient for joint quantile regression, which outputs a conditional prediction that is an *entire response distribution*.

With estimated quantile functions available for the Tobit model *and* the joint quantile regression model, diagnostics based on the probability integral transform are possible for both models. If the models are appropriate, the estimated quantile levels for the observations, $\hat{\tau}_{y_i} = \hat{Q}^{-1}(y_i|x_i)$, should follow a uniform distribution.

2.6.1 Obtaining estimated quantile levels

Under the Tobit model, $\hat{\tau}_{y_i}$ for $y_i > 0$ is estimated using the normal CDF, $\Phi((y_i - x_i\hat{\beta})/\hat{\sigma})$. Under the joint quantile regression model, $\hat{\tau}_{y_i} = \hat{Q}^{-1}(y_i|x_i)$. The `summary` function carries out this inverse calculation by interpolating the estimated quantile lines between τ-grid points. For either model, if $y_i = 0$, then $\hat{\tau}_{y_i}$ can be taken as a random draw from $Unif(0, \hat{Q}^{-1}(0|x_i))$. Estimated quantile levels for each observation and each draw of the MCMC sampler can be retrieved from the `summary` function for `qrjoint`. The function that follows obtains the quantile levels, corrects them under censoring (or in this case under zero-truncation) and summarises them across posterior draws. We demonstrate this using the 'Summary' option.

```
# Function to summarise posterior draws of tau_Y. When fit includes
# censored values, left-censored tau_Y are replaced with draw from
# Unif(0, tau_Y) and right censored tau_Y are replaced with draw
# from Unif(tau_Y,1)
#
# Inputs
# fit: qrjoint fit object
# plot: If TRUE, plot produces a histogram and qq-plot comparing
# to uniform distribution
# mcmc: Character string describing how to summarise over
# posterior draws. Options are
#        "Summary" - takes mean of tau over posterior draws
#        "One" - returns tau at a single random MCMC iteration
#        "Many" - returns tau at all MCMC iterations

modfit.qrjoint  <- function(fit, burn.perc=0.5, mcmc="Summary"){
  invisible(capture.output(ql <- summary(fit, plot.dev=FALSE)$ql))
  cens <- fit$cens; nsamp <- ncol(ql)
  ql <- ql[, 1:nsamp > nsamp * burn.perc]
  if(mcmc=="Summary") {
    MCMC <- apply(ql, 1, mean)
    if(!is.null(cens)){
      MCMC[cens==2] <- runif(sum(cens==2),0, MCMC[cens==2])
      MCMC[cens==1] <- runif(sum(cens==1), MCMC[cens==1], 1)
    }
  }
  if(mcmc=="One"){
    MCMC <- ql[,sample(1:ncol(ql),1)]
    if(!is.null(cens)){
      MCMC[cens==2] <- runif(sum(cens==2),0, MCMC[cens==2])
      MCMC[cens==1] <- runif(sum(cens==1), MCMC[cens==1], 1)
    }
  }
  if(mcmc=="Many")     {
    if(!is.null(cens)){
      ql[cens==2,] <- runif(length(ql[cens==2,]),0, ql[cens==2,])
      ql[cens==1,] <- runif(length(ql[cens==1,]), ql[cens==1,], 1)
    }
```

```
    MCMC <- q1
  }
  invisible(MCMC)
}

set.seed(22222) # Censoring corrections perform stochastic
operation
dat$pfit.qrj1 <- modfit.qrjoint(fit.qrj1, mcmc="Summary")
dat$pfit.tb1 <- pnorm(dat$baRedMaple, mean=predict(fit.tb1),
                      sd=summary(fit.tb1)$scale)
dat$pfit.tb1[dat$baRedMaple==0] <- runif(sum(dat$baRedMaple==0),
                               0,dat$pfit.tb1[dat$baRedMaple==0])
```

We store them in the data frame containing the original data for convenience when assessing assumptions of linearity.

2.6.2 Assessing overall fit

A PP-plot may be used to compare the estimated quantile levels to their equivalent uniform probabilities.

```
p.qqtb1 <- ggplot() +
  geom_qq(aes(sample=dat$pfit.tb1), distribution=stats::qunif) +
  ylab("actual") + ggtitle("Tobit Model") +
  geom_abline(intercept=0, slope=1)

p.qqqrj1 <- ggplot() +
  geom_qq(aes(sample=dat$pfit.qrj1), distribution=stats::qunif) +
  ylab("actual") + ggtitle("Joint QR Model") +
  geom_abline(intercept=0, slope=1)

grid.arrange(p.qqtb1, p.qqqrj1, ncol=2)
```

In Fig. 2.6, the joint quantile regression lies close to the 45-degree line, showing similarity to a uniform distribution and indicating good aggregate model fit, while the Tobit model is decidedly nonuniform, indicating a poor fit.

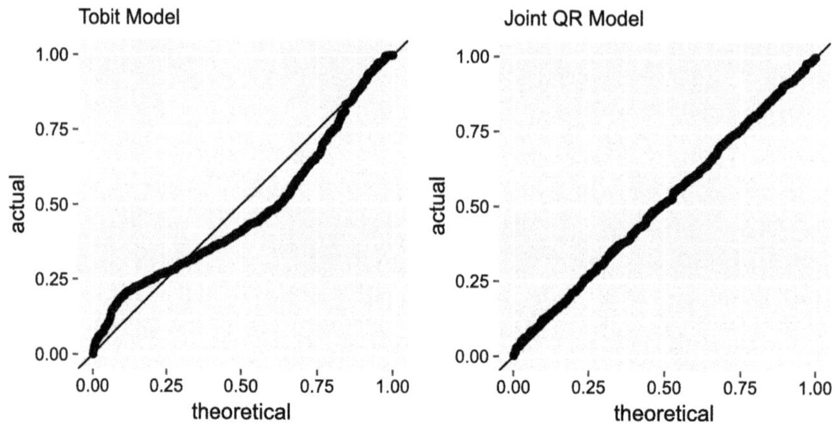

Figure 2.6 Estimated quantile-level plots for assessing overall model fit.

2.6.3 Assessing linearity

The estimated quantile levels, $\hat{\tau}_{y_i}$, also provide a way to diagnose design matrix misspecification and assess the assumption of linearity. At any given X, we expect the estimated quantile levels to be uniform. Therefore plotting a covariate against $\hat{\tau}_{y_i}$ and looking at any vertical cross-section, the estimated data quantile levels should be uniform within the swath.

We illustrate two options for quantile-level diagnostic plots using the joint quantile regression model. Scatter plots with mean trend gam/loess lines are illustrative for diagnosing potential nonlinearities; trend lines should lie close to a horizontal line at the constant value of 1/2. Violin plots, which cut the continuous variables into quantile bins (here deciles) and then display kernel density estimates within each bin can also assist in diagnosing nonlinearity. These violin plots should look uniform or blocky within each bin.

```
library(dplyr)        # for binning into deciles

qlplot <- function(data, x, y, plot=TRUE){
  if(is.numeric(data[,deparse(x)])){
    data$bin <- factor(ntile(data[,deparse(x)],10))   # bin numeric
    p.s <- ggplot(data, aes_q(x, y)) +
      geom_point() + geom_smooth(se=F, method="loess")
    p.v <- ggplot(data, aes_q(quote(bin), y)) + geom_violin() +
      xlab(paste("Decile bins of",x))
```

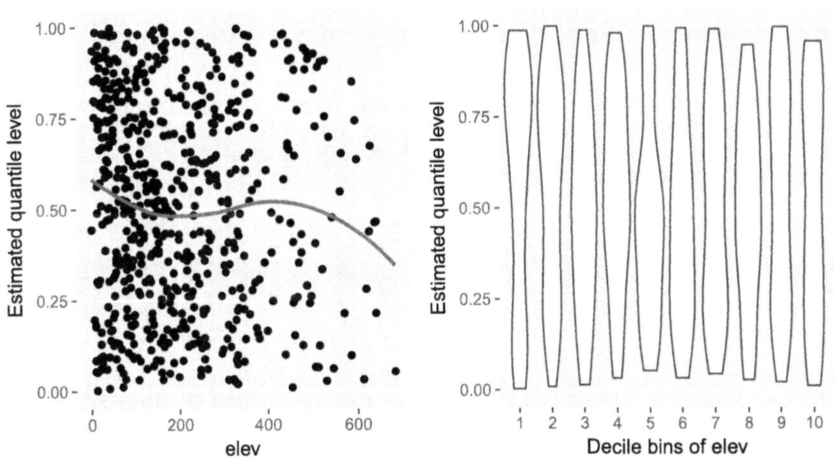

Figure 2.7 Covariate by estimated data quantile-levels plots for assessing linearity assumption.

```
    } else{
      p.s <- ggplot(data, aes_q(x, y)) + geom_point()
      p.v <- ggplot(data, aes_q(x, y)) + geom_violin()}

    yax <- list(ylim(0,1), ylab("Estimated quantile level"))
    if(plot) {grid.arrange(p.s + yax, p.v + yax, ncol=2)} else{
      invisible(arrangeGrob(p.s + yax, p.v + yax, ncol=2))
    }
}

qlplot(dat, x=quote(elev), y=quote(pfit.qrjl))
```

As shown in Fig. 2.7, the estimated data quantile levels plotted against `elev` show slight nonlinearity; for low elevations the mean trend line bows upward, away from zero, and the violin plot is somewhat top-heavy. The bowing downward at high elevations is likely driven by a few outlying-in-x elevation values and not a systematic departure from uniformity. The mostly uniform densities in decile bins 9 and 10 help to confirm this.

While the information in these two plots is similar, the violin plots can be helpful for consolidating sparse regions of the covariate space, e.g. with outlying `elev` values, or for spreading out dense regions. Overall, the mean trend line for `elev` does not depart egregiously from 0.5. Lacking some physically justified motive for a nonlinear elevation effect, some might reasonably elect to keep this covariate in its linear form. For illustration, we modify the design matrix by including a third-order b-spline for `elev`.

2.6.4 Model improvement

Using the quantile-level diagnostic plots of the previous section, we deduced that elevation's effect on red maple basal areas may not be linear and that our model might be improved by a b-spline transformation. As was mentioned previously, the linear model can be compared to the spline model using WAIC, which is calculated in `qrjoint`'s auxiliary `summary` function.

```
library(splines)   # for b-splines
set.seed(33333)
fit.qrj2 <- qrjoint(baRedMaple ~ ns(elev,3), data=dat,
        cens=ifelse(dat$baRedMaple==0,2,0),
        par="RQ", fbase="logistic", nsamp = 2000, thin = 20)
```

```
summary(fit.qrj2, plot.dev=FALSE)
#> WAIC.1 = 3531.35 , WAIC.2 = 3530.85
```

The spline-model run-time is longer both because of the increase in number of predictors and because more iterations were needed to reach convergence; however, it seems to pay off. The WAIC has decreased from ≈ 3550 to ≈ 3531, indicating an improved fit with the `elev` spline. Also, the quantile-level plots have less bowing near zero, as can be seen in Fig. 2.8. If the nonlinear effect of `elev` were of specific interest, additional degrees of freedom could be added to the b-spline basis until the practitioner is satisfied with the uniformity of quantile-level plots or until WAIC indicates overfitting. As our specific interest lies in the multiple regression model, we leave off further model modifications for now.

```
set.seed(44444)
dat$pfit.qrj2 <- modfit.qrjoint(fit.qrj2, mcmc="Summary")
qlplot(dat, x=quote(elev), y=quote(pfit.qrj2))
```

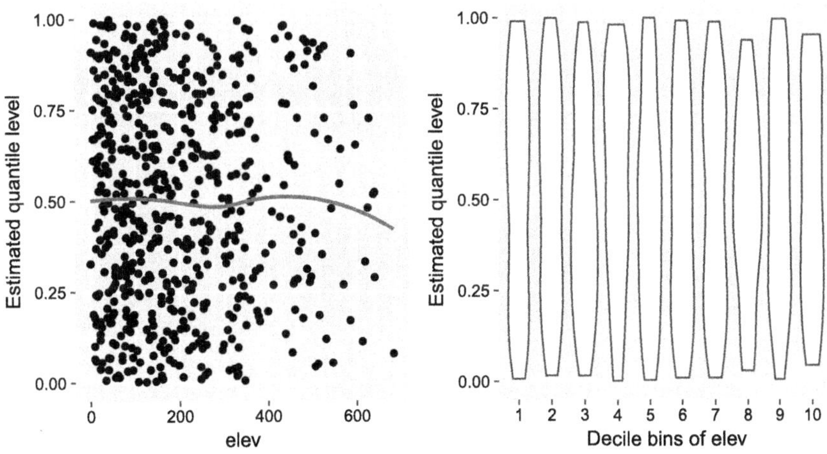

Figure 2.8 Covariate by estimated data quantile-levels plots after including b-spline.

2.7 Prediction and interpreting predicted responses

2.7.1 Quantiles for positive reals

We may desire to apply our fitted model to obtain predictions for a new data set. When doing this, it is important to remember that the joint quantile regression fit is only guaranteed to provide noncrossing quantile planes within the convex hull of the data upon which the model is fit. The code that follows uses the `predict` function to produce quantile line plots similar to those originally made using `coef`.

```
# Define new dataset and perform prediction
pred.grid <- seq(min(dat$elev),max(dat$elev), length=50)
dat.new <- data.frame(elev=pred.grid, baRedMaple=999)
pred1 <- predict(fit.qrj1, newdata=dat.new)
dimnames(pred1) <- list(elev=pred.grid, Level=tau)

library(reshape)      # for melting from wide to long for ggplot
pred1.long <- melt(pred1[,tau %in%tau.use])
pred1.long$Lev <- factor(pred1.long$Level,
    levels=levels(tau.factor))
p.dat + geom_line(data=pred1.long,
    aes(x=elev, y=value, col=Lev, group=Lev)) +
    coord_cartesian(ylim=c(0,43)) + labs(col="Level")
```

Alternately, we could build a new X matrix and get predictions through the matrix multiplication $X\beta$. This method is preferred when predicting on the spline model because it guarantees that the b-spline bases over the new data are the same bases upon which the regression is fit.

```
# Get beta from coef, X from predict on spline object,
prediction from matrix mult
library(splines)
beta2 <- coef(fit.qrj2)$beta.est
splines <- ns(dat$elev,3)
Xnew2 <- cbind(1,predict(splines, dat.new$elev))
pred2 <- Xnew2%*%t(beta2[,,"b.med",drop=TRUE])
dimnames(pred2) <- list(elev=pred.grid, Level=tau)
pred2.long <- melt(pred2[,tau %in%tau.use])

# Plot quantile lines using continuous gradient for tau
our.palette <- hcl(h=seq(375,55,length=9), l=65, c=100)
s.lev <- scale_color_gradientn(limits=c(0,1), colors=our.palette)
p.quants <- p.dat + coord_cartesian(ylim=c(0,43)) + s.lev +
      geom_line(data=pred2.long, aes(x=elev, y=value, col=Level,
                                         group=Level))
```

The first plot of Fig. 2.9, created from the code above, shows that even when there is more than one predictor, e.g. in this case three b-spline bases, the quantile planes do not cross.

2.7.2 Probability of zero

We may also desire to know the probability of having no red maple trees at a given site. These probabilities are equivalent to the probability of censoring (truncation) and can be obtained under the joint modelling context. Using the conditional quantile predictions for some x at every MCMC draw, we obtain $\tau_0 = Q^{-1}(0|x)$, the quantile level corresponding to when the conditional quantile equals zero, by linear interpolation between estimated grid points. Summarising these values across draws produces posterior intervals for the probability of having zero basal area at a site with given covariates, $P(\text{zero})$. In this case with all predictors derived from a single covariate, we are able to aggregate into one plot the effects of the three `elev` b-splines on the probability of zero using the code that follows.

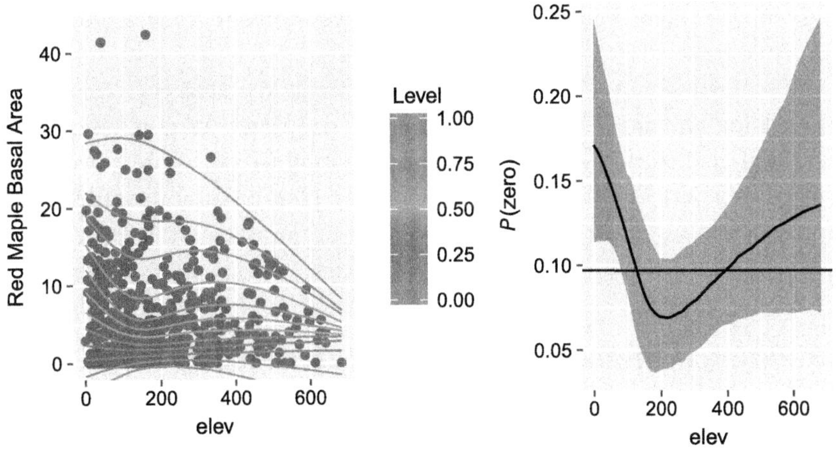

Figure 2.9 Predictions for elevation spline model. Left: Quantile lines. Right: Zero probabilities.

```
nsamp <- 500
coef2 <- coef(fit.qrj2, reduce=FALSE, nmc=nsamp)$beta.samp
tauplus <- round(fit.qrj2$tau.g,8)

# Probability of zero with error bars across elev
Q2 <- sapply(1:nsamp, function(f) Xnew2%*%t(coef2[,,f]),
             simplify="array")
tau0 <- apply(Q2,c(1,3), function(f) approx(f, tauplus,0)$y)
prob0 <- as.data.frame(t(apply(tau0, 1, quantile,
                               prob=c(0.025, 0.5, 0.975))))
prob0$elev <- pred.grid
p.p0 <- ggplot(prob0, aes(x=elev)) + geom_line(aes(y='50%')) +
  geom_ribbon(aes(ymin='2.5%', ymax='97.5%'), alpha=0.3) +
  ylab("P(zero)") +
  geom_hline(yintercept=mean(dat$baRedMaple==0))

grid.arrange(p.quants, p.p0, ncol=2)
```

In the output plot (second plot of Fig. 2.9), we compare the zero probability bands to the sample prevalence of zeroes, displayed as a black horizontal line. Bands that are fully above (or fully below) the sample prevalence indicate an increase (or decrease) in zero probability for values in that range of `elev`. Here we conclude that lower elevations are less likely to have red maple trees.

While estimating a given quantile or probability of zero is straightforward for any single observation's set of covariates, creating multiple regression analogues of the plots in Fig. 2.9 using two or more covariates is more difficult. The functional-β-coefficient plots and the quantile-level diagnostic plots translate seamlessly from a single covariate setting to a multiple regression setting.

2.8 Fitting multiple regression basal area models

2.8.1 Model terms, transformations and interactions

The four covariates that we are interested in exploring simultaneously in a multiple, quantile regression setting are `elev`, `region`, `aspect` and `slope`. Before starting, we compile a list of notes and questions to address during modelling:

- *Dealing with Directional Covariates.* The covariate `aspect` is radial or wrapping in nature, with values 360 and 1 being adjacent degree measurements. A common way to treat radial data is to include both `cos` and `sin` bases. This transformation makes `aspect` less unit-interpretable (i.e. slope can no longer be interpreted as 'a one unit increase in degrees corresponds to an x unit increase in basal area...') but more interpretable in terms of cardinal directionality. For these data, a `cos` transformation measures southerliness-to-northerliness (-1 to 1, respectively), while a `sin` transformation measures westerliness-to-easterliness (-1 to 1, respectively). Depending on sun and shade tolerance, some trees prefer north or south, east or west facing slopes. Do red maple trees?
- *Partially Deterministic Relations Between `aspect` and `slope`.* On a related note, a site cannot face a direction unless it is sloped. The `aspect` covariate records '0' for many sites that have zero or near-zero slopes. To prevent these values from influencing the directional effect of `aspect`, an indicator value can be added to let flat sites have their own adjusting intercept.
- *Interaction Effect.* One may well suspect some interaction between `slope` and `aspect`. For instance, the east-westerly effect on red maple basal areas may be different for moderately sloped sites than for steeply sloped sites. Is an interaction necessary for describing the quantiles of red maple basal areas?

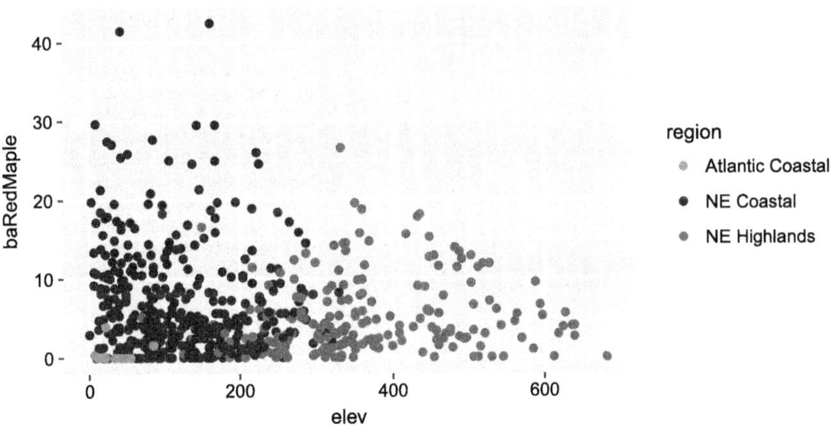

Figure 2.10 Region may share some of the same effects on basal area as elevation.

- *Categorical Covariate Encoding.* The EPA Level-III `region` variable transcends state boundaries to categorise sites into roughly similar geophysical regions. In these data, there are only three regions: the Atlantic Coastal Pine Barrens (13 sites), the Northeastern Coastal Zone (393 sites) and the Northeastern Highlands (202 sites). These regions may stand as rough proxy for soil covariates such as sand, rock or clay composition, which are not included in the data but could potentially be related to tree growth for a given species. By default, R will use the Atlantic Coastal Pine Barrens as a reference category and code the other two regions using indicator variables.
- *Dependence Between Region and Elevation.* Finally, the variables `region` and `elev` are highly related (see Fig. 2.10), having different though overlapping ranges of elevation per region. It would be interesting to know if both variables are needed in the regression model or if the effect of `region` on red maple basal areas subsumes the need for an `elev` effect or vice versa.

We have created a model that includes all covariates along with the necessary transformations and interactions to test for the effects listed.

```
set.seed(55555)
fit.qrj3 <- qrjoint(baRedMaple ~  slope*(I(cos(aspect*pi/180)) +
            I(sin(aspect*pi/180))) +
            I(aspect==0) + region + elev, data=dat,
```

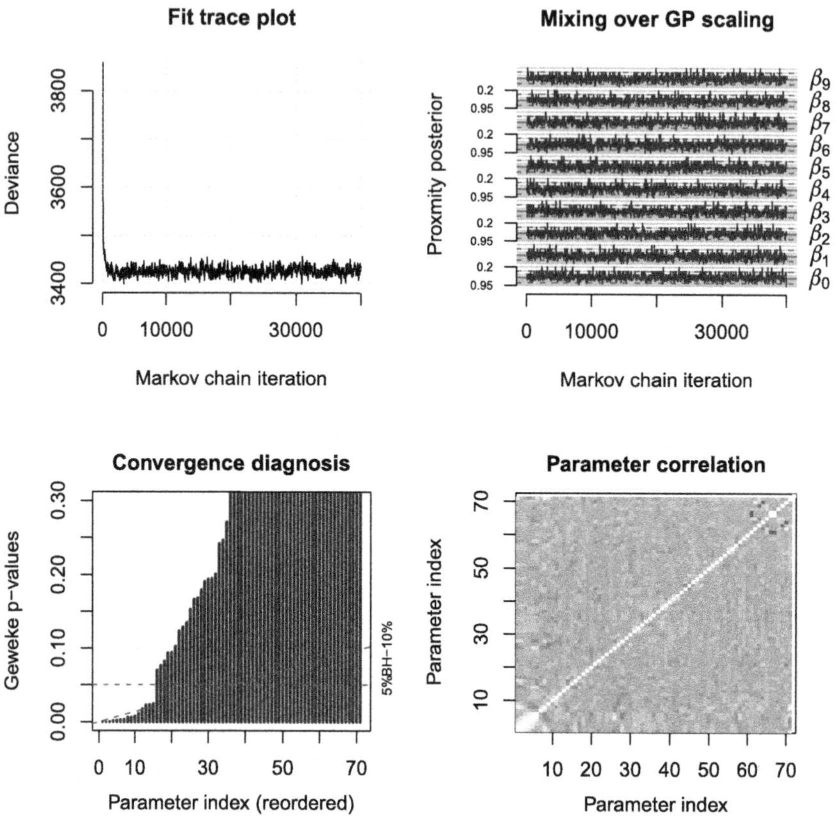

Figure 2.11 MCMC diagnostics for full `qrjoint` model, fit.qrj3.

```
            cens=ifelse(dat$baRedMaple==0,2,0),
            par="RQ", fbase="logistic", nsamp = 2000, thin = 20)
```

```
summary(fit.qrj3, more.details=TRUE)
#> WAIC.1 = 3455.15 , WAIC.2 = 3455.95
```

The plots of Fig. 2.11 give us some confidence that the MCMC sampler is converging and that we are able to continue with our model diagnostics.

```
dat$pfit.qrj3 <- modfit.qrjoint(fit.qrj3, mcmc="Summary")

p.ql1 <- qlplot(dat, x=quote(slope), y=quote(pfit.qrj3),
                plot=FALSE)
```

```
p.ql2 <- qlplot(dat, x=quote(elev), y=quote(pfit.qrj3),
               plot=FALSE)
p.ql3 <- qlplot(dat, x=quote(aspect), y=quote(pfit.qrj3),
               plot=FALSE)
p.ql4 <- qlplot(dat, x=quote(region), y=quote(pfit.qrj3),
               plot=FALSE)

grid.arrange(p.ql1, p.ql2, p.ql3, p.ql4, ncol=1)
```

2.8.2 Assessing model assumptions

The uniformity across quantile-level plots (Fig. 2.12) is sufficient that we feel confident in interpreting these regression parameters; however, there may yet be some room for improvement. The elevation variable exhibits similar bowing in its mean trend line as that seen in the single variate, elevation regression. Perhaps the model could be improved by reintroducing the b-spline for elevation? We register this modification for future model iterations but first take a look at the coefficients from the model.

```
coef(fit.qrj3, nmc = 500, plot=TRUE, show.intercept=FALSE)
```

2.8.3 Interpreting coefficients

The coefficient plots are shown in Fig. 2.13. A description of the effects follows here.

- The reference intercept distribution (not plotted) corresponds to an Atlantic Coastal, sea-level site that has some directional aspect, yet is supposedly flat. Since this site only exists in theory, the intercept is not worth interpreting.
- The indicator variable for `aspect==0` is nonzero for most τ and thereby performs an adjustment to the reference intercept distribution. Without an interpretable reference intercept, this adjusted intercept distribution will not be interpretable either.
- The two categorical `region` indicators have 95% interval bands fully above zero for all τ; we can say that a northeastern region site has basal areas about 6 ft^2/acre greater than an Atlantic Coastal site with otherwise equivalent covariates.
- It seems that both `region` and `elev` have effects, because the slope function of `elev` is constant above zero for all but the highest and lowest τ.

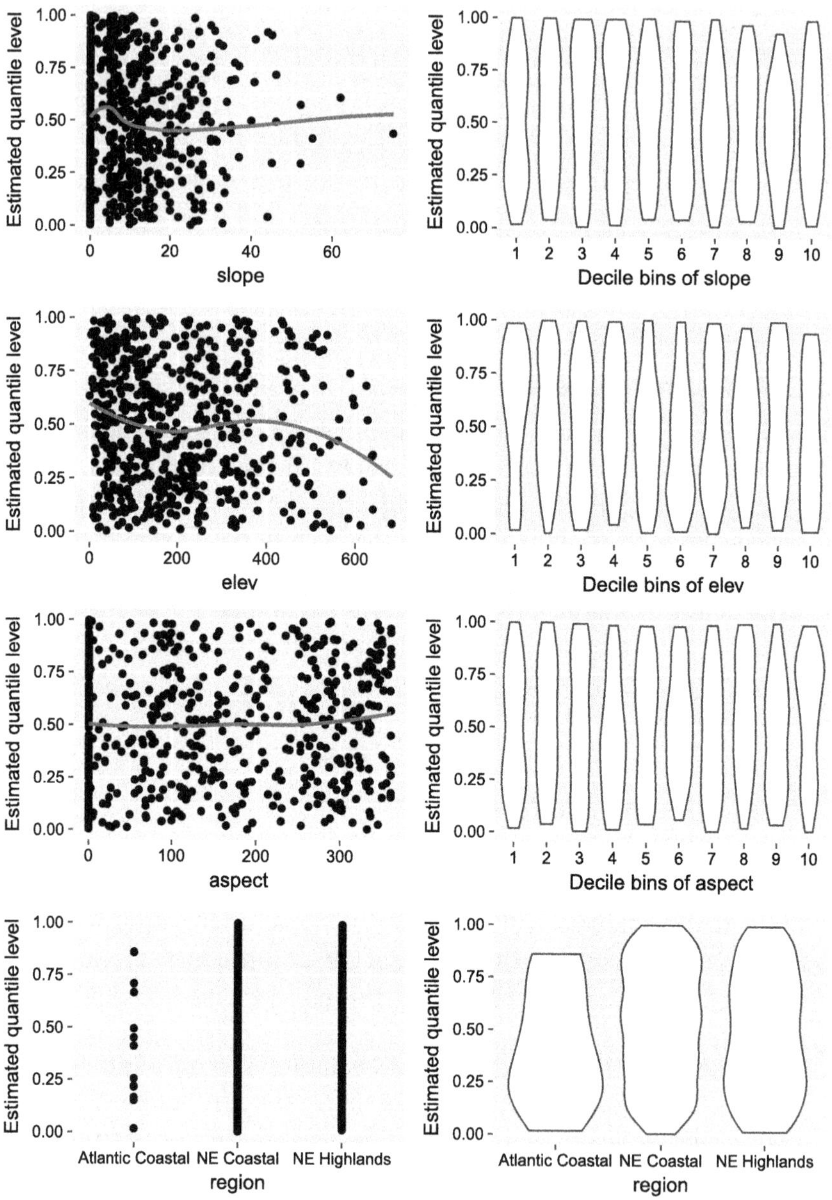

Figure 2.12 Quantile-level diagnostic plots from full regression model.

For quantile levels with bands fully above zero, we would conclude that increased elevation corresponds to greater red maple basal areas, at least

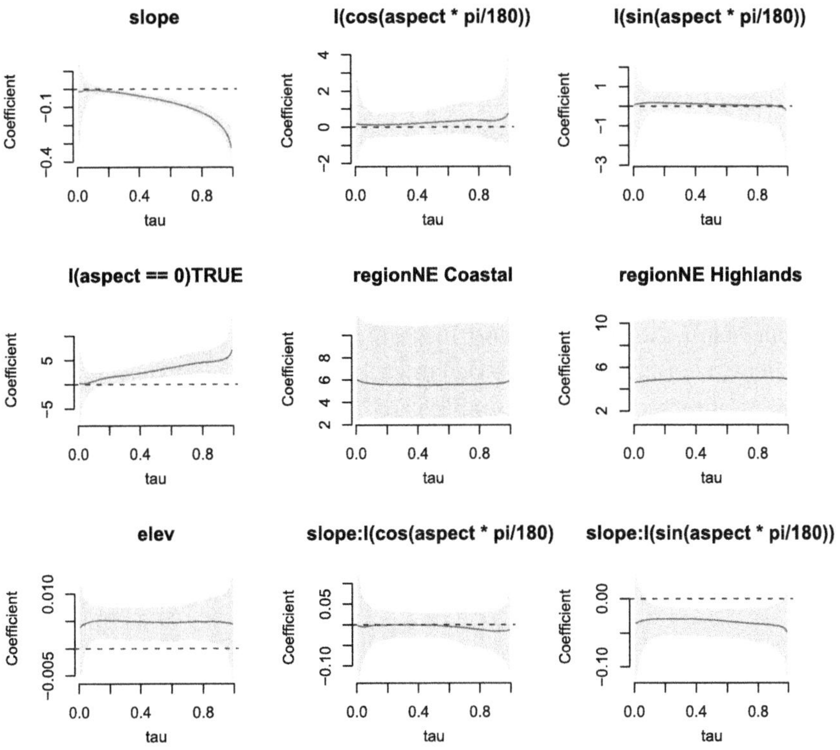

Figure 2.13 Joint quantile regression coefficients from full regression model.

within the range of `elev` considered (0 ft to 682 ft). Although a coefficient of 0.004 seems small, the cumulative effect over the sample range could amount to a 0.004⋆682 = 2.7 difference in basal areas. Contrasting this positive, τ-flat effect to the effect found in the linear-elevation model, the quantiles in the upper portion of the response distribution must be explained by some newly included variable because we no longer see negative coefficients for large τ.

- The coefficient for `slope` shows a differential effect, growing increasingly negative as τ increases. One can conclude that steeper sites have smaller red maple basal areas (bands below zero for τ greater than about 0.3). The decreasing differential effect also points to a decrease in variance of basal area as `slope` increases, i.e. heterogeneity of variance.
- Neither the marginal `cos` nor `sin` effect for `aspect` is significantly different from zero. Perhaps we should have anticipated this since these terms correspond to cardinal-direction effects when `slope==0`, and as we said

previously, `aspect` only has meaning when `slope` is nonzero. In future model iterations, leaving these marginal variables out will have the effect of fixing them equal to zero.

- The `slope:sin(aspect)` term has a negative coefficient, pointing to an interaction between `slope` and the west–east variable for quantile levels $\tau > 0.3$. We would like to understand this interaction better.

2.8.4 Understanding marginal and interaction effects

To understand the direction and magnitude of an interaction effect we `predict` over a data set in which the interacting covariates have been varied over some interpretable range (being careful not to extrapolate out of the convex hull created by the original data) and the remaining covariates have been fixed. Plots are then made of the predicted quantiles across the varied covariates for select τ to visualise their interaction effect. This technique can also be used to plot a single variable's marginal effect, but it is especially helpful when trying to understand interactions.

To tease out the `slope`-by-`aspect` interaction, we vary `slope` between 0 and 50 degrees and `aspect` between 0 and 360 degrees, while arbitrarily fixing `region=="NE Coastal"` and `elev==median(elev)`.

```
newdat <- expand.grid(slope=seq(0,50,by=5),
          aspect=seq(0,360,length=9)[-1],
          elev=median(dat$elev),
          region=factor("NE Coastal", levels=levels(dat$region)),
          baRedMaple=999)
newdat$cos <- round(cos(newdat$aspect*pi/180),2)
newdat$sin <- round(sin(newdat$aspect*pi/180),2)

pred3 <- as.data.frame(predict(newdata=newdat, fit.qrj3))
# default summary is posterior median
tau0 <- apply(pred3, 1,
        function(f) approx(f, seq(0,1,length=101), 0)$y)
pred <- cbind(newdat, pred3, tau0)

# Makes nicer radial plots when 0 and 360 in data.
Not true meaning of/prediction for aspect=0
pred.north <- pred[pred$aspect==360,]
pred.north$aspect <- 0
```

```
pred <- rbind(pred.north, pred)

plotrad <- function(y, ylabel){
  slp <- quote(slope); asp <- quote(aspect); qsin <- quote(sin);
  qcos <- quote(cos)

  p1 <- ggplot() +
        geom_line(data=pred, aes_q(x=asp, y, group=slp, col=slp)) +
        scale_x_continuous(breaks=c(90,180,270,360))
  p2 <- ggplot() +
        geom_line(data=pred, aes_q(x=asp, y, group=slp, col=slp)) +
        coord_polar() +
        scale_x_continuous(breaks=c(45,90,135,180,225,270,305,360),
                           labels=c("NE","E","SE","S","SW","W",
                                    "NW","N"))
  p3 <- ggplot() +
        geom_line(data=subset(pred, cos>=0),
                  aes_q(x=qsin, y, group=slp, col=slp)) +
        geom_line(data=subset(pred, cos<=0),
                  aes_q(x=qsin, y, group=slp, col=slp))
  p4 <- ggplot() +
        geom_line(data=subset(pred, sin>=0),
                  aes_q(x=qcos, y, group=slp, col=slp)) +
        geom_line(data=subset(pred, sin<=0),
                  aes_q(x=qcos, y, group=slp, col=slp))

  tmp <- ggplot_gtable(ggplot_build(p1))   # Only print one
  guide box
  legend <- tmp$grobs[[which(sapply(tmp$grobs,
            function(x) x$name) == "guide-box")]]
  addend <- list(theme(legend.position="none"), ylab(ylabel))

  grid.arrange(arrangeGrob(p1 + addend, p2 + addend,
               ncol=2, widths=c(4,5)),
               arrangeGrob(p3 + addend, p4 + addend, legend,
               ncol=3, widths=c(4,4,1)))}

plotrad(quote(`0.5`), "Median basal area")
```

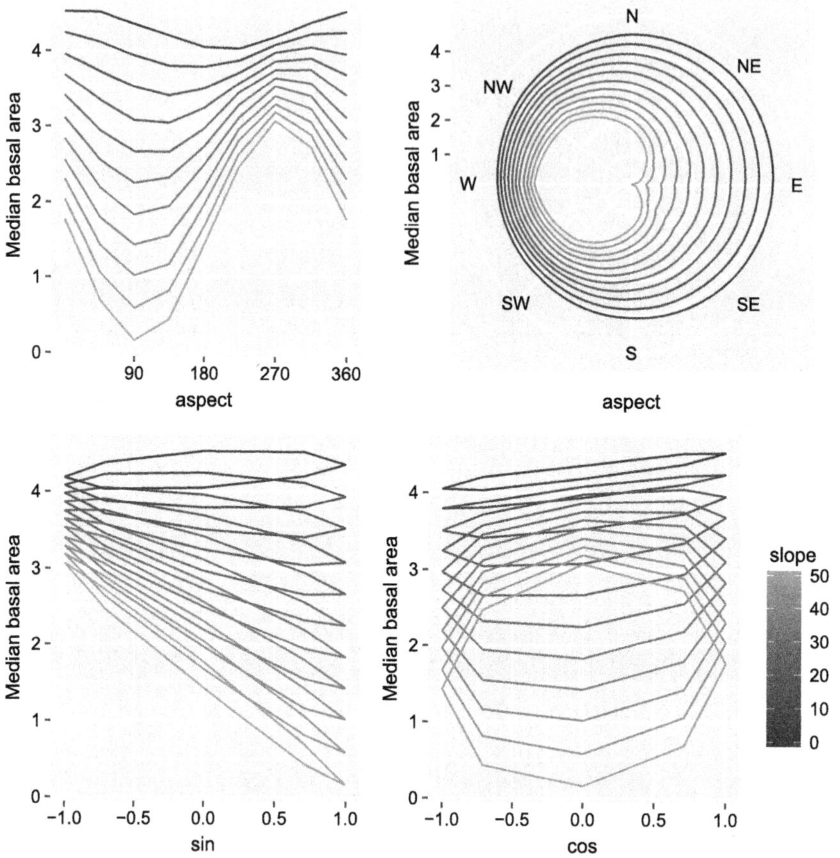

Figure 2.14 Marginal predicted medians over varying slope and aspect.

Fig. 2.14 shows a suite of median regression plots, each intended to aid in interpreting the `slope` by radial `aspect` interaction. Without adding error bars, which would make these already busy plots even more difficult to interpret, these plots can only suggest the magnitude and direction of the effects on red maple basal areas.

In the first plot, by picking a particular `slope` we generally see that the median basal area is greater for `aspect` near 270 (west) than it is for `aspect` near 90 (east); however, the differential is more pronounced the steeper the `slope` of the site is. Another way to think of the interaction is that there are bigger decreases in median basal areas when comparing an eastward facing 50-degree-sloped site to its mostly flat counterpart than there are when comparing a westward facing 50-degree-sloped site to *its* mostly flat counterpart.

This interaction plays out in the second, radial plot by having near-circles (no directional effect) for near-flat slopes, but then relatively bigger basal areas for westerly facing sites as slope increases.

In the third plot, the interaction shows up as differently sloped lines or 'rings' for different `slope` values across the `sin(aspect)` variable.

The fourth plot does not show differently sloped marginal 'rings' across `cos(aspect)` because that interaction effect is nonsignificant.

Here we arbitrarily picked the median quantile for illustration. If we were interested in the interaction effect on the 99th percentile we could use the code below to get a similar set of plots.

```
plotrad(quote(`0.99`), "99th percentile basal area")
```

2.8.5 Understanding effects on probability of zero

Perhaps more interesting than looking at additional τ-predicted quantiles would be to see the effect of the covariates on the probability of having zero basal area. These can be found as extensions of the marginal or interaction predictions from the previous section. We illustrate using the `slope` by trig-transformed `aspect` interaction, repurposing our custom function for use on the zero probabilities.

For a 'quick-and-dirty' approximation, we find the zero probabilities by interpolation over the already summarised `pred3` array. To include error bands around our zero probabilities, we would need to back up a step and get predicted values for each iteration of the MCMC sampler, interpolate to find the zero probabilities and *then* summarise, as laid out in Section 2.5.

```
plotrad(quote(`tau0`), "Prob(0)")
```

Directionally, the plots of Fig. 2.15 seem to tell a similar story to the median interaction plots; east facing sites are more likely to have zero basal areas than similarly sloped west facing sites. We interpret these cautiously though, lacking appropriate error bands to quantify our uncertainty and definitively declare the probabilities different than the sample prevalence of zeroes.

2.8.6 Further model refinement and comparison

By comparing WAIC, we see that the multiple regression fit `fit.qrj3` is a better fit than `fit.qrj2` of the simple quantile regression section. Seeking

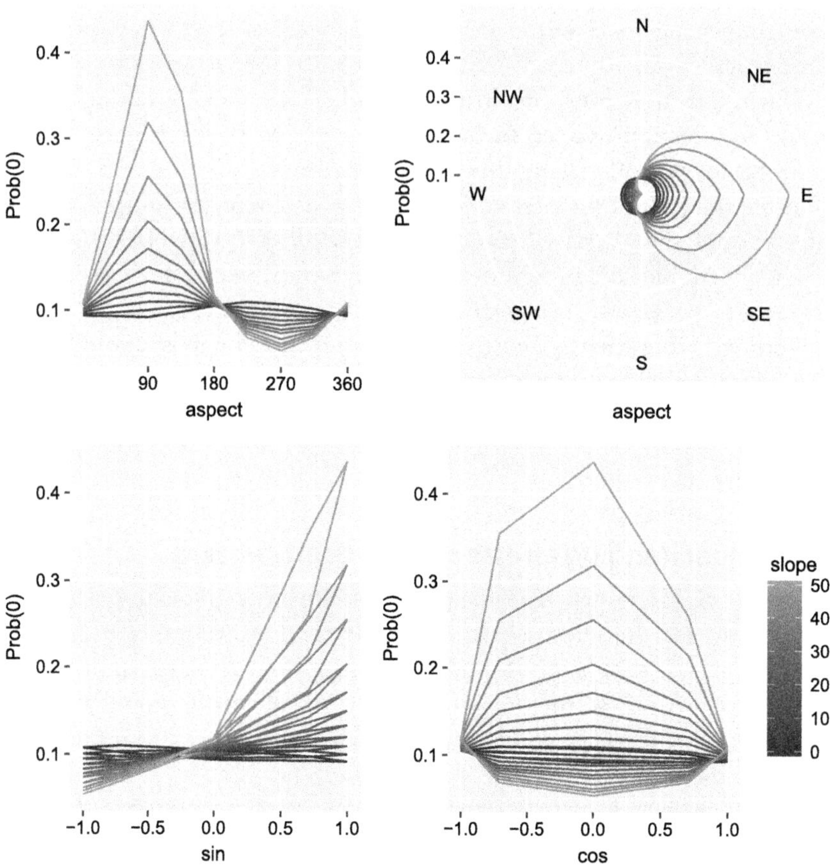

Figure 2.15 Marginal probability of zero over varying slope and aspect.

an even better fit, we make several refinements to the multiple regression model.

First, we add the b-spline on elevation that we used in the single covariate model, hoping to straighten out the quantile levels for that covariate. And second, we drop the marginal transformed `aspect` covariates from the model. Usually, dropping a nonsignificant main effect from a model when the interaction is significant and retained is not advocated; however, in this application we have a scientific justification.

For related but slightly different reasons, dropping part of a radial transformation is not usually advocated; however, in this application the covariate that corresponds to the north–south direction does not show a significant effect, and the inclusion of the east–west covariate could be justified under its own ecological moorings. We compare two models: one that has the nonsignificant `cos(aspect):slope` effect retained and one that drops it from the model.

```
library(splines)
set.seed(66666)
fit.qrj4 <- qrjoint(baRedMaple ~ slope +
            slope:I(sin(aspect*pi/180)) +
            slope:I(cos(aspect*pi/180)) +
            I(aspect==0) + region + ns(elev,3),
            data=dat, cens=ifelse(dat$baRedMaple==0,2,0),
            par="RQ", fbase="logistic", nsamp = 2000, thin = 20)

summary(fit.qrj4, plot.dev=FALSE)
#> WAIC.1 = 3446.18 , WAIC.2 = 3445.82

library(splines)
set.seed(77777)
fit.qrj5 <- qrjoint(baRedMaple ~
            slope + slope:I(sin(aspect*pi/180)) + I(aspect==0) +
            region + ns(elev,3), data=dat,
            cens=ifelse(dat$baRedMaple==0,2,0),
            par="RQ", fbase="logistic", nsamp = 2000, thin = 20)

summary(fit.qrj5, plot.dev=FALSE)
#> WAIC.1 = 3442.22 , WAIC.2 = 3442.57
```

Here we see that the WAIC is improved by the addition of the elevation b-spline and by dropping the marginal `cos` and `sin` effects. Also we see that WAIC improves slightly when `cos(aspect):slope` is also dropped from the model.

These models, fit on ~600 observations and <10 predictors, can each take 10 minutes or so to run, depending on computing resources. Models run on ~2000 observations and a similar number of predictors can take an hour to reach convergence and collect adequate samples from the MCMC chain. We see that model building and comparison for joint quantile regression is possible on moderately sized data sets and yields rich, interpretable and distribution-free results; however, it requires some time commitment for computing and interpretation. We suggest these methods to the practitioner who is willing to invest their time to achieve such rich, distribution-free results, but not to the casual user.

2.9 Conclusions and final remarks

In this chapter we have illustrated how joint quantile regression, as implemented in the `qrjoint` R package, can be used to carry out a model-based regression analysis of a zero-inflated but otherwise positive continuous response. Joint quantile regression is able to model the continuous response distribution with few distributional assumptions, making it more broadly applicable than Tobit regression. The censoring or latent-variable construct is only appropriate for modelling excess zero values when the same mechanisms that drive small-response values also drive zero-response values. We believe that to be reasonable in the case of the basal area case study.

We have shown how the quantile planes produced by the joint quantile regression obey the appropriate monotonicity constraints, something that cannot be said for traditional quantile regression methods. We have illustrated via a case study how to interpret the coefficient estimates obtained from a joint quantile regression. We also introduced visual diagnostics based on the probability integral transform that allow us to assess overall model fit and linearity assumptions, pointing us to areas where our design matrix could be refined. These diagnostics are not available for independently estimated quantile regressions, and therefore represent a valuable new tool for model refinement in the quantile regression context.

Additionally, by utilising the generative nature of our joint quantile regression model, we not only adjust for censoring but also make it a prominent inferential objective. For our case study, observing zero red maple basal area can be a phenomenon of independent scientific interest. The probability of this event, measured as $\tau_0(x) = Q^{-1}(0|x)$, can only be calculated by inverting the quantile function $Q(\tau|x)$ – which necessitates obtaining noncrossing, joint estimation of the function at all quantile levels. Such estimates are hard to obtain from an ensemble of single quantile-level quantile regressions.

We have approached this problem primarily from the perspective of inference on regression intercept and slopes, viewed as unknown functions of the quantile level. However, we have also illustrated elementary tools for prediction, including how-tos for estimating the probability of zero when data are left-truncated at zero. If prediction were the primary goal, we could train models on a subset of data and compare observed basal areas to the predictions on the held-out data. Comparison between `qrjoint`-fit models can be made on quantile predictions by using the check-loss metric and/or on the probability of zero by maximising the area under a receiver operating characteristic curve, depending on the focus of prediction.

Acknowledgement

This material is based upon work supported by the National Science Foundation under Grant No. 1613173.

References

[1] J. Abrevaya, The effects of demographics and maternal behavior on the distribution of birth outcomes, in: Economic Applications of Quantile Regression, Springer, 2002, pp. 247–257.

[2] C. Andrieu, J. Thoms, A tutorial on adaptive MCMC, Statistics and Computing 18 (4) (2008) 343–373.

[3] S. Banerjee, A.E. Gelfand, A.O. Finley, H. Sang, Gaussian predictive process models for large spatial data sets, Journal of the Royal Statistical Society: Series B (Statistical Methodology) 70 (4) (2008) 825–848.

[4] H.D. Bondell, B.J. Reich, H. Wang, Noncrossing quantile regression curve estimation, Biometrika 97 (4) (2010) 825–838.

[5] L.F. Burgette, J.P. Reiter, M.L. Miranda, Exploratory quantile regression with many covariates: an application to adverse birth outcomes, Epidemiology 22 (6) (2011) 859–866.

[6] J.B. Dunham, B.S. Cade, J.W. Terrell, Influences of spatial and temporal variation on fish-habitat relationships defined by regression quantiles, Transactions of the American Fisheries Society 131 (1) (2002) 86–98.

[7] D.B. Dunson, J.A. Taylor, Approximate Bayesian inference for quantiles, Nonparametric Statistics 17 (3) (2005) 385–400.

[8] J.B. Elsner, J.P. Kossin, T.H. Jagger, The increasing intensity of the strongest tropical cyclones, Nature 455 (7209) (2008) 92–95.

[9] Y. Feng, Y. Chen, X. He, et al., Bayesian quantile regression with approximate likelihood, Bernoulli 21 (2) (2015) 832–850.

[10] X. He, Quantile curves without crossing, The American Statistician 51 (2) (1997) 186–192.

[11] R. Koenker, G. Bassett, Regression quantiles, Econometrica: Journal of the Econometric Society 46 (1) (1978) 33–50.

[12] S. Portnoy, Censored regression quantiles, Journal of the American Statistical Association 98 (464) (2003) 1001–1012.

[13] J.L. Powell, Censored regression quantiles, Journal of Econometrics 32 (1) (1986) 143–155.

[14] B.J. Reich, M. Fuentes, D.B. Dunson, Bayesian spatial quantile regression, Journal of the American Statistical Association 106 (493) (2011) 6–20.

[15] J. Tobin, Estimation of relationships for limited dependent variables, Econometrica: Journal of the Econometric Society (1958) 24–36.

[16] S.T. Tokdar, Towards a faster implementation of density estimation with logistic Gaussian process priors, Journal of Computational and Graphical Statistics 16 (3) (2007) 633–655.
[17] S.T. Tokdar, J.B. Kadane, Simultaneous linear quantile regression: a semiparametric Bayesian approach, Bayesian Analysis 7 (1) (2012) 51–72.
[18] Y. Yang, S.T. Tokdar, Joint estimation of quantile planes over arbitrary predictor spaces, Journal of the American Statistical Association 112 (519) (2017) 1107–1120.

CHAPTER 3

Bayesian nonparametric density regression for ordinal responses

Maria DeYoreo[a], **Athanasios Kottas**[b]
[a]The RAND Corporation, 1776 Main St., Santa Monica, CA 90401, United States
[b]University of California, Santa Cruz, Department of Statistics, 1156 High Street, Santa Cruz, CA 95064, United States

Contents

3.1 Introduction

Ordinal data arise frequently in the social sciences, for instance, survey respondents often assign ratings on ordinal scales (such as 'agree', 'neutral' or 'disagree') to a set of questions. The relationship between the ordinal responses and other respondent characteristics are typically of interest. The environmental sciences also represents a broad area of application for ordinal regression models. Physical measurements might be recorded on a discrete scale, even though they are truly continuous. For example, in the data set **ozone** available through R [49], ozone concentration is recorded along with wind speed, radiation and temperature. While in this example ozone concentration is continuous, it is possible to imagine it being recorded as

Flexible Bayesian Regression Modelling
https://doi.org/10.1016/B978-0-12-815862-3.00009-3

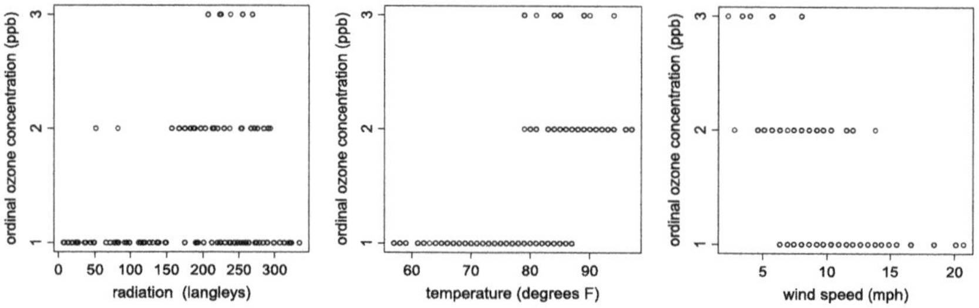

Figure 3.1 Ordinal ozone concentration versus radiation, temperature and wind speed.

simply 'low', 'medium' and 'high', where low might be defined as concentrations below 50 parts per billion (ppb) and high as concentrations above 100 ppb. In this application, the relationships between ordinal ozone concentration and the other environmental covariates, displayed in Fig. 3.1, are of interest.

As illustrated by the ozone data example, which we will refer to throughout this chapter, a natural way to model ordinal data is to envision the ordinal variable as representing a discretised version of an underlying latent continuous random variable. When a normal distribution is assumed for the latent variable this results in the commonly used ordinal probit model (e.g. [34,1]).

With multiple correlated ordinal variables, which can arise for instance when survey respondents answer multiple questions on an ordinal scale, a multivariate normal distribution can be used. This allows for inferring the relationship between the ordinal variables and results in a multivariate ordinal probit model [9].

Under the probit model for a single ordinal response Y with C categories and covariate vector $\boldsymbol{x}$, $\Pr(Y \leq m \mid \boldsymbol{x}) = \Phi(\gamma_m - \boldsymbol{x}^T\boldsymbol{\beta})$, for $m = 1, \ldots, C$. Here, $-\infty = \gamma_0 < \gamma_1 < \cdots < \gamma_{C-1} < \gamma_C = \infty$ are cut-off points for the response categories, where typically $\gamma_1 = 0$ for identifiability, and $\Phi(\cdot)$ is the standard normal cumulative distribution function (CDF). Working in a Bayesian framework, [1] have shown that posterior simulation is greatly simplified by augmenting the model with latent variables. In particular, assume that the ordinal response Y arises from a latent continuous response Z, such that $Y = m$ if and only if $Z \in (\gamma_{m-1}, \gamma_m]$, for $m = 1, \ldots, C$, and $Z \mid \boldsymbol{\beta} \sim \mathrm{N}(\boldsymbol{x}^T\boldsymbol{\beta}, 1)$, which yields $\Pr(Y = m \mid \boldsymbol{x}) = \int_{\gamma_{m-1}}^{\gamma_m} \mathrm{N}(z \mid \boldsymbol{x}^T\boldsymbol{\beta}, 1)\,dz$, where $\mathrm{N}(z \mid \mu, \sigma^2)$ denotes a normal density function evaluated at z with mean μ and standard deviation σ.

The multivariate probit model for binary or ordinal responses generalises the probit model to accommodate correlated ordinal responses $\boldsymbol{Y} = (Y_1, ..., Y_k)$, where $Y_j \in \{1, ..., C_j\}$ for $j = 1, ..., k$, using a multivariate normal distribution for the underlying latent variables $\boldsymbol{Z} = (Z_1, ..., Z_k)$. To obtain an identifiable model, restrictions must be imposed on the covariance matrix $\boldsymbol{\Sigma}$ of the multivariate normal distribution for $\boldsymbol{Z}$; for example, it may be restricted to be a correlation matrix. This yields challenges in developing an effective inferential algorithm for estimation of this model. Additionally, implementing the probit model (with either univariate or multivariate responses) requires estimation for the cut-off points, which are typically highly correlated with the latent responses [9,29,8].

The assumption of normality on the latent variables is restrictive, especially for data which contain a large proportion of observations at high or low ordinal levels and relatively few observations at moderate levels. As a consequence of the normal distribution shape, there are certain limitations on the effect that each covariate can have on the marginal probability response curves. In particular, $\Pr(Y_j = 1 \mid x)$ and $\Pr(Y_j = C_j \mid x)$ are monotonically increasing or decreasing as a function of covariate x, and they must have the opposite type of monotonicity. The direction of monotonicity changes exactly once in moving from category 1 to C_j (referred to as the single crossing property). In addition, the relative effect of covariates r and s, i.e. the ratio of $\partial \Pr(Y_j = m \mid \boldsymbol{x})/\partial x_r$ to $\partial \Pr(Y_j = m \mid \boldsymbol{x})/\partial x_s$, is equal to the ratio of the rth and sth regression coefficients for the jth response, which does not depend on m or $\boldsymbol{x}$. That is, the relative effect of one covariate to another is the same for every ordinal level and any covariate value [7].

To relax these assumptions, we turn to Bayesian nonparametric density regression modelling. In particular, our approach uses a nonparametric mixture model for the joint distribution of the covariates and latent responses which yields general inference for ordinal regression relationships and other functionals of the conditional response distribution. A practically important feature of this nonparametric modelling framework is that it can be applied with fixed cut-off points for the response categories, thus resulting in more flexible inference than parametric probit models, which can be implemented with simpler and more efficient posterior simulation methods.

The rest of this chapter is organised as follows. In Section 3.2, we provide a general overview of Bayesian nonparametric density regression, in the process introducing basic background on Dirichlet process (DP) priors and DP mixture models. Section 3.3 presents the ordinal regression methodology, including the mixture model formulation (Section 3.3.1), details on prior specification and posterior inference (Section 3.3.2), illustrations using the ozone data (Section 3.3.3) and a discussion of related work and extensions of the model (Section 3.3.4). Finally, Section 3.4 summarises the main points of this chapter.

3.2 Bayesian nonparametric density regression

There is by now a rich literature on Bayesian regression modelling that utilises nonparametric priors. Most of the work in this literature revolves around the traditional regression setting which focuses on a functional of the response distribution (mean, median, mode) to incorporate the relationship with covariates. More specifically, with a univariate continuous response Z and covariate vector $\boldsymbol{x}$, the traditional model formulation for the responses becomes $z_i = h(\boldsymbol{x}_i) + \varepsilon_i$, where $h(\boldsymbol{x})$ is the regression function and the ε_i arise, typically conditionally i.i.d., from an error distribution. The two main trends in the literature involve semiparametric modelling, either placing a nonparametric prior on the space of regression functions with a parametric error distribution or specifying the regression function parametrically (typically, in a linear regression form $h(\boldsymbol{x}) = \boldsymbol{x}^T\boldsymbol{\beta}$) and using a nonparametric prior for the space of error distributions. There is a wide variety of methods for either of these two directions, in terms of the different nonparametric prior models that have been developed, additional structure for the regression function (e.g. smoothness or monotonicity) or the error distribution (e.g. unimodality) and computational techniques for inference and prediction, as well as with respect to the applications explored. A more detailed review is beyond the scope of this chapter, but we refer to [19], [24], [36] and [39] for reviews of some of the methods.

Here, we focus on a different approach to the regression problem which builds from a nonparametric mixture model for the joint distribution of response(s) and covariates such that inference for regression relationships arises from the conditional response distribution. This approach provides the foundation for the ordinal regression methodology discussed in Section 3.3. In this section, we review it in a more generic setting, after introducing the DP and DP mixture models [18,2], the class of nonparametric priors for random densities underlying the methods reviewed in this chapter.

3.2.1 Dirichlet process priors and Dirichlet process mixtures

The DP was developed by [18] as a prior probability model for spaces of distributions (defined on a particular sample space $\mathcal{X}$); indeed, it is the first such prior introduced in the literature. It is defined as a stochastic process with realisations that are (random) probability measures, built from Dirichlet finite-dimensional distributions with specific structure for the Dirichlet distribution parameters that ensures consistent extension to a stochastic process. The DP is characterised by two parameters: a positive scalar parameter, α, and $G_0 \equiv G_0(\boldsymbol{\psi})$, a distribution (on $\mathcal{X}$) specified up to a number of parameters $\boldsymbol{\psi}$. We write $G \sim \mathrm{DP}(\alpha, G_0)$ to denote that the random distribution G follows a DP prior. For any (measurable) subset B of $\mathcal{X}$, $\mathrm{E}(G(B)) = G_0(B)$ and $\mathrm{Var}(G(B)) = (\alpha+1)^{-1} G_0(B)\{1 - G_0(B)\}$. Therefore, G_0 is a centering distribution for the DP whereas α can be interpreted as a precision parameter. The larger α is, the *closer* a DP realisation G is to G_0; as α gets smaller, the variability in the DP realisations increases, and they also become more discrete, concentrated on fewer effective atoms.

The discreteness of DP realisations is evident from the DP constructive definition [51], which is also key for the study of other model properties and for posterior inference. According to this definition, a realisation G from $\mathrm{DP}(\alpha, G_0)$ is (almost surely) of the form $G = \sum_{l=1}^{\infty} p_l \delta_{\boldsymbol{\vartheta}_l}$. Here, δ_a denotes a point mass at a, the atoms $\boldsymbol{\vartheta}_l$ are i.i.d. realisations from G_0 and the weights are determined through *stick breaking* from beta-distributed random variables: $p_1 = v_1$, and $p_l = v_l \prod_{r=1}^{l-1}(1 - v_r)$, for $l = 2, 3, \ldots$, with $v_l \overset{i.i.d.}{\sim} \mathrm{Beta}(1, \alpha)$. Moreover, $\{\boldsymbol{\vartheta}_l : l = 1, 2, ...\}$ and $\{v_l : l = 1, 2, ...\}$ are independent sequences of random variables.

The DP is more commonly used as a nonparametric prior for distributions in later stages of hierarchical models, for example in DP mixture models, $f(\boldsymbol{u} \mid G) = \int k(\boldsymbol{u} \mid \boldsymbol{\theta})\, \mathrm{d}G(\boldsymbol{\theta})$, where $k(\cdot \mid \boldsymbol{\theta})$ is the density for the mixture kernel family of distributions with parameters $\boldsymbol{\theta}$ and $G \sim \mathrm{DP}(\alpha, G_0)$. For data $\{\boldsymbol{u}_i : i = 1, ..., n\}$ assumed to arise i.i.d., given G, from $f(\boldsymbol{u} \mid G)$, the model can be expressed hierarchically by introducing a set of latent mixing parameters, $\{\boldsymbol{\theta}_i : i = 1, ..., n\}$, associated with the $\boldsymbol{u}_i$. More specifically, the hierarchical model formulation is given by $\boldsymbol{u}_i \mid \boldsymbol{\theta}_i \overset{ind.}{\sim} k(\boldsymbol{u}_i \mid \boldsymbol{\theta}_i)$, and $\boldsymbol{\theta}_i \mid G \overset{i.i.d.}{\sim} G$, for $i = 1, ..., n$. The model is typically completed with hyperpriors for the DP precision parameter α and for (some of) the parameters of the centering distribution G_0.

The DP mixture model setting can be very versatile as the kernel distribution may be univariate or multivariate, including continuous and/or discrete components. In this context, the discreteness of the DP is an asset as it allows ties in the mixing parameters, resulting in a flexible shape for the DP mixture density $f(\boldsymbol{u} \mid G)$. In fact, using the DP constructive definition, the model can be equivalently written as $f(\boldsymbol{u} \mid G) = \sum_{l=1}^{\infty} p_l k(\boldsymbol{u} \mid \boldsymbol{\vartheta}_l)$, that is, a discrete countable mixture of kernel densities with mixture weights given by the DP stick breaking weights.

DP mixture models combine the appealing features of mixture modelling with strong theoretical properties of nonparametric priors, such as full support (informally, the capacity to place positive prior probability on arbitrarily small neighbourhoods of any distribution) and posterior consistency. For a detailed account of theoretical properties for DP and DP mixture priors, we refer to [21]. Therefore, DP mixtures have become very popular in the Bayes nonparametrics literature and they have been widely explored for applications in various fields. It is thus not surprising that posterior simulation methods for DP mixture models have been extensively investigated. Markov chain Monte Carlo (MCMC) computational approaches include (i) algorithms that sample from the marginal posterior distribution of the mixing parameters that arises after marginalising G over its DP prior (e.g. [17,33,41]), with full inference available by additional sampling from the conditional posterior distribution of G [20]; (ii) blocked Gibbs samplers based on truncation approximations to G [26,25]; (iii) retrospective sampling techniques [45]; and (iv) slice sampling methods [59,30]. The more recent literature (both in statistics and machine learning) actively explores computational inference methods to scale DP mixture models to large amounts of data. Such methods go beyond MCMC and typically involve variational algorithms; two of the earlier examples are [6] and [63]. Details for one of the MCMC methods (the blocked Gibbs sampler) are given in Section 3.3.2 in the context of the ordinal regression model.

3.2.2 Dirichlet process mixture modelling for density regression

For simpler notation and to fix ideas, consider a univariate continuous response, Z, and a p-dimensional vector of covariates, $\boldsymbol{x}$. (The methodology can be applied to multivariate responses and, indeed, this is how it is discussed in Section 3.3 in the ordinal regression setting.) For problems involving random covariates, a natural approach to nonparametric regression is to estimate the joint response covariate density, $f(z, \boldsymbol{x})$, and the marginal covariate density, $f(\boldsymbol{x})$, and obtain regression estimates from the conditional response density, $f(z \mid \boldsymbol{x})$. This density regression approach (also referred to as 'implied conditional regression' or 'curve fitting') dates back at least to [40] and [61], where kernel smoothing estimation methods were used. Alternatively, a model-based, nonparametric framework can be built using Bayesian density estimation through nonparametric mixture models for $f(z, \boldsymbol{x})$. The first reference in that direction is [38], where DP mixtures of multivariate normal densities were used. The nonparametric mixture modelling approach to density regression is attractive because of the flexibility of well-established prior probability models for $f(z, \boldsymbol{x})$ and the model-based inferential framework that enables full uncertainty quantification for any functional of the conditional response distribution.

Consider a generic DP mixture model for the joint response covariate density,

$$f(z, \boldsymbol{x}) \equiv f(z, \boldsymbol{x} \mid G) = \int k(z, \boldsymbol{x} \mid \boldsymbol{\theta}) \, \mathrm{d}G(\boldsymbol{\theta}), \quad G \mid \alpha, \boldsymbol{\psi} \sim \mathrm{DP}(\alpha, G_0(\boldsymbol{\psi})),$$

where $k(z, \boldsymbol{x} \mid \boldsymbol{\theta})$ is an appropriate kernel density. Using the DP constructive definition with the notation of Section 3.2.1, the conditional response density can be written as

$$f(z \mid \boldsymbol{x}, G) = \frac{f(z, \boldsymbol{x} \mid G)}{f(\boldsymbol{x} \mid G)} = \frac{\sum_{l=1}^{\infty} p_l \, k(z, \boldsymbol{x} \mid \boldsymbol{\theta}_l)}{\sum_{l=1}^{\infty} p_l \, k(\boldsymbol{x} \mid \boldsymbol{\theta}_l)} = \sum_{l=1}^{\infty} \omega_l(\boldsymbol{x}) \, k(z \mid \boldsymbol{x}, \boldsymbol{\theta}_l)$$

where $\omega_l(\boldsymbol{x}) = p_l \, k(\boldsymbol{x} \mid \boldsymbol{\theta}_l)/\{\sum_{r=1}^{\infty} p_r \, k(\boldsymbol{x} \mid \boldsymbol{\theta}_r)\}$. Hence, the conditional response density admits a representation as a mixture of the conditional response kernel densities with covariate-dependent mixture weights. Such weights allow for local adjustment over the covariate space, thus enabling general shapes (tail, skewness and modal behaviour) for the response distribution across covariate values. Similar expressions can be derived for other linear functionals of the response distribution. In particular, the mean regression functional is given by $\mathrm{E}(Z \mid \boldsymbol{x}, G) = \sum_{l=1}^{\infty} \omega_l(\boldsymbol{x}) \mathrm{E}(Z \mid \boldsymbol{x}, \boldsymbol{\theta}_l)$. In general, (almost sure) finiteness of $\mathrm{E}(Z \mid \boldsymbol{x}, G)$ can be verified through sufficient conditions that involve the DP mixture kernel and G_0; see e.g. [47]. In the case of a multivariate normal mixture kernel, $\mathrm{E}(Z \mid \boldsymbol{x}, \boldsymbol{\theta}_l)$ is a linear regression function, and thus the mixture mean regression function, $\mathrm{E}(Z \mid \boldsymbol{x}, G)$, is a locally weighted mixture of linear regressions which allows estimation of nonlinear regression relationships. Here, it is instructive to draw the contrast with semiparametric mean regression models that target either the mean regression function *or* the error distribution. The nonparametric mixture density regression approach can model both nonlinear regression functions *and* nonstandard shapes for the response distribution, thus offering a flexible framework for the general regression problem.

The specification of the DP mixture kernel, $k(z, \boldsymbol{x} \mid \boldsymbol{\theta})$, is typically driven by the type of response and covariate variables in the particular application, as well as by computational considerations. A common choice is the multivariate normal density, which can handle (possibly after transformation) continuous variables for the response and covariates. As described in Section 3.3.1, the normal kernel density can also accommodate ordinal responses through latent continuous variables, and this modelling strategy can be further utilised for ordinal covariates. More generally, the kernel can be built from a density for the covariates, $k(\boldsymbol{x} \mid \boldsymbol{\theta}_1)$, and a parametric regression model, $k(z \mid \boldsymbol{x}, \boldsymbol{\theta}_2)$, where $\boldsymbol{\theta} = (\boldsymbol{\theta}_1, \boldsymbol{\theta}_2)$. The general form can be simplified by reducing $k(z \mid \boldsymbol{x}, \boldsymbol{\theta}_2)$ to a marginal density $k(z \mid \boldsymbol{\theta}_2)$ for the response. The full product kernel form involves the further simplification that assumes independence in the kernel distribution for the covariates. For problems with a moderate number of covariates, mixture kernels with partial/full independence structure result in more efficient posterior simulation by reducing the number of mixing parameters, but they may limit inferential flexibility. Although mixing over parameters of a product kernel induces dependence in the DP mixture distribution, there is an impact on model structure for regression functionals. For instance, if $k(z, \boldsymbol{x} \mid \boldsymbol{\theta}) = k(\boldsymbol{x} \mid \boldsymbol{\theta}_1)k(z \mid \boldsymbol{\theta}_2)$, the mean regression function becomes $\sum_{l=1}^{\infty} \omega_l(\boldsymbol{x})\,\mathrm{E}(Z \mid \boldsymbol{\theta}_l)$, where the kernel response means no longer depend on the covariates. This form can still uncover nonlinear regression relationships through the covariate-dependent weights, although this will typically occur at the expense of estimating a larger number of effective mixture components.

The density regression approach is based on the notion of a joint model for the response and the covariates, and it is thus meaningful for problems with random covariates. As discussed in [38], applying it to nonrandom covariates introduces artificial terms into the likelihood; in the same spirit, modelling only the response distribution in the presence of random covariates omits relevant likelihood terms. The main practical limitation of this modelling approach is that it becomes prohibitive for problems with a relatively large number of covariates (say, more than 20) as the sample sizes typically available are not sufficient for effective estimation of the rapidly increasing number of parameters, especially if one insists on general mixture kernels. However, the methodology is appealing for several important applications in the biological, environmental and social sciences involving a small to moderate number of random covariates.

Section 3.3.4 reviews relevant applications of DP mixture models for problems with categorical responses. In addition, variations and extensions of the DP mixture density regression model discussed here have been applied to functional data analysis [50], quantile regression [55], Markov switching regression [54] and mean residual life regression [47]. Moreover, the modelling framework has been explored for fully nonparametric inference for marked nonhomogeneous Poisson processes [53,56,62]. Finally, modifications and alternatives to the DP prior for the mixing distribution have been studied in order to control clustering more effectively; see e.g. [37], [46], [58] and [48].

3.3 Mixture modelling for ordinal responses

3.3.1 Modelling approach

Suppose that k ordinal categorical variables are recorded for each of n individuals, along with p continuous covariates, so that for individual i we observe a response vector $\boldsymbol{y}_i = (y_{i1}, \ldots, y_{ik})$ and a covariate vector $\boldsymbol{x}_i = (x_{i1}, \ldots, x_{ip})$, with $y_{ij} \in \{1, \ldots, C_j\}$ and $C_j > 2$. Introduce latent continuous random variables $\boldsymbol{z}_i = (z_{i1}, \ldots, z_{ik})$, $i = 1, \ldots, n$, such that $y_{ij} = l$ if and only if $\gamma_{j,l-1} < z_{ij} \leq \gamma_{j,l}$, for $j = 1, \ldots, k$ and $l = 1, \ldots, C_j$. For reasons previously mentioned, we focus on building a model for the joint density $f(\boldsymbol{z}, \boldsymbol{x})$, which is a continuous density of dimension $k + p$, which implies a model for the conditional response distribution $f(\boldsymbol{y} \mid \boldsymbol{x})$.

To model $f(\boldsymbol{z}, \boldsymbol{x})$ in a flexible way, we use a DP mixture of multivariate normals model, mixing on the mean vector and covariance matrix. We assume $(\boldsymbol{z}_i, \boldsymbol{x}_i) \mid G \overset{iid}{\sim} \int \mathrm{N}(\boldsymbol{z}_i, \boldsymbol{x}_i \mid \boldsymbol{\mu}, \boldsymbol{\Sigma}) \mathrm{d}G(\boldsymbol{\mu}, \boldsymbol{\Sigma})$, and we place a DP prior on the random mixing distribution G. The hierarchical model is formulated by introducing a latent mixing parameter $\boldsymbol{\theta}_i = (\boldsymbol{\mu}_i, \boldsymbol{\Sigma}_i)$ for each data vector, i.e.

$$(\boldsymbol{z}_i, \boldsymbol{x}_i) \mid \boldsymbol{\theta}_i \overset{i.n.d.}{\sim} \mathrm{N}(\boldsymbol{\mu}_i, \boldsymbol{\Sigma}_i), \quad \boldsymbol{\theta}_i \mid G \overset{i.i.d.}{\sim} G, \quad i = 1, \ldots, n, \tag{3.1}$$

where $G \mid \alpha, \boldsymbol{\psi} \sim \mathrm{DP}(\alpha, G_0(\cdot \mid \boldsymbol{\psi}))$, with base (centering) distribution $G_0(\boldsymbol{\mu}, \boldsymbol{\Sigma} \mid \boldsymbol{\psi}) = \mathrm{N}(\boldsymbol{\mu} \mid \boldsymbol{m}, \boldsymbol{V}) \mathrm{IW}(\boldsymbol{\Sigma} \mid \nu, \boldsymbol{S})$. The parameter ν is fixed, and the model is completed with hyperpriors on $\boldsymbol{\psi} = (\boldsymbol{m}, \boldsymbol{V}, \boldsymbol{S})$, and a prior on α, i.e.

$$\boldsymbol{m} \sim \mathrm{N}(\boldsymbol{a_m}, \boldsymbol{B_m}), \quad \boldsymbol{V} \sim \mathrm{IW}(a_{\boldsymbol{V}}, \boldsymbol{B_V}), \quad \boldsymbol{S} \sim \mathrm{W}(a_{\boldsymbol{S}}, \boldsymbol{B_S}), \quad \alpha \sim \mathrm{gamma}(a_\alpha, b_\alpha), \tag{3.2}$$

where $W(a_S, \boldsymbol{B}_S)$ denotes a Wishart distribution with mean $a_S\boldsymbol{B}_S$, and $IW(a_V, \boldsymbol{B}_V)$ denotes an inverse-Wishart distribution with mean $(a_V - (k+p) - 1)^{-1}\boldsymbol{B}_V$.

The discreteness of the DP prior for G results in ties among the $\boldsymbol{\theta}_i$, so that in practice fewer than n distinct values for the $\{\boldsymbol{\theta}_i\}$ are effective in the hierarchical model. The data are therefore clustered into a typically small number of groups relative to n, with the number of clusters, n^*, controlled by parameter α, where larger values favour more clusters.

Based on the DP constructive definition discussed in Section 3.2.1, the prior model for $f(\boldsymbol{z}, \boldsymbol{x})$ has an almost sure representation as a countable mixture of multivariate normals, and the proposed model can therefore be viewed as a nonparametric extension of the multivariate probit model with random covariates. This implies a countable mixture of normal distributions (with covariate-dependent weights) for $f(\boldsymbol{z} \mid \boldsymbol{x}, G)$, from which the latent $\boldsymbol{z}$ may be integrated out to reveal the induced model for the ordinal regression relationships. In general, for a multivariate response $\boldsymbol{Y} = (Y_1, \dots, Y_k)$ with an associated covariate vector $\boldsymbol{X}$, the probability that $\boldsymbol{Y}$ takes on the values $\boldsymbol{l} = (l_1, \dots, l_k)$, where $l_j \in \{1, \dots, C_j\}$, for $j = 1, \dots, k$, can be expressed as

$$\Pr(\boldsymbol{Y} = \boldsymbol{l} \mid \boldsymbol{x}, G) = \sum_{r=1}^{\infty} w_r(\boldsymbol{x}) \int_{\gamma_{k,l_k-1}}^{\gamma_{k,l_k}} \cdots \int_{\gamma_{1,l_1-1}}^{\gamma_{1,l_1}} \mathrm{N}(\boldsymbol{z} \mid \boldsymbol{m}_r(\boldsymbol{x}), \boldsymbol{S}_r)\mathrm{d}\boldsymbol{z}, \qquad (3.3)$$

with covariate-dependent weights $w_r(\boldsymbol{x}) \propto p_r\mathrm{N}(\boldsymbol{x} \mid \boldsymbol{\mu}_r^x, \boldsymbol{\Sigma}_r^{xx})$, mean vectors $\boldsymbol{m}_r(\boldsymbol{x}) = \boldsymbol{\mu}_r^z + \boldsymbol{\Sigma}_r^{zx}(\boldsymbol{\Sigma}_r^{xx})^{-1}(\boldsymbol{x} - \boldsymbol{\mu}_r^x)$ and covariance matrices $\boldsymbol{S}_r = \boldsymbol{\Sigma}_r^{zz} - \boldsymbol{\Sigma}_r^{zx}(\boldsymbol{\Sigma}_r^{xx})^{-1}\boldsymbol{\Sigma}_r^{xz}$. Here, $(\boldsymbol{\mu}_r, \boldsymbol{\Sigma}_r)$ are the atoms in the DP prior constructive definition, where $\boldsymbol{\mu}_r$ is partitioned into $\boldsymbol{\mu}_r^z$ and $\boldsymbol{\mu}_r^x$ according to random vectors $\boldsymbol{Z}$ and $\boldsymbol{X}$, and $(\boldsymbol{\Sigma}_r^{zz}, \boldsymbol{\Sigma}_r^{xx}, \boldsymbol{\Sigma}_r^{zx}, \boldsymbol{\Sigma}_r^{xz})$ are the components of the corresponding partition of covariance matrix $\boldsymbol{\Sigma}_r$.

To illustrate, consider a bivariate response $\boldsymbol{Y} = (Y_1, Y_2)$, with covariates $\boldsymbol{X}$. The probability assigned to the event $(Y_1 = l_1) \cap (Y_2 = l_2)$ is obtained using (3.3), which involves evaluating bivariate normal distribution functions. However, one may be interested in the marginal relationships between individual components of $\boldsymbol{Y}$ and the covariates. We may obtain the probability that Y_1 and Y_2 take on some combination of values as a function of $\boldsymbol{X}$, but also marginally how the first varies as a function of $\boldsymbol{X}$. The marginal inference, $\Pr(Y_1 = l_1 \mid \boldsymbol{x}, G)$, is given by the expression

$$\sum_{r=1}^{\infty} w_r(\boldsymbol{x}) \left\{ \Phi\left(\frac{\gamma_{1,l_1} - m_r(\boldsymbol{x})}{s_r^{1/2}} \right) - \Phi\left(\frac{\gamma_{1,l_1-1} - m_r(\boldsymbol{x})}{s_r^{1/2}} \right) \right\}, \qquad (3.4)$$

where $m_r(\boldsymbol{x})$ and s_r are the conditional mean and variance for z_1 conditional on $\boldsymbol{x}$ implied by the joint distribution $\mathrm{N}(\boldsymbol{z}, \boldsymbol{x} \mid \boldsymbol{\mu}_r, \boldsymbol{\Sigma}_r)$. Expression (3.4) provides also the form of the ordinal regression curves in the case of a single response.

Hence, the implied regression relationships have a mixture structure with component-specific kernels which take the form of parametric probit regressions and weights which are covariate-dependent. This structure enables inference for nonlinear response curves, by favouring a set of parametric models with varying probabilities depending on the location in the covariate space. The limitations of parametric probit models – including relative covariate effects which are constant in terms of the covariate and the ordinal level, monotonicity and the single crossing property of the response curves – are thereby overcome.

We noted in Section 3.1 that computational difficulties sometimes arise in fitting parametric ordinal probit models. The reason for this is that to obtain an identifiable model, restrictions must be imposed on the covariance matrix $\boldsymbol{\Sigma}$ of the multivariate normal distribution for $\boldsymbol{Z}$. One way to handle this is to restrict the covariance matrix to be a correlation matrix, which complicates Bayesian inference since there does not exist a conjugate prior for correlation matrices. Posterior simulation is further complicated by estimation of the cut-off points which are typically highly correlated with the latent responses.

In the Bayesian nonparametric model proposed, it can be shown that the mixture kernel covariance matrix can be left unstructured, and cut-offs can be fixed to arbitrary increasing values. [13] show that all parameters of the normal mixture kernel are identifiable provided each ordinal response comprises more than two classifications. This methodology focuses on multivariate ordinal responses with $C_j > 2$, for all j. However, if one or more responses is binary, then the full covariance matrix of the normal mixture kernel for $(\boldsymbol{Z}, \boldsymbol{X})$ is not identifiable. [13] also demonstrate that, with fixed cut-offs, the model can approximate arbitrarily well any set of probabilities on the ordinal outcomes. This large support property of normal DP mixture models for ordinal responses was suggested earlier by [31], who provided an informal argument that the normal DP mixture model for multivariate ordinal responses (without covariates) can approximate arbitrarily well any probability distribution for a contingency table. The basis for this argument is that, in the limit, one mixture component can be placed within each set of cut-offs corresponding to a specific ordinal vector, with the mixture weights assigned accordingly to each cell. This feature represents a significant advantage over parametric ordinal regression models in terms of computation.

3.3.2 Implementation details

3.3.2.1 Prior specification

To implement the model, we need to specify the parameters of the hyperpriors in (3.2). A default specification strategy is developed by considering the limiting case of the model as $\alpha \to 0^+$, which results in a single normal distribution for $(\boldsymbol{Z}, \boldsymbol{X})$. This limiting model is essentially the multivariate probit model, with the addition of random covariates. The only covariate information we use here is an approximate centre and range for each covariate, denoted by $\boldsymbol{c}^x = (c_1^x, \ldots, c_p^x)$ and $\boldsymbol{r}^x = (r_1^x, \ldots, r_p^x)$. Then c_m^x and $r_m^x/4$ are used as proxies for the marginal mean and standard deviation of X_m. We also seek to centre and scale the latent variables appropriately, using the cut-offs. Since Y_j is supported on $\{1, \ldots, C_j\}$, latent continuous variable Z_j must be supported on values slightly below $\gamma_{j,1}$, up to slightly above γ_{j,C_j-1}. We therefore use $r_j^z/4$, where $r_j^z = (\gamma_{j,C_j-1} - \gamma_{j,1})$, as a proxy for the standard deviation of Z_j.

Under $(\boldsymbol{Z}, \boldsymbol{X}) \mid \boldsymbol{\mu}, \boldsymbol{\Sigma} \sim \mathrm{N}(\boldsymbol{\mu}, \boldsymbol{\Sigma})$, we have $\mathrm{E}(\boldsymbol{Z}, \boldsymbol{X}) = \boldsymbol{a_m}$, and $\mathrm{Cov}(\boldsymbol{Z}, \boldsymbol{X}) = a_S \boldsymbol{B_S}(\nu - d - 1)^{-1} + \boldsymbol{B_V}(a_V - d - 1)^{-1} + \boldsymbol{B_m}$, with $d = p + k$. Then, assuming each set of cut-offs $(\gamma_{j,0}, \ldots, \gamma_{j,C_j})$ are centred at 0, we fix $a_m = (0, \ldots, 0, \boldsymbol{c}^x)$. Letting $\boldsymbol{D}$ be a diagonal matrix with elements $\{(r_1^z/4)^2, \ldots, (r_k^z/4)^2, (r_1^x/4)^2, \ldots, (r_p^x/4)^2\}$, each of the three terms in $\mathrm{Cov}(\boldsymbol{Z}, \boldsymbol{X})$ can be assigned an equal proportion of the total covariance and set to $(1/3)\boldsymbol{D}$, or to $(1/2)\boldsymbol{D}$ to inflate the variance slightly. For dispersed but proper priors with finite expectation, ν, a_V and a_S can be fixed to $d+2$. Fixing these parameters allows for $\boldsymbol{B_S}$ and $\boldsymbol{B_V}$ to be determined accordingly, completing the default specification strategy for the hyperpriors of $\boldsymbol{m}$, $\boldsymbol{V}$ and $\boldsymbol{S}$.

In the strategy outlined above, the form of $\mathrm{Cov}(\boldsymbol{Z}, \boldsymbol{X})$ was diagonal, such that a priori we favour independence between $\boldsymbol{Z}$ and $\boldsymbol{X}$ within a particular mixture component. Combined with the other aspects of the prior specification approach, this generally leads to prior means for the ordinal regression curves which do not have any trend across the covariate space. Moreover, the corresponding prior uncertainty bands span a significant portion of the unit interval.

3.3.2.2 Posterior inference

The MCMC posterior simulation method we utilise is based on a finite truncation approximation to the countable mixing distribution G, using the DP stick breaking representation. The blocked Gibbs sampler [26,25] replaces the countable sum with a finite sum, $G_N = \sum_{l=1}^{N} p_l \delta_{(\boldsymbol{\mu}_l, \boldsymbol{\Sigma}_l)}$, with $(\boldsymbol{\mu}_l, \boldsymbol{\Sigma}_l)$ i.i.d. from G_0, for $l = 1, ..., N$. Here, the first $N - 1$ elements of $\boldsymbol{p} = (p_1, ..., p_N)$ are equivalent to those in the countable representation of G, whereas $p_N = 1 - \sum_{l=1}^{N-1} p_l$. Under this approach, the posterior samples for model parameters yield posterior samples for G_N, and therefore full inference is available for mixture functionals.

The truncation level N can be chosen to any desired level of accuracy, using standard DP properties. In particular, the expectation for the partial sum of the original DP weights, $\mathrm{E}(\sum_{l=1}^{N} p_l \mid \alpha) = 1 - \{\alpha/(\alpha + 1)\}^N$, can be averaged over the prior for α to estimate the marginal prior expectation, $\mathrm{E}(\sum_{l=1}^{N} p_l)$, which is then used to specify N given a tolerance level for the approximation. For instance, $N = 50$ and a gamma$(0.5, 0.5)$ prior for α yields $\mathrm{E}(\sum_{l=1}^{50} p_l) \approx 0.99994$.

To express the hierarchical model for the data after replacing G with G_N, introduce configuration variables $(L_1, \ldots, L_n)$, such that $L_i = l$ if and only if $\boldsymbol{\theta}_i = (\boldsymbol{\mu}_l, \boldsymbol{\Sigma}_l)$, for $i = 1, ..., n$ and $l = 1, ..., N$. Then, the model for the data becomes

$$
\begin{aligned}
y_{ij} = l \quad \text{iff} \quad \gamma_{j,l-1} < z_{ij} \leq \gamma_{j,l}, \quad & i = 1, \ldots, n, \quad j = 1, \ldots, k, \\
(\boldsymbol{z}_i, \boldsymbol{x}_i) \mid \{(\boldsymbol{\mu}_l, \boldsymbol{\Sigma}_l) : l = 1, ..., N\}, L_i \overset{ind.}{\sim} \mathrm{N}(\boldsymbol{\mu}_{L_i}, \boldsymbol{\Sigma}_{L_i}), \quad & i = 1, \ldots, n, \\
L_i \mid \boldsymbol{p} \overset{iid}{\sim} \sum\nolimits_{l=1}^{N} p_l \delta_l(L_i), \quad & i = 1, ..., n, \\
(\boldsymbol{\mu}_l, \boldsymbol{\Sigma}_l) \mid \boldsymbol{\psi} \overset{iid}{\sim} \mathrm{N}(\boldsymbol{\mu}_l \mid \boldsymbol{m}, \boldsymbol{V}) \mathrm{IW}(\boldsymbol{\Sigma}_l \mid \nu, \boldsymbol{S}), \quad & l = 1, \ldots, N,
\end{aligned}
$$

where the prior density for $\boldsymbol{p}$ is given by $\alpha^{N-1} p_N^{\alpha-1} (1 - p_1)^{-1} (1 - (p_1 + p_2))^{-1} \times \cdots \times (1 - \sum_{l=1}^{N-2} p_l)^{-1}$, which is a special case of the generalised Dirichlet distribution. The full model is completed with the conditionally conjugate priors on $\boldsymbol{\psi}$ and α as given in (3.2).

Conditional on the latent responses $\boldsymbol{z}_i$, we have standard updates for the parameters of a normal DP mixture model. All full posterior conditional distributions are readily sampled, enabling efficient Gibbs sampling from the joint posterior distribution. The full conditional distributions for the components of $\boldsymbol{\psi}$ are easily found using standard conjugate updating. The updates for $\boldsymbol{p}$ and α are generic for any choice of mixture kernel (e.g. [26]), the former having a generalised Dirichlet distribution, and the latter a gamma distribution. Each L_i is sampled from a discrete distribution on $\{1, \ldots, N\}$, with probabilities proportional to $p_l \mathrm{N}(\boldsymbol{z}_i, \boldsymbol{x}_i \mid \boldsymbol{\mu}_l, \boldsymbol{\Sigma}_l)$, for $l = 1, \ldots, N$.

Let $\{L_j^* : j = 1, \ldots, n^*\}$ be the vector of distinct values of $\{L_1, \ldots, L_n\}$. For $l \notin \{L_j^*\}$, the full conditional for $\boldsymbol{\mu}_l$ is proportional to $\mathrm{N}(\boldsymbol{m}, \boldsymbol{V})$, and the full conditional for $\boldsymbol{\Sigma}_l$ is proportional to $\mathrm{IW}(\boldsymbol{\Sigma}_l \mid \nu, \boldsymbol{S})$. For $l \in \{L_j^*\}$, the full conditional for $\boldsymbol{\mu}_l$ is normal, with mean vector $(\boldsymbol{V}^{-1} + M_l \boldsymbol{\Sigma}_l^{-1})^{-1}(\boldsymbol{V}^{-1}\boldsymbol{m} + \boldsymbol{\Sigma}_l^{-1} \sum_{\{i:L_i=l\}} (\boldsymbol{z}_i, \boldsymbol{x}_i)^T)$ and covariance matrix $(\boldsymbol{V}^{-1} + M_l \boldsymbol{\Sigma}_l^{-1})^{-1}$, where $M_l = |\{i : L_i = l\}$ is the size of mixture component l. For $l \in \{L_j^*\}$, the full conditional for $\boldsymbol{\Sigma}_l$ is $\mathrm{IW}(\nu + M_l, \boldsymbol{S} + \sum_{\{i:L_i=l\}} ((\boldsymbol{z}_i, \boldsymbol{x}_i)^T - \boldsymbol{\mu}_l)((\boldsymbol{z}_i, \boldsymbol{x}_i)^T - \boldsymbol{\mu}_l)^T$.

Conditional on the mixture model parameters, each z_{ij}, for $i = 1, \ldots, n$ and $j = 1, \ldots, k$, has a truncated normal full conditional distribution supported on the interval $(\gamma_{j,y_{ij}-1}, \gamma_{j,y_{ij}}]$.

The regression functional $\Pr(\boldsymbol{Y} = \boldsymbol{l} \mid \boldsymbol{x}, G)$ (estimated by the truncated version of (3.3) implied by G_N) can be computed over a grid in $\boldsymbol{x}$ at every MCMC iteration. This yields an entire set of samples for ordinal response probabilities at any covariate value $\boldsymbol{x}$ (note that $\boldsymbol{x}$ may include just a portion of the covariate vector or a single covariate). As indicated in (3.4), in the multivariate setting, we may wish to report inference for individual components of $\boldsymbol{Y}$ over the covariate space.

In some applications, in addition to modelling how $\boldsymbol{Y}$ varies across $\boldsymbol{X}$, we may also be interested in how the distribution of $\boldsymbol{X}$ changes at different ordinal values of $\boldsymbol{Y}$. As a feature of the density regression modelling approach, we can obtain inference for $f(\boldsymbol{x} \mid \boldsymbol{y}, G)$, for any configuration of ordinal response levels $\boldsymbol{y}$. We refer to these inferences as inverse relationships, an example of which is provided in the data illustration of Section 3.3.3.

Under the multivariate response setting, the association between the ordinal variables may also be a key target of inference. In the social sciences, when a single multivariate normal distribution is used for the latent responses, the correlations between pairs of latent responses, $\mathrm{corr}(Z_r, Z_s)$, are termed polychoric correlations [43]. Under the mixture modelling framework presented here, one can obtain analogous inferences by sampling a single $\mathrm{corr}(Z_r, Z_s)$ at each MCMC iteration according to the corresponding $\boldsymbol{p}$, providing posterior predictive inference to assess overall agreement between pairs of response variables. As an alternative, and arguably more informative measure of association, we can obtain inference for probability of agreement over each covariate, or probability of agreement at each or-

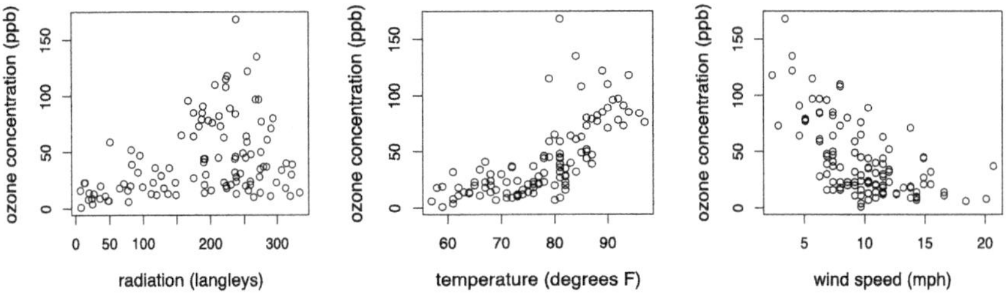

Figure 3.2 Ozone concentration versus radiation, temperature and wind speed.

dinal level. These inferences can be used to identify parts of the covariate space where there is agreement between response variables, as well as the ordinal values which are associated with higher levels of agreement. One common application arises in the social sciences, where the objective is to assess agreement among multiple raters or judges who are assigning a grade to the same item.

3.3.3 Illustration: ozone concentration

To illustrate the Bayesian nonparametric approach to ordinal regression, we work with the data set **ozone** from the **ElemStatLearn** package in R. This example contains four variables: ozone concentration (ppb), wind speed (mph), radiation (langleys) and temperature (degrees Fahrenheit). While these environmental characteristics are interrelated, we focus on estimating ozone concentration as a function of radiation, wind speed and temperature. Fig. 3.2 displays continuous ozone concentration as a function of the other environmental variables. Ozone concentration appears to be increasing with temperature and decreasing with wind speed, while its relationship with radiation is clearly nonlinear, taking larger values at moderate-high levels (in terms of the ozone concentration distribution) of ozone concentration.

3.3.3.1 Density regression

The density regression approach of [38] (described in Section 3.2) is used to estimate the distribution of ozone concentration, Z, conditional on covariates $\boldsymbol{X} = (X_1, X_2, X_3) =$ (radiation, temperature, wind speed). Specifically, we use a DP mixture of multivariate normals for the continuous vector $(Z, \boldsymbol{X})$, from which inference can be obtained for $f(z \mid \boldsymbol{x}) = \sum_{r=1}^{N} w_r(\boldsymbol{x}) \mathrm{N}(z \mid m_r(\boldsymbol{x}), S_r)$, where $w_r(\boldsymbol{x})$, $m_r(\boldsymbol{x})$ and S_r are defined after (3.3). We note that the **DPpackage** [27,28] provides a function **DPcden-**

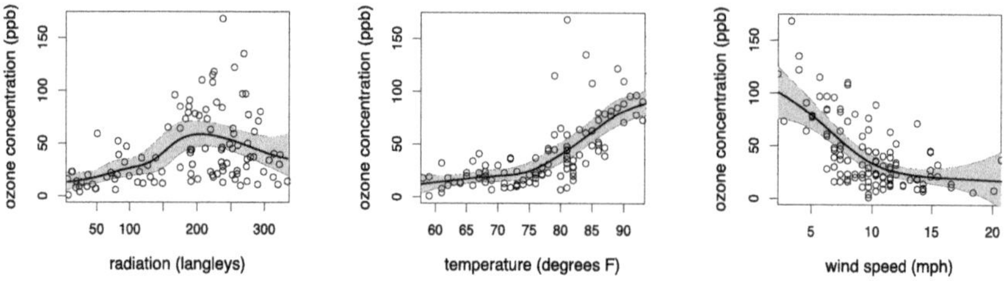

Figure 3.3 Posterior mean and 95% interval estimates for the regression function for ozone concentration conditional on radiation, temperature and wind speed.

sity for inference in this setting. Fig. 3.3 displays posterior mean estimates for the regression function, $E(Z \mid x_j) = \sum_{r=1}^{N} w_r(x_j)m_r(x_j)$, along with 95% interval bands, for each covariate X_j, based on results from the **DPcdensity** function. Note that the regression functions are all somewhat nonlinear and have shapes that would be difficult to capture with a linear regression model, as approximating these curves would require nonlinear functions and/or transformations.

We define ozone concentrations greater than 100 ppb as high; this can be considered an extreme level of ozone concentration, as only about 6% of the total of 111 observations are this high. Concentrations between 50 ppb and 100 ppb (approximately 25% of the observations) are considered medium, and values less than 50 ppb are considered low. The DP mixture of multivariate normals model applied to $(Z, \mathbf{X})$ can be used to obtain inference for the probability that ozone concentration is low, medium and high, conditional on X, via $\Pr(\gamma_{l-1} < Z \leq \gamma_l \mid x, G)$, for $l = 1, 2, 3$, where $\gamma = (-\infty, 50, 100, \infty)$, using the expressions for ordinal regression functions given in (3.3). Posterior means and 95% intervals for these probabilities are displayed in Fig. 3.4.

3.3.3.2 Ordinal regression

We now move to the topic of ordinal regression. Problems in the environmental sciences provide a broad area of application for which the proposed ordinal regression approach is particularly well suited. For such problems, it is of interest to estimate relationships between different environmental variables, some of which may be recorded on an ordinal scale even though they are, in fact, continuous variables. This is also a setting where it is natural to model the joint stochastic mechanism for all variables under study from which different types of conditional relationships can be explored.

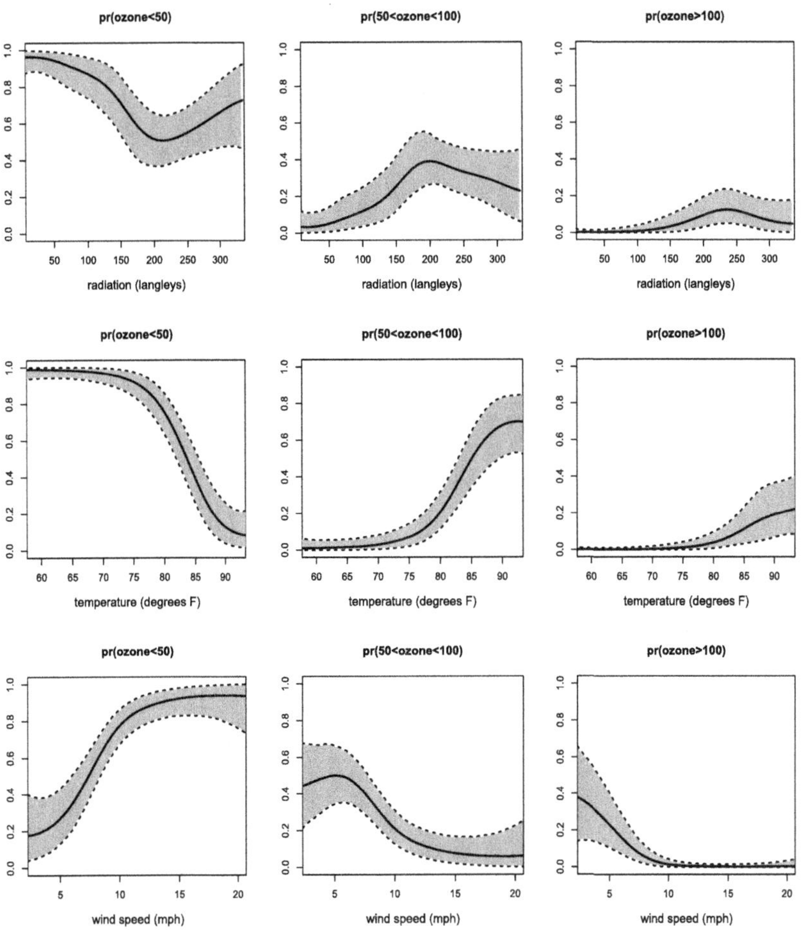

Figure 3.4 Posterior mean estimates and pointwise 95% intervals for the probability that ozone concentration is below 50 ppb (low, first column), between 50 and 100 ppb (medium, second column) and above 100 ppb (high, last column), conditional on radiation (first row), temperature (second row) and wind speed (last row).

To illustrate the ordinal regression methodology in this setting, rather than using directly the observed ozone concentration, we define an ordinal response containing three ozone concentration categories, using the cut-offs for low, medium and high described in the previous section. We use this to illustrate a practical setting in which an ordinal response may arise as a discretised version of a continuous response. Fig. 3.1 shows ozone concentration on an ordinal scale (1 = low, 2 = medium, 3 = high) as a function of the covariates.

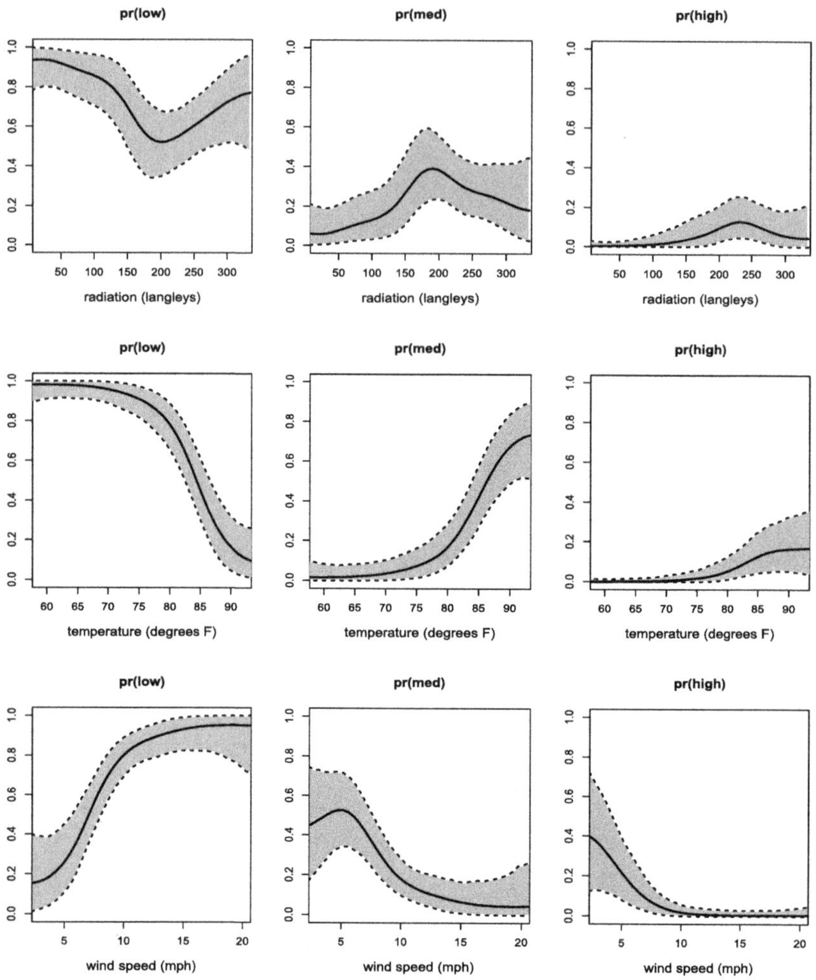

Figure 3.5 Posterior mean estimates and pointwise 95% intervals for the probability that ozone concentration is low (first column), medium (second column), high (last column), conditional on radiation (first row), temperature (second row) and wind speed (last row).

The ordinal regression model was applied with response variable, Y, given by discretised ozone concentration, and covariates, $\boldsymbol{X}$. We estimate the ordinal regression curves, $\Pr(Y = l \mid x, G)$, for $l = 1, 2, 3$, for each covariate x. The estimated ordinal regression functions are displayed in Fig. 3.5. We note the strong similarity to the analogous inferences from the model that directly uses the continuous ozone concentration (Fig. 3.4).

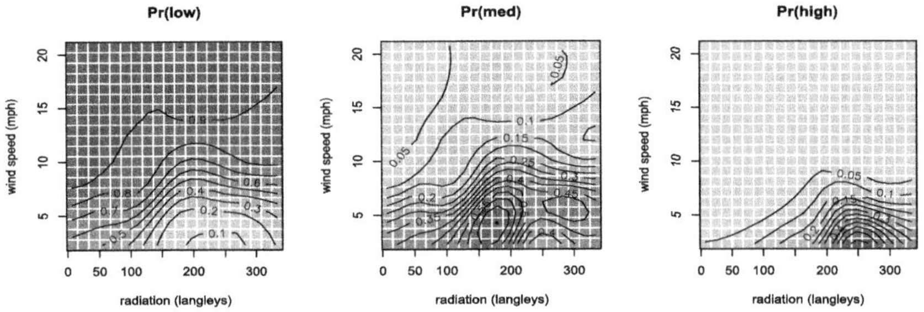

Figure 3.6 Posterior mean estimates for the probability that ordinal ozone concentration *Y* takes values low (1), medium (2) and high (3), as a function of radiation and wind speed.

In addition to typical univariate regression functions that describe how a response variable varies as a function of a single covariate, we can also estimate bivariate regression surfaces. Fig. 3.6 provides posterior mean estimates for the probability that ordinal ozone concentration Y takes values low, medium and high as a function of both radiation and wind speed. We see that the probability that $Y = 1$ is highest for faster wind speeds. The probability that $Y = 2$ is concentrated over a relatively small space in the figure, taking high values for moderate levels of radiation and slow winds. The probability that $Y = 3$ is even more sharply concentrated in terms of moderate-high radiation and slow winds.

One appealing feature of the joint modelling approach to regression is that inference for the covariate distribution, $f(x \mid G) = \sum_{r=1}^{\infty} p_r \mathrm{N}(x \mid \mu^x, \Sigma^{xx})$, or for the covariate distribution conditional on a particular value of Y, $f(x \mid y, G) = \sum_{r=1}^{\infty} w_r(y) \mathrm{N}(x \mid \mu^x, \Sigma^{xx})$, with $w_r(y) \propto p_r(\Phi((\gamma_{y-1} - m_r(x))/s_r^{1/2}) - \Phi((\gamma_y - m_r(x))/s_r^{1/2}))$, can also be obtained. These inverse inferences indicate how the covariates change with the ordinal response. Fig. 3.7 displays inference for the distribution of radiation conditional on ozone concentration taking values of low, medium and high. When ozone concentration is low, radiation has a bimodal distribution. This bimodality is easily accommodated by the mixture model for the joint response covariate distribution. When ozone concentration is medium or high, the distribution is unimodal, with left skewness. The distribution is more peaked under high ozone concentrations; however, the interval estimates are also widest here, reflecting the small sample size associated with $Y = 3$.

We have illustrated the Bayesian nonparametric model for ordinal regression on data which are truly continuous, but are transformed to an

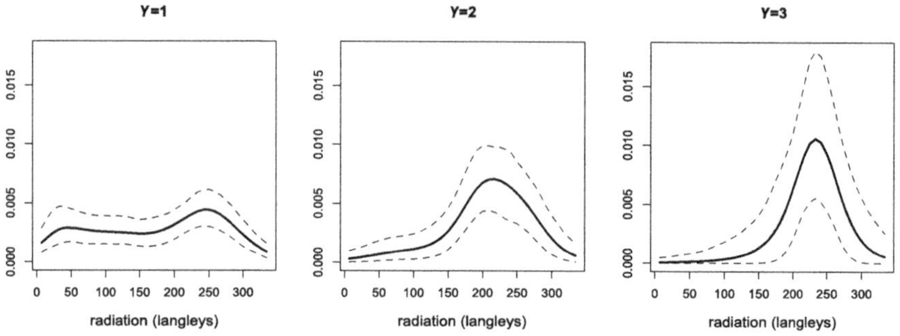

Figure 3.7 Posterior mean estimates and pointwise 95% intervals for the density of radiation conditional on $Y = 1$ (low ozone concentration), $Y = 2$ (medium ozone concentration) and $Y = 3$ (high ozone concentration).

ordinal scale through discretisation. This allows for presentation of the Bayesian nonparametric density regression approach for continuous data, which naturally can be extended to accommodate ordinal responses. The ordinal responses are seen to arise from underlying latent continuous random variables, modelled with a DP mixture of multivariate normals. While this particular ozone example was used for illustration, we refer the reader to [13] for examples involving truly ordinal responses. One example includes credit ratings, which are ordinal, and another involves grades assigned to essays on an ordinal 10-point scale.

3.3.4 Related work and extensions

The joint response covariate modelling approach with categorical variables has been explored by others, including [52], [15], [23], [12] and [44]. [52] considered classification of a univariate response using a multinomial logit kernel, and this was extended by [23] to accommodate alternative response types with mixtures of generalised linear models. [15] studied DP mixtures of independent kernels, and [12] developed a joint response covariate modelling approach for binary regression. However, these models would not be suitable for ordinal data, or for making inference on the association between the ordinal responses.

Related work on Bayesian nonparametric modelling for ordinal regression is relatively limited, particularly in the multivariate setting. In the special case of binary regression, there is only one probability response curve to be modelled, and this problem has received significant attention. Existing semiparametric approaches relax the normality assumption for the latent response using DP or DP mixture priors [42,5,4], while others have targeted the linearity assumption for the response function [35,60,11]. For a univariate ordinal response, [10] assume that the latent response arises from scale mixtures of normals and the covariate effects are additive upon transformation by cubic splines. This allows nonlinearities to be obtained in the marginal regression curves, albeit under the restrictive assumption of additive covariate effects. [22] extend the ordinal probit model by introducing subject-specific random effects terms modelled with a DP prior.

[8] model the latent variables for correlated ordinal responses with scale mixtures of normal distributions, with means linear on the covariates. Related, [3] assume the latent variables arise from mixtures of linear multivariate probit regressions, mixing on the regression coefficients and covariance matrices in the multivariate normal distribution. The latter modelling approach is an extension of the work in [31], where, in the context of multivariate ordinal data without covariates, the latent response distribution was modelled with a DP mixture of multivariate normals.

When developing the model for ordinal regression we have assumed that all covariates are continuous. To handle discrete covariates some modification of the kernel is needed. Ordinal covariates can be handled in the same way as the ordinal responses, so that some elements of the multivariate normal kernel are assumed to represent latent continuous covariates instead of ordinal covariates. [14] uses this approach to accommodate an ordinal covariate 'age', measured in years. To handle unordered categorical covariates, the kernel would need to be modified. For example, one could use a product of a multivariate normal distribution for the (latent) continuous variables and a categorical distribution for the discrete covariates.

Throughout this chapter, we have assumed a common vector of covariates $\boldsymbol{X} = (X_1, ..., X_p)$ for each response vector $\boldsymbol{Y}$. That is, the covariates are not specific to particular response variables, but rather $(\boldsymbol{Y}, \boldsymbol{X})$ arises as a multivariate vector. An alternative version of the probit model involves p_j covariates $(X_{j,1}, \ldots, X_{j,p_j})$ specific to response variable Y_j. This regression setting was described for multivariate continuous responses by [57], and this is the version of the multivariate binary probit model considered in [9].

Scenarios which make use of response-specific covariates fall broadly into two categories. The first consists of problems in which only a portion of the covariate vector is thought to affect a particular response, but there may be some overlap in the subset of covariates which generate the responses. [9] considered a voting behaviour problem of this kind in which the first of two responses was assumed to be generated by a subset of the covariates associated with the second response. This data structure can also be accommodated by modelling all covariates $\boldsymbol{X}$ jointly with $\boldsymbol{Y}$, and conditioning on the relevant subset of $\boldsymbol{X}$ in the regression inferences.

The other type of data structure which is occasionally handled with a multivariate regression model with response-specific covariates involves univariate ordinal responses that are related in a hierarchical/dynamic fashion. For instance, [9] illustrate their model with the commonly used Six Cities data, in which $\boldsymbol{Y} = (Y_1, \ldots, Y_4)$ represents wheezing status at ages 7 through 10. Such settings are arguably more naturally approached through hierarchical/dynamic modelling. Indeed, one extension of the methodology developed here involves dynamic modelling for ordinal regression relationships, such that at any particular time point a unique regression relationship is estimated in a flexible fashion, while dependence is incorporated across time. This methodology is presented in [14], where a dependent DP [32] is used to model dynamically evolving random distributions. The ordinal variable in this application is fish maturity, which is recorded on an ordinal three-point scale. [44] develop similar models for spatially indexed mixed categorical count-continuous data, using a probit stick breaking process [16], another type of dependent nonparametric prior, to induce dependence across spatial locations.

3.4 Summary

Ordinal data are challenging to model in a way that accounts for the ordinal nature of the responses and is computationally feasible to make inference from, and accommodating multiple ordinal responses is especially complex. Standard parametric models for ordinal responses enforce certain relationships between the response(s) and covariates, which may be too restrictive for data applications. We presented a Bayesian nonparametric mixture modelling approach to ordinal regression, which builds from the density regression modelling framework. The ordinal regression model can be used to flexibly estimate more than just the regression functions for the response conditional on covariates. It can also provide general inference for the covariate distribution, for the distribution of the covariates given the response variable, as well as for relationships between the ordinal responses in multivariate ordinal regression.

Acknowledgements

The authors wish to thank the book editors, and especially Yanan Fan, for the invitation to write this chapter. The work of the second author was supported in part by the National Science Foundation under award SES 1631963.

References

[1] J. Albert, S. Chib, Bayesian analysis of binary and polychotomous response data, Journal of the American Statistical Association 88 (1993) 669–679.
[2] C.E. Antoniak, Mixtures of Dirichlet processes with applications to Bayesian nonparametric problems, The Annals of Statistics 2 (1974) 1152–1174.
[3] J. Bao, T. Hanson, Bayesian nonparametric multivariate ordinal regression, Canadian Journal of Statistics 43 (3) (2015) 337–357.
[4] S. Basu, S. Chib, Marginal likelihood and Bayes factors for Dirichlet process mixture models, Journal of the American Statistical Association 98 (2003) 224–235.
[5] S. Basu, S. Mukhopadhyay, Bayesian analysis of binary regression using symmetric and asymmetric links, The Indian Journal of Statistics Series B 62 (2000) 372–387.
[6] D.M. Blei, M.I. Jordan, Variational inference for Dirichlet process mixtures, Bayesian Analysis 1 (2006) 121–144.
[7] S. Boes, R. Winkelmann, Ordered response models, Advances in Statistical Analysis 90 (2006) 165–179.
[8] M. Chen, D. Dey, Bayesian analysis for correlated ordinal data models, in: D. Dey, S. Ghosh, B. Mallick (Eds.), Generalized Linear Models: a Bayesian Perspective, Marcel Dekker, New York, 2000, pp. 135–162.
[9] S. Chib, E. Greenberg, Analysis of multivariate probit models, Biometrika 85 (1998) 347–361.
[10] S. Chib, E. Greenberg, Additive cubic spline regression with Dirichlet process mixture errors, Journal of Econometrics 156 (2010) 322–336.
[11] N. Choudhuri, S. Ghosal, A. Roy, Nonparametric binary regression using a Gaussian process prior, Statistical Methodology 4 (2007) 227–243.
[12] M. DeYoreo, A. Kottas, A fully nonparametric modeling approach to binary regression, Bayesian Analysis 10 (2015) 821–847.
[13] M. DeYoreo, A. Kottas, Bayesian nonparametric modeling for multivariate ordinal regression, Journal of Computational and Graphical Statistics 27 (2018) 71–84.
[14] M. DeYoreo, A. Kottas, Modeling for dynamic ordinal regression relationships: an application to estimating maturity of rockfish in California, Journal of the American Statistical Association 113 (2018) 68–80.
[15] D. Dunson, A. Bhattacharya, Nonparametric Bayes regression and classification through mixtures of product kernels, Bayesian Statistics 9 (2010) 145–164.
[16] D. Dunson, N. Pillai, J.H. Park, Bayesian density regression, Journal of the Royal Statistical Society: Series B 69 (2) (2007) 163–183.
[17] M. Escobar, M. West, Bayesian density estimation and inference using mixtures, Journal of the American Statistical Association 90 (1995) 577–588.
[18] T.S. Ferguson, A Bayesian analysis of some nonparametric problems, The Annals of Statistics 1 (1973) 209–230.
[19] A.E. Gelfand, Approaches for semiparametric Bayesian regression, in: S. Ghosh (Ed.), Asymptotics, Nonparametrics and Time Series, Marcel Dekker, New York, 1999, pp. 615–638.

[20] A.E. Gelfand, A. Kottas, A computational approach for full nonparametric Bayesian inference under Dirichlet process mixtures, Journal of Computational and Graphical Statistics 11 (2002) 289–305.
[21] S. Ghosal, A. van der Vaart, Fundamentals of Nonparametric Bayesian Inference, Cambridge University Press, 2017.
[22] J. Gill, G. Casella, Nonparametric priors for ordinal Bayesian social science models: specification and estimation, Journal of the American Statistical Association 104 (2009) 453–464.
[23] L.A. Hannah, D.M. Blei, W.B. Powell, Dirichlet process mixtures of generalized linear models, Journal of Machine Learning Research 1 (2011) 1–33.
[24] T.E. Hanson, A.J. Branscum, W.O. Johnson, Bayesian nonparametric modeling and data analysis: an introduction, in: D.K. Dey, C.R. Rao (Eds.), Bayesian Thinking: Modeling and Computation (Handbook of Statistics, vol. 25), Elsevier, Amsterdam, 2005, pp. 245–278.
[25] H. Ishwaran, L.F. James, Gibbs sampling methods for stick-breaking priors, Journal of the American Statistical Association 96 (2001) 161–173.
[26] H. Ishwaran, M. Zarepour, Markov chain Monte Carlo in approximate Dirichlet and Beta two-parameter process hierarchical models, Biometrika 87 (2000) 371–390.
[27] A. Jara, Applied Bayesian non- and semi-parametric inference using DPpackage, R News 7 (3) (2007) 17–26.
[28] A. Jara, T. Hanson, F. Quintana, P. Müller, Gary Rosner, DPpackage: Bayesian semi- and nonparametric modeling in R, Journal of Statistical Software 40 (5) (2011) 1–30.
[29] V.E. Johnson, J.H. Albert, Ordinal Data Modeling, Springer, New York, 1999.
[30] M. Kalli, J.E. Griffin, S. Walker, Slice sampling mixture models, Statistics and Computing 21 (2011) 93–105.
[31] A. Kottas, P. Müller, F. Quintana, Nonparametric Bayesian modelling for multivariate ordinal data, Journal of Computational and Graphical Statistics 14 (2005) 610–625.
[32] S. MacEachern, Dependent Dirichlet Processes, Tech. rept., Department of Statistics, The Ohio State University, 2000.
[33] S.N. MacEachern, P. Müller, Estimating mixture of Dirichlet process models, Journal of Computational and Graphical Statistics 7 (1998) 223–238.
[34] P. McCullagh, Regression models for ordinal data, Journal of the Royal Statistical Society, Series B (1980) 109–142.
[35] S. Mukhopadyay, A.E. Gelfand, Dirichlet process mixed generalized linear models, Journal of the American Statistical Association 92 (1997) 633–639.
[36] P. Müller, R. Mitra, Bayesian nonparametric inference – why and how (with discussion), Bayesian Analysis 8 (2013) 269–360.
[37] P. Müller, F. Quintana, Random partition models with regression on covariates, Journal of Statistical Planning and Inference 140 (2010) 2801–2808.
[38] P. Müller, A. Erkanli, M. West, Bayesian curve fitting using multivariate normal mixtures, Biometrika 83 (1996) 67–79.
[39] P. Müller, F. Quintana, A. Jara, T. Hanson, Bayesian Nonparametric Data Analysis, Springer, 2015.
[40] E.A. Nadaraya, On estimating regression, Theory of Probability & Its Applications 9 (1964) 141–142.
[41] R. Neal, Markov chain sampling methods for Dirichlet process mixture models, Journal of Computational and Graphical Statistics 9 (2000) 249–265.
[42] M.A. Newton, C. Czado, R. Chappell, Bayesian inference for semiparametric binary regression, Journal of the American Statistical Association 91 (1996) 142–153.

[43] U. Olsson, Maximum likelihood estimation of the polychoric correlation coefficient, Psychometrika 44 (1979) 443–460.
[44] G. Papageorgiou, S. Richardson, N. Best, Bayesian nonparametric models for spatially indexed data of mixed type, Journal of the Royal Statistical Society, Series B 77 (2015) 973–999.
[45] O. Papaspiliopoulos, G.O. Roberts, Retrospective Markov chain Monte Carlo methods for Dirichlet process hierarchical models, Biometrika 95 (2008) 169–186.
[46] J.H. Park, D.B. Dunson, Bayesian generalized product partition model, Statistica Sinica 20 (2010) 1203–1226.
[47] V. Poynor, A. Kottas, Bayesian Nonparametric Mean Residual Life Regression, Tech. rept. UCSC-SOE-17-08, Jack Baskin School of Engineering, University of California, Santa Cruz, 2017.
[48] J.J. Quinlan, G.L. Page, F.A. Quintana, Density regression using repulsive distributions, Journal of Statistical Computation and Simulation (2018), https://doi.org/10.1080/00949655.2018.1491578.
[49] R Core Team, R: A Language and Environment for Statistical Computing, R Foundation for Statistical Computing, Vienna, Austria, 2017.
[50] A. Rodriguez, D.B. Dunson, A.E. Gelfand, Nonparametric functional data analysis through Bayesian density estimation, Biometrika 96 (2009) 149–162.
[51] J. Sethuraman, A constructive definition of Dirichlet priors, Statistica Sinica 4 (1994) 639–650.
[52] B. Shahbaba, R. Neal, Nonlinear modeling using Dirichlet process mixtures, Journal of Machine Learning Research 10 (2009) 1829–1850.
[53] M. Taddy, Autoregressive mixture models for dynamic spatial Poisson processes: application to tracking the intensity of violent crime, Journal of the American Statistical Association 105 (2010) 1403–1417.
[54] M. Taddy, A. Kottas, Markov switching Dirichlet process mixture regression, Bayesian Analysis 4 (2009) 793–816.
[55] M. Taddy, A. Kottas, A Bayesian nonparametric approach to inference for quantile regression, Journal of Business and Economic Statistics 28 (2010) 357–369.
[56] M. Taddy, A. Kottas, Mixture modeling for marked Poisson processes, Bayesian Analysis 7 (2012) 335–362.
[57] G. Tiao, A. Zellner, On the Bayesian estimation of multivariate regression, Journal of the Royal Statistical Society, Series B 26 (1964) 277–285.
[58] S. Wade, D.B. Dunson, S. Petrone, L. Trippa, Improving prediction from Dirichlet process mixtures via enrichment, Journal of Machine Learning Research 15 (2014) 1041–1071.
[59] S. Walker, Sampling the Dirichlet mixture model with slices, Communications in Statistics, Simulation and Computation 36 (2007) 45–54.
[60] S. Walker, B. Mallick, Hierarchical generalized linear models and frailty models with Bayesian nonparametric mixing, Journal of the Royal Statistical Society B 59 (1997) 845–860.
[61] G.S. Watson, Smooth regression analysis, Sankhya: The Indian Journal of Statistics, Series A 26 (1964) 359–372.
[62] S. Xiao, A. Kottas, B. Sansó, Modeling for seasonal marked point processes: an analysis of evolving hurricane occurrences, The Annals of Applied Statistics 9 (2015) 353–382.
[63] O. Zobay, Mean field inference for the Dirichlet process mixture model, Electronic Journal of Statistics 3 (2009) 507–545.

CHAPTER 4

Bayesian nonparametric methods for financial and macroeconomic time series analysis

Maria Kalli
University of Kent, School of Mathematics, Statistics & Actuarial Science, Sibson Building, Parkwood Road, Canterbury, CT2 7FS, United Kingdom

Contents

4.1 Introduction

Bayesian nonparametric methods were introduced by [20], who defined the Dirichlet process and showed how it could be used as a prior over probability measures. [1] then extended Ferguson's work to mixtures of Dirichlet processes and [55] showed how the Dirichlet process can be used in density estimation as the prior for the underlying mixing measure in a mixture model. Analytical inference using these models was facilitated by [18], who popularised the algorithm of [55] by showing how Markov chain Monte Carlo (MCMC) methods could be used to sample from the posterior distribution. Subsequently, the popularity of Bayesian nonparametric methods has grown exponentially. This is due to the ability of these methods to combine the flexibility of nonparametrics with the simplicity of the Bayesian modelling framework (such as hierarchical structure, automatic dimension penalisation and simple combination of different models).

In the 2010s alone a plethora of models, priors and related computational methods have been developed and applied to a range of statistical modelling problems from density estimation, nonparametric regression and nonparametric spatial modelling to clustering. For a book length review of

Flexible Bayesian Regression Modelling
https://doi.org/10.1016/B978-0-12-815862-3.00012-3

these methods see [37] and [59]. In this chapter we are going to focus on the use of Bayesian nonparametric methods in time series analysis.

Time series data are at the heart of time series analysis, and the overarching aim is to analyse such data in order to extract meaningful information about their dynamic structure and use it in forecasting future observations. We are going to look at both financial and macroeconomic times series, the former collected at a daily frequency and the latter collected at a monthly frequency, at the level of national and international economies.

Modelling such data is not an easy task. The models developed for financial time series, like asset returns, are mostly univariate ones. The challenge in this case is to adequately capture their distributional characteristics or 'stylised facts', such as the unimodality and asymmetry of their unconditional distribution around zero, the heavy-tailed behaviour of both the conditional and unconditional distributions, volatility clustering, the negative correlation between volatility and returns ('leverage-effect') and the slow decay of the autocorrelation function of absolute returns, to simply name a few. For further details, see [14]. With macroeconomic data, such as inflation, interest rates and output growth (used to describe the state of the aggregate economy), the focus is on correctly estimating their joint dynamic relationship and so the models developed should be multivariate ones. The challenge in this case is to adequately model the transition mechanism, which is important not only in identifying the dynamic relationships between the variables, but also in forecasting future values of the variables involved. A clear understanding of the joint dynamic behaviour of macroeconomic variables and the ability to predict with a high degree of accuracy are important to Central Banks for monetary policy decisions and to Governments when deciding their strategy on fiscal policy.

Whether we are interested in univariate time series models for asset returns or multivariate time series models for macroeconomic variables, simple parametric models rarely capture the key 'stylised facts' of the former and rarely describe well the dynamic relationships of the latter. This has led to the increased use of classical nonparametric procedures which avoid making strong distributional assumptions. However, there has been less work in Bayesian nonparametric modelling, reflecting the relative lack of familiarity of econometricians and financial economists with Bayesian nonparametric methods and their computational complexity.

The early adopters of Bayesian nonparametric methods focused on univariate models for the analysis of financial and economic time series, and used the Dirichlet process mixture (DPM) model, introduced in [55]. The

DPM is an infinite mixture model where the Dirichlet process is chosen as a prior over the parameters of a distribution, with density $k(\cdot|\theta)$ and parameters θ, facilitating the modelling of complex densities $f(\cdot)$. Under the DPM model

$$f(\cdot) = \int k(\cdot|\boldsymbol{\theta})G(d\boldsymbol{\theta}),$$

where $\boldsymbol{\theta}$ is the parameter vector and G is the unknown random distribution drawn from a Dirichlet process. [33] use a variation of the DPM, the order-based dependent Dirichlet process (πDDP) to model the volatility process of a stochastic volatility (SV) model and apply it to daily returns of the S&P 500 stock market index. [60] and [70] use the DPM for the analysis of time series data that are subject to regime changes where no specific economic theory exists about the structure of the series. [36] and [53] use the DPM to model the innovation distribution of a random-effects autoregressive model, and a heteroscedastic linear regression model, respectively. Finally, [43] and [15] use the DPM to model the distribution of asset returns using an SV model. This initial work is reviewed in [32].

We firmly believe that Bayesian nonparametric methods will play an important role in developing financial and macroeconomic time series models with excellent forecasting performance. Here we focus on more recent developments which concentrate on density estimation within a volatility model, long-memory models and vector autoregressive (VAR) models. This chapter is structured as follows. In Section 4.2 we concentrate on volatility models where Bayesian nonparametric methods are used to model the innovation distribution of financial asset returns. In Section 4.3 we describe how the Dirichlet process can be used to explain long-range dependence in SV models, and in Section 4.4 we depart from univariate volatility models and focus on how Bayesian nonparametric methods can be used to build multivariate models to explain the joint dynamic behaviour of macroeconomic time series. We conclude in Section 4.5 with our vision on the future of Bayesian nonparametric methods for financial time series analysis.

4.2 Bayesian nonparametric methods for the innovation distribution in volatility models

Modelling of the distribution of financial time series, y_t, observed at regularly spaced times $t = 1 \ldots, n$, is important for measuring risk. The starting point for volatility models is the following:

$$y_t = \sigma_t \epsilon_t \qquad \text{for} \qquad t = 1, 2, \ldots, n, \tag{4.1}$$

where y_t is the log return, ϵ_t is the innovation following some distribution F_ϵ with mean zero and variance $\sigma_\epsilon^2 = 1$. The volatility process, σ_t, observed at time t can either have a GARCH-type or an SV setup. The choice of F_ϵ plays a key role in capturing the 'stylised facts' of returns, because it determines their conditional distribution (often used to derive value at risk thresholds) and impacts on distributions of future returns.

The normal distribution had been the standard choice for F_ϵ but since it fails to capture the heavy tails and slight asymmetry of the conditional distribution of returns, it has been replaced by other distributional choices such as a Student t distribution [7], a skewed Student t distribution [35], a generalised t distribution [74], a mixture of normal distributions [4] and the asymmetric Laplace distribution [11], to name a few. All of these choices are parametric and limited by the properties of the chosen distributional family.

The Bayesian nonparametric approach adds more flexibility in modelling F_ϵ. [14] demonstrated with his detailed empirical analysis of returns how complex their distributional characteristics are, and this is where Bayesian nonparametric methods can add value. These methods place a prior on an infinite-dimensional parameter space and adapt their complexity to the data. This implies that models developed with such methods will not underfit the data. A more appropriate term for Bayesian nonparametric models is infinite-capacity models, emphasising the crucial property that they allow their complexity (i.e. the number of parameters) to grow as more data are observed; in contrast, finite-capacity models assume a fixed complexity. The other benefit with Bayesian nonparametric methods is that we do not have to worry about overfitting the data, because if we have a well-specified Bayesian model it should not overfit. Correctly specifying the Bayesian model is important because a well-specified Bayesian model that grows with the amount of data (like the Bayesian nonparametric models do) will neither overfit nor underfit the data, and this leads to better out-of-sample forecasts; see [63].

The majority of volatility models use the DPM to model F_ϵ. Under the DPM, the unknown distribution is

$$f_\epsilon(\cdot) = \int k(\cdot|\theta) G(d\theta),$$

where θ is the parameter vector and G the unknown random distribution drawn from a stick breaking prior, such as

$$G(\cdot) = \sum_{j=1}^{\infty} w_j \delta_{\theta_j}(\cdot), \tag{4.2}$$

where δ_{θ_j} is the Dirac measure giving mass one at location θ_j, with weight w_j. The weights must satisfy two conditions in order for G to be a probability measure: $0 < w_j < 1$ and $\sum_{j=1}^{\infty} w_j = 1$ with probability one. The locations θ_j are i.i.d. random variables with distribution G_0 and are independent of the random weights w_j. The distribution G_0 is often referred to as the *base or centering distribution*. This is so because for any measurable set B of a σ-field $\mathcal{B}$, we have $E[G(B)] = G_0(B)$. The random weights w_j are transformations of i.i.d. beta random variables, $v_j \sim Be(1, M)$ (with $M > 0$), represented as follows:

$$w_1 = v_1 \text{ and } w_j = v_j \prod_{\ell<j}(1 - v_\ell). \tag{4.3}$$

Eq. (4.3) gives rise to the *stick breaking* representation of the DPM (see [69]), and we can write $f_\epsilon(\cdot)$ as an infinite mixture, i.e.

$$f_\epsilon(\cdot) = \sum_{j=1}^{\infty} w_j k(\cdot|\theta_j).$$

Inference is simplified by choosing a conjugate model for θ_j and often both $k(\cdot|\theta)$ and G_0 are chosen to be normal distributions. [43] and [15] use the DPM in their SV model and find that the out-of-sample predictive performance of their models is superior to most parametric alternatives.

The stick breaking notion, Eq. (4.3), of constructing infinite-dimensional priors has a very long history and dates back to the work of [34], [22], [51] and [39]. The Dirichlet process is actually a subclass of more general stick breaking processes (SBPs). In the general SBP, the $v_j \sim Be(a_j, b_j)$, and the Dirichlet process arises when we set $a_j = 1$ and $b_j = M$. The positive constant M is often referred to as the *precision* parameter, because it controls how close realisations of G are to G_0. It also controls the rate of decay of the mixture weights, and thus the number of nonnegligible weights. Since the conditional distribution of returns plays a key role in risk management, a good model should be able to account for its heavy-tailed behaviour well. It is therefore sensible to choose a Bayesian nonparametric prior because it provides more flexibility, where components with small weights could be used to account for the heavy tails. Looking at the expectation of the weights under the Dirichlet process we have

$$E[w_j] = \frac{1}{1+M}\left(1 - \frac{1}{1+M}\right)^{j-1} \quad \text{for} \quad j > l. \tag{4.4}$$

It is clear that $E[w_j]$ in Eq. (4.4) is decreasing in j and that the value of M controls the weight decay. This exponential decay can be a disadvantage as more mixture components may be needed to capture the heavy tails of the conditional returns' distribution. A more flexible prior is the two-parameter Poisson Dirichlet process of [66], where the parameters of the beta distribution of the v_j's are $a_j = 1 - \alpha$ with $\alpha \in [0, 1)$ and $b_j = M + j\alpha$. This prior is often referred to as the Pitman–Yor process and it is also a subclass of the general SBP. [49] construct a more general SBP, which centres over a distribution for the weights on $E[w_j]$.

They choose $E[w_j] = \xi_j$, where ξ_j is $Pr(X = j)$ for a random variable X with a discrete distribution on $1, 2, 3, \ldots$. This allows for more control over the rate of weight decay and therefore the generation of nonnegligible components. In [49] the random variable X is given a beta-geometric distribution resulting in a more flexible model as more mixture components with small weights are used to capture the heavy tail behaviour. For more details see [49].

[49] also departs from the standard conjugate structure of the DPM. The continuous density function $k(\cdot|\theta)$ and centering distribution G_0 are not chosen to be Gaussian. An infinite mixture (see [8]) of uniform distributions is chosen for the density of the innovations, $f_\epsilon(\cdot)$ represented by

$$f_\epsilon(\cdot) = \int \upsilon(\epsilon|\xi, \lambda) G(d\xi), \tag{4.5}$$

where $\upsilon(\epsilon|\xi, \lambda)$ is the density function of the scaled uniform distribution $U(-e^{-\lambda}\xi, e^{\lambda}\xi)$ with asymmetry parameter λ and scale ξ. The unknown distribution G is generated from an SBP(a_j, b_j), and G_0 is chosen to be the standard exponential distribution. The choice of the scaled uniform kernel ensures unimodality of the conditional return distribution and captures any level of kurtosis while avoiding the risk of artificial modes at extreme returns, as may be the case under the DPM model.

Take the simplest case of $U(-\xi, \xi)$. This ensures unimodality for the innovations' distribution with mode at zero. The random distribution G ranges over all distribution functions on $(0, \infty)$ and therefore f_ϵ ranges over all unimodal and symmetric density functions on $(-\infty, \infty)$; see [19]. To capture the slight asymmetry of returns the skewness parameter λ is introduced as per [21].

The flexible construction of this infinite mixture of uniforms (IUM) has the following hierarchical setup for the innovations' distribution:

$$\begin{aligned} y_t = \sigma_t \epsilon_t, \qquad & \epsilon_t \sim U(-\xi_{d_t} e^{-\lambda}, \xi_{d_t} e^{\lambda}) \qquad \text{for } t = 1, \ldots, n, \\ Pr(d_t = j) = w_j, \qquad & \xi_j \sim G_0(\cdot) \qquad \text{for } j = 1, 2, \ldots, \\ w_1 = v_1, w_j = v_j \prod_{\ell<j} (1 - v_\ell) & \text{ and } v_j \sim Be(a_j, b_j), \end{aligned}$$

where G_0 is a standard exponential distribution. The distribution of ϵ_t is therefore

$$f_{v,\xi}(\epsilon_t) = \sum_{j=1}^{\infty} w_j \upsilon(-\xi_j e^{-\lambda}, \xi_j e^{\lambda})$$

and the conditional return distribution is

$$f_{G,\lambda}(y_t|\sigma_t) = \sum_{j=1}^{\infty} w_j \upsilon(y_t| - \xi_j \sigma_t e^{-\lambda}, \xi_j \sigma_t e^{\lambda}), \tag{4.6}$$

where the volatility is modelled using the GARCH(1, 1), the GJR-GARCH(1, 1) [26] and the EGARCH(1, 1) [62]. The latter two choices model the 'leverage effect'. Even though the pair $k(\cdot|\theta)$ and G_0 is not a conjugate one, inference is possible by using the slice-efficient sampler of [46]. For details on the MCMC sampler please refer to [49].

To illustrate the impact of the IUM representation on out-of-sample predictive performance, we are going to look at the returns of the S&P500 from 3 January 1980 to 30 December 1987 and the returns of the FTSE100 from 3 January 1997 to 12 March 2009. To measure the accuracy of predictions, we will calculate the log predictive score (LPS) as well as the log predictive tail score (LPTS) of [15]. The LPTS is a variation of the LPS used when our aim is to forecast extreme returns (which is the case in risk management). The LPTS is given as follows:

$$\text{LPTS} = -\frac{1}{\sum_{t=1}^{T} \mathbf{1}(|y_t^\star| > z_\alpha)} \sum_{t=1}^{T} \mathbf{1}(|y_t^\star| > z_\alpha) \log f(y_t|y_{1:(t-1)}, \hat{\vartheta}), \tag{4.7}$$

where z_α, is the upper $100\alpha\%$ of the absolute values of the standardised returns y_t and $f(y_t|y_{(1:t-1)}, \vartheta)$ is the one-step-ahead predictive density, with ϑ representing the model parameters and $\hat{\vartheta}$ their estimates. We are going to consider the upper 5% and 1% of values.

This forecasting example focuses on how the IUM model choice for the innovations' distribution compares to the skewed Student t and the DPM (with normal kernel). Volatility is modelled with a GJR-GARCH(1, 1). In addition we will also compare these models with the SV model with leverage and Student t innovations and the SV-DPM of [43]. Our aim is to demonstrate that the flexible IUM model for the innovations' distribution leads to better out-of-sample forecasts when compared to the popular parametric choice of the skewed Student t distribution and the DPM (with normal kernel).

Table 4.1 displays the LPS and LPTS scores for each model for the S&P500 and FTSE100 returns. The calculation of LPS and LPTS, $t = 1, \ldots, T$, in Eq. (4.7) refers to the second half of the data sets, the evaluation (out-of-sample) set. The first half is the training (in sample) set which is used to get the parameter estimates $\hat{\vartheta}$. We can see that for the FTSE100 returns the GJR-GARCH(1, 1) with IUM innovations outperforms all other models, whereas for the S&P500 the GJR-GARCH(1, 1) with IUM innovations outperforms all other models in terms of the LPTSs. This demonstrates that having a very flexible model for the innovations' distribution provides better forecasts of extreme returns, something invaluable to asset and risk managers.

Table 4.1 Log predictive scores and log predictive tail scores at 1% and 5% for S&P 500 and FTSE 100. The first two rows show the scores of the parametric models, and the last three rows show the scores of the nonparametric models. The smallest LPS and LPTS are in bold.

	S&P 500			FTSE 100		
	LPS	LPTS-01	LPTS-05	LPS	LPTS-01	LPTS-05
Bayesian parametric models						
GJR-Garch(1, 1)-skewed t	1.314	8.039	4.588	1.337	5.402	3.490
SV(1)-t (leverage)	1.325	9.023	4.879	1.343	5.705	3.567
Bayesian nonparametric models						
GJR-Garch(1, 1)-DPM	**1.311**	6.017	4.059	1.327	5.831	3.600
GJR-Garch(1, 1)-IUM	1.319	**5.650**	**3.598**	**1.319**	**4.897**	**3.094**
SV-DPM	1.313	7.231	4.811	1.349	5.963	3.712

4.3 Bayesian nonparametric methods for long-range dependence in SV models

In the previous section we discussed the use of DPM and SBP to define the prior of the innovation distribution of a volatility model. Here we are going to focus on how a Bayesian nonparametric prior can be incorporated in an aggregation model to flexibly describe the dynamics of a stationary SV model given by

$$y_t = \beta \exp\{h_t/2\}\epsilon_t, \qquad t = 1, 2, \ldots, T, \tag{4.8}$$

where y_t is the asset return at time t, ϵ_t are i.i.d. draws from some distribution (usually, taken to be normal) and $\exp\{h_t/2\}$ is the volatility on the tth day. In an SV model the log volatility process, h_t, is often assumed to follow an AR(1), i.e.

$$h_t = \phi h_{t-1} + \eta_t, \qquad t = 1, 2, \ldots, T, \tag{4.9}$$

where η_t is normally distributed with mean 0 and variance $\sigma^2(1-\phi^2)$, which results in the stationary distribution of h_t being normal with mean 0 and variance σ^2. The autoregressive coefficient or persistence parameter ϕ controls the behaviour of the autocorrelation function of h_t.

Empirical analyses of financial time series, see [17] and [14], show evidence of slow decay of the sample autocorrelation function. This slow decay is linked to the concept of long-range dependence. [47] focus on the result of [28] and assume that h_t is the aggregate of weakly stationary processes, with a clearly defined covariance function. Then long-range dependence occurs when this covariance function is unsummable. Following the work of [68,29,77] they assume that h_t is the aggregate of AR(1) processes to account for long-range dependence.

Cross-sectional aggregation models are usually defined in the following way. We have m time series $h_{i,1}, h_{i,2}, \ldots, h_{i,T}$ for $i = 1, \ldots, m$ of the form

$$h_{i,t} = \phi_i h_{i,t-1} + \eta_{i,t}, \tag{4.10}$$

where $\eta_{i,t} \sim N(0, \sigma^2(1-\phi_i^2))$ are idiosyncratic shocks, and the persistence parameter $\phi_i \overset{i.i.d.}{\sim} F_\phi$, with support on $(0, 1)$. The aggregate process is

$$h_t = \frac{1}{m}\sum_{i=1}^{m} h_{i,t}, \qquad t = 1, 2, \ldots, T. \tag{4.11}$$

Both [28] and [77] prove that long-range dependence is affected by the choices of a single parameter, let us call it b, which characterises the distribution F_ϕ. In [28] F_ϕ is a beta distribution on $(0, 1)$ with shape parameters a and b, and when $b \to \infty$ the autocovariance function of the aggregate approximates that of an ARMA process. [77] generalises this result to distributions with density $f_\phi(\phi) \propto g(\phi)(1-\phi)^b$ on $(0,1)$ and considers the limit of the process $h_t \Big/ \sqrt{Var[h_t]}$ showing that the process is stationary if $b > 0$ but nonstationary if $b < 0$.

It is clear from [28] and [77] that the choice of F_ϕ has an effect on long-range dependence. To provide more flexibility on the choice of F_ϕ, [47] use a Bayesian nonparametric prior. They begin by constructing a suitable limiting process for a cross-sectional aggregation model as the number of elements tends to infinity. Using the notation $h_t(\phi, \sigma^2)$ to represent an AR(1) process with persistence parameter ϕ and stationary variance σ^2,

$$h_t(\phi, \sigma^2) = \phi h_{t-1}(\phi, \sigma^2) + \eta_t,$$

where $\eta_t \sim N\left(0, \sigma^2(1-\phi^2)\right)$, so the marginal distribution of $h_t(\phi, \sigma^2)$ is $N(0, \sigma^2)$. They define the aggregate in (4.11) as follows.

Definition 1. A finite cross-sectional aggregation (FCA) process $h_t^{(m)}$ with parameters m, σ^2 and F_ϕ is defined by

$$h_t^{(m)} = \frac{1}{m}\sum_{i=1}^{m} h_t\left(\phi_i, \sigma^2\right), \qquad t = 1, 2, \ldots, T, \tag{4.12}$$

where $\phi_1, \ldots, \phi_m \overset{i.i.d.}{\sim} F_\phi$.

[47] chose the Dirichlet process as the prior for F_ϕ. This implies that F_ϕ is discrete with an infinite number of atoms, and it can be written as Eq. (4.12), i.e.

$$F_\phi = \sum_{j=1}^{\infty} w_j \delta_{\theta_j} \qquad \text{for} \qquad j = 1, \cdots, \infty. \tag{4.13}$$

Under Eq. (4.13) each ϕ_i must take a value in $\theta_1, \theta_2, \ldots$. and there can be ties in these values. This means that we can group all the ϕ_i's that are equal to θ_j allowing for arbitrary levels of long-range dependence to exist. We can therefore model the effect of uneven information flows on volatility which can be linked to the differences in effects caused by different types of information. For example, in the study of stock returns one type of information that can affect their volatility is a profit warning announcement. Profit warnings may have a longer lasting effect when compared to other types of announcements like stock splits or rights issues.

We can now define the infinite cross-sectional aggregation (ICA) process as the limit of the FCA when the number of AR(1) processes $m \to \infty$ and with F_ϕ having the form in Eq. (4.13) as follows:

$$h_t^{(\infty)} = \sum_{j=1}^{\infty} h_t\left(\theta_j, \sigma^2 w_j\right), \qquad t = 1, 2, \ldots, T. \tag{4.14}$$

We will refer to the resulting volatility model as stochastic volatility with infinite cross-sectional aggregation (SV-ICA).

To proceed to inference we need to address the issue of the infinite sum of Eq. (4.13). [40,41] showed how to construct a finite-dimensional random probability measure with n atoms that limits to the Dirichlet process as $n \to \infty$. Using this result leads to the following finite approximation of F_ϕ:

$$F_\phi^{(n)} = \sum_{j=1}^{n} w_j^{(n)} \delta_{\theta_j^{(n)}}, \tag{4.15}$$

where $\left(w_1^{(n)}, \ldots, w_n^{(n)}\right) \sim \mathrm{Dir}(M/n, \ldots, M/n)$ and $\theta_j^{(n)} \overset{i.i.d.}{\sim} Be(1, b)$. The relationship between the Dirichlet distribution and the gamma distribution can be used to rewrite Eq. (4.15) as

$$F_\phi^{(n)} = \sum_{j=1}^{n} \frac{\sigma_j^2}{\sum_{k=1}^{n} \sigma_k^2} \delta_{\theta_j} \tag{4.16}$$

with $\sigma_j^2 \overset{i.i.d.}{\sim} Ga(M/n, M/\zeta)$.

Inference is further complicated by the nonlinear state space form of the SV-ICA model. This is addressed by using the linearised form of the SV model for MCMC [50,64,61], and employing the Forward Filtering Backward Sampling (FFBS) algorithm [10,23]. For more details on the SV-ICA and the related MCMC see [47].

To illustrate how the SV-ICA model can be used to account for long-range dependence we use the daily returns of HSBC plc from 16 May 2000 to 14 July 2010 and the daily returns of Apple Inc. from 1 January 2000 to 26 July 2010. We chose these two companies because they operate in different industry sectors, the former in the banking and the latter in the technology sector. Then it is reasonable to think that they will exhibit different volatility dynamics, demonstrated by the persistence parameter distribution, F_ϕ. The plots of these returns are shown in Fig. 4.1. The returns of HSBC appear more volatile than those of Apple, especially during

2007/2008, when the U.S. housing market collapsed, leading to a global financial market crash.

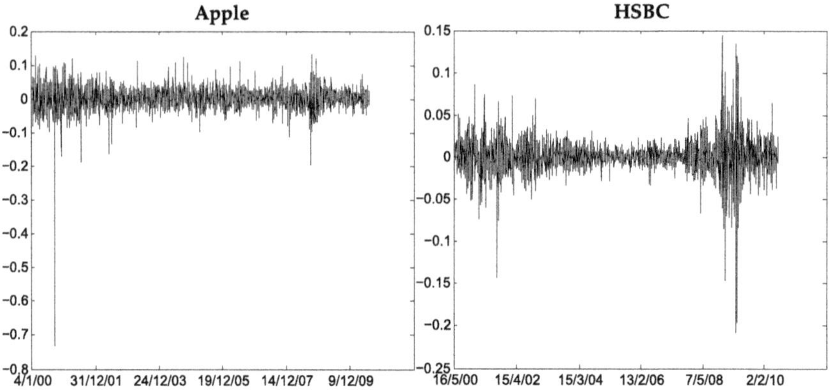

Figure 4.1 The daily returns for Apple and HSBC.

Since F_ϕ represents the decomposition of the volatility process in terms of AR(1) processes with different first-lag dependences, we construct plots of the posterior expectation of $F_\phi^{(n)}([0, x])$ for $x \in (0, 1)$, the cumulative distribution function, at different values of n (where n is the truncation required for the MCMC). Informally, convergence of the posterior occurs if there are only small changes in the posterior summaries (posterior expectation and 95% credible interval) for n larger than some n_0. [47] choose the following values for the truncation: $n = 30$, $n = 50$ and $n = 70$. These are sufficient to judge convergence for both the HSBC and Apple examples.

The plots in Fig. 4.2 show the posterior expectation of $F_\phi^{(n)}$ and its 95% credible intervals for HSBC plc, while Fig. 4.3 provides the same plots for Apple Inc., for the three different values of n. The last plot in both Fig. 4.2 and Fig. 4.3 shows the posterior distribution of ϕ under a simple SV model. For HSBC, there is only a marginal difference in the convergence of $F_\phi^{(n)}$ to F_ϕ for the three values of n; for Apple it is for the last two values of n that we observe this. We can therefore say that for Apple convergence occurs around $n = 50$ with the 95% credible intervals being wider than those of HSBC. Regarding $n = 70$, we can see that for HSBC plc much of ϕ's mass is placed close to one. This is not similar to the fit of the simple SV model with a single AR(1) process for h_t, where the posterior median of ϕ is around 0.984 with a 95% credible interval of (0.976, 0.992). A closer look at the three convergence plots shows that mass is placed at much smaller and much larger values of ϕ, implying that values of ϕ_i are more spread out within the interval (0.5, 1), compared to what the simple SV model, which uses a single value of ϕ, is able to accommodate. For Apple things are quite different; much of ϕ's mass is placed around the smaller values. This implies that the behaviour of persistence in volatility is different between the two sets of returns.

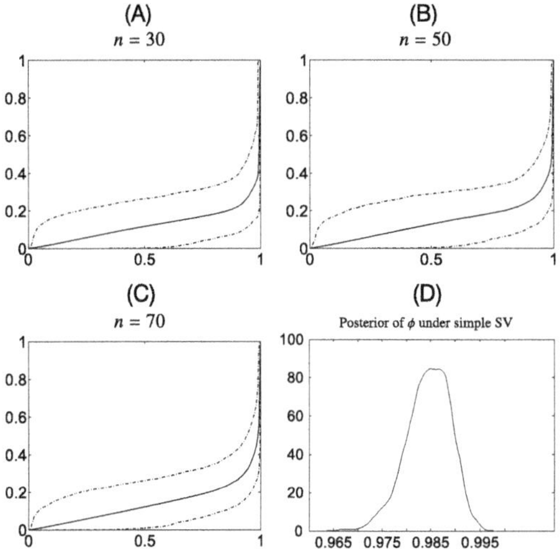

Figure 4.2 HSBC data: Posterior expectation of $F_\phi^{(n)}$ (solid line) with 95% credible interval (dot-dashed lines) for (A) $n = 30$, (B) $n = 50$ and (C) $n = 70$. The x-axis shows ϕ and the y-axis shows the posterior expectation of $F_\phi^{(n)}$. Panel (D) displays the posterior density of ϕ under the simple SV model.

To fully understand the difference in persistence of volatility between the two returns series and gain more insight into the decomposition of their persistence, [47] calculate the proportion of processes for which the dependence is small by lag κ. This measure is defined as

$$\gamma_\kappa = F_\phi^{(n)}(\{\lambda \,|\, \lambda^\kappa < \varepsilon\})$$

for some small value ε (we take $\varepsilon = 0.01$). We can then interpret γ_κ as the proportion of processes with an autocorrelation less than 0.01 after k lags. Table 4.2 and Table 4.3 provide the values of γ_κ when $n = 70$, for HSBC and Apple, respectively. The lags displayed in both tables are in terms of trading weeks and trading years.[1] The first entry for γ_κ in Table 4.2

[1] A trading week has five days and a trading year approximately 252.

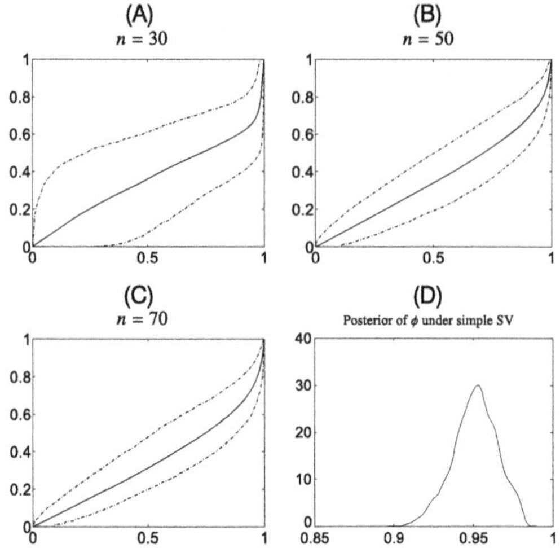

Figure 4.3 Apple data: Posterior expectation of $F_{\phi}^{(n)}$ (solid line) with 95% credible interval (dot-dashed lines) for (A) $n = 30$, (B) $n = 50$ and (C) $n = 70$. The x-axis shows ϕ and the y-axis shows the posterior expectation of $F_{\phi}^{(n)}$. Panel (D) displays the posterior density of ϕ under the simple SV model.

indicates that 10% of the variation in volatility is explained by processes which decay after one week (decay quickly). Moving along the table we see that 45% of the variation is explained by processes that decay after one year. The posterior median estimate of the persistence parameter for the simple AR(1) model suggests that autocorrelation falls below 0.01 by the 286th lag. This is roughly a little over one trading year. This is an interesting point because under the SV-ICA model a higher proportion of the variation in volatility is placed on processes that take two to five years to decay. This is clearly seen in Table 4.2, where the autocorrelation of 19% of processes has not decayed below 0.01 after five years, providing evidence of very long persistence in the data. For Apple (Table 4.3), the values of γ_κ are larger for all lags when compared to HSBC. In Apple's case 85% of the variation in volatility is explained by processes with autocorrelation decaying below 0.01 before one year. For HSBC this occurs after five years (or more). With Apple the autocorrelation of only 4% of the processes has decayed below 0.01 after five years. This confirms the conclusions about the difference in volatility persistence between the returns of two different companies operating in two different industry sectors. This could also be due to investors' belief of the riskiness not only of the two sectors but also of the two stocks.

Table 4.2 HSBC data: Values of γ_K at various lags when $n = 70$.

1 week	2 weeks	8 weeks	1/2 year	1 year	2 years	5 years
0.10	0.16	0.26	0.38	0.45	0.54	0.81

Table 4.3 Apple data: Values of γ_K at various lags when $n = 70$.

1 week	2 weeks	8 weeks	1/2 year	1 year	2 years	5 years
0.24	0.40	0.65	0.78	0.85	0.90	0.96

We conclude this section by comparing the out-of-sample predictive performance of the SV-ICA model with that of a simple SV model with an AR(1) process for the log volatility, and the SV-DPM with normal kernel, proposed by [43]. Recall that [43] model the return distribution using the DPM with normal kernel, and the log volatility h_t with an AR(1) process. Both the SV-ICA and the SV-DPM use the Bayesian nonparametric approach. The SV-ICA models the dependence in the volatility process but retains a normal return distribution whereas [43] use a nonparametric return distribution with a parametric volatility process.

Predictive performance is assessed by the LPS [27] at different prediction horizons τ. In this case, the LPS is

$$\mathrm{LPS}(\tau) = -\frac{1}{T - \tau - \lfloor T/2 \rfloor + 1} \sum_{i=\lfloor T/2 \rfloor}^{T-\tau} \log p\left(y_i^\tau \,|\, y_1, \ldots, y_{i-1}\right),$$

where τ is a positive integer and $y_i^\tau = y_{i+\tau} - y_i$ is the log return over τ days. The results are presented for time horizon up to 150 days, and smaller values of the LPS identify the model with better forecasts. Fig. 4.4 displays the LPS as a function of the forecasting horizon. The SV-ICA model dominates the SV-DPM model at all time horizons for the Apple returns and at longer time horizons for the HSBC returns. This suggests that it is better to model the volatility dynamics of returns using the Bayesian nonparametric approach, rather than the return distribution.

4.4 Bayesian nonparametric methods for the analysis of macroeconomic time series

In Sections 4.2 and 4.3 we focused on the analysis of univariate time series, where we demonstrated that the Bayesian nonparametric approach led to better out-of-sample forecasts, both in the case of modelling conditional returns' distribution using the SBP and in the case of flexibly

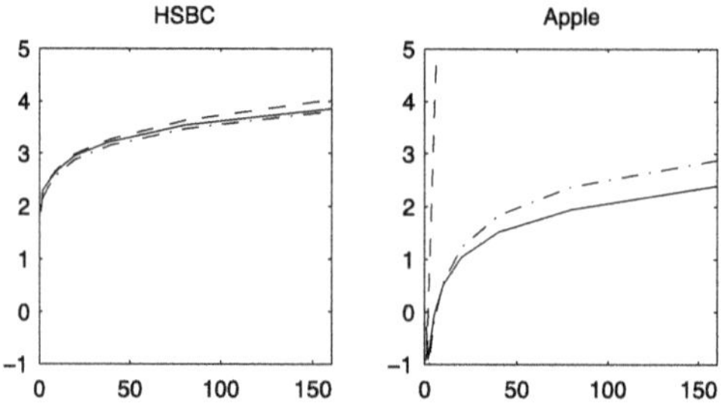

Figure 4.4 Log predictive score (τ) as a function of forecasting horizon (τ) for the SV-ICA model with $n = 70$ (solid line), the simple SV model (dot-dashed line) and the Bayesian nonparametric model (dashed line) for HSBC and Apple.

capturing the dynamics of an SV model by using the Dirichlet process as the prior for the distribution of the persistence parameter in an aggregation model. Here we are going to concentrate on multivariate time series models. Such models are used in macroeconomic modelling to understand the dynamic relationship between different economic variables (such as unemployment and inflation interest rates) in a particular economy or across different economies.

The VAR model has been the benchmark for analysing macroeconomic time series. In its basic form, the L-lag VAR model represents a p-dimensional vector of variables measured at time t, $y_t = (y_{t,1}, \ldots, y_{t,p})'$, as a linear combination of past realisations,

$$y_t = \mu + B_1 y_{t-1} + \ldots + B_L y_{t-L} + e_t, \tag{4.17}$$

where $\{B_l\}_{l=1}^{L}$ are $(p \times p)$-dimensional matrices of unknown coefficients and $e_t = (e_{1,t}, \ldots, e_{p,t})'$ is a $(p \times 1)$-dimensional multivariate normally distributed random innovation vector with mean zero and covariance matrix Σ. This simple linear representation of the joint dynamics of y_t is the reason behind the popularity of VAR models. It facilitates the study of the effects of shocks (such as monetary and fiscal policy shocks) through computation of response functions and forecast error variance decompositions; see [56,65, 72,16].

However, this linear representation of the variables' joint dynamic behaviour, with a constant conditional mean and variance, and Gaussian innovations (which are the key assumptions of VAR models) have come under heavy criticism and can be considered unrealistic. For example, empirical evidence suggests that macroeconomic variables may have nonlinear relationships (see [30]), the nature of shocks may not be Gaussian (see [76]) and the effects of these shocks may not be linear (see [67] and [58] for monetary policy studies and [5,3,24] for fiscal policy studies).

These limitations of the VAR(p) model are now well understood. The two prevailing modelling directions are regime switching (RS) models and time-varying vector autoregressive (TV-VAR) models. RS models can be seen as a form of a dynamic mixture model which can more accurately capture the structure of the data (for a comprehensive review see [38]). TV-VAR models allow the system's conditional mean and/or variance to vary over time by modelling the VAR coefficients and innovation covariance matrix with a linear time series model, often a random walk or an AR(1) process (for a comprehensive review see [52]). Both of these approaches have been proven to provide better out-of-sample forecasts when compared to the benchmark VAR model, though it is the TV-VAR that is now seen as the 'gold standard' by Central Banks; see [13] and [12].

[48] take a different approach and directly model the joint stationary and transition densities of the system using the stick breaking representation of the DPM. This implies that both densities are infinite mixtures (with the Dirichlet process as the mixing measure), where the data dictate if and when a new component is needed. The advantages of this Bayesian nonparametric approach over classical nonparametric methods are that we do not need to tune any smoothing parameters, uncertainty about the unknown stationary and transition densities is expressed through the posterior and, most importantly, out-of-sample predictive performance is superior to other models; see [63]. [71] take an alternative approach, where they model the margins nonparametrically.

To construct their multivariate model, [48] build on [2], where a prior with full support for the transition density and stationary density (i.e. any transition density and stationary density can be represented arbitrarily well by the prior) was defined for the univariate case. [48] call their multivariate stationary time series model Bayesian nonparametric VAR (BayesNP-VAR).

To derive the transition densities of the BayesNP-VAR, we start from the joint distribution of y_t and its L lags y_t^L, which is given an infinite mixture expressed as follows:

$$p(y_t, y_t^L) = \sum_{j=1}^{\infty} w_j\, k(y_t, y_t^L|\theta_j), \tag{4.18}$$

where $k(y_t, y_t^L|\theta_j)$ is an $((L+1)p)$-dimensional probability density function which does not depend on t and θ_j are the locations of the mixture components with $\theta_j \overset{i.i.d.}{\sim} G_0$. To ensure that the overall process is stationary, we assume that $k(y_{t-i}, \ldots, y_{t-i-\kappa}|\theta_j)$ for $i = 0, \ldots, L-\kappa$ and $\kappa = 0, \ldots, L-1$ depends on κ only (which can be achieved by assuming that $k(y_t, y_t^L|\theta_j)$ is the joint distribution of a stationary process). The mixture weights w_j are defined using the stick breaking representation, $w_1 = v_1$, $w_j = v_j \prod_{m<j}(1-v_m)$ and $v_j \overset{i.i.d.}{\sim} Be(1, M)$. We complete the multivariate DPM setup of Eq. (4.18) by assuming that the locations θ_j are independent of the weights, w_j.

The joint density in Eq. (4.18) leads to a transition density that is also an infinite mixture with the following form:

$$p(y_t|y_t^L) = \frac{p(y_t, y_t^L)}{p(y_t^L)} = \frac{\sum_{j=1}^{\infty} w_j\, k(y_t, y_t^L|\theta_j)}{\sum_{j=1}^{\infty} w_j\, k(y_t^L|\theta_j)} \tag{4.19}$$

$$= \sum_{j=1}^{\infty} \omega_j(y_t^L)\, k(y_t|y_t^L, \theta_j),$$

where $k(y_t|y_t^L, \theta_j)$ is the transition density of the jth component and $\omega_j(y_t^L) = \frac{w_j\, k(y_t^L|\theta_j)}{\sum_{k=1}^{\infty} w_k\, k(y_t^L|\theta_k)}$ is the weight of the jth component which depends on previous lags, the key feature of our model. The transition density can be seen as a multivariate mixture of experts. Mixtures of experts are extensions of smooth regression models and popular within the machine learning community. They are used in regression to estimate the conditional density $p(y|x)$ of a univariate y for all values of an (often high-dimensional) covariate x, using mixtures where the component weights depend on a covariate x; see [42], [45], [25] and [75]. The weights of the transition density in Eq. (4.19) depend on the observed lagged values which allows different component transition densities to be favoured in different periods. For example, contractionary and expansionary periods could have different transition densities. In the BayesNP-VAR model, we can consider each component ('expert') as a regime, with changes of regime determined by the observed lagged values of y_t^L.

To address the risk of overfitting the data, when either p (the number of time series variables) or the number of components increases, or both, [48] considered a two-stage approach.

- A structure similar to a factor model for $k(y_t, y_t^L|\theta_j)$. This choice divides the variation of the data into a part which describes the dependence between variables and a part which is idiosyncratic to each variable. To shrink to low-rank structures, they use the multiplicative gamma process shrinkage prior of [6].

- A prior for the precision parameter M, which strikes a balance between having too few and too many components. Recall from Section 4.2 that M controls the relative values of the weights. The expectation of the jth weight is $\mathrm{E}[w_j] = \frac{M^{j-1}}{(M+1)^j}$ and so, as M increases, the average size of the jth weight becomes smaller and the number of components with nonnegligible weights becomes larger.

For more detail on the construction of the BayesNP-VAR model and the related MCMC for inference refer to [48]. We conclude this section with the application of the BayesNP-VAR to seasonally adjusted, monthly macroeconomic time series from the U.S. collected from the Federal Reserve Bank of St Louis (FRED). The sample period is from 1 January 1959 to 1 August 2016, and the details of the variables together with the transformations used are displayed in Table 4.4

Table 4.4 U.S. data.

Name	Description	Growth rates
UNR	Unemployment rate	none
PCE	Personal consumption expenditure index: 2009=100	$1200\ ln(\frac{y_t}{y_{t-1}})$
NFP	Total nonfarm payroll, thousands of persons	$1200\ ln(\frac{y_t}{y_{t-1}})$
FEDR	Federal funds rate	none
IPRO	Industrial production index: 2012=100	$1200\ ln(\frac{y_t}{y_{t-1}})$
LTR	Long-term interest rate	none

Source: FRED.

To illustrate that the BayesNP-VAR correctly identifies economic regimes where shocks are transmitted in different ways, [48] select the MCMC sample with the highest posterior density value. This allows for the approximation of the posterior mode of the BayesNP-VAR mixture model. We can then identify the most probable component in $p(y_t|y_t^L)$ for the selected MCMC sample. These components are highlighted in time plots and shown together with their related weights. The idea is to show that for different time periods, different components are identified, and this is informed by the weights of the mixture model, which depend on previously observed lagged values. Figs 4.5, 4.6 and 4.7 display these time plots, and six distinct components/regimes are identified. The first two rows show the time series for each variable highlighting the regime with

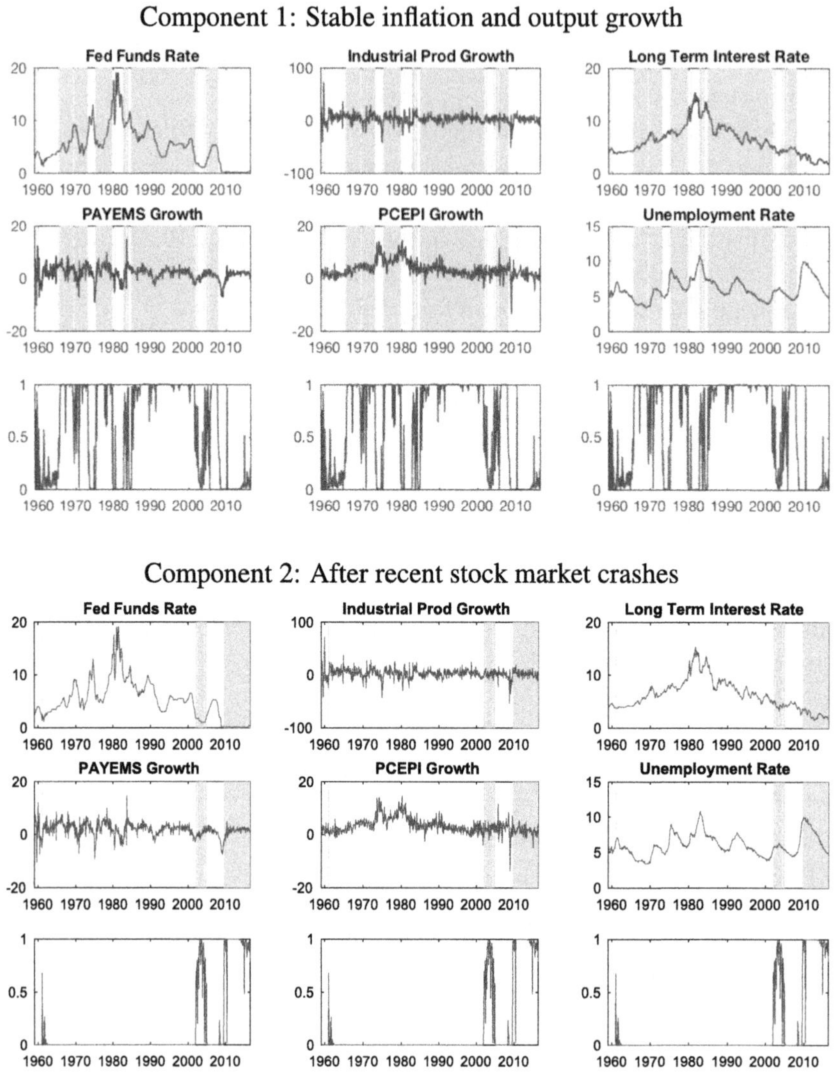

Figure 4.5 Plots identifying the first and second components of the U.S. data in growth rates. The first two rows of each set of nine plots display the time series highlighting, in cyan (mid grey in print version), the component/regime, and the third row displays the nonnegligible weight of the respective regime.

the largest mixture weight. The weight for that is displayed in the last row. The first component covers periods of sustained growth, including *'The Great Moderation'* of the mid-1980s to the mid-2000s. This was a period

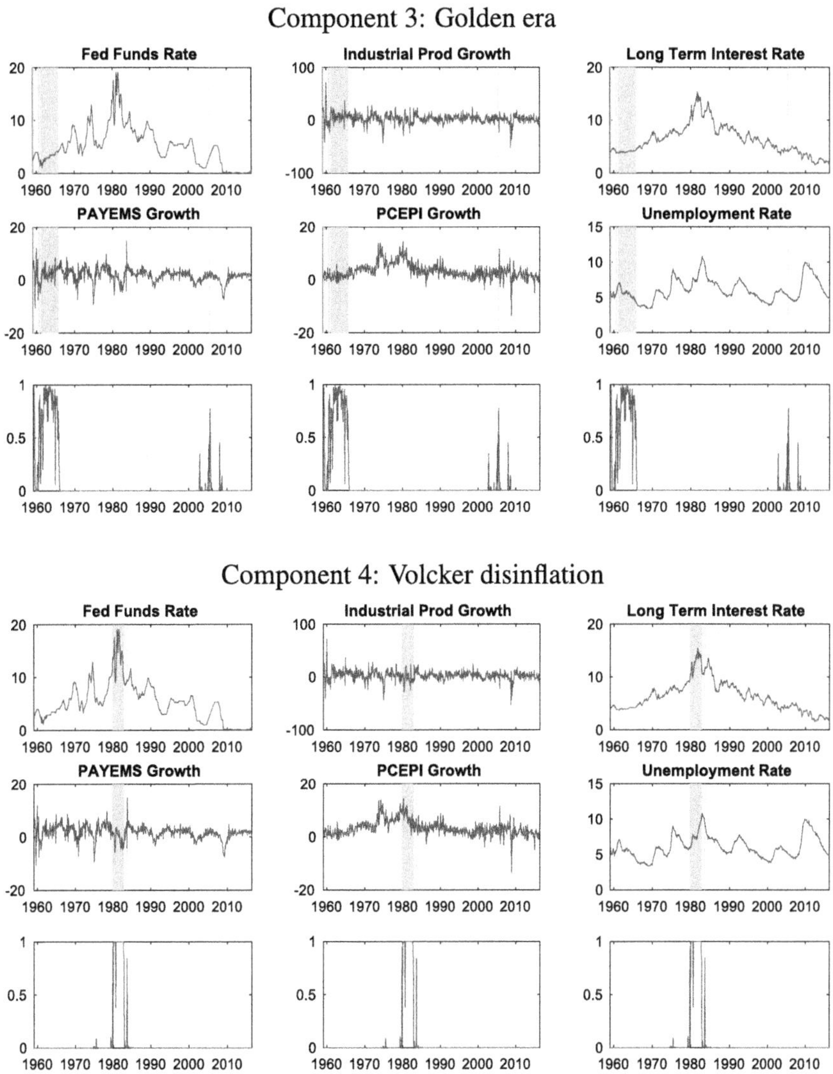

Figure 4.6 Plots identifying the third and fourth components of the U.S. data in growth rates. The first two rows of each set of nine plots display the time series highlighting, in cyan (mid grey in print version), the component/regime, and the third row displays the nonnegligible weight of the respective regime.

when the fluctuations in the business cycle were less pronounced. The second component is characterised by periods after economic downturns. The first one was the burst of the 2000 'Dot.com' bubble and the second one the

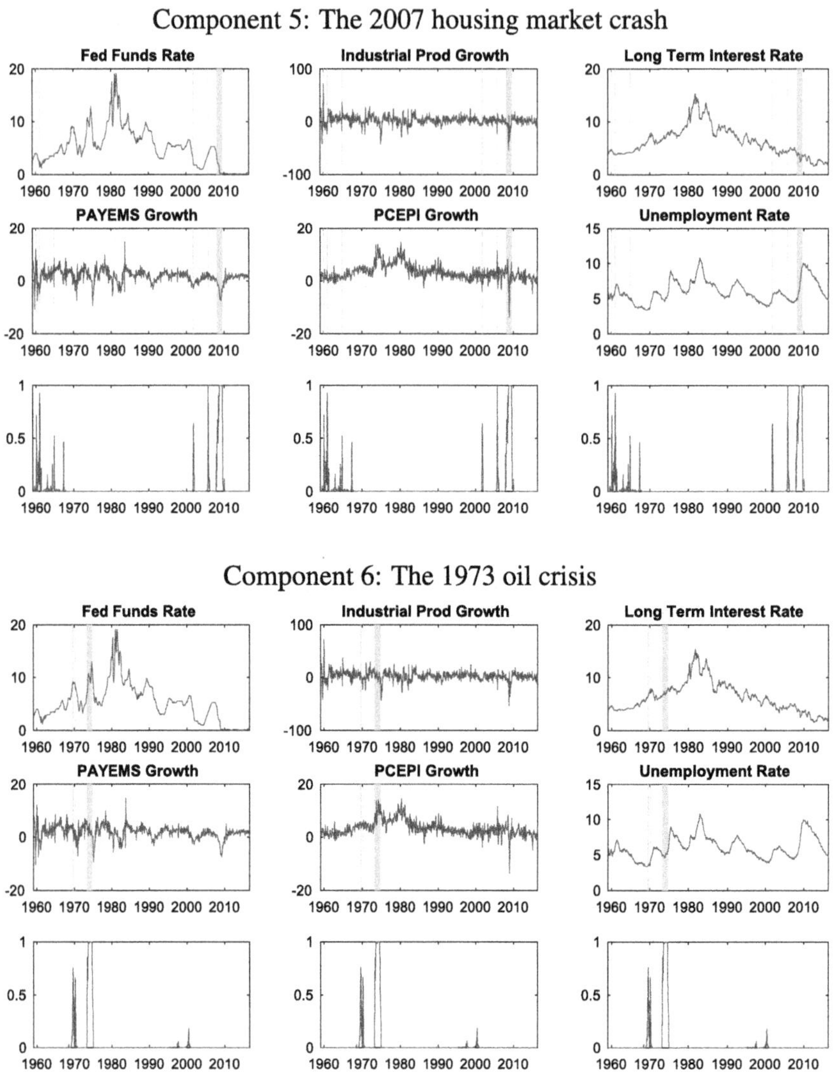

Figure 4.7 Plots identifying the fifth and sixth components of the U.S. data in growth rates. The first two rows of each set of nine plots display the time series highlighting, in cyan (mid grey in print version), the component/regime, and the third row displays the nonnegligible weight of the respective regime.

2007 U.S. housing market meltdown. Components three and four represent the *'Golden Era'* of U.S. capitalism and the *'Volcker disinflation'*, respectively. The last two components identify two of the worst recessions in recent U.S.

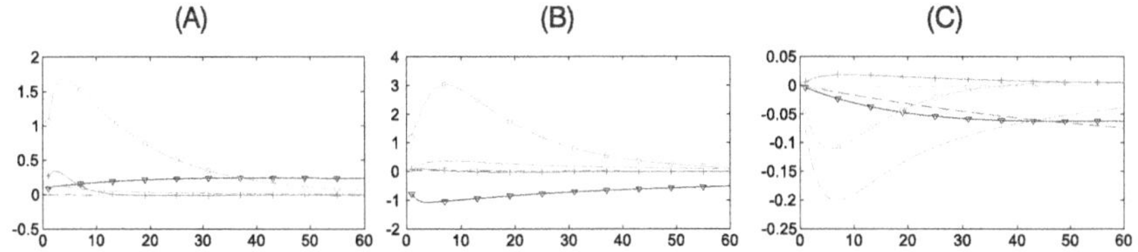

Figure 4.8 IRFs to a 1% increase in federal funds rate. (A) Inflation response. (B) Industrial production growth response. (C) Unemployment response. *Blue dash inverted triangle,* component 1; *red dash,* component 2; *green dot dash,* component 3; *yellow solid,* component 4; *cyan circle dash,* component 5; *pink plus dash,* component 6.

history; the fifth component captures the *'U.S. housing meltdown'* of 2007, whereas the sixth component captures the *'Oil Shock'* of the early 1970s. The difference between the two is that the latter was characterised by high inflation.

For the BayesNP-VAR, the transition density within each component is a VAR. This means that impulse response functions (IRFs) can be constructed. IRFs describe the evolution of a macroeconomic time series along a specified horizon after a specified shock at some time point t. An IRF is a polynomial function of the estimated VAR coefficients. Fig. 4.8 displays the IRFs for 60 months ahead following a unit shock in the chosen time series. Each component is coloured differently, with the following colour scheme: blue dash inverted triangle for the first component, red dash for the second, green dot dash for the third, yellow solid for the fourth, cyan circle dash for the fifth and pink plus dash for the sixth component. The effects of a 1% increase in the federal funds rate is shown in Fig. 4.8, where panel (A) displays the IRFs of inflation, panel (B) the IRF output growth and panel (C) the IRF of the unemployment rate. There are clear differences in the effects of the monetary policy shock, in periods of economic growth, periods of contraction and periods of economic stability. For further in depth discussion of the results, see [48].

Like the examples of the previous sections the out-of-sample predictive performance is assessed by calculating the LPS. [48] calculate the LPS for all the variables (using their joint predictive distribution) as follows:

$$-\sum_{i=s}^{T-h} \log p(y_{i+h}|y_1, \ldots, y_i), \tag{4.20}$$

where T is the size of the time series, s is the time from where the prediction starts and h is the predictive horizon. They also calculate the LPS for each variable (using its marginal predictive distribution,

$$-\sum_{i=s}^{T-h} \log p(y_{i+h,j}|y_1,\ldots,y_i). \tag{4.21}$$

A smaller LPS value indicates better predictive performance. In the paper, forecasting horizons of $h = 1$, 2 and 4 months are considered. Table 4.5 displays these LPSs. The BayesNP-VAR(1) is compared to the TVP-SV-VAR(1), which is the most popular model choice by Central banks. Regardless of the time horizon the BayesNP-VAR(1) model outperforms the TVP-SV-VAR(1) in both overall and marginal LPSs. For comparisons with other multivariate models as well as use of other predictive performance metrics, such as the root mean squared error, see [48].

Table 4.5 Log predictive scores for growth rates of U.S. data.

Model	Horizon	Joint and marginal scores						
		Overall	FEDR	IPRO	LTR	NFP	PCE	UNR
BayesNP-VAR(1)	1	322	52	109	39	48	52	22
	2	335	51	107	38	47	51	21
	4	321	58	102	36	45	49	20
TV-SV-VAR(1)	1	332	48	120	38	50	63	16
	2	351	54	119	45	51	64	21
	4	367	62	121	50	55	65	26

4.5 Conclusion

In this chapter, we showed how Bayesian nonparametric priors can be used to estimate the conditional distribution of asset returns, capture long-range dependence in SV models and explain the joint dynamic behaviour of macroeconomic time series. For all three cases we showed that the out-of-sample predictive performance of the resulting Bayesian nonparametric model was superior to other competitive models.

However, the Dirichlet process, DPM and SBP are not the only Bayesian nonparametric priors that can be used in the analysis of financial and macroeconomic time series. In the 2010s other Bayesian nonparametric priors have been developed using normalisations of complete random measures (see [54]). We believe that these priors should be used in the analysis of financial time series, because they provide a more flexible construction for the weights of mixture models. For example, they can be used in the analysis of ultrahigh-frequency data, where evidence of nonstationarity together with long-range dependence exists.

Since the seminal work of [57] there has been a lot of work in developing dependent random measures based on stick breaking constructions but these had not been used in financial time series analysis until recently. [44] use the hierarchical Dirichlet process (HDP) of [73] to capture the time dependence of the realised covariance (RCOV) matrix and estimate its conditional distribution. The HDP is a distribution over multiple correlated probability measures, $G_1, \ldots, G_r$, sharing the same atom locations. Each probability measure is generated from independent Dirichlet processes with shared precision parameter and base measure, which is generated from a Dirichlet process itself. [9] generalise the HDP to hierarchical constructions with normalised random measures, while [31] develop correlated random measures which do not involve such hierarchical construction. We believe that these measures are a more flexible alternative to the stick breaking constructed ones, as they are not constrained by the stochastic ordering of the mixture weights. These methods will be useful for modelling more complex financial and macroeconomic data.

References

[1] C.E. Antoniak, Mixtures of Dirichlet processes with applications to Bayesian nonparametric problems, The Annals of Statistics 2 (1974) 1152–1174.

[2] I. Antoniano-Villalobos, S.G. Walker, A nonparametric model for stationary time series, Journal of Time Series Analysis 37 (2016) 126–142.

[3] A.J. Auerbach, Y. Gorodnichenko, Fiscal multipliers in recession and expansion, in: A. Alesina, F. Giavazzi (Eds.), Fiscal Policy After the Financial Crisis, University of Chicago Press, 2013, pp. 63–98.

[4] X. Bai, J. Russell, G. Tiao, Kurtosis of GARCH and stochastic volatility models with non-normal innovations, Journal of Econometrics 114 (2) (2003) 349–360.

[5] A. Baum, G.B. Koester, The Impact of Fiscal Policy on Economic Activity Over the Business Cycle: Evidence From a Threshold VAR Analysis, Discussion paper, Series 1 Economic Studies N03/2011, Deutsche Bundesbank, 2011.

[6] A. Bhattacharya, D.B. Dunson, Sparse Bayesian infinite factor models, Biometrika 98 (2) (2011) 291–306.

[7] T. Bollerslev, A conditionally heteroskedastic time series model for speculative prices and rates of return, Review of Economics and Statistics 69 (1987) 542–547.

[8] D. Brunner, A.Y. Lo, Bayes methods for a symmetric unimodal density and its mode, Annals of Statistics 17 (1989) 1550–1566.

[9] F. Camerlenghi, A. Lijoi, P. Orbanz, I. Prünster, Distribution theory for hierarchical processes, The Annals of Statistics 47 (2019) 67–92.

[10] C.K. Carter, R. Kohn, On Gibbs sampling for state space models, Biometrika 81 (1994) 541–553.

[11] Q. Chen, R. Gerlach, Z. Lu, Bayesian value at risk and expected shortfall forecasting via the asymmetric Laplace distribution, Computational Statistics and Data Analysis 56 (2012) 3498–3516.

[12] T. Clark, F. Ravazzolo, Macroeconomic forecasting performance under alternative specifications of time-varying volatility, Journal of Applied Econometrics 30 (2015) 551–575.

[13] T.E. Clark, Real-time density forecasts from Bayesian vector autoregressions with stochastic volatility, Journal of Business and Economic Statistics 29 (2011) 327–341.

[14] R. Cont, Empirical properties of asset returns: stylized facts and statistical issues, Quantitative Finance 1 (2) (2001) 223–236.

[15] E.I. Delatola, J.E. Griffin, Bayesian nonparametric modelling of the return distribution with stochastic volatility, Bayesian Analysis 6 (2011) 901–926.

[16] F.X. Diebold, G.D. Rudebusch, Five questions about business cycles, FRBSF Economic Review (2001) 1–15.

[17] Z. Ding, C. Granger, R.F. Engle, A long memory property of stock market returns and a new model, Journal of Empirical Finance 1 (1993) 83–106.

[18] M.D. Escobar, M. West, Bayesian density estimation and inference using mixtures, Journal of the American Statistical Association 90 (1995) 577–588.

[19] W. Feller, Introduction to Probability Theory and Its Applications, vol. 1, John Wiley and Sons, 1957.

[20] T. Ferguson, A Bayesian analysis of some nonparametric problems, The Annals of Statistics 1 (2) (1973) 209–230.

[21] C. Fernandez, M.F.J. Steel, On Bayesian modelling of fat tails and skewness, Journal of the American Statistical Association 93 (1998) 359–371.

[22] D.A. Freedman, On the asymptotic behaviour of Bayes estimates in the discrete case, Annals of Mathematical Statistics 34 (1963) 1386–1403.

[23] S. Frühwirth-Schnatter, Data augmentation and dynamic linear models, Journal of Time Series Analysis 15 (1994) 183–202.

[24] L. Gambacorta, B. Hofmann, G. Peersman, The effectiveness of unconventional monetary policy at the zero lower bound: a cross-country analysis, Journal of Money, Credit and Banking 46 (2014) 615–642.

[25] J. Geweke, M. Keane, Smoothly mixing regressions, Journal of Econometrics 138 (2007) 252–290.

[26] L. Glosten, R. Jagannathan, D. Runkle, On the relation between the expected value and the volatility of the nominal excess return on stocks, The Journal of Finance 48 (5) (1993) 1779–1801.

[27] T. Gneiting, A.E. Raftery, Strictly proper scoring rules, prediction and estimation, Journal of the American Statistical Association 102 (2007) 359–378.

[28] C. Granger, Long memory relationships and the aggregation of dynamic models, Journal of Econometrics 14 (1980) 227–238.

[29] C. Granger, Long memory relationships and the autoregression of dynamic models, Journal of Econometrics 14 (1980) 227–238.

[30] C. Granger, T. Terasvirta, Modelling nonlinear economic relationships, International Journal of Forecasting 10 (1994) 169–171.

[31] J.E. Griffin, F. Leisen, Compound random measures and their use in Bayesian nonparametric models, Journal of the Royal Statistical Society, Series B 79 (2018) 525–545.
[32] J.E. Griffin, F.A. Quintana, M.F.J. Steel, Flexible and nonparametric methods, in: G. Koop, H.K. van Dijk, J. Geweke (Eds.), Handbook of Bayesian Econometrics, Oxford University Press, 2011.
[33] J.E. Griffin, M.F.J. Steel, Order-based dependent Dirichlet processes, Journal of the American Statistical Association 101 (2006) 179–194.
[34] P. Halmos, Random alms, The Annals of Mathematical Statistics 15 (1944) 182–189.
[35] B.E. Hansen, Autoregressive conditional density estimation, International Economic Review 35 (1994) 705–730.
[36] K. Hirano, Semiparametric Bayesian inference in autoregressive panel data models, Econometrica 70 (2002) 781–799.
[37] N.L. Hjort, C. Holmes, P. Müller, S.G. Walker (Eds.), Bayesian Nonparametrics, 1st ed., Statistic and Probabilistic Mathematics, Cambridge University Press, 2010, April.
[38] K. Hubrich, T. Teräsvirta, Thresholds and smooth transitions in vector autoregressive models, in: T.B. Fomby, L. Kilian, A. Murphy (Eds.), VAR Models in Macroeconomics-New Developments and Applications: Essays in Honor of Christopher A. Sims, in: Advances in Econometrics, vol. 32, Emerald Group Publishing Limited, 2013.
[39] H. Ishwaran, L.F. James, Gibbs sampling methods for stick-breaking priors, Journal of the American Statistical Association 96 (2001) 161–173.
[40] H. Ishwaran, M. Zarepour, Markov chain Monte Carlo in approximate Dirichlet and two-parameter process hierarchical models, Biometrika 87 (2000) 371–390.
[41] H. Ishwaran, M. Zarepour, Exact and approximate sum-representations for the Dirichlet process, The Canadian Journal of Statistics 30 (2002) 269–283.
[42] R. Jacobs, M. Jordan, S. Nowlan, G. Hinton, Adaptive mixtures of local experts, Neural Computation 3 (1991) 79–87.
[43] M.J. Jensen, J.M. Maheu, Bayesian semiparametric stochastic volatility modeling, Journal of Econometrics 157 (2) (2010) 306–316.
[44] X. Jin, J.M. Maheu, Bayesian semiparametric modelling of realized covariance matrices, Journal of Econometrics 192 (2016) 19–39.
[45] M. Jordan, R. Jacobs, Hierarchical mixtures of experts and the EM algorithm, Neural Computation 6 (1994) 181–214.
[46] M. Kalli, J. Griffin, S.G. Walker, Slice sampling mixture models, Statistics and Computing 21 (2011) 93–105.
[47] M. Kalli, J.E. Griffin, Flexible modelling of dependence in volatility processes, Journal of Business and Economic Statistics 33 (2015) 102–113.
[48] M. Kalli, J.E. Griffin, Bayesian nonparametric vector autoregressive model, Journal of Econometrics 203 (2018) 267–282.
[49] M. Kalli, S.G. Walker, P. Damien, Modelling the conditional distribution of daily stock index returns: an alternative Bayesian semiparametric model, Journal of Business and Economic Statistics 31 (2013) 371–383.
[50] S. Kim, N. Shephard, S. Chib, Stochastic volatility: likelihood inference and comparison with ARCH models, Review of Economic Studies 65 (1998) 361–393.
[51] J.F.C. Kingman, Random discrete distributions, Journal of the Royal Statistical Society, Series B 37 (1974) 1–22.
[52] G. Koop, D. Korobilis, Bayesian multivariate time series methods for empirical macroeconomics, Foundations and Trends in Econometrics 3 (2010) 267–358.

[53] D. Leslie, R. Kohn, D. Nott, A general approach to heteroscedastic linear regression, Statistics and Computing 17 (2007) 131–146.
[54] A. Lijoi, I. Prünster, Models beyond the Dirichlet process, in: N. Hjort, C. Holmes, P. Müller, S. Walker (Eds.), Bayesian Nonparametrics, 1st ed., Cambridge University Press, 2010, pp. 80–136.
[55] A.Y. Lo, On a class of Bayesian nonparametric estimates: I. Density estimates, The Annals of Statistics 12 (1984) 351–357.
[56] R.E. Lucas, Methods and problems in business cycle theory, Journal of Money, Credit and Banking 12 (1980) 696–715.
[57] S.N. MacEachern, Dependent Dirichlet Processes, Technical report, Department of Statistics, Ohio State University, 2000.
[58] C. Matthes, R. Barnichon, Measuring the nonlinear effects of monetary policy, Number 49 in 2015 Meeting Papers, Society of Economic Dynamics, 2015.
[59] P. Müller, F. Quintana, A. Jara, T. Hanson, Bayesian Nonparametric Data Analysis, 1st ed., Springer, 2015.
[60] P. Müller, M. West, S.N. MacEachern, Bayesian models for non-linear auto-regressions, Journal of Time Series Analysis 18 (1997) 593–614.
[61] J. Nakajima, Y. Omori, Leverage, heavy-tails and correlated jumps in stochastic volatility models, Computational Statistics & Data Analysis 53 (2009) 2335–2353.
[62] D.B. Nelson, Conditional heteroscedasticity in asset returns: a new approach, Econometrica 59 (1991) 347–370.
[63] A. Norets, D. Pati, Adaptive Bayesian estimation of conditional densities, Econometric Theory 33 (2017) 980–1012.
[64] Y. Omori, S. Chib, N. Shephard, J. Nakajima, Stochastic volatility with leverage: fast and efficient likelihood inference, Journal of Econometrics 140 (2007) 425–449.
[65] A. Pagan, Towards an understanding of some business cycle characteristics, Australian Economic Review 30 (1997) 1–15.
[66] J. Pitman, M. Yor, Two parameter Poisson-Dirichlet distribution derived from a stable subordinator, The Annals of Probability (1997) 855–900.
[67] M.O. Ravn, M. Sola, Asymmetric effects of monetary policy in the US, Federal Reserve Bank of St. Louis Review 86 (2004) 41–60.
[68] P. Robinson, Statistical inference for a random coefficient autoregressive model, Scandinavian Journal of Statistics 5 (1978) 163–168.
[69] J. Sethuraman, A constructive definition of Dirichlet priors, Statistica Sinica 4 (2) (1994) 639–650.
[70] B. Shahbaba, Discovering hidden structures using mixture models: application to nonlinear time series processes, Studies in Nonlinear Dynamics and Econometrics 13 (5) (2009).
[71] M. Smith, S. Vahey, Asymmetric forecast densities for U.S. macroeconomic variables from a Gaussian copula model of cross-sectional and serial dependence, Journal of Business and Economic Statistics 34 (416–434) (2016).
[72] J. Stock, M. Watson, Business cycle fluctuations in US macroeconomic time series, in: Handbook of Macroeconomics, vol. 1, Part A, Elsevier, 1999, Chapter 1.
[73] Y.W. Teh, M.I. Jordan, M.J. Beal, D.M. Blei, Hierarchical Dirichlet processes, Journal of the American Statistical Association 101 (2006) 1566–1581.
[74] P. Theodossiou, Financial data and the skewed generalized T distribution, Management Science 44 (12) (1998) 1650–1661.

[75] M. Villani, R. Kohn, D. Nott, Generalized smooth finite mixtures, Journal of Econometrics 171 (2012) 121–133.
[76] C.L. Weise, The asymmetric effects of monetary policy: a nonlinear vector autoregression approach, Journal of Money, Credit and Banking 31 (1999) 85–108.
[77] P. Zaffaroni, Contemporaneous aggregation of linear dynamic models in large economies, Journal of Econometrics 120 (2004) 75–102.

CHAPTER 5

Bayesian mixed binary-continuous copula regression with an application to childhood undernutrition

Nadja Klein[a], Thomas Kneib[b,c], Giampiero Marra[d], Rosalba Radice[e]
[a]Humboldt Universität zu Berlin, School of Business and Economics, Unter den Linden 6, 10099 Berlin, Germany
[b]Georg-August-Universität Göttingen, Faculty of Business and Economic Sciences, Humboldtallee 3, 37073 Göttingen, Germany
[d]University College London, Department of Statistical Science, Gower Street, London WC1E 6BT, United Kingdom
[e]Cass Business School, City University of London, Faculty of Actuarial Science and Insurance, 106 Bunhill Row, London EC1Y 8TZ, United Kingdom

Contents

5.1 Introduction

Many empirical phenomena studied via regression models are multidimensional such that reducing them to one single response variable naturally leads to a loss of information on the true data generating process. In particular, regression models with univariate response variables do not allow

[c] Thomas Kneib received financial support from the German Research Foundation (DFG) within the research project KN 922/9-1.

Flexible Bayesian Regression Modelling
https://doi.org/10.1016/B978-0-12-815862-3.00011-1

the analyst to study the dependence between the different response variables. As one example on a multidimensional response variable, we will investigate determinants of child health in developing countries. This is a particularly relevant research area since improving child health is among the most important goals for developing countries and consequently also figures prominently in the sustainable development goals set out by the United Nations.

In our application, we make use of the wealth of information provided by the Demographic and Health surveys, which are nationally representative surveys covering aspects such as fertility, family planning, maternal and child health, child survival and child nutrition (www.measuredhs.com). Currently, information is available on more than 300 surveys conducted in 90 countries, and we chose India as a particularly interesting case since it is among the countries with the highest rates of childhood undernutrition [13]. As two important dimensions of child health, we will consider *wasting* as a continuous indicator for acute malnutrition as reflected by low weight for height (in comparison to a reference population) and a binary indicator for fever within the two weeks preceding the survey interview. More precisely, wasting is usually reported as a z-score that compares the nutritional status of a child with a predefined reference population via

$$z = \frac{\text{observed value} - \text{median value in reference population}}{\text{standard deviation in reference population}}. \tag{5.1}$$

Based on the definition of the World Health Organization [43], an individual is considered to suffer from wasting if the score is two standard deviations below the median of the reference population.

Both indicators are representatives of adverse health risks and measure different yet potentially interrelated aspects of child health. As a consequence, it is very likely to observe dependence between the two health dimensions even after adjusting for explanatory variables. We therefore deal with the challenge of identifying determinants of child health risks by developing Bayesian bivariate regression models where the full distribution of the two response variables can be investigated simultaneously. This will comprise

- the flexible, modular specification of the joint distribution of a discrete and a continuous response based on copulas,
- regression predictors on all parameters of the bivariate response distribution including the dependence parameter of the copula but also all parameters characterising the marginal distributions,

- flexible regression predictors comprising various types of regression effects such as nonlinear effects of continuous covariates, spatial effects and random effects,
- efficient fully Bayesian inference based on Markov chain Monte Carlo (MCMC) simulations,
- tools for model choice and model checking.

Our model developments can be cast into the framework of generalised additive models for location, scale and shape (GAMLSS) as originally proposed by Rigby and Stasinopoulos [32] and Stasinopoulos and Rigby [40]. The basic idea of GAMLSS is to assume a parametric type of distribution for the response variable of interest and to place regression predictors on potentially all parameters characterising the response distribution. This allows one to leave the restrictive realm of mean regression models where all parameters but the mean are treated as nuisance parameters. The original proposal of GAMLSS relied on penalised maximum likelihood inference while later developments have considered functional gradient descent boosting [26] or Bayesian inference based on MCMC simulations [17].

While originally being associated with univariate responses, GAMLSS can easily be extended to bivariate (or more generally multivariate) responses as long as a suitable type of parametric response distribution is still available. Inspired by seemingly unrelated regression models [48,37,22], Klein, Kneib, Klasen and Lang [15] developed such multivariate GAMLSS based on the bivariate normal and/or the bivariate t distribution, while Marra and Radice [24] proposed recursive bivariate probit models. The main limitation in these developments was the determination of appropriate bivariate or multivariate response distributions. To gain additional flexibility in this respect, the construction via copulas [27] proved to be very useful since it allows to separately specify the marginal distributions and the dependence structure. This construction principle has been used for bivariate continuous response vectors in Klein and Kneib ([14], based on MCMC simulations) Marra and Radice [25] and Radice et al. ([31], penalised maximum likelihood inference), or Yee ([47], in the context of vector generalised additive models). A similar framework has also been proposed in [4] utilising random walk proposals. However, they only consider normal marginals with constant variances and a linear predictor for the marginal expectations. The predictor of the copula parameter is furthermore restricted to cubic splines. Klein et al. [18] extended the approach of Marra and Radice [25] to allow also for responses of a mixed discrete-continuous type and developed corresponding penalised maximum likelihood inference. Additional flexibility is obtained as the marginal and copula parameters are related to regression predictors of structured additive form [8,44]. A somewhat different perspective on bivariate response models is often taken in economics to account for endogeneity of a regressor that is treated as the response in the second equation. Linear copula specifications are also gaining in popularity in this area; see for instance Park and Gupta [29] and references therein for the particular case of marketing-related applications.

In this chapter, we develop the fully Bayesian analogue to Klein et al. [18] to provide access to the full posterior distribution via MCMC simulation techniques. Beside what has been developed in Vatter and Chavez-Demoulin [41] and Klein et al. [18], to the best of our knowledge, other existing bivariate copula regression approaches and software implementations (see e.g. [1,10,20,19,34,46]) cover only parts of the flexibility of our approach. The approach of [41] is based on a two-stage technique where the parameters of the marginal distributions and of the copula function are estimated separately. In contrast, we adopt a simultaneous estimation approach since [25] showed empirically that estimating all parameters simultaneously offers computation and efficiency gains. Further simultaneous copula regression methods in a fully parametric approach to likelihood estimation are considered in [5,45] albeit restricted to the case of linear dependence via a Gaussian copula. Alternatively if the dimension of the response is larger than two, semi/nonparametric extensions where, for instance, the margins and/or copula function are estimated using kernels, wavelets or orthogonal polynomials may be considered (e.g. [12,21,35,36]). While such techniques are in principle more flexible in determining the shape of the underlying bivariate distribution, in practice they are limited with regard to the inclusion of flexible covariate effects, and may require large sample sizes to produce reliable results.

The rest of this chapter is structured as follows: Section 5.2 contains the corresponding model developments including the copula-based construction of mixed discrete-continuous distributions and the specification of the regression predictors. Section 5.3 develops the Bayesian inferential scheme while Sections 5.4 and 5.5 discuss the application of the models in the context of child health. More precisely, Section 5.4 focuses on questions of model selection and model evaluation while Section 5.5 discusses the empirical results and their implications. The final Section 5.6 considers issues for future research.

5.2 Bivariate copula models with mixed binary-continuous marginals

5.2.1 Copula-based construction of bivariate binary-continuous distributions

Copulas provide a flexible, modular possibility for constructing multivariate (in our case bivariate) distributions that allows for the separation between the specification for the marginals and the specification of the dependence structure. The foundation for this construction is Sklar's theorem that implies that any bivariate, strictly continuous cumulative distribution function (CDF) $F(y_1, y_2) = P(Y_1 \leq y_1, Y_2 \leq y_2)$ related to a pair of response variables (Y_1, Y_2) can be uniquely represented as

$$F(y_1, y_2) = C(F_1(y_1), F_2(y_2)), \tag{5.2}$$

where $C: [0, 1]^2 \to [0, 1]$ denotes a copula (i.e. a bivariate CDF defined on the unit square with standard uniform marginals) and $F_d(y_d) = P(Y_d \leq y_d)$, for $d = 1, 2$, correspond to the marginal CDFs of the two random variables Y_1 and Y_2. When assuming a parametric structure for both the marginal distributions and the copula, representation (5.2) yields a completely parametric model for the bivariate CDF which, in turn, allows one to relate copulas with distributional regression models. In the resulting class of copula regression models, the parameters from (5.2) are related to regression predictors via suitable link functions yielding a flexible and versatile way of defining regression models for bivariate response variables with regression effects not only on the marginals but also on the dependence structure as represented by the copula.

If one of the two components Y_1 or Y_2 is discrete, Eq. (5.2) is still valid but the copula is in general no longer unique which renders the data-based identification of parameters challenging. In this chapter, we focus on the particular case where one of the two components is binary and circumvent the nonuniqueness of the copula by using the latent variable representation of binary regression models. For the rest of the chapter we assume, without loss of generality, that the first response component Y_1 is binary (i.e. $Y_1 \in \{0, 1\}$) but is related to the (unobserved) latent variable Y_1^* via the threshold mechanism $Y_1 = \mathbb{1}(Y_1^* > 0)$, where $\mathbb{1}(\cdot)$ denotes the indicator function. From this it follows that the CDF of the observed response Y_1 ($F_1(y_1)$) and the CDF of the latent variable Y_1^* ($F_1^*(y_1^*)$) coincide at $y_1 = y_1^* = 0$, i.e.

$$P(Y_1 = 0) = P(Y_1 \leq 0) = F_1(0) = F_1^*(0) = P(Y_1^* \leq 0).$$

Utilising the latent variable, the copula representation (5.2) yields

$$P(Y_1 = 0, Y_2 \leq y_2) = P(Y_1^* \leq 0, Y_2 \leq y_2) = C(F_1^*(0), F_2(y_2))$$

and

$$P(Y_1 = 1, Y_2 \leq y_2) = P(Y_1^* > 0, Y_2 \leq y_2) = F_2(y_2) - C(F_1^*(0), F_2(y_2)),$$

leading to the mixed binary-continuous density

$$p(y_1, y_2) = \left(\frac{\partial C(F_1^*(0), F_2(y_2))}{\partial F_2(y_2)}\right)^{1-y_1} \cdot \left(1 - \frac{\partial C(F_1^*(0), F_2(y_2))}{\partial F_2(y_2)}\right)^{y_1} \cdot p_2(y_2), \tag{5.3}$$

where $p_2(y_2) = \frac{\partial F_2(y_2)}{\partial y_2}$ is the marginal density of Y_2. Eq. (5.3) will provide the basis for calculating the likelihood of our copula regression specification and will therefore be an integral component of the Bayesian inferential scheme that we are going to develop later.

5.2.2 Specifying the marginal distributions

As a major advantage of the copula approach, we can separately specify the two marginal distributions and the dependence structure. Concerning the former, we have to make a specific assumption about the binary response component Y_1 (or the corresponding latent variable Y_1^*) and the continuous response component Y_2.

Since we are interested in imputing the unobserved latent variables Y_1^* as a part of our MCMC approach, we will assume a normal distribution for the latent variable, i.e. $Y_1^* \sim \mathrm{N}(\eta_1, 1)$, where η_1 is a regression predictor that determines the location parameter of the latent variable, and therefore implicitly the success probability of the binary response variable. The CDF of Y_1^* is then given by $F_1^*(y_1^*) = \Phi(y_1^* - \eta_1)$ (with the standard normal CDF $\Phi(\cdot)$) and the success probability is $\pi = \mathbb{P}(Y_1 = 1) = \mathbb{P}(Y_1^* > 0) = \Phi(\eta_1)$. Of course other latent variable specifications are conceivable, e.g. the logistic distribution leading to a marginal logit model for the binary response Y_1 or the Gumbel distribution leading to a marginal complementary log-log model, but we will exclusively focus on the probit specification in the following since it considerably facilitates the imputation of Y_1^*.

For the continuous marginal, any strictly continuous CDF $F_2(y_2)$ can be employed and the exact choice should be guided by the specific application. In our case, we will rely on a normal specification for Y_2 with

CDF $F_2(y_2) = \Phi\left(\frac{y_2-\mu}{\sigma}\right)$, where μ and σ^2 denote the mean and variance that will be related to regression predictors later. The choice of the normal distribution is in line with most previous univariate analyses of undernutrition indicators where the normal distribution (in particular with regression effects also on the variance) provided a very reasonable fit.

5.2.3 Specifying the copula

The most prominent choice for copulas is the Gaussian copula

$$C(u_1, u_2) = \Phi_2\left(\Phi^{-1}(u_1), \Phi^{-1}(u_2)\right),$$

where $\Phi_2(\cdot, \cdot)$ corresponds to the CDF of the bivariate normal distribution with expectation zero, unit variances and correlation coefficient $\rho \in [-1, 1]$. In our case, this would imply not only that the copula model reduces to a bivariate normal model on the latent scale but it also has the disadvantage that only linear correlation can be modelled while tail dependence (i.e. stronger dependence of extreme events) cannot be accounted for. In most bivariate regression situations, however, the simultaneous occurrence of two extreme events (in our case for example a low nutritional status and a high probability of fever) are of particular interest and therefore relaxing this restrictive assumption would be relevant. We therefore consider the Clayton copula

$$C(u_1, u_2) = (u_1^{-\theta} + u_2^{-\theta} - 1)^{-1/\theta},$$

with dependence parameter $\theta > 0$, as a competitor to the Gaussian copula. The Clayton copula allows for lower tail dependence but is restricted to positive dependence in its standard form. To overcome this limitation, we also consider rotated versions of the Clayton copula obtained from

$$\begin{aligned}
C_{90}(u_1, u_2) &= u_2 - C(1 - u_1, u_2), \\
C_{180}(u_1, u_2) &= u_1 + u_2 - 1 + C(1 - u_1, 1 - u_2), \\
C_{270}(u_1, u_2) &= u_1 - C(u_1, 1 - u_2),
\end{aligned}$$

where $C(\cdot, \cdot)$ denotes the standard Clayton copula and the rotation shifts the tail dependence to either of the four corners of the unit square. This yields upper tail (rotation by 180°) or negative tail dependence (rotation by 90° to relate large values of Y_2 with small values of Y_1 and vice versa for rotation by 270°). A visualisation of the resulting four versions of the

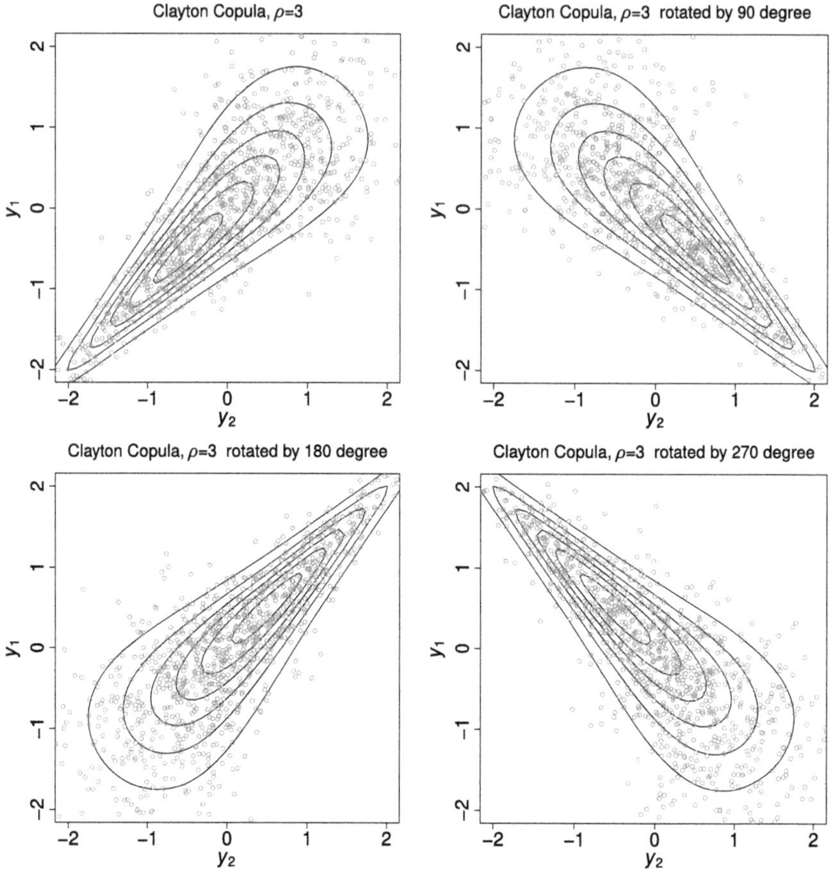

Figure 5.1 Contour lines (in 0.02 steps) of various bivariate distributions, all with standard normal marginal distributions and linear correlation coefficient of 0.5 (for positive dependence) and -0.5 (for negative dependence). The distributions are generated by rotating the Clayton copula by 0, 90, 180 and 270 degrees and where the copula parameter is denoted by θ.

Clayton copula can be found in Fig. 5.1, where all marginal distributions are standard normal and the value of the correlation coefficient is equal to 0.5 for positive and -0.5 for negative dependence.

5.2.4 Embedding copula regression in the distributional regression framework

The copula-based specification of the distribution for the bivariate response vector enables us to embed our model structure in the framework of distributional regression, where potentially all parameters of the joint distribution can be related to regression predictors formed from covariates collected in the vector $\boldsymbol{\nu}_i$ (containing e.g. binary, categorical, continuous and spatial variables). More precisely, we assume that for observed response vectors $\boldsymbol{y}_i = (y_{i1}, y_{i2})$, $i = 1, \ldots, n$ (or equivalently $\boldsymbol{y}_i = (y^*_{i1}, y_{i2})$), the conditional density $f(\boldsymbol{y}_i|\boldsymbol{\nu}_i)$ given covariates $\boldsymbol{\nu}_i$ depends on, in total, $K = K_1 + K_2 + K_c$ parameters $\boldsymbol{\vartheta}_i = (\vartheta_{i1}, \ldots, \vartheta_{iK})'$ comprising

- $K_1 = 1$ parameters for the binary regression model for y_{i1} (the success probability),
- K_2 parameters for the marginal of y_{i2} (i.e. $K_2 = 2$ in case of the Gaussian distribution) and
- K_c parameters for the copula $C(\cdot, \cdot)$ (in our case, we will always have $K_c = 1$).

Each of the parameters ϑ_{ik} is then related to a corresponding regression predictor η_{ik} based on a one-to-one response function h_k via

$$\vartheta_{ik} = h_k(\eta_{ik}), \qquad \eta_{ik} = g_k(\vartheta_{ik}).$$

The response functions h_k map the real line to the parameter space and can be inverted to the link functions $g_k = h_k^{-1}$ mapping the parameter space back to the real line. In our model specification, we rely on (i) the probit response function for the success probability of the binary response y_{i1}, (ii) the exponential response function for nonnegative parameters such as the variance of the normally distributed continuous response variable and the dependence of the Clayton copula and (iii) Fisher's z-transformation for parameters from a bounded interval such as the correlation coefficient of the Gaussian copula.

For each of the predictors η_{ik} we assume a semiparametric, additive structure (as proposed in [8]),

$$\eta_{ik} = \beta_0^{\vartheta_k} + \sum_{j=1}^{J_k} s_j^{\vartheta_k}(\boldsymbol{\nu}_i), \tag{5.4}$$

consisting of an intercept $\beta_0^{\vartheta_k}$ and an additive combination of J_k functional effects $s_j^{\vartheta_k}(\boldsymbol{\nu}_i)$ depending on (different subsets of) the covariate vector $\boldsymbol{\nu}_i$ (see the next subsection for details).

5.2.5 Predictor specification

Dropping the parameter index ϑ_k for notational simplicity, we assume a representation in terms of D_j basis functions $B_{j,d_j}(\boldsymbol{\nu}_i)$ for the different additive effect components in (5.4), yielding

$$s_j(\boldsymbol{\nu}_i) = \sum_{d_j=1}^{D_j} \beta_{j,d_j} B_{j,d_j}(\boldsymbol{\nu}_i). \tag{5.5}$$

As a consequence, each vector of function evaluations $(s_j(\boldsymbol{\nu}_1), \ldots, s_j(\boldsymbol{\nu}_n))'$ can be written as $\boldsymbol{Z}_j\boldsymbol{\beta}_j$ with basis coefficient vector $\boldsymbol{\beta}_j = (\beta_{j1}, \ldots, \beta_{j,D_j})'$ and design matrix $\boldsymbol{Z}_j$ containing the evaluated basis functions, i.e. $\boldsymbol{Z}_j[i, d_j] = B_{j,d_j}(\boldsymbol{\nu}_i)$. In matrix-vector notation the predictor vector $\boldsymbol{\eta} = (\eta_1, \ldots, \eta_n)'$ for all n observations of a given distributional parameter can therefore be represented as

$$\boldsymbol{\eta} = \beta_0 \mathbf{1}_n + \boldsymbol{Z}_1\boldsymbol{\beta}_1 + \ldots + \boldsymbol{Z}_J\boldsymbol{\beta}_J,$$

where $\mathbf{1}_n$ is a vector of ones of length n. To ensure identifiability of the model, specific constraints may have to be applied to the parameter vectors $\boldsymbol{\beta}_j$, for example to centre certain effect types.

Since the parameter vectors $\boldsymbol{\beta}_j$ are often of considerably high dimension, we enforce specific properties such as smoothness or shrinkage by assigning multivariate normal priors

$$p\left(\boldsymbol{\beta}_j|\tau_j^2\right) \propto \exp\left(-\frac{1}{2\tau_j^2}\boldsymbol{\beta}_j'\boldsymbol{K}_j\boldsymbol{\beta}_j\right) \mathbb{1}(\boldsymbol{A}_j\boldsymbol{\beta}_j = \mathbf{0}) \tag{5.6}$$

to the coefficient vectors $\boldsymbol{\beta}_j$. The positive semidefinite penalty matrix $\boldsymbol{K}_j$ is chosen to achieve the desired type of regularisation and we will discuss specific choices below. The variance parameter τ_j^2 determines the relevance of the prior distribution relative to the information provided by the data and is typically assigned a hyperprior to allow for a data-driven amount of regularisation. A conjugate default choice is to use an inverse gamma prior for τ_j^2. The constraint matrix $\boldsymbol{A}_j$ is supplemented to the prior to achieve an identifiable model (for example by implementing a centering constraint). The prior (5.6) has a close connection to the specification of [28] and also regularised maximum likelihood inference with quadratic penalty terms $\lambda_j\boldsymbol{\beta}_j'\boldsymbol{K}_j\boldsymbol{\beta}_j$, where $\lambda_j = 1/(2\tau_j^2)$ is the smoothing parameter controlling the trade-off between fit and smoothness.

Different model components are now obtained by making more specific choices on the basis functions in (5.5) and the penalty matrix $\boldsymbol{K}_j$ in (5.6).

Linear effects

For parametric, linear effects, the design matrix is formed by stacking individual covariate vectors $\boldsymbol{z}_{ij}$ into $\boldsymbol{Z}_j$ such that the basis functions reduce to the selection of individual entries from the complete vector of covariates. To obtain flat priors for the parameters of the linear effects, we set $\boldsymbol{K}_j = \boldsymbol{0}$ and drop the corresponding smoothing variance from the model specification. If $\boldsymbol{z}_{ij}$ is of considerably high dimension or represents categorical covariates with some factor levels being only weakly identified by the data, then it can make sense to use the Bayesian analogue of a ridge penalty where $\boldsymbol{K}_j = \boldsymbol{I}_{D_j}$ with $\boldsymbol{I}_{D_j}$ being the D_j-dimensional identity matrix. This implies that the regression coefficients are considered as i.i.d. random effects and τ_j^2 represents the variance of the random effects.

Nonlinear effects

For nonlinear effects of continuous variables, we rely on the idea of Bayesian penalised splines [23] where the basis functions are given by B-splines of a prespecified degree obtained from an equidistant set of knots. A moderately large number of basis functions (20 to 40, say) is then usually sufficient to provide enough flexibility to represent common shapes of nonlinear effects observed in empirical data. To avoid overfitting and to enforce smoothness of the nonlinear effect, we specify a random walk prior on the sequence of B-spline coefficients with flat priors for initial values. This is equivalent to the frequentist approach of using a difference-based penalty as introduced by Eilers and Marx [7]. As a consequence, we obtain $\boldsymbol{K}_j = \boldsymbol{D}_j'\boldsymbol{D}_j$, where $\boldsymbol{D}_j$ is a difference matrix with difference order corresponding to the order of the chosen random walk. To render additive models comprising multiple nonlinear effects identifiable, we have to impose a centering constraint on the corresponding effects. This can be achieved by the constraint matrix $\boldsymbol{A}_j$ and in our case setting $\boldsymbol{A}_j = \boldsymbol{1}_{D_j}$ (i.e. specifying $\boldsymbol{A}_j$ as a D_j-dimensional vector of ones) leads to the desired constraint.

Spatial effects

For modelling spatial effects based on regional data where observations are assigned to distinct administrative regions but no exact coordinate information is available, we rely on Gaussian Markov random field specifications. In this case the number of basis functions coincides with the number of distinct regions while the basis functions are simply indicator functions for the different regions. As a consequence, the design matrix corresponds to a collection of dummy variables coding the assignment of the observations to the regions, i.e.

$$\boldsymbol{Z}_j[i, d] = \begin{cases} 1 & \text{if the observation belongs to region } d, \\ 0 & \text{otherwise,} \end{cases}$$

where $d = 1, \ldots, D_j$. A Gaussian Markov random field prior is then obtained by assuming

$$\beta_{jd} | \beta_{jd'}, d' \in \delta_d \sim \mathrm{N}\left(\frac{1}{N_d} \sum_{d' \in \delta_d} \beta_{jd'}, \frac{\tau_j^2}{N_d} \right),$$

where δ_d is the set of neighbours of region d and $N_d = |\delta_d|$ is the size of the neighbourhood. As a consequence, the conditional distribution of the spatial effect in a given region given its neighbours is normal with the expectation given by the average of the neighbouring effects and the variance given as the ratio of a common smoothness variance and the number of neighbours. One can now show that this assumption of spatial similarity is equivalent to our general prior structure (5.6) with

$$\boldsymbol{K}_j[d, d'] = \begin{cases} -1 & \text{if } d' \in \delta_d, \\ 0 & \text{if} d' \notin \delta_d, d \neq d', \\ N_d & \text{if } d = d'; \end{cases}$$

see Rue and Held [33]. Again a centering constraint is usually applied via $\boldsymbol{A}_j = \mathbf{1}_{D_j}$.

Other effect types

Several other specifications can be employed. These include varying coefficient smooths obtained by multiplying one or more smooth components by some covariate(s) and smooth functions of two or more continuous covariates (e.g. [9,44]).

5.3 Bayesian inference

Bayesian inference for conditional copula models can be carried out by a generic and modular updating scheme based on MCMC simulations via iteratively updating all model parameters of the joint posterior. To deal with the mixed binary-continuous nature of the response vector, we will rely on a data augmentation scheme where the unobserved, latent responses y_{i1}^* are imputed as a part of the MCMC scheme. Once these imputed responses are available, we can proceed in analogy to the case of bivariate continuous responses discussed in detail in Klein and Kneib [14].

After imputing the latent responses y_{i1}^*, the likelihood contribution of observation i is given by

$$p_i(y_{i1}^*, y_{i2}) = c_i(F_{i1}^*(y_{i1}^*), F_{i2}(y_{i2})) \cdot p_{i1}^*(y_{i1}^*) \cdot p_{i2}(y_{i2}),$$

where

$$c_i(F_{i1}^*(y_{i1}^*), F_{i2}(y_{i2})) = \frac{\partial^2 C(F_{i1}^*(y_{i1}^*), F_{i2}(y_{i2}))}{\partial F_{i1}^*(y_{i1}^*) \partial F_{i2}(y_{i2})}$$

denotes the density of the copula, $F_{i1}^*(y_{i1}^*) = \Phi(y_{i1}^* - \eta_{i1})$ and $p_{i1}^*(y_{i1}^*) = \varphi(y_{i1}^* - \eta_{i1})$ are the CDF and the density of the latent responses y_{i1}^* and $p_{i2}(y_{i2})$ is the density of the continuous response y_{i2}. Already at this point, it should be noted that parameters related to the marginal distributions are showing up both in the copula density and the respective marginal density while parameters related to the copula are not included in the marginal densities. This gives rise to a modular implementation where updating parameters of the marginals and the copula requires only limited knowledge about the exact specifications for the other model components (see below for details).

Data augmentation for the binary response

The conditional distribution of the first response given the second one can easily be derived from the copula as

$$F_{i,1|2}(y_{i1}^* | y_{i2}) = \frac{\partial C(F_{i1}(y_{i1}^*), F_{i2}(y_{i2}))}{\partial F_{i2}(y_{i2})}. \tag{5.7}$$

When imputing the latent responses y_{i1}^*, we additionally condition on the observed binary response y_{i1}, which leads to

$$F_{y_{i1}^* | y_{i2}, y_{i1}}(y_{i1}^* | y_{i2}, y_{i1}) = \begin{cases} \frac{F_{i,1|2}(y_{i1}^* | y_{i2}) - F_{i,1|2}(0 | y_{i2})}{1 - F_{i,1|2}(0 | y_{i2})} & \text{if } y_{i1} = 1, \\ \frac{F_{i,1|2}(y_{i1}^* | y_{i2})}{F_{i,1|2}(0 | y_{i2})} & \text{if } y_{i1} = 0. \end{cases} \tag{5.8}$$

Generating random numbers from these truncated distributions was originally proposed by Pitt et al. [30], Smith and Khaled [38] and can be facilitated by applying the inversion method (or a numerical approximation thereof) to (5.7) when a specific copula and marginal distribution for the second response are given and then adjusting the resulting sample according to (5.8). More precisely, if u_i is a sample from a uniform distribution, then a sample from the conditional distribution of $Y_{i1}^* | Y_{i2}, Y_{i1}$ is given by

$$F_{i,1|2}^{-1}(u_i^* | y_{i2}),$$

where

$$u_i^* = \begin{cases} u_i \cdot \left[1 - F_{i,1|2}(0|y_{i2})\right] + F_{i,1|2}(0|y_{i2}) & \text{if } y_{i1} = 1, \\ u_i \cdot F_{i,1|2}(0|y_{i2}) & \text{if } y_{i1} = 0. \end{cases}$$

For both copulas considered in this chapter, explicit solutions for the simulation from the conditional distributions (5.7) are available. Let u_i be a realisation from the standard uniform distribution $U[0, 1]$. Then for the Gaussian copula, we have

$$y_{i1}^* = \sqrt{1 - \rho_i^2}\,\Phi^{-1}(u_i) + \rho_i \Phi^{-1}(F_{i2}(y_{i2})),$$

while for the Clayton copula we obtain

$$y_{i1}^* = \left(\left(\frac{-F_{i2}(y_{i2})^{-\theta_i - 1}}{u_i} \right)^{\frac{\theta_i}{1+\theta_i}} - F_{i2}(y_{i2})^{-\theta_i} + 1 \right)^{\theta_i}.$$

When working with the rotated version of the Clayton copula, we use the equations introduced in Section 5.2.3 to adjust the simulation of the latent responses.

Iteratively weighted least squares proposals

Updating the regression coefficients for the different effects relies on iteratively weighted least squares proposals that construct a Gaussian proposal density matching the mode and the curvature of the full conditional for a given vector of regression coefficients $\boldsymbol{\beta}_j$. More precisely, we assume the working model $\tilde{\boldsymbol{y}} \sim \mathrm{N}(\boldsymbol{\eta}, \boldsymbol{W}^{-1})$ with $\boldsymbol{\eta}$ corresponding to the predictor $\boldsymbol{\beta}_j$ belongs to, working observations $\tilde{\boldsymbol{y}} = \boldsymbol{\eta} + \boldsymbol{W}^{-1}\boldsymbol{v}$, score vectors $\boldsymbol{v}$ with elements $v_i = \frac{\partial}{\partial \eta_i} \log(p_i)$ and diagonal weight matrices $\boldsymbol{W}$ consisting of working weights $w_i = -\frac{\partial^2}{(\partial \eta_i)^2} \log(p_i)$. This working model then induces a normal proposal with mean and precision matrix given by

$$\boldsymbol{\mu}_j = \boldsymbol{P}_j^{-1}\boldsymbol{Z}_j'\boldsymbol{W}(\tilde{\boldsymbol{y}} - \boldsymbol{\eta}_{-j}), \qquad \boldsymbol{P}_j = \boldsymbol{Z}_j'\boldsymbol{W}\boldsymbol{Z}_j + \frac{1}{\tau_j^2}\boldsymbol{K}_j, \tag{5.9}$$

where $\boldsymbol{\eta}_{-j}$ is the predictor without the jth component; see Brezger and Lang [3] or Klein, Kneib and Lang [16] for details in the context of structured additive regression and distributional regression, respectively.

Updating parameters of the marginal distributions

For a parameter ϑ_{ik} corresponding to the marginal distribution of the dth response y_{id}, $d = 1, 2$, the score elements and working weights can be determined via

$$v_i = \frac{\partial \log(c_i(F_{i1}(y_{i1}), F_{i2}(y_{i2})))}{\partial F_{id}(y_{id})} \frac{\partial F_{id}(y_{id})}{\partial \eta_i^{\vartheta_k}} + \frac{\partial \log(p_{id})}{\partial \eta_i^{\vartheta_k}}, \qquad w_i = -\frac{\partial v_i}{\partial \eta_i^{\vartheta_k}},$$

where $\eta_i^{\vartheta_k}$ is the predictor corresponding to ϑ_k. Note that we dropped the * from all quantities related to the first response component to simplify notation but all derivations in this section in fact relate to the latent, continuous responses y_{i1}^*.

Note that the evaluation of the first and second derivatives can be decomposed into different components reflecting different parts of the copula regression specification. The derivative of the log-copula density is with respect to the corresponding marginal CDF $F_{id}(y_{id})$ and does not require any knowledge about the second marginal other than the evaluated CDF. As a consequence, the derivative can be evaluated without knowing the exact distributional specification for the other response but only requires the current values of the CDF. The derivative of the marginal CDF $F_{id}(y_{id})$ with respect to the predictor $\eta_i^{\vartheta_k}$ depends on the chosen marginal and the particular parameter but is independent of the chosen copula and the specification for the other marginal. Finally, the derivative of the log-density of the marginal with respect to the predictor coincides with the derivative that would be required for a univariate distributional regression model and will therefore be readily available for most of the standard distributions. Similar expressions can be derived for the working weights w_i where again one component will correspond to $\frac{\partial^2 \log(p_{id})}{\partial(\eta_i^{\vartheta_k})^2}$ which is already available from the univariate model specifications.

Updating parameters of the copula

The log-copula density of the Gaussian copula is given by

$$\begin{aligned}\log(c_i(u_{i1}, u_{i2})) = & -\frac{1}{2}\log\left(1-\rho_i^2\right) + \frac{\rho_i}{1-\rho_i^2}\Phi^{-1}(u_{i1})\Phi^{-1}(u_{i2}) \\ & - \frac{\rho_i^2}{2\left(1-\rho_i^2\right)}\left(\Phi^{-1}(u_{i1})^2 + \Phi^{-1}(u_{i2})^2\right),\end{aligned}$$

where $u_{id} = F_{id}(y_{id})$, $d = 1, 2$. Therefore the elements of the score vector are given by

$$\begin{aligned}v_i = & \rho_i\sqrt{1-\rho_i^2} + \left(\sqrt{1+\eta_i^{2\rho_i}} + \rho_i\eta_i\right)\Phi^{-1}(u_{i1})\Phi^{-1}(u_{i2}) \\ & - \eta_i\left(\Phi^{-1}(u_{i1})^2 + \Phi^{-1}(u_{i2})^2\right)\end{aligned}$$

and the working weights can be determined as

$$\begin{aligned}w_i = & \left(1-\rho_i^2\right)^2 - \rho_i^2\left(1-\rho_i^2\right) + \left(2\rho_i + \rho_i\left(1-\rho_i^2\right)\right)\Phi^{-1}(u_{i1})\Phi^{-1}(u_{i2}) \\ & - \Phi^{-1}(u_{i1})^2 - \Phi^{-1}(u_{i2})^2.\end{aligned}$$

In this case, the working weights can be significantly simplified by replacing them with their expectations, which are given by

$$\mathbb{E}(w_i) = 1 - \rho_i^4.$$

For the Clayton copula, the log-copula density is given by

$$\begin{aligned}\log(c_i(u_{i1}, u_{i2})) = & \log(\theta_i + 1) - (1+\theta_i)(\log u_{i1} + \log u_{i2}) \\ & - \left(2 + \frac{1}{\theta_i}\right)\log\left(u_{i1}^{-\theta_i} + u_{i2}^{-\theta_i} - 1\right),\end{aligned}$$

such that the score vector contains elements

$$\begin{aligned}v_i = & \frac{\theta_i}{\theta_i + 1} - \theta_i(\log u_{i1} + \log u_{i2}) + \frac{1}{\theta_i}\log\left(u_{i1}^{-\theta_i} + u_{i2}^{-\theta_i} - 1\right) \\ & + \left(2 + \frac{1}{\theta_i}\right)\frac{\theta_i\left(u_{i1}^{-\theta_i}\log u_{i1} + u_{i2}^{-\theta_i}\log u_{i2}\right)}{u_{i1}^{-\theta_i} + u_{i2}^{-\theta_i} - 1}\end{aligned}$$

and the working weights are given by

$$w_i = \frac{\theta_i}{(\theta_i+1)^2} - \theta_i(\log u_{i1} + \log u_{i2}) - \frac{1}{\theta_i}\left(u_1^{-\theta_i} + u_{i2}^{-\theta_i} - 1\right)$$
$$- (1-2\theta_i)\frac{u_{i1}^{-\theta_i}\log u_{i1} + u_{i2}^{-\theta_i}\log u_{i2}}{u_{i1}^{-\theta_i} + u_{i2}^{-\theta_i} - 1}$$
$$+ \frac{\left(2+\frac{1}{\theta_i}\right)\theta_i^2}{u_1^{-\theta_i} + u_{i2}^{-\theta_i} - 1}\left[\frac{\left(u_{i1}^{-\theta_i}\log u_{i1} + u_{i2}^{-\theta_i}\log u_{i2}\right)^2}{u_{i1}^{-\theta_i} + u_{i2}^{-\theta_i} - 1}\right.$$
$$\left. - (\log u_{i1})^2 u_{i1}^{-\theta_i} - (\log u_{i2})^2 u_{i2}^{-\theta_i}\right].$$

If rotated versions of the Clayton copula are employed, the copula densities have to be replaced accordingly by

$$c_{90}(u_{i1}, u_{i2}) = \frac{\partial^2}{\partial \tilde{u}_{i1}\partial u_{i2}} C(\tilde{u}_{i1}, u_{i2}),$$
$$c_{180}(u_{i1}, u_{i2}) = \frac{\partial^2}{\partial \tilde{u}_{i1}\partial \tilde{u}_{i2}} C(\tilde{u}_{i1}, \tilde{u}_{i2}),$$
$$c_{270}(u_{i1}, u_{i2}) = \frac{\partial^2}{\partial u_{i1}\partial \tilde{u}_{i2}} C(u_{i1}, \tilde{u}_{i2}),$$

with $\tilde{u}_{i1} = 1 - u_{i1}$ and $\tilde{u}_{i2} = 1 - u_{i2}$.

Similar to the case of the marginal distributions, updating the regression coefficients in the copula parameter does not require precise knowledge about the marginal distributions but rather only relies on the marginal CDFs evaluated at the observed response values.

Updating the smoothing variances

Since the inverse gamma prior for τ_j^2 is conjugate to the multivariate normal prior (5.6), the smoothing variances τ_j^2 can always be updated by a Gibbs update from $\tau_j^2|\cdot \sim \text{IG}(a_j', b_j')$, with updated parameters $a_j' = \frac{\text{rk}(\boldsymbol{K}_j)}{2} + a_j$, $b_j' = \frac{1}{2}\boldsymbol{\beta}_j'\boldsymbol{K}_j\boldsymbol{\beta}_j + b_j$.

Implementation

An efficient implementation making use of fast sparse matrix multiplications is available in a developer version of the software package BayesX [2] and as part of the supplementary material to this chapter.

5.4 Model selection and model evaluation

In any application of distributional regression, one faces important model choice decisions: choosing the most appropriate out of a set of potential response distributions and selecting adequate predictor specifications for each parameter of these distributions. In the case of copula regression models, one has additionally to determine a reasonable conditional dependence structure between the outcomes. In order to arrive at the final model, for which results will be discussed in Section 5.5, we rely on the following three tools.

Quantile residuals for the marginal fits

The fit of the marginal distributions can be checked visually using the quantile residual plots suggested by Stasinopoulos et al. [39]. For continuous univariate random variables, it is a well-known result that the cumulative distribution function $F(\cdot)$ evaluated at the random variable y_i yields a uniform distribution on $[0, 1]$. As a consequence, quantile residuals defined as $\hat{r}_i = \Phi^{-1}(F(y_i|\hat{\boldsymbol{\vartheta}}_i))$, with the inverse CDF of a standard normal distribution Φ^{-1} and $F(\cdot|\hat{\boldsymbol{\vartheta}}_i)$ denoting CDF with estimated parameters $\hat{\boldsymbol{\vartheta}}_i = (\hat{\vartheta}_{i1}, \ldots, \hat{\vartheta}_{iK})'$ plugged in, should at least approximately be standard normally distributed if the correct model has been specified [6]. In practice, the residuals can be assessed graphically in terms of quantile-quantile plots: the closer the residuals are to the bisecting line, the better is the fit to the data. Unfortunately the idea of quantile residuals is not easily transferred to multivariate response models since there is no multivariate analogue to the probability integral transform. As a consequence, quantile residuals can only be applied to the marginal distributions separately which will not allow us to detect model deviations in the dependence but is still a helpful device for the marginal specification of the continuous stunting score y_{i1}. In principle, such residuals can also be computed for the binary component y_{i2}. However, note that u_i becomes a random variable in the interval $[F(y_i - 1|\hat{\boldsymbol{\vartheta}}_i), F(y_i|\hat{\boldsymbol{\vartheta}}_i)]$.

Fig. 5.2 shows the quantile residuals for both marginal distributions and suggests an appropriate marginal fit for the wasting model despite slight deviations from the bisecting line in the upper right corner. For the binary model for the presence of fever, we do not observe any strong deviations from the bisecting line but this is likely a result of the discreteness of the response and the corresponding generation of random values u_i as mentioned above. As long as the model gets the fractions of successes and

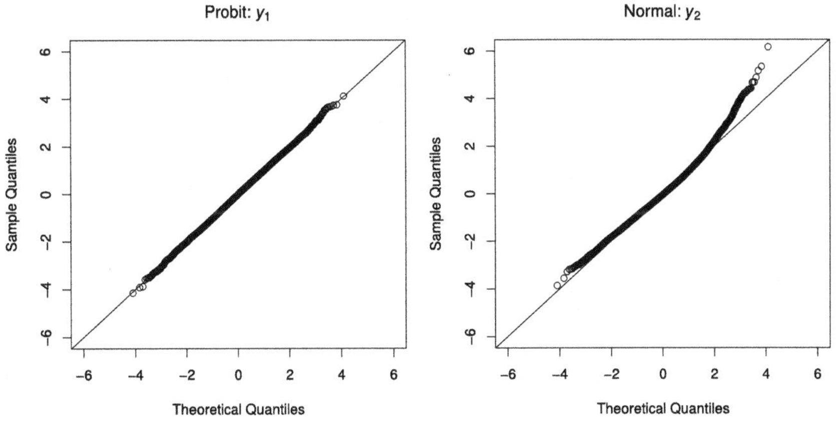

Figure 5.2 Marginal quantile residuals of fever (left) and wasting (right).

failures in covariate-dependent classes of observations roughly right, one should not expect strong deviations. By construction, the possibility to detect model misspecification for binary models based on quantile residuals therefore seems limited.

Model choice via information criteria

The deviance information criterion (DIC) is a commonly used criterion for model choice in Bayesian inference that has become quite popular due to the fact that it can easily be computed from the MCMC output. If $\boldsymbol{\theta}^{[1]}, \ldots, \boldsymbol{\theta}^{[T]}$ is an MCMC sample from the posterior for the complete parameter vector $\boldsymbol{\theta}$, the DIC is given by $\overline{D(\boldsymbol{\theta})} + pd = 2\overline{D(\boldsymbol{\theta})} - D(\overline{\boldsymbol{\theta}}) = \frac{2}{T}\sum D(\boldsymbol{\theta}^{[t]}) - D(\frac{1}{T}\sum \boldsymbol{\theta}^{[t]})$, where $D(\boldsymbol{\theta}) = -2\log(f(\boldsymbol{y}|\boldsymbol{\theta}))$ is the model deviance and $pd = \overline{D(\boldsymbol{\theta})} - D(\overline{\boldsymbol{\theta}})$ is an effective parameter count.

However, the DIC suffers from a number of well-known limitations. For example, it implicitly requires the assumption of a multivariate normal posterior and depends on the chosen parameterisation of the model. As a consequence, the widely applicable information criterion (WAIC), also referred to as Watanabe information criterion, was introduced in Watanabe [42] in the context of singular learning theory and is more and more replacing the DIC in applied model choice problems based on Bayesian inference. Both DIC and WAIC are implemented in the software package BayesX [2] and are readily available from the MCMC output without additional computational costs.

Table 5.1 Comparison of DIC and WAIC values under different copula assumptions.

Copula	DIC	WAIC
Gaussian	92,627	92,980
Clayton	92,900	93,066
Clayton 90°	92,761	92,997
Clayton 180°	92,905	93,073
Clayton 270°	**92,524**	**92,979**

To determine the form of the dependence between the two response variables, we compare the Gaussian copula and the four rotated versions of the Clayton copula based on the most complex model specification where predictor (5.10) is applied to all distributional parameters. Table 5.1 shows the resulting DIC/WAIC values, indicating that a Clayton copula rotated by 270° gives the best fit. This supports the presence of tail dependence which could not be modelled with the Gaussian copula. It also implies that the data support a strong association between the presence of fever (reflected by large values of y^*_{i1}) and severe forms of malnutrition (reflected by small values of y_{i2}); compare Fig. 5.1. This intuitively makes sense since undernourished children will be more vulnerable to diseases and it is also more likely that diseased children become malnourished.

Given the copula specification, we now turn to the selection of relevant effects in the regression predictors. Since a full model search over $= 2^{\text{number predictors} \times \text{number effects}} = 2^{4\times 5}$ models is clearly infeasible, we fix the full predictor specification for the marginal distributions and only focus on effect selection in the copula parameter to identify determinants of the dependence structure which are of particular relevance in our application. The full predictor specification of the parameters of the marginal distributions are chosen based on the analyses in Klein, Kneib, Klasen and Lang [15], i.e.

$$\begin{aligned}\eta_{i,k} = \beta_{0,k} + \beta_{1,k} csex_i + f_{1,k}(cage_i) + f_{2,k}(breastfeeding_i) \\ + f_{3,k}(mbmi_i) + f_{mrf,k}(dist_i),\end{aligned} \tag{5.10}$$

where *csex* is a binary indicator of the sex of the child, *cage*, *breastfeeding* and *mbmi* are continuous covariates representing the age of the child in months, duration of breastfeeding in months and the body mass index of the mother that we model with cubic Bayesian P-splines based on an equidistant grid

Table 5.2 Comparison of DIC and WAIC values under different predictor specifications for the dependence parameter θ.

Predictor for θ	DIC	WAIC
$f_1(cage)$	92,692	93,012
$f_2(breastfeeding)$	92,742	93,009
$f_3(mbmi)$	92,968	93,008
$\beta_1 csex$	92,645	93,007
$f_{mrf}(dist)$	92,571	92,982
$f_1(cage) + f_{mrf}(dist)$	92,597	92,988
$f_1(cage) + f_2(breastfeeding)$	92,713	93,010
$f_1(cage) + f_2(mbmi)$	92,596	93,003
$f_1(cage) + \beta_1 csex$	92,711	93,006
$f_1(breastfeeding) + \beta_1 csex$	92,645	93,008
$f_1(cage) + f_{mrf}(dist) + \beta_1 csex$	92,609	92,983
$f_1(breastfeeding) + f_{mrf}(dist) + \beta_1 csex$	92,623	92,982
$f_1(cage) + f_2(breastfeeding) + f_{mrf}(dist) + \beta_1 csex$	92,583	92,991
$f_1(cage) + f_3(mbmi) + f_{mrf}(dist) + \beta_1 csex$	92,615	92,992
$f_1(cage) + f_2(breastfeeding) + f_3(mbmi) + \beta_1 csex$	92,619	93,005
$f_2(breastfeeding) + f_3(mbmi) + f_{mrf}(dist) + \beta_1 csex$	92,585	92,985
$f_1(cage) + f_2(breastfeeding) + f_3(mbmi) + f_{mrf}(dist) + \beta_1 csex$	**92,524**	**92,979**

of 20 inner knots (resulting in a total of 22 basis functions), and *dist* is one of 438 districts in India the children are living in which we model this spatial effect with a Gaussian Markov random field prior where the neighbourhood is defined through common borders of the districts.

For the copula parameter, we tested 16 possible predictor specifications for the dependence parameter arising from the inclusion/exclusion of distinct predictor components leading to the DIC/WAIC values in Table 5.2. The results provide support for the most complex model where all effects are included and we will use this specification as the basis for further investigations in the following.

Predictive ability

Gneiting and Raftery [11] propose proper scoring rules as summary measures for the evaluation of probabilistic forecasts, i.e. to evaluate the predictive ability of a statistical model. In order to check whether a joint model indeed provides an improvement upon two separate marginal models for Y_1 and Y_2, we compute the average logarithmic predictive score based on ten-fold cross-validation. For this purpose, we randomly split the data set in 10 parts of roughly equal size, estimate the model on nine-tenths of the data and determine estimated predictive log-densities $\log(\hat{p}_i(y_{i1}, y_{i2}))$ for the hold-out data. Let $\boldsymbol{y}_1, \ldots, \boldsymbol{y}_{n_r}$ be data in one of the $R = 10$ hold-out samples and $\hat{p}_{i,r}$ the predictive distributions with predicted parameter vectors $\hat{\boldsymbol{\vartheta}}_r = (\hat{\vartheta}_{i,r,1}, \ldots, \hat{\vartheta}_{i,r,K})'$, $r = 1, \ldots, 10$. Competing forecasts are then ranked by averaged scores $S = \frac{1}{10}\sum_{r=1}^{10}\frac{1}{n_r}\sum_{i=1}^{n_r}\log(\hat{p}_{i,r}(y_{i,r,1}, y_{i,r,2}))$ such that higher scores deliver better probabilistic forecasts when comparing different models. The resulting values for our best copula model and the independent model are -1.881 and -1.883, respectively, such that the copula model has a slightly better predictive performance.

5.5 Results

Effects of covariates

In a first step, we examine the raw (centred) nonlinear estimated effects of $f_{1,k}(cage)$, $f_{2,k}(breastfeeding)$ and $f_{3,k}(mbmi)$ in Figs 5.3 to 5.5 for the predictors of μ, σ^2 of the normal marginal of Y_2 (first row), the predictor for the occurrence probability π for *fever* (second row, left) and the copula parameter θ of the rotated Clayton copula (second row, right). In each subfigure, the posterior mean (solid line) is shown together with 95% pointwise credible intervals (dashed).

From these raw effects we find that the age of the child is only moderately associated with any of the distributional parameters. In contrast, both the body mass index of the mother and the duration of breastfeeding are important determinants at least for the parameters related to the marginal distributions. Surprisingly, longer durations of breastfeeding are associated with both a higher risk of fever and reduced wasting scores. While this seems counterintuitive at first sight since breastfeeding is usually considered a protective factor, increased durations of breastfeeding may also be associated with the nonavailability of other food sources and may therefore proxy poverty of the household the children live in.

Another surprising finding is that none of the continuous covariates has a significant association with the dependence parameter θ when determining significance via the pointwise 95% credible intervals. This is in contrast to the indication of DIC/WAIC that both favoured the most complex model specification for the dependence parameter. However, it should be taken into account that in fact DIC and WAIC are evaluating the predictive ability of a model which is not directly related to the (in)significance of effects.

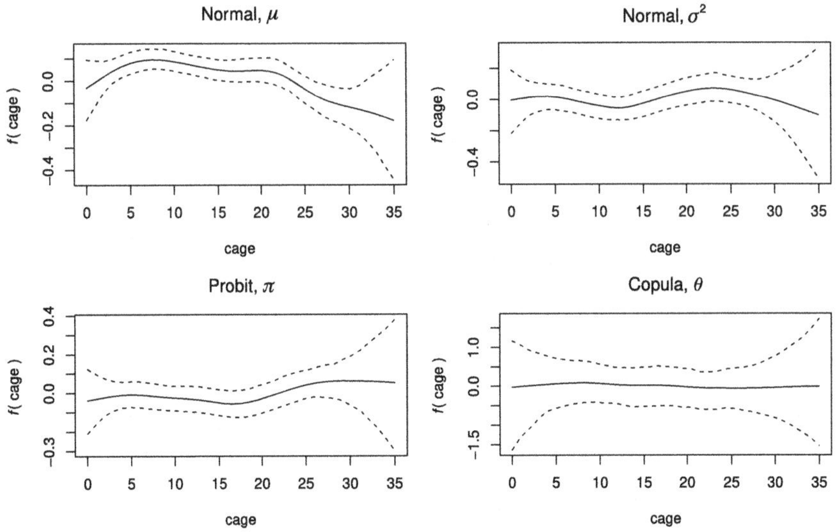

Figure 5.3 Estimated nonlinear effects of $f_{1,k}(cage)$ on the predictors of μ, σ^2 of the normal marginal of Y_2 (first row), the predictor for the probability π of *fever* (second row, left) and the copula parameter θ of the rotated Clayton copula (second row, right). In each subfigure, the posterior mean (solid) together with the 95% pointwise credible interval (dashed) is depicted.

Fig. 5.6 shows the estimated posterior mean spatial effects of all predictors where we find significant spatial variation in all parameters including the dependence parameter. As a consequence, there seems to be a considerable amount of unobserved spatial heterogeneity which is not too surprising given the relatively small set of covariates that we are using in our analysis.

Finally, Table 5.3 gives a summary of the posterior of the intercepts $\beta_{0,k}$ and the linear coefficients $\beta_{1,k}$ of the gender of the child; it turns out the constants are all significantly negative despite the one in the predictor of μ and that *csex* is significant only in the predictor of π.

Joint probabilities

While the visualisation of raw effect estimates already provides some interesting insights, it is sometimes hard to interpret these effect estimates alone. For example, it is tempting to relate the estimated spatial effect on the dependence parameter with a significant north-south gradient in the strength of the dependence. However, the exact value of dependence ob-

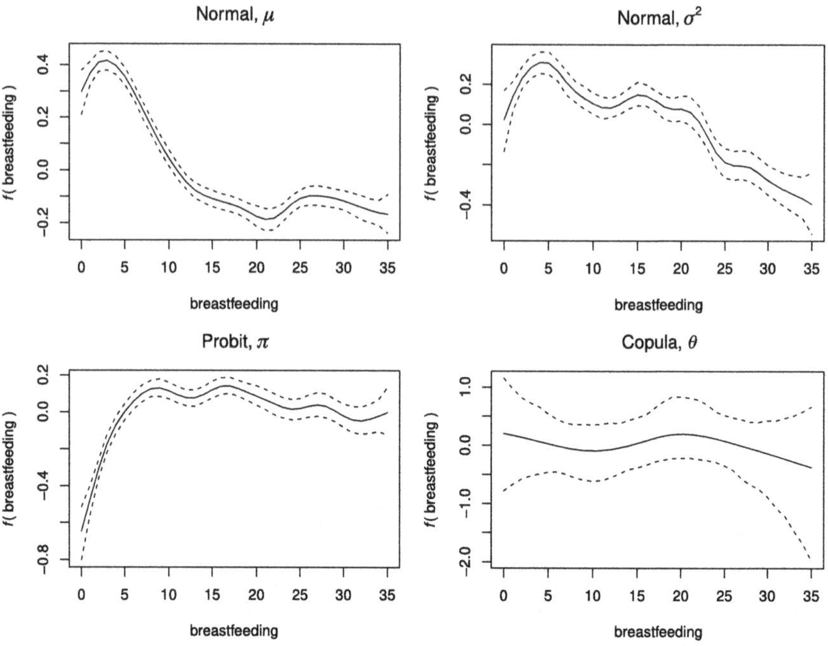

Figure 5.4 Estimated nonlinear effects of $f_{2,k}(\textit{breastfeeding})$ on the predictors of μ, σ^2 of the normal marginal of Y_2 (first row), the predictor for the probability π of *fever* (second row, left) and the copula parameter θ of the rotated Clayton copula (second row, right). In each subfigure, the posterior mean (solid) together with the 95% pointwise credible interval (dashed) is depicted.

served in a given region does not only depend on the estimate spatial effect but also on the covariate characteristics observed for the children in this region. We therefore study the spatial variation in the joint relative risks (in %) of having fever and being undernourished by computing corresponding model-implied probabilities where all covariates are set to the means within the regions. For these probabilities, a child is said to be moderately wasted if $-3 < Y_2 < -2$ and severely wasted for scores ≤ -3. Fig. 5.7 shows the resulting probabilities not only for the copula regression model but also for two independent marginal models.

The first striking consideration is that there are strong differences between the joint model and the marginal models. While for moderate wasting both variants agree in identifying the central region of India as being associated with the highest simultaneous health risks, the exact numbers assigned to the regions differ considerably. In particular, the copula regres-

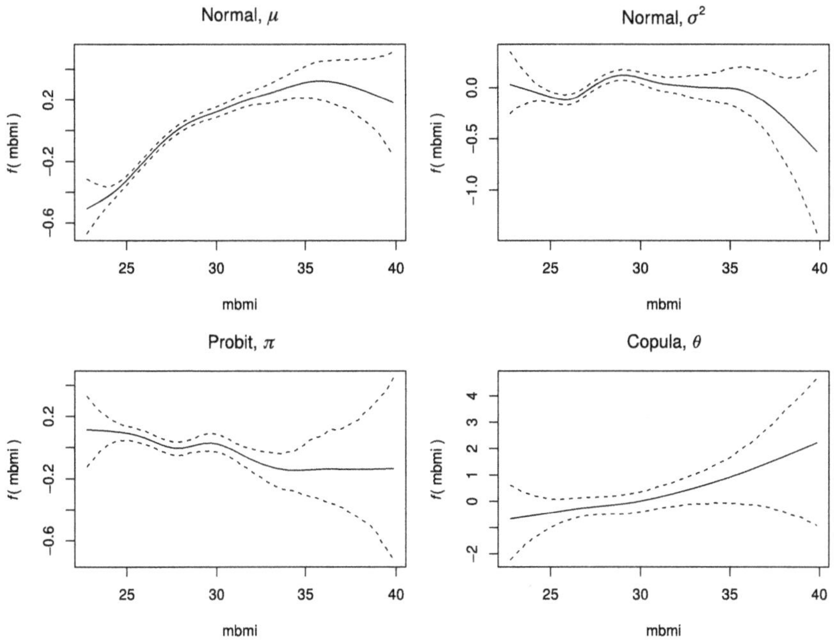

Figure 5.5 Estimated nonlinear effects of $f_{3,k}(mbmi)$ on the predictors of μ, σ^2 of the normal marginal of Y_2 (first row), the predictor for the probability π of *fever* (second row, left) and the copula parameter θ of the rotated Clayton copula (second row, right). In each subfigure, the posterior mean (solid) together with the 95% pointwise credible interval (dashed) is depicted.

sion model is more selective and identifies a smaller subset of regions that show an increased health risk. This may be very helpful for policy makers to design targeted interventions that focus on regions where there is strong dependence between different health outcomes. When considering severe wasting, the picture is quite different since the independent marginal models identify hardly any likelihood for simultaneously observing fever and severe forms of wasting while the copula specification reveals some regions with higher health risks.

Since the duration of breastfeeding appeared to be an important determinant of both health dimensions when studying the raw effect estimates, we also visualise the joint relative risks (in %) of having fever and being undernourished as a function of the breastfeeding duration in Fig. 5.8. Again, we consider different breastfeeding durations while setting the other covariates to the means at the different observed breastfeeding durations. Here the deviation between the independent marginal models and the copula

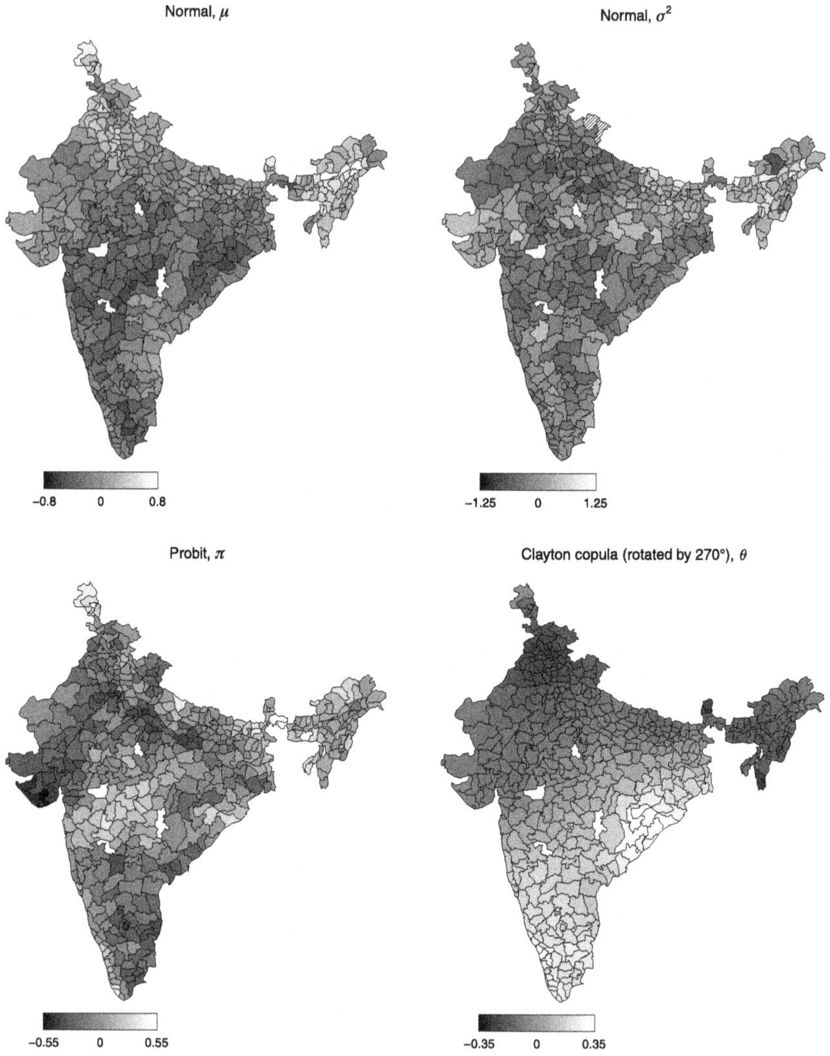

Figure 5.6 Estimated posterior mean spatial effects of $f_{3,k}(mbmi)$ on the predictors of μ, σ^2 of the normal marginal of Y_2 (first row), the predictor for the probability π of *fever* (second row, left) and the copula parameter θ of the rotated Clayton copula (second row, right).

regression model is stronger for moderate forms of wasting. While both approaches identify an increased risk associated with moderate durations of breastfeeding around 12 to 24 months, the risk is evaluated to be way higher based on the copula specification.

Table 5.3 Summary statistics of the posteriors of the intercepts $\beta_{0,k}$ and the linear coefficients $\beta_{1,k}$ of the gender of the child.

coefficient	mean	std	2.5%	10%	50%	90%	97.5%
	Normal	μ					
$\beta_{0,1}$	−0.036	0.025	−0.087	−0.068	−0.036	−0.005	0.007
$\beta_{1,1}$	0.005	0.011	−0.018	−0.01	0.005	0.02	0.028
	Normal	σ^2					
$\beta_{0,2}$	−0.284	0.04	−0.365	−0.334	−0.284	−0.232	−0.204
$\beta_{1,2}$	−0.005	0.018	−0.04	−0.028	−0.005	0.019	0.031
	Probit	π					
$\beta_{0,3}$	−0.531	0.035	−0.598	−0.574	−0.532	−0.485	−0.462
$\beta_{1,3}$	−0.051	0.017	−0.084	−0.074	−0.052	−0.029	−0.017
	Copula	θ					
$\beta_{0,4}$	−2.429	0.241	−2.905	−2.759	−2.426	−2.125	−1.998
$\beta_{1,4}$	−0.026	0.202	−0.431	−0.278	−0.022	0.228	0.382

5.6 Summary and discussion

We have developed a Bayesian framework for fitting flexible bivariate copula regression models with binary and continuous margins motivated and illustrated by a bivariate analysis of child health in India. Posterior estimation is carried out within a fully Bayesian framework with MCMC simulations implemented efficiently in the software package BayesX [2]. One advantage of the Bayesian framework is that the complete joint posterior distribution can be computed easily from the MCMC output. In addition, we provide guidelines for model choice and variable selection with a focus on selecting and specifying the copula such that predictions are optimal amongst the candidate models.

In our application, it turns out that the presence of fever is strongly associated with acute undernutrition measured as wasting, and that the association is more complex than what a linear correlation could capture. Moreover, log-scores favour the joint copula model over separate marginal models which would assume independence of the two responses. Related to this, the joint probabilities from the copula model for observing a child with fever and moderate/severe undernutrition vary considerably, with respect to both spatial allocation and breastfeeding time of the children, and differ from two of the marginal models. In particular, ignoring the dependence structure would lead to overestimation of the relative risk for children

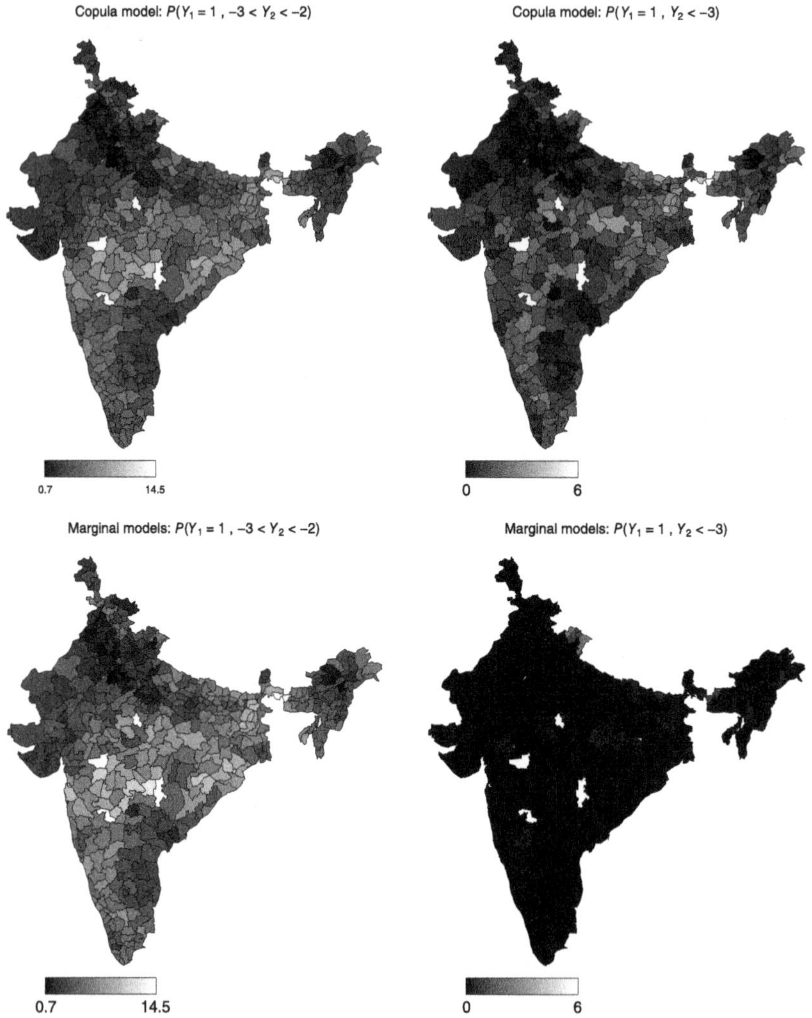

Figure 5.7 Joint probabilities (in %) for having fever and being moderately undernourished (left) and severely undernourished (right) by county of residence. The first row shows the estimated probabilities from the copula model and the second one those based on the marginal models.

suffering from fever and moderate undernutrition and underestimation of those having fever and severe undernutrition.

Particular challenges for multivariate distribution regression models such as the one considered in this chapter remain the checking of model assumptions and model selection. While we provided some guidance in this

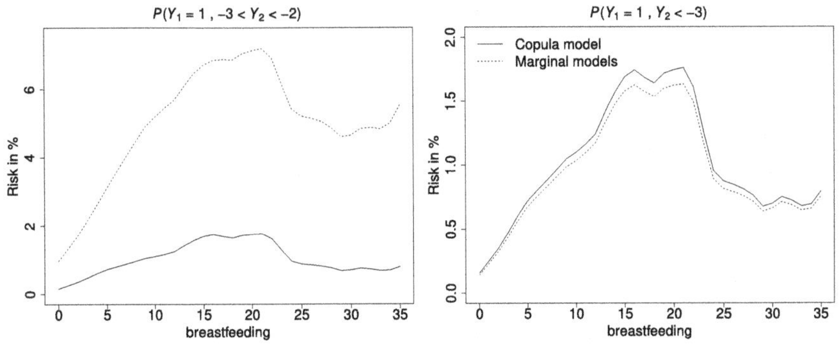

Figure 5.8 Joint probabilities (in %) for having fever and being moderately undernourished (left) and severely undernourished (right) by duration of breastfeeding (in months). The solid line shows the estimated probabilities from the copula model and the dashed line the one based on the marginal models.

respect, the corresponding methods clearly still have limitations (e.g. the restriction of quantile residuals to only the marginal fits) or easily get untractable for complex models with several predictors and covariates.

Acknowledgements

We are grateful for helpful and critical comments from the Editor.

References

[1] E.F. Acar, V.R. Craiu, F. Yao, Statistical testing of covariate effects in conditional copula models, Electronic Journal of Statistics 7 (2013) 2822–2850.

[2] C. Belitz, A. Brezger, N. Klein, T. Kneib, S. Lang, N. Umlauf, BayesX - software for Bayesian inference in structured additive regression models, version 3.0.1, available from http://www.bayesx.org, 2015.

[3] A. Brezger, S. Lang, Generalized structured additive regression based on Bayesian P-splines, Computational Statistics & Data Analysis 50 (2006) 967–991.

[4] V.R. Craiu, A. Sabeti, In mixed company: Bayesian inference for bivariate conditional copula models with discrete and continuous outcomes, Journal of Multivariate Analysis 110 (2012) 106–120.

[5] A.R. de Leon, B. Wu, Copula-based regression models for a bivariate discrete and continuous outcome, Statistics in Medicine 30 (2) (2011) 175–185.

[6] P.K. Dunn, G.K. Smyth, Randomized quantile residuals, Journal of Computational and Graphical Statistics 5 (1996) 236–245.

[7] P.H.C. Eilers, B.D. Marx, Flexible smoothing with B-splines and penalties, Statistical Science 11 (1996) 89–121.

[8] L. Fahrmeir, T. Kneib, S. Lang, Penalized structured additive regression for space-time data: a Bayesian perspective, Statistica Sinica 14 (2004) 731–761.

[9] L. Fahrmeir, T. Kneib, S. Lang, B. Marx, Regression - Models, Methods and Applications, Springer, Berlin, 2013.

[10] I. Gijbels, N. Veraverbeke, M. Omelka, Conditional copulas, association measures and their applications, Computational Statistics & Data Analysis 55 (2011) 1919–1932.

[11] T. Gneiting, A.E. Raftery, Strictly proper scoring rules, prediction, and estimation, Journal of the American Statistical Association 102 (2007) 359–378.

[12] G. Kauermann, C. Schellhase, D. Ruppert, Flexible copula density estimation with penalized hierarchical B-splines, Scandinavian Journal of Statistics 40 (2013) 685–705.

[13] S. Klasen, Poverty, undernutrition, and child mortality: some inter-regional puzzles and their implications for research and policy, Journal of Economic Inequality 6 (2008) 89–115.

[14] N. Klein, T. Kneib, Simultaneous inference in structured additive conditional copula regression models: a unifying Bayesian approach, Statistics and Computing 26 (2016) 841–860.

[15] N. Klein, T. Kneib, S. Klasen, S. Lang, Bayesian structured additive distributional regression for multivariate responses, Journal of the Royal Statistical Society. Series C (Applied Statistics) 64 (2015) 569–591.

[16] N. Klein, T. Kneib, S. Lang, Bayesian generalized additive models for location, scale and shape for zero-inflated and overdispersed count data, Journal of the American Statistical Association 110 (2015) 405–419, https://doi.org/10.1080/01621459.2014.912955.

[17] N. Klein, T. Kneib, S. Lang, A. Sohn, Bayesian structured additive distributional regression with an application to regional income inequality in Germany, The Annals of Applied Statistics 9 (2015) 1024–1052.

[18] N. Klein, T. Kneib, R. Radice, G. Marra, S. Rokicki, M. McGovern, Mixed binary-continuous copula regression models with application to adverse birth outcomes, Statistics in Medicine 38 (3) (2019) 413–436.

[19] N. Kraemer, D. Silvestrini, CopulaRegression: bivariate copula based regression models, R package version 0.1-5, http://CRAN.R-project.org/package=CopulaRegression, 2015.

[20] N. Kramer, E.C. Brechmann, D. Silvestrini, C. Czado, Total loss estimation using copula-based regression models, Insurance: Mathematics and Economics 53 (2012) 829–839.

[21] P. Lambert, Archimedean copula estimation using Bayesian splines smoothing techniques, Computational Statistics & Data Analysis 51 (2007) 6307–6320.

[22] S. Lang, S.B. Adebayo, L. Fahrmeir, W.J. Steiner, Bayesian geoadditive seemingly unrelated regression, Computational Statistics 18 (2003) 263–292.

[23] S. Lang, A. Brezger, Bayesian P-splines, Journal of Computational and Graphical Statistics 13 (2004) 183–212.

[24] G. Marra, R. Radice, Estimation of a semiparametric recursive bivariate probit model in the presence of endogeneity, The Canadian Journal of Statistics 39 (2011) 259–279.

[25] G. Marra, R. Radice, Bivariate copula additive models for location, scale and shape, Computational Statistics and Data Analysis 112 (2017) 99–113.

[26] A. Mayr, N. Fenske, B. Hofner, T. Kneib, M. Schmid, Generalized additive models for location, scale and shape for high dimensional data: a flexible approach based on boosting, Journal of the Royal Statistical Society, Series C (Applied Statistics) 61 (2012) 403–427.

[27] R. Nelsen, An Introduction to Copulas, Springer, New York, 2006.

[28] A. Panagiotelis, M.S. Smith, Bayesian identification, selection and estimation of functions in high-dimensional additive models, Journal of Econometrics 143 (2008) 291–316.

[29] S. Park, S. Gupta, Handling endogenous regressors by joint estimation using copulas, Marketing Science 31 (4) (2012) 567–586.

[30] M. Pitt, D. Chan, R. Kohn, Efficient Bayesian inference for Gaussian copula regression models, Biometrika 93 (2006) 537–554.

[31] R. Radice, G. Marra, M. Wojtys, Copula regression spline models for binary outcomes, Statistics and Computing 26 (2016) 981–995.

[32] R.A. Rigby, D.M. Stasinopoulos, Generalized additive models for location, scale and shape (with discussion), Journal of the Royal Statistical Society, Series C (Applied Statistics) 54 (2005) 507–554.

[33] H. Rue, L. Held, Gaussian Markov Random Fields, Chapman & Hall/CRC, New York/Boca Raton, 2005.

[34] A. Sabeti, M. Wei, R.V. Craiu, Additive models for conditional copulas, Stat 3 (2014) 300–312.

[35] J. Segers, R. van den Akker, B.J.M. Werker, Semiparametric Gaussian copula models: geometry and efficient rank-based estimation, Annals of Statistics 42 (2014) 1911–1940.

[36] X. Shen, Y. Zhu, L. Song, Linear B-spline copulas with applications to nonparametric estimation of copulas, Computational Statistics & Data Analysis 52 (2008) 3806–3819.

[37] M. Smith, R. Kohn, Nonparametric seemingly unrelated regression, Journal of Econometrics 98 (2000) 257–281.

[38] M.S. Smith, M.A. Khaled, Estimation of copula models with discrete margins via Bayesian data augmentation, Journal of the American Statistical Association 107 (2012) 290–303.

[39] D.M. Stasinopoulos, B. Rigby, C. Akantziliotou, Instructions on How to Use the GAMLSS Package in R, second edition, 2008, available at www.gamlss.org.

[40] D.M. Stasinopoulos, R.A. Rigby, Automatic smoothing parameter selection in GAMLSS with an application to centile estimation, Statistical Methods in Medical Research 23 (2014) 318–332, https://doi.org/10.1177/0962280212473302.

[41] T. Vatter, V. Chavez-Demoulin, Generalized additive models for conditional dependence structures, Journal of Multivariate Analysis 141 (2015) 147–167.

[42] S. Watanabe, Asymptotic equivalence of Bayes cross validation and widely applicable information criterion in singular learning theory, The Journal of Machine Learning Research 11 (2010) 3571–3594.

[43] WHO, Food security indicator data base, World Health Organization, http://apps.who.int/gho/data/node.main.52?lang=en, 2016.

[44] S.N. Wood, Generalized Additive Models: An Introduction With R, 2nd edn, Chapman & Hall/CRC, New York/Boca Raton, 2017.

[45] B. Wu, A.R. de Leon, Gaussian copula mixed models for clustered mixed outcomes, with application in developmental toxicology, Journal of Agricultural, Biological & Environmental Statistics 19 (1) (2014) 39–56.

[46] J. Yan, Enjoy the joy of copulas: with a package copula, Journal of Statistical Software 21 (2007) 1–21.

[47] T. Yee, Vector Generalized Linear and Additive Models: With an Implementation in R, Springer, New York, 2015.
[48] A. Zellner, An efficient method of estimating seemingly unrelated regression equations and tests for aggregation bias, Journal of the American Statistical Association 57 (1962) 348–368.

CHAPTER 6

Nonstandard flexible regression via variational Bayes

John T. Ormerod[a,b]

[a]School of Mathematics and Statistics, University of Sydney, Sydney, NSW 2006, Australia
[b]ARC Centre of Excellence for Mathematical & Statistical Frontiers, University of Melbourne, Parkville, VIC 3010, Australia

Contents

Chapter Points

- Several nonstandard semiparametric models are considered including robust semiparametric regression, heteroscedastic semiparametric regression, semiparametric regression for overdispersed count data and logistic regression with missing data.
- Mean field variational Bayes (VB) is introduced and various tricks are described for dealing with situations where VB is not easily applied.

Flexible Bayesian Regression Modelling
https://doi.org/10.1016/B978-0-12-815862-3.00010-X

- Several R scripts are available analysing data sets exhibiting each of the complications considered using the methods described.

6.1 Introduction

The Bayesian inferential paradigm is a natural framework for fitting complex models and nonstandard problems due to the availability of Markov chain Monte Carlo (MCMC) software such as JAGS [26] and stan [3]. However, for large data sets or complex problems MCMC methods can be considered to be too slow to be used in practice. For such problems mean field variational Bayes (VB) can be used as a computationally efficient albeit approximate alternative to MCMC [1,25]. These VB methods approximate marginal posterior distributions by convenient (often parametric) forms using posterior independence between subsets of parameters as a driving assumption. While direct and fair comparison between MCMC and VB is difficult in sacrificing some accuracy the VB approach is often orders of magnitude faster than MCMC methods. However, unlike MCMC, methods based on VB cannot achieve an arbitrary accuracy in the estimation of the posterior distribution. Typically VB methods underestimate posterior variances, and as such, their use in the context of inference is sometimes questionable.

Despite this shortcoming VB has shown to be an effective approach to several practical problems, including document retrieval [19], functional magnetic resonance imaging [11,23] and cluster analysis for gene expression data [33]. We believe that VB can still be useful in the context of statistical prediction and exploratory data analysis, and where decisions need to be made within a short time frame.

The models we consider in this chapter largely fall under the umbrella of semiparametric regression. Semiparametric regression is a rich field which combines traditional parametric regression models (e.g. [6,9]) and more modern nonparametric regression methods (e.g. [35,17,15]). This field spans several fields in statistics: parametric and nonparametric regression, longitudinal and spatial data analysis, mixed and hierarchical Bayesian models, expectation maximisation (EM) and MCMC algorithms. Semiparametric regression consists of a class of models which includes generalised additive models, generalised additive mixed models, varying coefficient models, geoadditive models and subject-specific curve models, among others (for a relatively comprehensive summary see [29]).

Penalised splines form the foundation of semiparametric regression models and include, as special cases, smoothing splines (e.g. [35]), P-splines [10] and pseudosplines [16]. A key feature of penalised splines is that the number of basis functions is much smaller than the sample size. In the generalised additive (mixed) model `R` package `mgcv` [40] the univariate function estimates use a further variant of penalised splines – low-rank thin-plate splines [39].

In this chapter we focus on nonstandard semiparametric regression models. For standard problems typical software packages exist so there would be no motivation to discuss them in the current work. Hence, by 'nonstandard' we mean semiparametric regression models which deal with some modelling complication and as such fall outside the conventional setup in which the response distributions are in the one-parameter exponential family and all data are cleanly observed. Examples of nonstandard situations include, but are not limited to:

1. outliers;
2. heteroscedastic noise;
3. overdispersed count data; and
4. missing data.

In this chapter we give a tutorial style introduction to VB to fit nonstandard flexible regression methods in the above cases. The VB methodology itself does not stray far from techniques already developed in the literature [25,37]. However, when the complications above arise standard application of VB methodology is not straightforward to apply. We show here how some simple tricks can be brought to bear to handle these complications.

This chapter is arranged as follows. Section 6.2 outlines some preparatory infrastructure for the rest of the chapter including mixed model-based penalised splines, semiparametric regression, our choice of prior, (mean field) VB and some tricks when standard VB cannot be easily applied, and we describe how we make comparisons with a gold standard (MCMC). Section 6.3 applies the methods described in Section 6.2 to a standard semiparametric regression model (a generalised additive model) which provides a basis for the rest of the chapter. Section 6.4 to Section 6.7 describe our approaches for handing outliers, heteroscedastic noise, overdispersed count data and missing data, respectively. In Section 6.8 we make some concluding remarks.

6.2 Preparatory modelling components

Before we can get into specific models we will introduce modelling components which are common for many of the models considered in the chapter and the associated notation.

6.2.1 Mixed model-based penalised splines

Mixed model-based penalised splines are a convenient way to model nonparametric functional relationships in semiparametric regression models. In general the mixed model representations of these have the form

$$f(x) = \beta_0 + \beta_1 x + \sum_{k=1}^{K} z_k(x) u_k, \quad \text{where} \quad \mathbf{u}|\sigma_u^2 \sim N(\mathbf{0}, \sigma_u^2 \mathbf{\Omega}),$$

the matrix $\mathbf{\Omega}$ is some $K \times K$ positive definite penalty matrix and the basis functions $\{z_k(\cdot)\}_{k=1}^{K}$ are nonlinear functions. In this chapter we choose the $z_k(\cdot)$ functions corresponding to O'Sullivan splines as described in [36] which are constructed to closely approximate smoothing splines. O'Sullivan splines are constructed in such a way that $\mathbf{\Omega} = \mathbf{I}$ which eases their implementation and incorporation using popular computing packages for fitting linear mixed models. An alternative is the P-splines of [10] which use B-splines for $\{z_k(\cdot)\}_{k=1}^{K}$ and use a penalty matrix $\mathbf{\Omega}$ of the form $\mathbf{\Omega} = \mathbf{D}_k^T \mathbf{D}_k$, where $\mathbf{D}_k$ is the kth-order differencing matrix. Geoadditive models specify the basis using thin-plate splines [29,39] can also be used in this modelling framework.

O'Sullivan splines are constructed using a B-spline basis which are defined using knots defined on the same space as x. [36] recommend quantile spaced knots, while [10] use equally spaced knots. This choice has little effect on the fitted function provided a sufficiently large number of knots are used. A simple rule of thumb for the number of knots K is $K = \min(n_U/4, 35)$, where n_U is the number of uniquely observed x's. Using a large number of knots leads to increased computational cost without greatly affecting the quality of the fitted functions. Hence, using too many knots is computationally wasteful.

6.2.2 Semiparametric regression

A general semiparametric regression model is of the form

$$\ln p(y_i|\boldsymbol{\beta}, \mathbf{u}, \boldsymbol{\phi}) \equiv \ell\left(y_i, (\mathbf{X}\boldsymbol{\beta} + \mathbf{Z}\mathbf{u})_i, \boldsymbol{\phi}\right), \tag{6.1}$$

where $y_i \subseteq \mathbb{R}$, $\mathbf{X} \in \mathbb{R}^{n\times p}$ and $\mathbf{Z} \in \mathbb{R}^{n\times q}$ are design matrices corresponding to fixed and random effects, respectively, $\boldsymbol{\beta} \in \mathbb{R}^p$ and $\mathbf{u} \in \mathbb{R}^q$ are vectors of coefficients corresponding to fixed and random effects, respectively, $\boldsymbol{\phi}$ is a vector of nuisance parameters and ℓ is an appropriate function. For example, if $y_i|\boldsymbol{\beta}, \mathbf{u}, \boldsymbol{\phi} \sim N((\mathbf{X}\boldsymbol{\beta} + \mathbf{Z}\mathbf{u})_i, \sigma^2)$, then $\boldsymbol{\phi} = \sigma^2$ and $\ell(y_i, (\mathbf{X}\boldsymbol{\beta} + \mathbf{Z}\mathbf{u})_i, \boldsymbol{\phi}) = -\ln(2\pi\sigma^2)/2 - [y_i - (\mathbf{X}\boldsymbol{\beta} + \mathbf{Z}\mathbf{u})_i]^2/(2\sigma^2)$.

Often the 'fixed' components of the model $\mathbf{X}$ and $\boldsymbol{\beta}$ are of the form

$$\mathbf{X} = \begin{bmatrix} 1 & x_{11} & x_{12} & \cdots & x_{1d} \\ 1 & x_{21} & x_{22} & \cdots & x_{2d} \\ \vdots & \vdots & \vdots & \ddots & \vdots \\ 1 & x_{n1} & x_{n2} & \cdots & x_{nd} \end{bmatrix} \quad \text{and} \quad \boldsymbol{\beta} = \begin{bmatrix} \beta_0 \\ \beta_1 \\ \vdots \\ \beta_d \end{bmatrix},$$

with d being the number of available predictors and $p = d + 1$.

The random effects components $\mathbf{Z}$ and $\mathbf{u}$ are of the form

$$\mathbf{Z} = \left[\mathbf{Z}_1, \ldots, \mathbf{Z}_R\right], \quad \mathbf{u} = \begin{bmatrix} \mathbf{u}_1 \\ \vdots \\ \mathbf{u}_R \end{bmatrix} \quad \text{and}$$

$$\mathbf{u}_r|\sigma_r^2 \sim N(\mathbf{0}, \sigma_r^2\mathbf{P}_r^{-1}), \qquad 1 \le r \le R,$$

where R is the number of modelling components, $\mathbf{Z}_r \in \mathbb{R}^{n\times q_r}$ are design matrices, $\mathbf{u}_r \in \mathbb{R}^{q_r}$, σ_r^2 are variance components and $\mathbf{P}_r$ are $q_r \times q_r$ positive definite (often diagonal) matrices. Here $q = \sum_{r=1}^R q_r$. The above specification means we can represent the model for $\mathbf{u}$ in the form

$$\mathbf{u}|\boldsymbol{\sigma}^2 \sim N(\mathbf{0}, \text{blockdiag}(\sigma_1^2\mathbf{P}_1^{-1}, \ldots, \sigma_R^2\mathbf{P}_R^{-1})), \tag{6.2}$$

where $\boldsymbol{\sigma}^2 = (\sigma_1^2, \ldots, \sigma_R^2)$.

The above modelling structure is quite rich and includes:

- Penalised splines: Suppose $\{z_k(x)\}_{k=1}^K$ are the set of basis functions described in Section 6.2.1. In the context of generalised additive models we may want to have several nonlinear smooth fits corresponding to several predictors. Let $\{z_{rk}(\cdot)\}_{k=1}^{K_r}$ be the set of basis functions for the rth predictor and let x_{ir} denote the ith sample of the rth predictor. Then

$$\mathbf{Z}_r = \begin{bmatrix} z_{r1}(x_{1r}) & \cdots & z_{rK_r}(x_{1r}) \\ \vdots & \ddots & \vdots \\ z_{r1}(x_{nr}) & \cdots & z_{rK_r}(x_{nr}) \end{bmatrix} \quad \text{and} \quad \mathbf{P}_r = \boldsymbol{\Omega}_r,$$

where $\mathbf{\Omega}_r$ is a penalty matrix for the rth predictor.

- Random intercepts: Suppose that the n samples are partitioned into m groups of size n_i with $n = \sum_{i=1}^{m} n_i$. Then

$$\mathbf{Z}_r = \begin{bmatrix} \mathbf{1}_{n_1} & \mathbf{0} & \cdots & \mathbf{0} \\ \mathbf{0} & \mathbf{1}_{n_2} & \cdots & \mathbf{0} \\ \vdots & \vdots & \ddots & \vdots \\ \mathbf{0} & \mathbf{0} & \cdots & \mathbf{1}_{n_m} \end{bmatrix} \qquad \text{and} \qquad \mathbf{P}_r = \mathbf{I}_m,$$

  where $\mathbf{1}_a$ is a vector of ones of length a.

Other modelling components that can be used are crossed-random effects and geoadditive models. For the interested reader details of how these modelling components can be incorporated can be found in [41]. These require specific specifications of $\mathbf{Z}_r$ and $\mathbf{P}_r$ and can be included without loss of generality.

We can generalise the random intercept components above to general random effects but this will require modelling the $\mathbf{u}_r$ vectors as $\mathbf{u}_r|\mathbf{\Sigma}_r \sim N(\mathbf{0}, \mathbf{\Sigma}_r)$ whose natural conjugate priors for $\mathbf{\Sigma}_r$ are inverse-Wishart distributions.

6.2.3 Priors

The remaining modelling components require the specification of priors for $\boldsymbol{\beta}$ and the σ_r^2's. To keep the exposition simple we will use priors

$$\boldsymbol{\beta} \sim N(\mathbf{0}, \sigma_\beta^2 \mathbf{I}) \qquad \text{and} \qquad \sigma_r^2 \sim \text{IG}(s_r, t_r), \quad 1 \le r \le R, \tag{6.3}$$

where $\sigma_\beta^2 = 10^8$ and $\text{IG}(s_r, t_r)$ denotes the inverse-gamma distribution with shape s_r and scale t_r with $s_r = t_r = 0.01$. These are conjugate priors and simplify algebra. In general we recommend the half-Cauchy priors advocated in [13]. These have a convenient conjugate gamma-gamma representation (e.g. [24]), but add to notation and expand the complexity of the model hierarchy without greatly changing the model fits for the data considered in this chapter.

6.2.4 Mean field variational Bayes

Mean field VB seeks to perform approximate Bayesian inference by seeking convenient parametric approximations to posterior quantities by an iterative process seeking to minimise the Kullback–Leibler (KL) divergence between the parametric approximation and the true posterior distribution.

Given a model's parameter $\boldsymbol{\theta}$ and data $\mathcal{D}$, the posterior density of $\boldsymbol{\theta}$ may be expressed as

$$p(\boldsymbol{\theta} \mid \mathcal{D}) = \frac{p(\mathcal{D}, \boldsymbol{\theta})}{p(\mathcal{D})}.$$

The denominator is known as the *marginal likelihood* of the data and involves the evaluation of an integral or a sum that may be computationally infeasible. The end point of a VB approximation algorithm is to choose an approximation $q(\boldsymbol{\theta})$ to the posterior density $p(\boldsymbol{\theta}|\mathcal{D})$ from a set of functions $\mathcal{F}$ that are more computationally feasible by minimising the KL divergence, i.e.

$$D_{KL}(q||p) = \mathbb{E}_q\left[\ln\left\{\frac{q(\boldsymbol{\theta})}{p(\boldsymbol{\theta} \mid \mathcal{D})}\right\}\right], \tag{6.4}$$

where $\mathbb{E}_q$ refers to the expectation with respect to $q(\boldsymbol{\theta})$. Since

$$\mathbb{E}_q\left[\ln\left\{\frac{q(\boldsymbol{\theta})}{p(\boldsymbol{\theta} \mid \mathcal{D})}\right\}\right] = \mathbb{E}_q\left[\ln\left\{\frac{q(\boldsymbol{\theta})p(\mathcal{D})}{p(\mathcal{D}, \boldsymbol{\theta})}\right\}\right] = \ln p(\mathcal{D}) - \mathbb{E}_q\left[\ln\left\{\frac{p(\mathcal{D}, \boldsymbol{\theta})}{q(\boldsymbol{\theta})}\right\}\right],$$

minimising (6.4) is also equivalent to maximising the expected lower bound order (ELBO) given by

$$\text{ELBO} = \mathbb{E}_q\left[\ln\left\{\frac{p(\mathcal{D}, \boldsymbol{\theta})}{q(\boldsymbol{\theta})}\right\}\right]. \tag{6.5}$$

One common choice for $\mathcal{F}$ is the set of mean field functions

$$\mathcal{F} = \left\{ q(\boldsymbol{\theta}) \text{ such that } q(\boldsymbol{\theta}) = \prod_{j=1}^{J} q_j(\boldsymbol{\theta}_j) \right\}.$$

This choice of $\mathcal{F}$ leads to the optimal approximating densities

$$q_j(\boldsymbol{\theta}_j) \propto \exp\left[\mathbb{E}_{-q_j}\left\{\ln p(\mathcal{D}, \boldsymbol{\theta})\right\}\right], \qquad j = 1, \ldots, J \tag{6.6}$$

(for details see [1,25]). The notation $\mathbb{E}_{-q_j}$ refers to expectation to all parameters except $q_j(\boldsymbol{\theta}_j)$, i.e. if all parameters are continuous then

$$\mathbb{E}_{-q_j}\left[\ln p(\mathcal{D}, \boldsymbol{\theta})\right] = \int \prod_{k \neq j} q_j(\boldsymbol{\theta}_j) \ln p(\mathcal{D}, \boldsymbol{\theta}) d\boldsymbol{\theta}_{-j}, \tag{6.7}$$

and integrals are replaced with appropriate summands when parameters are discrete.

It can be shown that updating $q_j(\boldsymbol{\theta}_j)$ via (6.6) for fixed forms of the remaining q-densities (i.e. $\{q_k(\boldsymbol{\theta}_k)\}_{k\neq j}$) results in an increase in the lower bound ELBO. Hence, cycling through the updates $j = 1, \ldots, J$, for each $q_j(\boldsymbol{\theta}_j)$ can be interpreted as a coordinate ascent method for maximising ELBO which, under mild regularity conditions, will converge to a local maximiser of the lower bound [21].

If a Gibbs sampling scheme is available for this model based on the full conditionals for $(\boldsymbol{\theta}_1, \ldots, \boldsymbol{\theta}_J)$ the q-densities take the same parametric form as the full conditionals for each $\boldsymbol{\theta}_j$, $1 \leq j \leq J$. In this chapter we will use the R-like function convention to denote specific known densities. Subscripts for prior parameters and (approximate) posterior parameters will be used to identify these hyperparameters, and 'tildered' values correspond to posterior parameters. For example, if $\boldsymbol{\alpha} \sim N(\boldsymbol{\mu}_\alpha, \boldsymbol{\Sigma}_\alpha)$ and the approximate posterior for $\boldsymbol{\alpha}$ is multivariate normal, then the q-density for $\boldsymbol{\alpha}$ will be denoted $q(\boldsymbol{\alpha}) = \text{dmvnorm}(\boldsymbol{\alpha} \,|\, \widetilde{\boldsymbol{\mu}}_\alpha, \widetilde{\boldsymbol{\Sigma}}_\alpha)$.

6.2.5 Tricks when VB is not easy to apply

Two common complications arise when attempting to use VB. To describe these complications let

$$f_j(\boldsymbol{\theta}_j) = \mathbb{E}_{-q_j}\left[\ln p(\mathcal{D}, \boldsymbol{\theta})\right]$$

so that we can write

$$q_j(\boldsymbol{\theta}_j) = Z_j^{-1} \exp\left[f_j(\boldsymbol{\theta}_j)\right] \qquad \text{and} \qquad Z_j = \int \exp\left[f_j(\boldsymbol{\theta}_j)\right] d\boldsymbol{\theta}_j.$$

The two complications are the following:

1. The function $f_j(\boldsymbol{\theta}_j)$ may not be available analytically since taking expectations of $\ln p(\mathcal{D}, \boldsymbol{\theta})$ may not be possible for some elements $q_j(\boldsymbol{\theta}_j)$.
2. The normalising constant Z_j may not be available analytically.

Here we will explore analytic approximations to these complications. However, the approaches here do not cover all such approaches to these problems. There is a growing literature on stochastic VB methods. Key references include [30,20,28].

The first complication can be handled by a first- or second-order delta method [32]. To fix ideas suppose $q(\boldsymbol{\theta}) = q_1(\boldsymbol{\theta}_1)q_2(\boldsymbol{\theta}_2)q_3(\boldsymbol{\theta}_3)$. Then

$$f_1(\boldsymbol{\theta}_1) = \int q_2(\boldsymbol{\theta}_2)q_3(\boldsymbol{\theta}_3) \ln p(\mathcal{D}, \boldsymbol{\theta}_1, \boldsymbol{\theta}_2, \boldsymbol{\theta}_3) d\boldsymbol{\theta}_2 d\boldsymbol{\theta}_3.$$

Suppose it is not easy to integrate out $\boldsymbol{\theta}_2$ from the above equation. A first-order delta method approximation uses a first-order Taylor series around $\boldsymbol{\theta}_2 = \mathbb{E}_q(\boldsymbol{\theta}_2)$ before taking expectations. The result uses

$$f_1(\boldsymbol{\theta}_1) \approx \int q_3(\boldsymbol{\theta}_3) \ln p(\mathcal{D}, \boldsymbol{\theta}_1, \mathbb{E}_q(\boldsymbol{\theta}_2), \boldsymbol{\theta}_3) d\boldsymbol{\theta}_3.$$

Similarly, a second-order delta method approximation to f_1 takes a second-order Taylor series around $\boldsymbol{\theta}_2 = \mathbb{E}_q(\boldsymbol{\theta}_2)$ before taking expectations. This results in the approximation

$$\begin{aligned} f_1(\boldsymbol{\theta}_1) \approx \int q_3(\boldsymbol{\theta}_3)\big[&\ln p(\mathcal{D}, \boldsymbol{\theta}_1, \mathbb{E}_q(\boldsymbol{\theta}_2), \boldsymbol{\theta}_3) \\ &+ \tfrac{1}{2}\text{tr}\left\{\text{cov}_q(\boldsymbol{\theta}_2)\mathbf{H}(\boldsymbol{\theta}_1, \mathbb{E}_q(\boldsymbol{\theta}_2), \boldsymbol{\theta}_3)\right\}\big]d\boldsymbol{\theta}_3, \end{aligned}$$

where

$$\mathbf{H}(\boldsymbol{\theta}_1, \boldsymbol{\theta}_2, \boldsymbol{\theta}_3) = \frac{\partial^2 \ln p(\mathcal{D}, \boldsymbol{\theta}_1, \boldsymbol{\theta}_2, \boldsymbol{\theta}_3)}{\partial \boldsymbol{\theta}_2 \partial \boldsymbol{\theta}_2^T}.$$

In this chapter we only use the first-order delta method approximation.

The second complication can be dealt with using a Laplace approximation, i.e.

$$q_j(\boldsymbol{\theta}_j) \approx \text{dmvnorm}(\boldsymbol{\theta}_j | \widetilde{\boldsymbol{\mu}}_j, \widetilde{\boldsymbol{\Sigma}}_j),$$

where $\widetilde{\boldsymbol{\mu}}_j$ is the maximiser of $f_j(\boldsymbol{\theta}_j)$ with respect to $\boldsymbol{\theta}_j$, and $\widetilde{\boldsymbol{\Sigma}}_j = [-\mathbf{H}_j(\widetilde{\boldsymbol{\theta}}_j)]^{-1}$, where $\mathbf{H}_j(\boldsymbol{\theta}_j)$ is the jth Hessian matrix defined by

$$\left[\mathbf{H}_j(\boldsymbol{\theta}_j)\right]_{k,k'} = \frac{\partial^2 f_j(\boldsymbol{\theta}_j)}{\partial \theta_k \partial \theta_{k'}}, \qquad 1 \le k, k' \le d_j,$$

where $\boldsymbol{\theta}_j \in \mathbb{R}^{d_j}$. This can be found using Newton–Raphson iterations, i.e.

$$\widetilde{\boldsymbol{\mu}}_j^{(t+1)} = \widetilde{\boldsymbol{\mu}}_j^{(t)} + \left[-\mathbf{H}_j(\widetilde{\boldsymbol{\mu}}_j^{(t)})\right]^{-1} \mathbf{g}_j(\widetilde{\boldsymbol{\mu}}_j^{(t)}),$$

where $\widetilde{\boldsymbol{\mu}}_j^{(0)}$ is a given starting point and $\left[\mathbf{g}_j(\boldsymbol{\theta}_j)\right]_k = \partial f_j(\boldsymbol{\theta}_j)/\partial \theta_k$, $1 \le k \le d_j$. An alternative to Newton–Raphson iterations is the Broyden–Fletcher–Goldfarb–Shanno (BFGS) quasi-Newton method [2,12,14,31], which only requires implementation of $f_j(\boldsymbol{\theta}_j)$ and possibly $\mathbf{g}_j(\boldsymbol{\theta}_j)$ (which can also be approximated numerically) and, as a biproduct, can provide an approximation to $\left[-\mathbf{H}_j(\widetilde{\boldsymbol{\mu}}_j^*)\right]^{-1}$, where $\widetilde{\boldsymbol{\mu}}_j^*$ is the maximiser of $f_j(\boldsymbol{\theta}_j)$.

As an alternative approach to complication 2, if $\theta_j \in \mathbb{R}$ is a scalar, then numerical quadrature can be used, i.e.

$$q_j(\theta_j) \approx \frac{\exp\left[f_j(\theta_j)\right]}{\sum_{k=1}^{N} w_k \exp\left[f_j(\theta_{jk})\right]},$$

where $\{w_k\}_{k=1}^{N}$ and $\{\theta_{jk}\}_{k=1}^{N}$ are appropriate quadrature weights and abscissa, respectively. We have found Gaussian quadrature to be quite effective (see for example Chapter 4 of [27]) for univariate integration. Note that the numerator and denominator of the above expression should be divided by the maximum value of $\exp\left[f_j(\theta_{jk})\right]$ to avoid numerical overflow when implemented. Similarly, the mth moment of $q(\theta_j)$ can be approximated using

$$\mathbb{E}_q(\theta_k^m) = \frac{\sum_{k=1}^{N} \theta_{jk}^m w_k \exp\left[f_j(\theta_{jk})\right]}{\sum_{k=1}^{N} w_k \exp\left[f_j(\theta_{jk})\right]}. \tag{6.8}$$

6.2.6 Comparisons

For purposes of comparison of our VB methodology with a gold standard, we will compare the accuracy of our VB-based method with MCMC via `stan` [3]. The `stan` computer package is a state-of-the-art platform for statistical modelling and high-performance statistical computation; it implements full Bayesian statistical inference with MCMC sampling (using Hamiltonian Monte Carlo) [18]. All examples were run on the author's laptop computer (64-bit Windows 8 Intel i7-4930MX central processing unit at 3 GHz with 32 GB of random access memory), where we use 1000 samples for burn-in and 10,000 for inference with no thinning.

While we will not explicitly outline code here, code for all of the examples in this chapter will be made available from

http://www.maths.usyd.edu.au/u/jormerod/

Note that `stan` converts a model into `C++` code which it compiles before sampling begins. We do not include this compile time when reporting computing times for `stan` to provide a fairer comparison. Our VB implementation of the algorithms in this chapter is entirely in the `R` programming language. Since `stan` is largely implemented in `C++` comparisons are not entirely fair since `C++` is well known to be faster than `R`. Despite this in each case our VB approach implemented in `R` is still an order of magnitude faster than MCMC via `stan`.

6.3 A standard semiparametric regression model

Before we consider some nonstandard semiparametric regression model examples we begin with a standard semiparametric regression model. This will form the basis for some nonstandard extensions. In place of (6.1) we will use

$$\mathbf{y}|\boldsymbol{\beta}, \mathbf{u}, \sigma_\varepsilon^2 \sim N(\mathbf{X}\boldsymbol{\beta} + \mathbf{Z}\mathbf{u}, \sigma_\varepsilon^2\mathbf{I}), \tag{6.9}$$

where $\sigma_\varepsilon^2 > 0$ is the residual variance. The model specification is completed by specifying the prior for σ_ε^2, where we will use

$$\sigma_\varepsilon^2 \sim \text{IG}(s_\varepsilon, t_\varepsilon). \tag{6.10}$$

Given the above model description we are now in a place to derive the VB algorithm. We will consider the VB approximation corresponding to $q(\boldsymbol{\theta}) = q(\boldsymbol{\nu})q(\sigma_\varepsilon^2, \boldsymbol{\sigma}^2)$, where $\boldsymbol{\nu} = [\boldsymbol{\beta}^T, \mathbf{u}^T]^T$. This leads to

$$\begin{aligned}
q(\boldsymbol{\nu}) &\propto \exp\big[-\tfrac{1}{2}\boldsymbol{\nu}^T\mathbb{E}_q\{\sigma_\varepsilon^{-2}\mathbf{C}^T\mathbf{C} \\
&\qquad +\text{blockdiag}(\sigma_\beta^{-2}\mathbf{I}, \sigma_1^{-2}\mathbf{P}_1, \ldots, \sigma_R^{-2}\mathbf{P}_R)\}\boldsymbol{\nu} \\
&\qquad +\mathbb{E}_q\{\sigma_\varepsilon^{-2}\}\mathbf{y}^T\mathbf{C}\boldsymbol{\nu}\big], \\
q(\sigma_\varepsilon^2) &\propto \exp\big[-\big(s_\varepsilon + \tfrac{n}{2} + 1\big)\ln(\sigma_\varepsilon^2) - \sigma_\varepsilon^{-2}\mathbb{E}_q\{t_\varepsilon + \tfrac{1}{2}\|\mathbf{y} - \mathbf{C}\boldsymbol{\nu}\|^2\}\big] \quad \text{and} \\
q(\sigma_r^2) &\propto \exp\big[-\big(s_r + \tfrac{q_r}{2} + 1\big)\ln(\sigma_r^2) - \sigma_r^{-2}\mathbb{E}_q\{t_r + \tfrac{1}{2}\mathbf{u}_r^T\mathbf{P}_r\mathbf{u}_r\}\big], \quad 1 \le r \le R,
\end{aligned} \tag{6.11}$$

where $\mathbf{C} = [\mathbf{X}, \mathbf{Z}]$. Looking at the forms of the q-densities in (6.11) we can identify $q(\boldsymbol{\nu})$ as multivariate Gaussian and $q(\sigma_\varepsilon^2)$, $q(\sigma_r^2)$'s as inverse-gamma densities, i.e.

$$\begin{aligned}
q(\boldsymbol{\nu}) &= \text{dmvnorm}(\,\boldsymbol{\nu}\,|\,\widetilde{\boldsymbol{\mu}}_\nu\,,\,\widetilde{\boldsymbol{\Sigma}}_\nu\,), \\
q(\sigma_\varepsilon^2) &= \text{dinvgamma}(\,\sigma_\varepsilon^2\,|\,\widetilde{s}_\varepsilon\,,\,\widetilde{t}_\varepsilon\,) \qquad \text{and} \\
q(\sigma_r^2) &= \text{dinvgamma}(\,\sigma_r^2\,|\,\widetilde{s}_r\,,\,\widetilde{t}_r\,), \qquad 1 \le r \le R,
\end{aligned} \tag{6.12}$$

where

$$\begin{gathered}
\widetilde{\boldsymbol{\Sigma}}_\nu = \Big[\Big(\tfrac{\widetilde{s}_\varepsilon}{\widetilde{t}_\varepsilon}\Big)\mathbf{C}^T\mathbf{C} + \text{blockdiag}\Big(\sigma_\beta^{-2}\mathbf{I}_p, \tfrac{\widetilde{s}_1}{\widetilde{t}_1}\mathbf{P}_1, \ldots \tfrac{\widetilde{s}_R}{\widetilde{t}_R}\mathbf{P}_R\Big)\Big]^{-1}, \\
\widetilde{\boldsymbol{\mu}}_\nu = \Big(\tfrac{\widetilde{s}_\varepsilon}{\widetilde{t}_\varepsilon}\Big)\widetilde{\boldsymbol{\Sigma}}_\nu\mathbf{C}^T\mathbf{y}, \\
\widetilde{s}_\varepsilon = s_\varepsilon + \tfrac{n}{2}, \qquad \widetilde{t}_\varepsilon = t_\varepsilon + \tfrac{1}{2}\|\mathbf{y} - \mathbf{C}\widetilde{\boldsymbol{\mu}}_\nu\|^2 + \tfrac{1}{2}\text{tr}(\mathbf{C}^T\mathbf{C}\widetilde{\boldsymbol{\Sigma}}_\nu), \\
\widetilde{s}_r = s_r + \tfrac{q_r}{2} \quad \text{and} \quad \widetilde{t}_r = t_r + \tfrac{1}{2}\widetilde{\boldsymbol{\mu}}_{\mathbf{u}_r}^T\mathbf{P}_r\widetilde{\boldsymbol{\mu}}_{\mathbf{u}_r} + \tfrac{1}{2}\text{tr}(\mathbf{P}_r\widetilde{\boldsymbol{\Sigma}}_{\mathbf{u}_r}), \quad 1 \le r \le R,
\end{gathered} \tag{6.13}$$

and the values $\widetilde{\boldsymbol{\mu}}_{\mathbf{u}_r}$ and $\widetilde{\boldsymbol{\Sigma}}_{\mathbf{u}_r}$ correspond to the subcomponents of $\widetilde{\boldsymbol{\mu}}_{\boldsymbol{\nu}}$ to the elements $\mathbf{u}_r$. Algorithm 1 concisely summarises the updates below.

Algorithm 1 Fitting a GAM using VB.

Require: $\widetilde{t}_\varepsilon, \widetilde{t}_r > 0$, $1 \le r \le R$

Set $\widetilde{s}_\varepsilon = s_\varepsilon + \frac{n}{2}$ and $\widetilde{s}_r = s_r + \frac{q_r}{2}$, $1 \le r \le R$.

while the change in $\widetilde{t}_\varepsilon$ and $\widetilde{t}_r$, $1 \le r \le R$ is not small **do**

$$\widetilde{\boldsymbol{\Sigma}}_{\boldsymbol{\nu}} \leftarrow \left[(\widetilde{s}_\varepsilon/\widetilde{t}_\varepsilon)\mathbf{C}^T\mathbf{C} + \text{blockdiag}\left(\sigma_\beta^{-2}\mathbf{I}_p, (\widetilde{s}_1/\widetilde{t}_1)\mathbf{P}_1, \ldots, (\widetilde{s}_R/\widetilde{t}_R)\mathbf{P}_R\right) \right]^{-1}$$

$$\widetilde{\boldsymbol{\mu}}_{\boldsymbol{\nu}} \leftarrow (\widetilde{s}_\varepsilon/\widetilde{t}_\varepsilon)\widetilde{\boldsymbol{\Sigma}}_{\boldsymbol{\nu}}\mathbf{C}^T\mathbf{y}$$

$$\widetilde{t}_\varepsilon \leftarrow t_\varepsilon + \tfrac{1}{2}\|\mathbf{y} - \mathbf{C}\widetilde{\boldsymbol{\mu}}_{\boldsymbol{\nu}}\|^2 + \tfrac{1}{2}\text{tr}(\mathbf{C}^T\mathbf{C}\widetilde{\boldsymbol{\Sigma}}_{\boldsymbol{\nu}})$$

$$\widetilde{t}_r \leftarrow t_r + \tfrac{1}{2}\widetilde{\boldsymbol{\mu}}_{\mathbf{u}_r}^T\mathbf{P}_r\widetilde{\boldsymbol{\mu}}_{\mathbf{u}_r} + \tfrac{1}{2}\text{tr}(\mathbf{P}_r\widetilde{\boldsymbol{\Sigma}}_{\mathbf{u}_r}), \qquad 1 \le r \le R$$

end while

6.3.1 Generalised additive model for air quality data

For this example we consider the daily air quality measurements in New York, May to September 1973. The data were obtained from the New York State Department of Conservation (ozone data) and the National Weather Service (meteorological data). These data can be found in the `datasets` package in `R` in the data set `airquality` and contain the following measurements:

- `Ozone`: Mean ozone in parts per billion from 13:00 to 15:00 hours at Roosevelt Island;
- `Solar.R`: Solar radiation in Langleys in the frequency band 4000-7700 Angstroms from 8:00 to 12:00 hours at Central Park;
- `Wind`: Average wind speed in miles per hour at 7:00 and 10:00 hours at LaGuardia Airport; and
- `Temp`: Maximum daily temperature in degrees Fahrenheit at La Guardia Airport.

We also have the day at which the data was collected (`day`).

For this example we will use the abovementioned predictors with $d = 4$. We will fit a model of the form $y_i \sim f(\mathbf{x}_i) + \varepsilon_i$, where $y_i = \texttt{Ozone}_i$, $\varepsilon_i \sim N(0, \sigma_\varepsilon^2)$, $1 \le i \le n$, and

$$\begin{aligned} f(\mathbf{x}_i) &= \beta_0 + \texttt{Solar.R}_i\beta_1 + \texttt{Wind}_i\beta_2 + \texttt{Temp}_i\beta_3 + \texttt{Day}_i\beta_4 \\ &\quad + f_1(\texttt{Solar.R}_i) + f_2(\texttt{Wind}_i) + f_3(\texttt{Temp}_i) + f_4(\texttt{day}_i). \end{aligned}$$

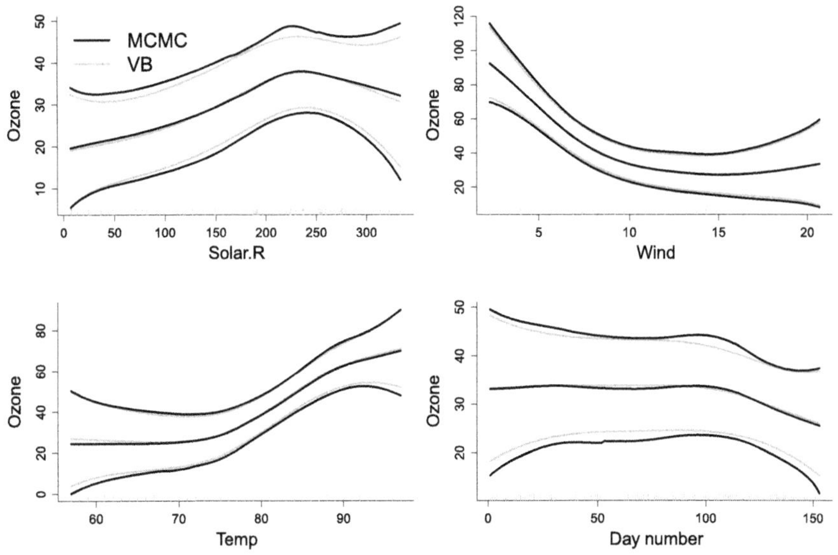

Figure 6.1 ***Fitted functions for the generalised model applied to the*** `airquality` ***data.*** Inner lines correspond to fitted additive components. Outer lines correspond to pointwise 95% credible intervals.

Using the semiparametric framework for penalised splines described in Section 6.2.3 the matrix $\mathbf{X}$ contains an intercept term along with linear terms for $\texttt{Solar.R}_i$, $\texttt{Wind}_i$, $\texttt{Temp}_i$ and $\texttt{Day}_i$, while the matrices $\mathbf{Z}_1$, $\mathbf{Z}_2$, $\mathbf{Z}_3$ and $\mathbf{Z}_4$ are constructed using O-Spline bases for the variables $\texttt{Solar.R}_i$, $\texttt{Wind}_i$, $\texttt{Temp}_i$ and $\texttt{Day}_i$, respectively.

Figs 6.1 and 6.2 illustrate the fitted functions for each covariate for the `airquality` data set, 95% confidence intervals for the mean and MCMC diagnostics. From these we see that the VB approximation gives a quite comparable fit to those obtained by MCMC. The approximate 95% credible intervals obtained using VB are only slightly underestimated. From Fig. 6.2 we see that posterior variances for the variance components are underestimated, but that the VB approximate posterior distribution for σ_ε^2 is almost exact.

6.4 Robust nonparametric regression

We now consider the situation where one or more outliers could have a significant effect on the quality of the fitted functions. We do so by replacing a normal distribution for the response with a t-distributed one. This dis-

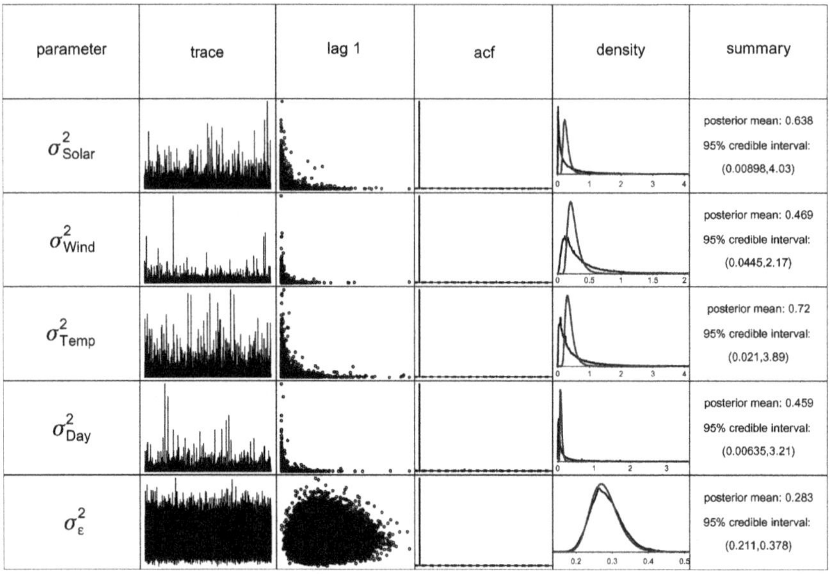

Figure 6.2 ***Summary of MCMC-based inference for parameters in the generalised model applied to the*** `airquality` ***data.*** The columns are: parameter, trace plot of MCMC sample, plot of sample against 1-lagged sample, sample autocorrelation function, kernel estimates of posterior densities, and basic numerical summaries. Blue (dark grey in print version) densities correspond to posterior density approximations obtained using VB.

tribution has thicker tails than the normal distribution leading to samples with large residuals to be downweighted during the fitting process.

Thus we consider the model

$$y_i|\boldsymbol{\beta}, \mathbf{u}, \sigma_\varepsilon^2, \nu \sim t((\mathbf{X}\boldsymbol{\beta} + \mathbf{Z}\mathbf{u})_i, \sigma_\varepsilon^2\mathbf{I}, \nu_y), \tag{6.14}$$

where the parameters of interest are $\boldsymbol{\theta} = (\boldsymbol{\beta}, \mathbf{u}, \sigma_\varepsilon^2, \boldsymbol{\sigma}^2, \nu_y)$. We adopt the priors (6.2), (6.3) and (6.10) for $\mathbf{u}$, $\boldsymbol{\beta}$ and $\boldsymbol{\sigma}^2$, and σ_ε^2, respectively. For ν_y we will use the prior $\nu_y \sim \text{Uniform}(L, U)$ for two positive constants L and U.

Noting that (6.14) is difficult to deal with using VB we instead adopt an auxiliary representation of (6.14). This entails replacing (6.14) with

$$\begin{aligned}
&y_i|\boldsymbol{\beta}, \mathbf{u}, \sigma_\varepsilon^2, a_i \stackrel{\text{ind}}{\sim} N((\mathbf{X}\boldsymbol{\beta} + \mathbf{Z}\mathbf{u})_i, \sigma_\varepsilon^2 a_i^{-1}),\\
&a_i \stackrel{\text{iid}}{\sim} \text{Gamma}(\nu_y/2, \nu_y/2), \quad 1 \le i \le n,
\end{aligned}$$

where $\mathbf{a} = (a_1, \ldots, a_n)^T$ is a vector of auxiliary variables. The original representation (6.14) can be recovered by noting that $p(y_i|\boldsymbol{\beta}, \mathbf{u}, \sigma_\varepsilon^2, \nu_y) = \int_0^\infty p(a_i|\boldsymbol{\beta}, \mathbf{u}, \sigma_\varepsilon^2, a_i)p(a_i|\nu_y)da_i$, $1 \le i \le n$.

We will consider a VB approximation corresponding to the partition

$$q(\boldsymbol{\theta}) = q(\boldsymbol{\nu})q(\sigma_\varepsilon^2, \boldsymbol{\sigma}^2)\left[\prod_{i=1}^{n} q(a_i)\right]q(\nu_y),$$

where again $\boldsymbol{\nu} = (\boldsymbol{\beta}^T, \mathbf{u}^T)^T$. The parametric forms for the q-densities for $\boldsymbol{\nu}$, σ_ε^2, σ_r^2, $1 \le r \le R$ are given by (6.12) and the terms $\widetilde{\boldsymbol{\Sigma}}_{\boldsymbol{\nu}}$, $\widetilde{\boldsymbol{\mu}}_{\boldsymbol{\nu}}$ and $\widetilde{t}_\varepsilon$ in (6.13) are replaced with

$$\begin{aligned}
\widetilde{\boldsymbol{\Sigma}}_{\boldsymbol{\nu}} &= \left[\left(\frac{\widetilde{a}_\varepsilon}{\widetilde{b}_\varepsilon}\right)\mathbf{C}^T\mathbf{W}\mathbf{C} + \text{blockdiag}\left(\sigma_\beta^{-2}\mathbf{I}_p, \frac{\widetilde{s}_1}{\widetilde{t}_1}\mathbf{P}_1, \ldots, \frac{\widetilde{s}_R}{\widetilde{t}_R}\mathbf{P}_R\right)\right]^{-1}, \\
\widetilde{\boldsymbol{\mu}}_{\boldsymbol{\nu}} &= \left(\frac{\widetilde{s}_\varepsilon}{\widetilde{t}_\varepsilon}\right)\widetilde{\boldsymbol{\Sigma}}_{\boldsymbol{\nu}}\mathbf{C}^T\mathbf{W}\mathbf{y} \qquad \text{and} \\
\widetilde{t}_\varepsilon &= t_\varepsilon + \tfrac{1}{2}(\mathbf{y} - \mathbf{C}\widetilde{\boldsymbol{\mu}}_{\boldsymbol{\nu}})^T\mathbf{W}(\mathbf{y} - \mathbf{C}\widetilde{\boldsymbol{\mu}}_{\boldsymbol{\nu}}) + \tfrac{1}{2}\text{tr}(\mathbf{C}^T\mathbf{W}\mathbf{C}\widetilde{\boldsymbol{\Sigma}}_{\boldsymbol{\nu}}),
\end{aligned}$$

with $\mathbf{W}$ being the diagonal matrix $\mathbf{W} = \text{diag}(w_1, \ldots, w_n)$ whose entries are given by $w_i = \mathbb{E}_q(a_i)$. We can interpret the above equations as corresponding to a weighted least squares fit where the weights are given by w_i. Note that in the limit as $w_i \to 0$ the ith observation does not contribute to the computed values of the variational parameters. Furthermore, if all w_i's are set to 1 the fit from Section 6.3 for a normal response is recovered.

The forms of the q-densities for $q(a_i)$ are given by $q(a_i) = \text{dgamma}(a_i\,|\,\widetilde{c}, \widetilde{d}_i)$, where

$$\begin{aligned}
\widetilde{c} &= \frac{\widetilde{\nu}_y + 1}{2} \qquad \text{and} \\
\widetilde{d}_i &= \frac{\widetilde{\nu}_y}{2} + \frac{1}{2}\left(\frac{\widetilde{s}_\varepsilon}{\widetilde{t}_\varepsilon}\right)\left[(\mathbf{y} - \mathbf{C}\widetilde{\boldsymbol{\mu}}_{\boldsymbol{\nu}})_i^2 + (\mathbf{C}\widetilde{\boldsymbol{\Sigma}}_{\boldsymbol{\nu}}\mathbf{C}^T)_{ii}\right], \qquad 1 \le i \le n,
\end{aligned}$$

where $\widetilde{\nu}_y = \mathbb{E}_q(\nu_y)$. The q-density $q(\nu_y)$ does not have a known normalising constant and is given by

$$\begin{aligned}
q(\nu_y) \propto \exp\Bigg[&\tfrac{n\nu_y}{2}\ln(\nu_y) - n\ln\Gamma\left(\tfrac{\nu_y}{2}\right) \\
&- \nu_y\left\{\tfrac{n}{2}\ln(2) + \tfrac{1}{2}\sum_{i=1}^{n}(w_i - \psi(c) + \ln(d_i))\right\}\Bigg], \qquad (6.15)
\end{aligned}$$

where $\psi(x) = d\ln\Gamma(x)/dx$ is the digamma function.

This means that the normalising constant and the first moment $\mathbb{E}_q(\nu_y)$ need to be estimated. We approximate both these quantities using composite trapezoidal integration between L and U using 300 quadrature points, i.e. using (6.8).

Given the above notation,

$$w_i = \mathbb{E}_q(a_i) = \frac{\widetilde{c}}{\widetilde{d}_i} = \frac{\widetilde{\nu}_y + 1}{\widetilde{\nu}_y + (\widetilde{s}_\varepsilon/\widetilde{t}_\varepsilon)\left[(\mathbf{y} - \mathbf{C}\widetilde{\boldsymbol{\mu}}_\nu)_i^2 + (\mathbf{C}\widetilde{\boldsymbol{\Sigma}}_\nu\mathbf{C}^T)_{ii}\right]}.$$

The term $(\mathbf{y} - \mathbf{C}\widetilde{\boldsymbol{\mu}}_\nu)_i$ is the ith residual, while the term $(\mathbf{C}\widetilde{\boldsymbol{\Sigma}}_\nu\mathbf{C}^T)_{ii}$ is analogous to the ith leverage statistic. In the limit as $\widetilde{\nu}_y \to \infty$ we have $w_i \to 1$. When $\widetilde{\nu}_y$ is small and/or either the ith residual or the ith leverage-like statistic becomes large the corresponding w_i will be small. Thus, samples with large residuals or high leverage points will be downweighted. This means that the resulting fit is doubly robust in the sense that it is resistant to both outliers and high leverage points. Algorithm 2 concisely summarises the updates for the VB approximation developed in this section.

6.4.1 Hauser respiratory experiment

We test the above methodology using a data set on a respiratory experiment conducted by Professor Russ Hauser at Harvard School of Public Health, Boston, USA. The data correspond to 60 measurements on one subject during two separate respiratory experiments. The response variable y_i represents the logarithm of the adjusted time of exhalation for x_i equal to the time in seconds since exposure to air containing particulate matter. The adjusted time of exhalation is obtained by subtracting the average time of exhalation at baseline, prior to exposure to filtered air. We interest ourselves in modelling the mean response as a function of time.

For this model we are fitting

$$y_i \overset{\text{ind}}{\sim} t(f(x_i), \sigma_\varepsilon^2, \nu_y), \qquad 1 \leq i \leq n,$$

where we use $L = 1$ and $U = 20$ as the prior hyperparameters for ν_y. We fit the equivalent model using `stan`; the results are plotted in Fig. 6.3.

In Fig. 6.3 we see the difference between the fitted means and 95% credible intervals. The variance of the posterior approximation for ν_y is slightly underestimated although the posterior mean for ν_y is quite well approximated.

The VB fit of these data took 0.3 seconds while `stan` took 84.1 seconds to produce 10,000 MCMC samples. We note that in [22] fitting this same

Algorithm 2 Fitting a robust GAM using VB.

Require: $\widetilde{t}_\varepsilon, \widetilde{t}_r > 0$, $1 \le r \le R$, $\widetilde{\nu}_y > 0$ large (say $\widetilde{\nu}_y = 30$)

Set $\widetilde{s}_\varepsilon = s_\varepsilon + \frac{n}{2}$, $\widetilde{s}_r = s_r + \frac{q_r}{2}$, $1 \le r \le R$, and $w_i = 1$, $1 \le i \le n$.

while the change in $\widetilde{t}_\varepsilon$ and $\widetilde{t}_r$, $1 \le r \le R$ is not small **do**

$$\widetilde{\mathbf{\Sigma}}_\nu \leftarrow \left[(\widetilde{s}_\varepsilon/\widetilde{t}_\varepsilon)\mathbf{C}^T\mathbf{W}\mathbf{C} + \text{blockdiag}\left(\sigma_\beta^{-2}\mathbf{I}_p, (\widetilde{s}_1/\widetilde{t}_1)\mathbf{P}_1, \ldots, (\widetilde{s}_R/\widetilde{t}_R)\mathbf{P}_R\right) \right]^{-1}$$

$$\widetilde{\boldsymbol{\mu}}_\nu \leftarrow (\widetilde{s}_\varepsilon/\widetilde{t}_\varepsilon)\widetilde{\mathbf{\Sigma}}_\nu\mathbf{C}^T\mathbf{W}\mathbf{y}$$

$$\widetilde{t}_\varepsilon \leftarrow t_\varepsilon + \tfrac{1}{2}(\mathbf{y} - \mathbf{C}\widetilde{\boldsymbol{\mu}}_\nu)^T\mathbf{W}(\mathbf{y} - \mathbf{C}\widetilde{\boldsymbol{\mu}}_\nu) + \tfrac{1}{2}\text{tr}(\mathbf{C}^T\mathbf{W}\mathbf{C}\widetilde{\mathbf{\Sigma}}_\nu)$$

$$\widetilde{t}_r \leftarrow t_r + \tfrac{1}{2}\widetilde{\boldsymbol{\mu}}_{\mathbf{u}_r}^T\mathbf{P}_r\widetilde{\boldsymbol{\mu}}_{\mathbf{u}_r} + \tfrac{1}{2}\text{tr}(\mathbf{P}_r\widetilde{\mathbf{\Sigma}}_{\mathbf{u}_r}), \qquad 1 \le r \le R$$

$$\widetilde{c} \leftarrow \tfrac{\widetilde{\nu}_y+1}{2}$$

$$\widetilde{d}_i \leftarrow \tfrac{\widetilde{\nu}_y}{2} + \tfrac{1}{2}\left(\tfrac{\widetilde{s}_\varepsilon}{\widetilde{t}_\varepsilon}\right)\left[(\mathbf{y} - \mathbf{C}\widetilde{\boldsymbol{\mu}}_\nu)_i^2 + (\mathbf{C}\widetilde{\mathbf{\Sigma}}_\nu\mathbf{C}^T)_{ii}\right], \qquad 1 \le i \le n$$

$$w_i \leftarrow \widetilde{c}/\widetilde{d}_i, \qquad 1 \le i \le n$$

Let $f(\nu_y) = \frac{n\nu_y}{2}\ln(\nu_y) - n\ln\Gamma\left(\frac{\nu_y}{2}\right) - \nu_y\Big[\frac{n}{2}\ln(2) + \frac{1}{2}\sum_{i=1}^n(w_i - \psi(c) + \ln(d_i))\Big]$

Approximate $\widetilde{\nu}_y = \mathbb{E}_q(\nu_y)$ via (6.15) using numerical quadrature via (6.8).

end while

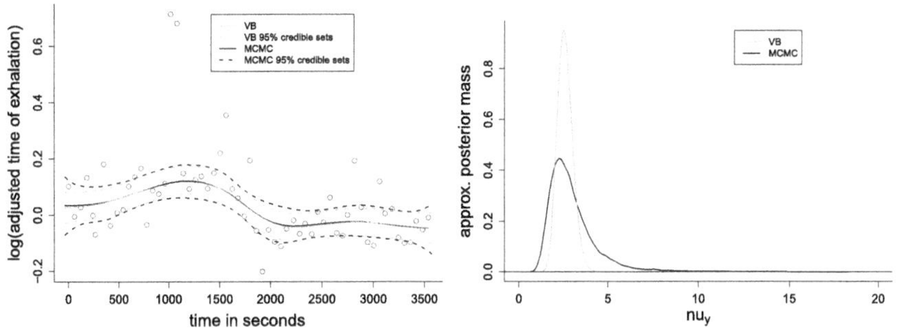

Figure 6.3 ***Fits of the Hauser respiratory experiment data using VB and MCMC (via*** `stan`***) of the robust nonparametric regression model.*** Left: Posterior mean and pointwise 95% credible sets for the regression function. Right: Approximate posterior function for the degrees of freedom parameter ν_y.

model in `Infer.NET` took 80.4 seconds and using `BUGS` it took 22.56 seconds on the same laptop and the same number of MCMC samples. Our `R` implementation of the VB method developed here compares very well to all of these.

6.5 Generalised additive model with heteroscedastic variance

In many real situations the assumption of homoscedasticity, i.e. constant variance, is unrealistic and may lead to false conclusions. Adverse effects of holding this assumption include incorrect confidence intervals, incorrect inferences on particular parameter values and calibration inference (predicting an x based on a y). The converse situation where the variance may change is called heteroscedasticity and is examined in, amongst others, [8], [4], [29] and [7]. A model that allows for heteroscedasticity may lead to more robust results as we can exploit heteroscedasticity to obtain better fits in regions where there is less noise corrupting the response.

In order to handle heteroscedasticity we will replace $\sigma_\varepsilon^2\mathbf{I}$ in (6.9) with $\text{diag}(\exp(\mathbf{X}_\varepsilon\boldsymbol{\beta}_\varepsilon + \mathbf{Z}_\varepsilon\mathbf{u}_\varepsilon))$, where $\mathbf{X}_\varepsilon$, $\boldsymbol{\beta}_\varepsilon$, $\mathbf{Z}_\varepsilon$ and $\mathbf{u}_\varepsilon$ play analogous roles for modelling the logarithm of the variance to those modelling the mean. Hence, we model the response as

$$\mathbf{y}|\boldsymbol{\beta}_\mu, \mathbf{u}_\mu, \boldsymbol{\beta}_\varepsilon, \mathbf{u}_\varepsilon \sim N(\mathbf{X}_\mu\boldsymbol{\beta}_\mu + \mathbf{Z}_\mu\mathbf{u}_\mu, \text{diag}(\exp(\mathbf{X}_\varepsilon\boldsymbol{\beta}_\varepsilon + \mathbf{Z}_\varepsilon\mathbf{u}_\varepsilon))),$$

where $\mathbf{X}_\mu \in \mathbb{R}^{n\times p_\mu}$, $\mathbf{X}_\varepsilon \in \mathbb{R}^{n\times p_\varepsilon}$, $\mathbf{Z}_\mu = [\mathbf{Z}_{\mu,1}, \ldots, \mathbf{Z}_{\mu,R_\mu}]$, $\mathbf{Z}_\varepsilon = [\mathbf{Z}_{\varepsilon,1}, \ldots, \mathbf{Z}_{\varepsilon,R_\varepsilon}]$, $\mathbf{Z}_{\mu,r} \in \mathbb{R}^{n\times q_{\mu,r}}$, $1 \le r \le R_\mu$ and $\mathbf{Z}_{\varepsilon,r} \in \mathbb{R}^{n\times q_{\varepsilon,r}}$, $1 \le r \le R_\varepsilon$. Here $\mathbf{X}_\mu$ and $\mathbf{X}_\varepsilon$ play the role of 'fixed effects' matrices corresponding to the mean and variance of elements for $\mathbf{y}$, respectively. Similarly, $\mathbf{Z}_\mu$ and $\mathbf{Z}_\varepsilon$ play an analogous role as design matrices for the random effects. We specify the distribution of the random effect coefficients $\mathbf{u}_\mu$ and $\mathbf{u}_\varepsilon$ as

$$\begin{aligned}
\mathbf{u}_\mu|\boldsymbol{\sigma}_\mu^2 &\sim N(\mathbf{0}, \text{blockdiag}(\sigma_{\mu,1}^2\mathbf{P}_{\mu,r}^{-1}, \ldots, \sigma_{\mu,R_\mu}^2\mathbf{P}_{\mu,r}^{-1})),\\
\mathbf{u}_\varepsilon|\boldsymbol{\sigma}_\varepsilon^2 &\sim N(\mathbf{0}, \text{blockdiag}(\sigma_{\varepsilon,1}^2\mathbf{P}_{\varepsilon,r}^{-1}, \ldots, \sigma_{\varepsilon,R_\varepsilon}^2\mathbf{P}_{\varepsilon,r}^{-1}))
\end{aligned}$$

and specify the priors for $\boldsymbol{\beta}_\mu$, $\boldsymbol{\beta}_\varepsilon$, $\boldsymbol{\sigma}_\mu^2$ and $\boldsymbol{\sigma}_\varepsilon^2$ with

$$\begin{aligned}
&\boldsymbol{\beta}_\mu \sim N(\mathbf{0}, \sigma_{\mu,\beta}^2\mathbf{I}_{p_\mu}), && \sigma_{\mu,r}^2 \sim \text{IG}(s_{\mu,r}, t_{\mu_r}), && 1 \le r \le R_\mu,\\
&\boldsymbol{\beta}_\varepsilon \sim N(\mathbf{0}, \sigma_{\varepsilon,\beta}^2\mathbf{I}_{p_\varepsilon}) \text{ and } && \sigma_{\varepsilon,r}^2 \sim \text{IG}(s_{\varepsilon,r}, t_\varepsilon), && 1 \le r \le R_\varepsilon.
\end{aligned}$$

For this model we consider a VB approximation corresponding to the factorisation

$$q(\boldsymbol{\nu}_\mu, \boldsymbol{\nu}_\varepsilon, \boldsymbol{\sigma}_\mu^2, \boldsymbol{\sigma}_\varepsilon^2) = q(\boldsymbol{\nu}_\mu, \boldsymbol{\nu}_\varepsilon)q(\boldsymbol{\sigma}_\mu^2, \boldsymbol{\sigma}_\varepsilon^2).$$

Then the optimal densities corresponding to this partition are of the form

$$q(\boldsymbol{\nu}_\mu,\boldsymbol{\nu}_\varepsilon)\ \propto \exp\Big[-\tfrac{1}{2}\mathbf{1}^T\mathbf{C}_\varepsilon\boldsymbol{\nu}_\varepsilon-\tfrac{1}{2}(\mathbf{y}-\mathbf{C}_\mu\boldsymbol{\nu}_\mu)^T\text{diag}(\exp(-\mathbf{C}_\varepsilon\boldsymbol{\nu}_\varepsilon))(\mathbf{y}-\mathbf{C}_\mu\boldsymbol{\nu}_\mu)\\ -\tfrac{1}{2}\boldsymbol{\nu}_\mu^T\mathbf{B}\mu\boldsymbol{\nu}_\mu-\tfrac{1}{2}\boldsymbol{\nu}_\varepsilon^T\mathbf{B}_\varepsilon\boldsymbol{\nu}_\varepsilon\Big],$$

for $1\le r\le R_\mu$ we have

$$q(\sigma^2_{\mu,r})\propto\exp\Big[-\big(s_{\mu,r}+\tfrac{q_{\mu,r}}{2}+1\big)\ln(\sigma^2_{\mu,r})-\sigma^{-2}_{\mu,r}\Big\{t_{\mu,r}+\tfrac{1}{2}\text{tr}\Big(\mathbf{P}_{\mu,r}\mathbb{E}_q\Big(\mathbf{u}_{\mu,r}\mathbf{u}^T_{\mu,r}\Big)\Big)\Big\}\Big],$$

and for $1\le r\le R_\varepsilon$ we have

$$q(\sigma^2_{\varepsilon,r})\propto\exp\big[-\big(s_{\varepsilon,r}+\tfrac{q_{\varepsilon,r}}{2}+1\big)\ln(\sigma^2_{\varepsilon,r})-\sigma^{-2}_{\varepsilon,r}\big\{t_{\varepsilon,r}+\tfrac{1}{2}\text{tr}\big(\mathbf{P}_{\varepsilon,r}\mathbb{E}_q\big(\mathbf{u}_{\varepsilon,r}\mathbf{u}^T_{\varepsilon,r}\big)\big)\big\}\big].$$

We identify the q-densities for the $q(\sigma^2_{\mu,r})$'s and $q(\sigma^2_{\varepsilon,r})$'s as inverse-gamma densities with

$$q(\sigma^2_{\mu,r})=\text{dinvgamma}\big[\sigma^2_{\mu,r}\,|\,s_{\mu,r}+\tfrac{q_{\mu,r}}{2},\ t_{\mu,r}+\tfrac{1}{2}\text{tr}\big(\mathbf{P}_{\mu,r}\mathbb{E}_q\big(\mathbf{u}_{\mu,r}\mathbf{u}^T_{\mu,r}\big)\big)\big],\\ 1\le r\le R_\mu,$$
$$q(\sigma^2_{\varepsilon,r})=\text{dinvgamma}\big[\sigma^2_{\varepsilon,r}\,|\,s_{\varepsilon,r}+\tfrac{q_{\varepsilon,r}}{2},\ t_{\varepsilon,r}+\tfrac{1}{2}\text{tr}\big(\mathbf{P}_{\varepsilon,r}\mathbb{E}_q\big(\mathbf{u}_{\varepsilon,r}\mathbf{u}^T_{\varepsilon,r}\big)\big)\big],\\ 1\le r\le R_\varepsilon.$$

The optimal q-density does not take the form of a recognisable density, so we approximate $q(\boldsymbol{\nu}_\mu,\boldsymbol{\nu}_\varepsilon)$ by a multivariate Gaussian density using Laplace's method. To this end let

$$\mathbf{B}_\mu\ =\text{blockdiag}\big(\sigma^{-2}_{\mu,\beta}\mathbf{I}_{p_\mu},(\widetilde{s}_{\mu,1}/\widetilde{t}_{\mu,1})\mathbf{P}_{\mu,1},\ldots,(\widetilde{s}_{\mu,R_\mu}/\widetilde{t}_{\mu,R_\mu})\mathbf{P}_{R_\mu}\big)\quad\text{and}$$
$$\mathbf{B}_\varepsilon\ =\text{blockdiag}\big(\sigma^{-2}_{\varepsilon,\beta}\mathbf{I}_{p_\varepsilon},(\widetilde{s}_{\varepsilon,1}/\widetilde{t}_{\varepsilon,1})\mathbf{P}_{\varepsilon,1},\ldots,(\widetilde{s}_{\varepsilon,R_\varepsilon}/\widetilde{t}_{\varepsilon,R_\varepsilon})\mathbf{P}_{R_\varepsilon}\big).$$

Then the gradient function is given by

$$\mathbf{g}(\boldsymbol{\nu}_\mu,\boldsymbol{\nu}_\varepsilon)=\begin{bmatrix}\mathbf{C}^T_\mu\text{diag}(\mathbf{w})\mathbf{d}-\mathbf{B}_\mu\boldsymbol{\nu}_\mu\\ \tfrac{1}{2}\mathbf{C}^T_\varepsilon\big\{\mathbf{d}^2\odot\mathbf{w}-\mathbf{1}\big\}-\mathbf{B}_\varepsilon\boldsymbol{\nu}_\varepsilon\end{bmatrix},$$

where $\mathbf{w}=\exp(-\mathbf{C}_\varepsilon\boldsymbol{\nu}_\varepsilon)$, $\mathbf{d}=\mathbf{y}-\mathbf{C}_\mu\boldsymbol{\nu}_\mu$, and $\odot$ denotes the Hadamard product. Next, the Hessian function is given by

$$\mathbf{H}(\boldsymbol{\nu}_\mu,\boldsymbol{\nu}_\varepsilon)=\begin{bmatrix}-\mathbf{C}^T_\mu\text{diag}(\mathbf{w})\mathbf{C}_\mu-\mathbf{B}_\mu & -\mathbf{C}^T_\mu\text{diag}(\mathbf{d}\odot\mathbf{w})\mathbf{C}_\varepsilon\\ -\mathbf{C}^T_\mu\text{diag}(\mathbf{d}\odot\mathbf{w})\mathbf{C}_\varepsilon & -\tfrac{1}{2}\mathbf{C}^T_\varepsilon\text{diag}(\mathbf{d}^2\odot\mathbf{w})\mathbf{C}_\varepsilon-\mathbf{B}_\varepsilon\end{bmatrix}.$$

Then updates for Laplace's method are of the form

$$\begin{aligned}
\widetilde{\boldsymbol{\Sigma}}_{\boldsymbol{\nu}}^{(t+1)} &= \left[-\mathbf{H}(\widetilde{\boldsymbol{\mu}}_{\mu}^{(t)}, \widetilde{\boldsymbol{\mu}}_{\varepsilon}^{(t)})\right]^{-1}, \\
\begin{bmatrix} \widetilde{\boldsymbol{\mu}}_{\boldsymbol{\nu}_\mu}^{(t+1)} \\ \widetilde{\boldsymbol{\mu}}_{\boldsymbol{\nu}_\varepsilon}^{(t+1)} \end{bmatrix} &= \begin{bmatrix} \widetilde{\boldsymbol{\mu}}_{\boldsymbol{\nu}_\mu}^{(t)} \\ \widetilde{\boldsymbol{\mu}}_{\boldsymbol{\nu}_\varepsilon}^{(t)} \end{bmatrix} + \widetilde{\boldsymbol{\Sigma}}_{\boldsymbol{\nu}}^{(t+1)} \mathbf{g}(\widetilde{\boldsymbol{\nu}}_{\mu}^{(t)}, \widetilde{\boldsymbol{\nu}}_{\varepsilon}^{(t)})
\end{aligned}$$

and upon convergence

$$q(\boldsymbol{\nu}_\mu, \boldsymbol{\nu}_\varepsilon) \approx \text{dmvnorm}\left[\left(\begin{array}{c} \boldsymbol{\nu}_\mu \\ \boldsymbol{\nu}_\varepsilon \end{array}\right) \Big| \left(\begin{array}{c} \widetilde{\boldsymbol{\mu}}_{\boldsymbol{\nu}_\mu} \\ \widetilde{\boldsymbol{\mu}}_{\boldsymbol{\nu}_\varepsilon} \end{array}\right), \widetilde{\boldsymbol{\Sigma}}_{\boldsymbol{\nu}}\right].$$

The algorithm for fitting a GAM with heteroscedastic variance using VB is summarised in Algorithm 3.

6.5.1 Milan air pollution example

This example is based on the Milan air pollution data set from [29]. These data consists of daily data over 10 years for mortality and several other meteorological variables for the city of Milan, Italy including 'total suspended particles in ambient air' (`TSP`), 'number of days since 31 December 1979' (`day.num`), 'mean daily temperature in degrees Celcius' (`mean.temp`) and 'relative humidity' (`rel.humid`).

For this example we will use the abovementioned predictors with $d = 4$. We will fit a model of the form $y_i \sim f(\mathbf{x}_i) + \varepsilon_i$, where $\varepsilon_i \sim N(0, \sigma_\varepsilon^2)$, $1 \le i \le n$, and

$$\begin{aligned}
f(\mathbf{x}_i) &= \beta_0 + \texttt{TSP}_i\beta_1 + \texttt{day.num}_i\beta_2 + \texttt{mean.temp}_i\beta_3 + \texttt{rel.humid}_i\beta_4 \\
&\quad + f_2(\texttt{mean.temp}_i) + f_3(\texttt{mean.temp}_i) + f_4(\texttt{rel.humid}_i).
\end{aligned}$$

Using the semiparametric framework for penalised splines described in Section 6.2.3 the matrix $\mathbf{X}$ contains an intercept term along with linear terms for $\texttt{TSP}_i$, $\texttt{day.num}_i$, $\texttt{mean.temp}_i$ and $\texttt{rel.humid}_i$, while the matrices $\mathbf{Z}_2$, $\mathbf{Z}_3$ and $\mathbf{Z}_4$ are constructed using O-spline bases for the variables $\texttt{day.num}_i$, $\texttt{mean.temp}_i$ and $\texttt{rel.humid}_i$, respectively. A minor modification of Algorithm 1 is required to fit this model, where the index r ranges from 2 to 4 rather than 1 to R.

Fig. 6.4 illustrates the fitted functions for each covariate for the Milan air pollution data set and 95% credible intervals for the mean. Fig. 6.5 gives a blown-up plot of the mean function for `day` along with 95% credible intervals. From these we see that the VB approximation gives a quite

Algorithm 3 Fitting a GAM with heteroscedastic variance using VB.

Require: $\widetilde{t}_{\mu,r},\ 1 \le r \le R_\mu; \qquad \widetilde{t}_{\varepsilon,r},\ 1 \le r \le R_\varepsilon$

Set $\widetilde{s}_{\mu,r} = s_{\mu,r} + \frac{q_{\mu,r}}{2}, \qquad 1 \le r \le R_\mu$

Set $\widetilde{s}_{\varepsilon,r} = s_{\varepsilon,r} + \frac{q_{\varepsilon,r}}{2}, \qquad 1 \le r \le R_\varepsilon$

while changes in $\widetilde{t}_{\mu,r}$ and $\widetilde{t}_{\varepsilon,r}$ are too large **do**

$\mathbf{B}_\mu \leftarrow \text{blockdiag}\left(\sigma_{\mu,\beta}^{-2}\mathbf{I}_{p_\mu}, (\widetilde{s}_{\mu,1}/\widetilde{t}_{\mu,1})\mathbf{P}_{\mu,1}, \ldots, (\widetilde{s}_{\mu,R_\mu}/\widetilde{t}_{\mu,R_\mu})\mathbf{P}_{R_\mu}\right)$

$\mathbf{B}_\varepsilon \leftarrow \text{blockdiag}\left(\sigma_{\varepsilon,\beta}^{-2}\mathbf{I}_{p_\varepsilon}, (\widetilde{s}_{\varepsilon,1}/\widetilde{t}_{\varepsilon,1})\mathbf{P}_{\varepsilon,1}, \ldots, (\widetilde{s}_{\varepsilon,R_\varepsilon}/\widetilde{t}_{\varepsilon,R_\varepsilon})\mathbf{P}_{R_\varepsilon}\right)$

$t = 0; \qquad \widetilde{\boldsymbol{\mu}}_{\mathbf{v}_\mu}^{(0)} \leftarrow \widetilde{\boldsymbol{\mu}}_{\mathbf{v}_\mu}; \qquad \widetilde{\boldsymbol{\mu}}_{\mathbf{v}_\varepsilon}^{(0)} \leftarrow \widetilde{\boldsymbol{\mu}}_{\mathbf{v}_\varepsilon}$

repeat

$\mathbf{d} \leftarrow \mathbf{y} - \mathbf{C}_\mu \widetilde{\boldsymbol{\mu}}_{\mathbf{v}_\mu}^{(t)}; \qquad \mathbf{w} \leftarrow \exp(-\mathbf{C}_\varepsilon \widetilde{\boldsymbol{\mu}}_{\mathbf{v}_\varepsilon}^{(t)})$

$$\mathbf{g}(\widetilde{\boldsymbol{\mu}}_\mu^{(t)}, \widetilde{\boldsymbol{\mu}}_\varepsilon^{(t)}) \leftarrow \begin{bmatrix} \mathbf{C}_\mu^T \text{diag}(\mathbf{w})\mathbf{d} - \mathbf{B}_\mu \widetilde{\boldsymbol{\mu}}_\mu^{(t)} \\ \frac{1}{2}\mathbf{C}_\varepsilon^T \{\mathbf{d}^2 \odot \mathbf{w} - \mathbf{1}\} - \mathbf{B}_\varepsilon \widetilde{\boldsymbol{\mu}}_\varepsilon^{(t)} \end{bmatrix}$$

$$\mathbf{H}(\widetilde{\boldsymbol{\mu}}_\mu^{(t)}, \widetilde{\boldsymbol{\mu}}_\varepsilon^{(t)}) \leftarrow \begin{bmatrix} -\mathbf{C}_\mu^T \text{diag}(\mathbf{w})\mathbf{C}_\mu - \mathbf{B}_\mu & -\mathbf{C}_\mu^T \text{diag}(\mathbf{d} \odot \mathbf{w})\mathbf{C}_\varepsilon \\ -\mathbf{C}_\mu^T \text{diag}(\mathbf{d} \odot \mathbf{w})\mathbf{C}_\varepsilon & -\frac{1}{2}\mathbf{C}_\varepsilon^T \text{diag}(\mathbf{d}^2 \odot \mathbf{w})\mathbf{C}_\varepsilon - \mathbf{B}_\varepsilon \end{bmatrix}$$

$$\widetilde{\boldsymbol{\Sigma}}_{\mathbf{v}}^{(t+1)} \leftarrow \left[-\mathbf{H}(\widetilde{\boldsymbol{\mu}}_\mu^{(t)}, \widetilde{\boldsymbol{\mu}}_\varepsilon^{(t)})\right]^{-1}$$

$$\begin{bmatrix} \widetilde{\boldsymbol{\mu}}_{\mathbf{v}_\mu}^{(t+1)} \\ \widetilde{\boldsymbol{\mu}}_{\mathbf{v}_\varepsilon}^{(t+1)} \end{bmatrix} \leftarrow \begin{bmatrix} \widetilde{\boldsymbol{\mu}}_{\mathbf{v}_\mu}^{(t)} \\ \widetilde{\boldsymbol{\mu}}_{\mathbf{v}_\varepsilon}^{(t)} \end{bmatrix} + \widetilde{\boldsymbol{\Sigma}}_{\mathbf{v}}^{(t+1)} \mathbf{g}(\widetilde{\boldsymbol{\mu}}_\mu^{(t)}, \widetilde{\boldsymbol{\mu}}_\varepsilon^{(t)})$$

$t \leftarrow t + 1$

until $\|\mathbf{g}(\widetilde{\boldsymbol{\mu}}_\mu^{(t)}, \widetilde{\boldsymbol{\mu}}_\varepsilon^{(t)})\|_\infty < \tau$

$\widetilde{\boldsymbol{\mu}}_{\mathbf{v}_\mu} \leftarrow \widetilde{\boldsymbol{\mu}}_{\mathbf{v}_\mu}^{(t)}; \qquad \widetilde{\boldsymbol{\mu}}_{\mathbf{v}_\varepsilon} \leftarrow \widetilde{\boldsymbol{\mu}}_{\mathbf{v}_\varepsilon}^{(t)}; \qquad \widetilde{\boldsymbol{\Sigma}}_{\mathbf{v}} \leftarrow \widetilde{\boldsymbol{\Sigma}}_{\mathbf{v}}^{(t)}$

$\widetilde{t}_{\mu,r} \leftarrow t_{\mu,r} + \frac{1}{2}\widetilde{\boldsymbol{\mu}}_{\mathbf{u}_{\mu,r}}^T \mathbf{P}_{\mu,r}\widetilde{\boldsymbol{\mu}}_{\mathbf{u}_{\mu,r}} + \frac{1}{2}\text{tr}(\mathbf{P}_{\mu,r}\widetilde{\boldsymbol{\Sigma}}_{\mathbf{u}_{\mu,r}}), \qquad 1 \le r \le R_\mu$

$\widetilde{t}_{\varepsilon,r} \leftarrow t_{\varepsilon,r} + \frac{1}{2}\widetilde{\boldsymbol{\mu}}_{\mathbf{u}_{\varepsilon,r}}^T \mathbf{P}_{\varepsilon,r}\widetilde{\boldsymbol{\mu}}_{\mathbf{u}_{\varepsilon,r}} + \frac{1}{2}\text{tr}(\mathbf{P}_{\varepsilon,r}\widetilde{\boldsymbol{\Sigma}}_{\mathbf{u}_{\varepsilon,r}}), \qquad 1 \le r \le R_\varepsilon$

end while

comparable fit to those obtained by MCMC, except for the mean of the smoothed function for day where the posterior credible intervals are noticeably underestimated. For all other fitted functions the approximate 95% credible intervals obtained using VB are only slightly underestimated.

6.6 Generalised additive negative binomial model

Models for count data are quite common in statistics where a natural model for count data might involve the Poisson distribution. This model however

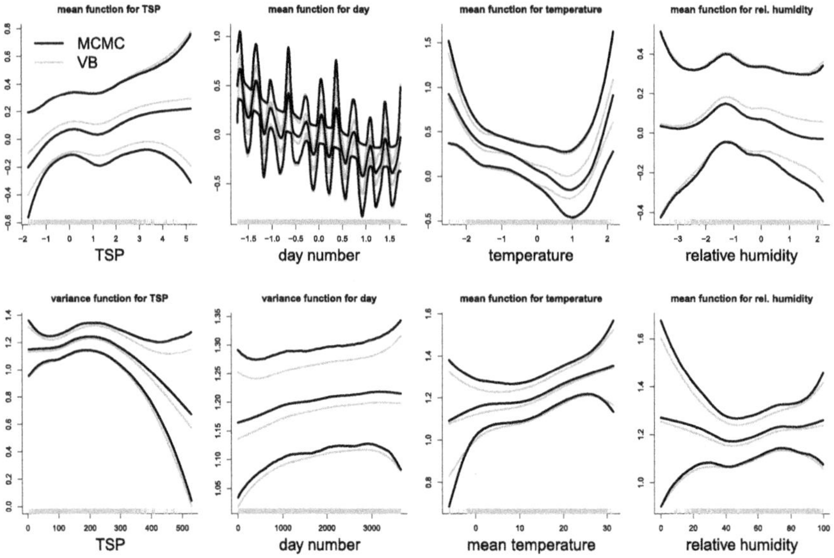

Figure 6.4 ***Fits of the Milan air pollution data using VB and MCMC (via*** `stan`***) of the heteroscedastic nonparametric regression model.*** Top four panels: Posterior mean and pointwise 95% credible sets for the four smoothed functions corresponding to the mean. Bottom four panels: Posterior means and pointwise 95% credible sets for the four variance functions.

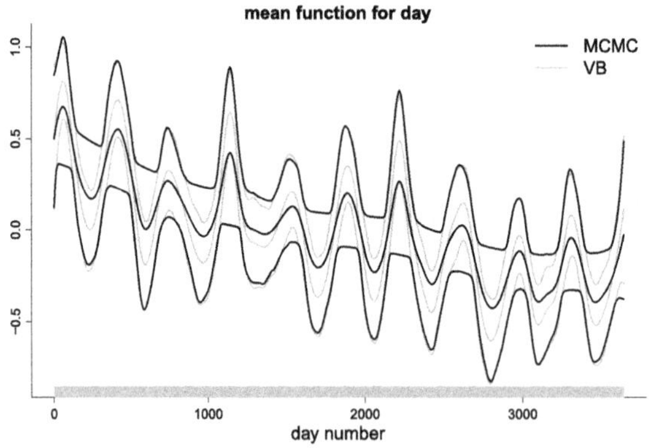

Figure 6.5 ***Fit of the Milan air pollution data using VB and MCMC (via*** `stan`***) of the heteroscedastic nonparametric regression model.*** An enlarged plot of the posterior means and pointwise 95% credible sets for the mean fit for day.

implicitly assumes equality of mean and variance, which is often not met in real data. More commonly data exhibit greater variance than expected under the assumed model (called overdispersion). An alternative model for count data where the response variance is greater than the response mean uses the negative binomial distribution. For the negative binomial distribution, if

$$Y \sim \text{Negative-Binomial}(\mu, \kappa), \quad \text{then} \quad \mathbb{E}(Y) = \mu \quad \text{and}$$
$$\text{Var}(Y) = \mu + \mu^2/\kappa,$$

where we have used the parameterisation of the density function given by

$$\text{dnegbin}(y|\mu, \kappa) = \binom{y+\kappa-1}{y}\left(\frac{\mu}{\mu+\kappa}\right)^y\left(\frac{\kappa}{\mu+\kappa}\right)^\kappa.$$

Using penalised spline infrastructure developed we set

$$\mu_i = \exp\left[(\mathbf{X}\boldsymbol{\beta} + \mathbf{Z}\mathbf{u})_i\right],$$

with priors (6.2) and (6.3) for $\mathbf{u}$, and both $\boldsymbol{\beta}$ and $\boldsymbol{\sigma}^2$, respectively. For κ we will adopt the prior $\kappa \sim \text{Gamma}(s_\kappa, t_\kappa)$.

We will use a VB-Laplace approximation corresponding to the factorisation

$$q(\boldsymbol{\nu}, \kappa, \boldsymbol{\sigma}_u^2) = q(\boldsymbol{\nu}, \kappa)q(\boldsymbol{\sigma}_u^2).$$

Then

$$\begin{aligned} q(\boldsymbol{\nu}, \kappa) &\propto \exp\big[\mathbf{y}^T\mathbf{C}\boldsymbol{\nu} - (\mathbf{y} + \kappa\mathbf{1})^T \ln(\kappa + \exp(\mathbf{C}\boldsymbol{\nu})) \\ &\quad -\tfrac{1}{2}\boldsymbol{\nu}^T\mathbf{B}\boldsymbol{\nu} + \mathbf{1}^T \ln\Gamma(\mathbf{y} + \kappa\mathbf{1}) \\ &\quad -n\ln\Gamma(\kappa) + n\kappa\ln(\kappa) + (s_\kappa - 1)\ln(\kappa) - t_\kappa\kappa\big], \\ q(\sigma_r^2) &= \text{dinvgamma}\left[\sigma_r^2|\widetilde{s}_r, \widetilde{t}_r\right], \qquad 1 \le r \le R. \end{aligned}$$

For each $1 \le r \le R$ we have

$$\widetilde{s}_r = s_r + \tfrac{q_r}{2} \qquad \text{and} \qquad \widetilde{t}_r = t_r + \tfrac{1}{2}\widetilde{\boldsymbol{\mu}}_{\mathbf{u}_r}^T\mathbf{P}_r\widetilde{\boldsymbol{\mu}}_{\mathbf{u}_r} + \tfrac{1}{2}\text{tr}(\mathbf{P}_r\widetilde{\boldsymbol{\Sigma}}_{\mathbf{u}_r}),$$

and $\mathbf{B} = \text{blockdiag}\left(\sigma_\beta^{-2}\mathbf{I}_p, (\widetilde{s}_1/\widetilde{t}_1)\mathbf{P}_1, \ldots, (\widetilde{s}_R/\widetilde{t}_R)\mathbf{P}_R\right)$.

Direct application of Newton–Raphson optimisation can lead to problems due to the restriction $\kappa > 0$. For this reason we use the transformation $\kappa = \exp(k)$. Then $q(\boldsymbol{\nu}, \kappa) \propto \exp[f(\boldsymbol{\nu}, k)]$, where

$$\begin{aligned} f(\boldsymbol{\nu}, k) &= \mathbf{y}^T\mathbf{C}\boldsymbol{\nu} - (\mathbf{y} + \exp(k)\mathbf{1})^T \ln(\exp(k) + \exp(\mathbf{C}\boldsymbol{\nu})) - \tfrac{1}{2}\boldsymbol{\nu}^T\mathbf{B}\boldsymbol{\nu} \\ &\quad +\mathbf{1}^T \ln\Gamma(\mathbf{y} + \exp(k)\mathbf{1}) - n\ln\Gamma(\exp(k)) + nk\exp(k) \\ &\quad +(s_\kappa - 1)k - t_\kappa \exp(k). \end{aligned}$$

Then

$$
\begin{aligned}
\frac{\partial f(\boldsymbol{\nu},k)}{\partial \boldsymbol{\nu}} &= \mathbf{C}^T\left\{\mathbf{y} - \frac{\mathbf{y}+\exp(k)}{\exp(k)+\exp(\mathbf{C}\boldsymbol{\nu})}\right\} - \mathbf{B}\boldsymbol{\nu},\\
\frac{\partial f(\boldsymbol{\nu},k)}{\partial k} = \frac{\partial f(\boldsymbol{\nu},k)}{\partial \kappa}\frac{\partial \kappa}{\dot{\mathrm{k}}} &= \kappa\Big\{\mathbf{1}^T\psi(\mathbf{y}+\kappa\mathbf{1}) - \mathbf{1}^T\ln(\kappa+\exp(\mathbf{C}\boldsymbol{\nu}))\\
&\quad -\mathbf{1}^T\left(\frac{\mathbf{y}+\kappa\mathbf{1}}{\kappa+\exp(\mathbf{C}\boldsymbol{\nu})}\right)\\
&\quad -n\psi(\kappa)+n\ln(\kappa)+n+(s_k-1)\kappa^{-1}+t_k\Big\}.
\end{aligned}
$$

For this problem we use BFGS optimisation to find the maximiser of f and make the approximation $q(\boldsymbol{\nu},k)\approx N(\widetilde{\boldsymbol{\mu}},\widetilde{\boldsymbol{\Sigma}})$, where $\widetilde{\boldsymbol{\mu}}$ is the maximiser of f and $\widetilde{\boldsymbol{\Sigma}}$ is an approximation of the inverse Hessian matrix evaluated at $\widetilde{\boldsymbol{\mu}}$. The marginal posterior distribution of k is normal and after transformation the marginal posterior distribution of κ is log-normal. Algorithm 4 summarises our approach.

Algorithm 4 Fitting a Negative Binomial Additive Model using VB.

Require: $\widetilde{t}_r$, $1\leq r\leq R$;
  Set $\widetilde{s}_r = s_r + \frac{q_r}{2}$, $\quad 1\leq r\leq R$
  while change in $\widetilde{t}_r$ is too large **do**
    $\mathbf{b}\leftarrow \text{blockdiag}\left(\sigma_\beta^{-2}\mathbf{I}_p, (\widetilde{s}_1/\widetilde{t}_1)\mathbf{P}_1,\ldots,(\widetilde{s}_R/\widetilde{t}_R)\mathbf{P}_R\right)$
    Maximise $f(\boldsymbol{\nu},k)$ with respect to $\boldsymbol{\nu}$ and k via BFGS optimisation using

$$
\mathbf{g}(\boldsymbol{\nu},k) = \begin{bmatrix} \frac{\partial f(\boldsymbol{\nu},k)}{\partial \boldsymbol{\nu}} \\ \frac{\partial f(\boldsymbol{\nu},k)}{\partial k} \end{bmatrix}
$$

    to obtain $\widetilde{\boldsymbol{\mu}}$ and $\widetilde{\boldsymbol{\Sigma}}$.
    $\widetilde{t}_r \leftarrow t_r + \frac{1}{2}\widetilde{\boldsymbol{\mu}}_{\mathbf{u}_r}^T\mathbf{P}_r\widetilde{\boldsymbol{\mu}}_{\mathbf{u}_r} + \frac{1}{2}\text{tr}(\mathbf{P}_r\widetilde{\boldsymbol{\Sigma}}_{\mathbf{u}_r})$, $\quad 1\leq r\leq R$
  end while

6.6.1 Lung cancer data

In this example we revisit the data set and model given in [34]. The response variable data consist of adduct counts (`adductCount`) for 77 former smokers in a lung cancer study (source: [38]). Four predictors are available:

- `ageInit`: Age of smoking initiation.
- `yearsSmoking`: Number of years of smoking.

- `cigsPerDay`: Number of cigarettes smoked per day.
- `yearsSinceQuit`: Number of years since quitting.

As explained in [34], `adductCount` is overdispersed and a Poisson additive model is not realistic. They make a case for a model of the following form:

$$\texttt{adductCount}_i|\mu_i,\kappa \overset{\text{ind.}}{\sim} \text{Negative-Binomial}(\mu_i,\kappa), \tag{6.16}$$

where

$$\mu_i = \exp\big[f_1(\texttt{ageInit}_i) + f_2(\texttt{yearsSmoking}_i) + f_3(\texttt{yearsSinceQuit}_i) + f_4(\texttt{cigsPerDay}_i)\big],$$

where the f_j's are smooth functions.

[34] devised kernel methods to fit negative binomial additive models such as (6.16). Instead we take a hierarchical Bayesian approach with penalised spline modelling for the f_j's (Section 6.2.2). Section 6.2.3 describes the choice of priors for the fixed effects and standard deviation parameters.

Fig. 6.6 illustrates the fitted functions along with 95% confidence intervals on the fitted means. Fig. 6.7 illustrates posterior distribution summaries for $\boldsymbol{\sigma}^2$ and κ. Again we see that the estimated posterior fitted functions and posterior densities for VB are quite close to those using MCMC, but that the posterior variances are underestimated. The computational time using VB is 17 seconds while for `stan` it is 107 seconds.

6.7 Logistic regression with missing covariates

Missing data are a ubiquitous problem in real data analysis. The most common approach to dealing with missing data is by simply omitting a combination of samples/covariates in order to obtain a complete data set which is then analysed using standard tools. However, depending on the modelling assumptions made, this can lead to biased estimates of the model parameters if these modelling assumptions do not hold.

To fix ideas we will focus on the problem where we have a completely observed binary response $\mathbf{y} = (y_1, \ldots, y_n)^T$ where each $y_i \in \{0, 1\}$ and matrix of covariate $\mathbf{X} \in \mathbb{R}^{n\times d}$, where $\mathbf{x}_i$ denotes the ith row of $\mathbf{X}$ and certain elements of $\mathbf{X}$ are observed and others are not observed or missing. We also assume that we know which elements of $\mathbf{X}$ are observed. This knowledge

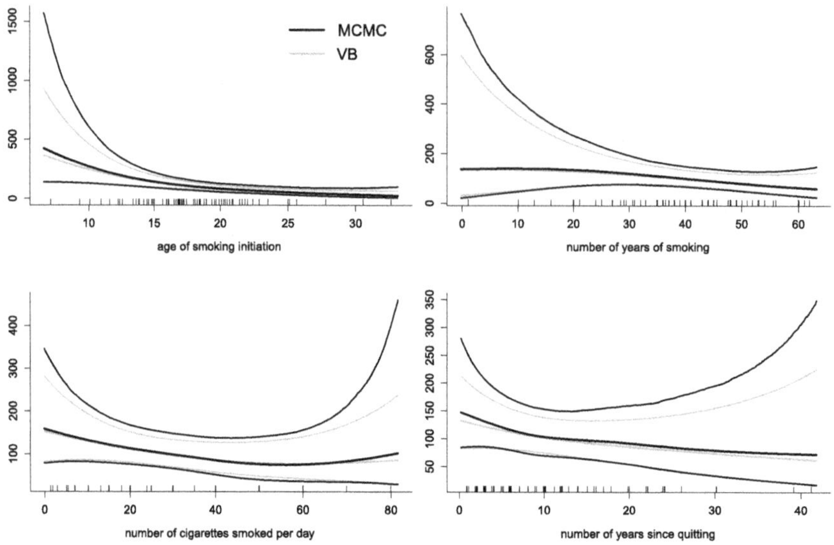

Figure 6.6 ***Fits of the Hauser respiratory experiment data using VB and MCMC (via*** `stan`***) of the robust nonparametric regression model.*** Posterior mean and pointwise 95% credible sets for the regression function.

is encoded in a matrix $\mathbf{R} \in \mathbb{R}^{n \times d}$ whose elements are

$$r_{ij} = \begin{cases} 1 & \text{if } x_{id} \text{ is observed,} \\ 0 & \text{if } x_{id} \text{ is missing.} \end{cases}$$

Similarly we denote the ith row of $\mathbf{R}$ by $\mathbf{r}_i$.

We will assume that the joint model for $(\mathbf{y}, \mathbf{X}, \mathbf{R})$ is of the form

$$p(\mathbf{y}, \mathbf{X}, \mathbf{R}|\boldsymbol{\theta}) = \prod_{i=1}^{n} p(y_i|\mathbf{x}_i, \boldsymbol{\theta}_Y) p(\mathbf{r}_i|\mathbf{x}_i, \boldsymbol{\theta}_R) p(\mathbf{x}_i|\boldsymbol{\theta}_X),$$

where we have assumed conditional independence, the components $p(y_i|\mathbf{x}_i, \boldsymbol{\theta}_Y)$, $p(\mathbf{r}_i|\mathbf{x}_i, \boldsymbol{\theta}_R)$, and $p(\mathbf{x}_i|\boldsymbol{\theta}_X)$ model the response, missing data mechanism and covariate distributions, respectively, and the parameter vectors $\boldsymbol{\theta}_Y$, $\boldsymbol{\theta}_R$ and $\boldsymbol{\theta}_X$ correspond to these respective modelling components with $\boldsymbol{\theta} = (\boldsymbol{\theta}_Y, \boldsymbol{\theta}_R, \boldsymbol{\theta}_X)$. Note that if the distribution of $\mathbf{r}_i$ does not depend on any missing values and the priors for $(\boldsymbol{\theta}_Y, \boldsymbol{\theta}_X)$ are independent of $\boldsymbol{\theta}_R$, then inferences on $(\boldsymbol{\theta}_Y, \boldsymbol{\theta}_X)$ can be performed separately from $\boldsymbol{\theta}_R$ since $p(\boldsymbol{\theta}|\mathcal{D}) = p(\boldsymbol{\theta}_Y, \boldsymbol{\theta}_X|\mathcal{D}) p(\boldsymbol{\theta}_R|\mathcal{D})$. In this case the missing data mechanism $p(\mathbf{r}_i|\mathbf{x}_i, \boldsymbol{\theta}_R)$ is said to be *ignorable*, and *nonignorable* otherwise.

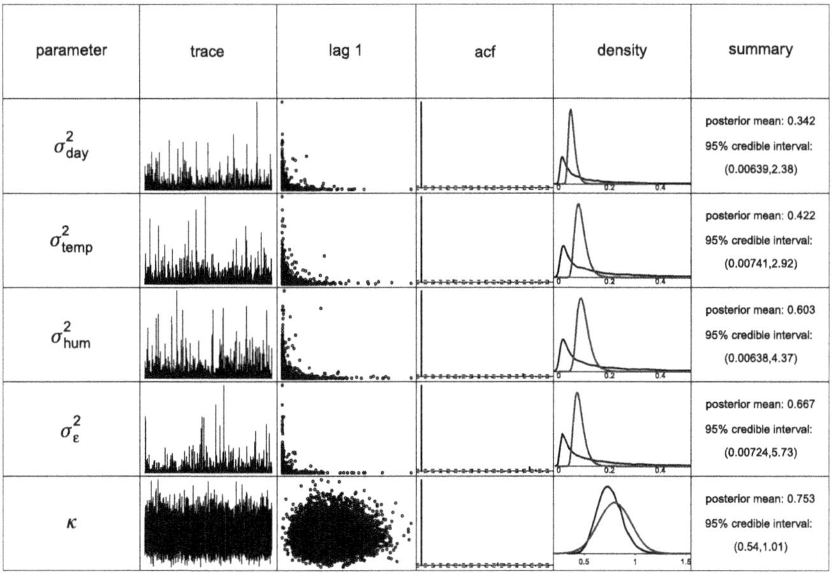

From Reptile Communities

Figure 6.7 ***Summary of MCMC-based inference for parameters in the model of the Lung cancer data.*** The columns are: parameter, trace plot of MCMC sample, plot of sample against 1-lagged sample, sample autocorrelation function, kernel estimates of posterior densities, and basic numerical summaries. Blue (dark grey in print version) densities correspond to posterior density approximations obtained using VB.

Assuming an ignorable missing data mechanism we will model $(y_i, \mathbf{x}_i)$ via

$$\begin{aligned} y_i|\boldsymbol{\beta}, \mathbf{x}_i &\sim \text{Bernoulli}\left[\text{expit}\left(\beta_0 + \beta_1 x_{i1} + \ldots + \beta_d x_{id}\right)\right], \\ \mathbf{x}_i|\boldsymbol{\mu}, \boldsymbol{\Sigma} &\sim N(\boldsymbol{\mu}, \boldsymbol{\Sigma}) \qquad \text{and} \qquad r_{ij}|\rho_j \sim \text{Bernoulli}(\rho_j), \end{aligned}$$

where $\text{expit}(x) = [1 + \exp(-x)]^{-1}$. Then $\ln p(\mathbf{y}|\mathbf{X}, \boldsymbol{\beta}) = \mathbf{y}^T\mathbf{C}\boldsymbol{\beta} - \mathbf{1}^T b(\mathbf{C}\boldsymbol{\beta})$, where the matrix $\mathbf{X}$ is the $n \times d$ matrix whose ith row is $\mathbf{x}_i$, $\mathbf{C} = [\mathbf{1}, \mathbf{X}]$, $\boldsymbol{\beta} = (\beta_0, \beta_1, \ldots, \beta_d)^T$ and $b(x) = \ln(1 + \exp(x))$.

We will employ the priors

$$\boldsymbol{\beta} \sim N(\mathbf{0}, \sigma_\beta^2 \mathbf{I}), \qquad \boldsymbol{\mu}_x|\boldsymbol{\Sigma}_x \sim N(\mathbf{0}, \sigma_\mu^2 \boldsymbol{\Sigma}_x) \qquad \text{and} \qquad \boldsymbol{\Sigma}_x \sim IW(\boldsymbol{\Psi}_\Sigma, \nu_\Sigma),$$

where $\sigma_\beta^2 = \sigma_\mu^2 = 10^8$, $\boldsymbol{\Psi} = 0.01\mathbf{I}$ and $\nu = d$.

Let $\mathcal{C} = \{j\colon r_{ij} = 0 \text{ for some } j = 1, \ldots, p\}$ and $\mathcal{M}_j = \{i\colon r_{ij} = 0\}$, $j = 1, \ldots, p$. We will consider a VB approximation corresponding to a factorisation of the form

$$q(\boldsymbol{\beta}, \boldsymbol{\mu}, \boldsymbol{\Sigma}, \mathbf{X}_{\mathcal{M}}) = q(\boldsymbol{\beta})q(\boldsymbol{\mu})q(\boldsymbol{\Sigma})\prod_{j\in C} q(\mathbf{x}_{\mathcal{M}_j,j}),$$

where $\mathbf{X}_{\mathcal{M}}$ denotes the missing x_{ij}'s. Given the form for $q(\boldsymbol{\beta}, \boldsymbol{\mu}, \boldsymbol{\Sigma}, \mathbf{X}_{\mathcal{M}})$ the q-densities for $\boldsymbol{\beta}$, $\boldsymbol{\mu}_x$, $\boldsymbol{\Sigma}_x$ and the missing x_{ij}'s are given by

$$\begin{aligned}
q(\boldsymbol{\beta}) &\propto \exp\left[\mathbf{y}^T\widetilde{\mathbf{C}}\boldsymbol{\beta} - \mathbf{1}^T\mathbb{E}_{-q(\boldsymbol{\beta})}(b(\mathbf{C}\boldsymbol{\beta})) - \tfrac{1}{2\sigma_\beta^2}\|\boldsymbol{\beta}\|^2\right],\\
q(\boldsymbol{\mu}_x) &= \text{dmvnorm}\left[\boldsymbol{\mu} \,|\, \widetilde{\boldsymbol{\mu}}_\mu, \widetilde{\boldsymbol{\Sigma}}_\mu\right], \qquad q(\boldsymbol{\Sigma}_x) = \text{diw}\left[\boldsymbol{\Sigma} \,|\, \widetilde{\boldsymbol{\Psi}}, \widetilde{\nu}\right],\\
q(\mathbf{x}_{\mathcal{M}_j,j}) &= \prod_{i:\ r_{ij}=0} q(\mathbf{x}_{ij}),
\end{aligned}$$

where

$$\begin{aligned}
\widetilde{\boldsymbol{\mu}}_\mu &= \frac{\mathbf{1}^T\widetilde{\mathbf{x}}}{n+\sigma_\mu^{-2}}, & \widetilde{\boldsymbol{\Sigma}}_\mu &= \frac{\widetilde{\boldsymbol{\Omega}}_x^{-1}}{n+\sigma_\mu^{-2}},\\
\widetilde{\boldsymbol{\Psi}} &= \boldsymbol{\Psi} + n\widetilde{\boldsymbol{\Sigma}}_\mu + \sum_{i=1}^n (\widetilde{\mathbf{x}}_i - \widetilde{\boldsymbol{\mu}}_\mu)(\widetilde{\mathbf{x}}_i - \widetilde{\boldsymbol{\mu}}_\mu)^T, & \widetilde{\nu} &= n + d + \nu \qquad \text{and}
\end{aligned}$$

$$\begin{aligned}
q(\mathbf{x}_{ij}) &\propto \exp\Big[-\tfrac{1}{2}\widetilde{\Omega}_{x,jj}x_{ij}^2 + x_{ij}\left\{(\widetilde{\boldsymbol{\Omega}}_x\widetilde{\boldsymbol{\mu}}_x)_j - \boldsymbol{\Omega}_{x,j,-j}\widetilde{\mathbf{x}}_{i,-j} + y_i\widetilde{\mu}_{\beta,j}\right\}\\
&\quad -\mathbb{E}_q\left\{b(\mathbf{x}_i^T\boldsymbol{\beta})\right\}\Big],
\end{aligned}$$

with $\widetilde{\boldsymbol{\Omega}}_x = \widetilde{\boldsymbol{\Sigma}}_x^{-1}$, $\widetilde{\mathbf{C}} = [\mathbf{1}, \widetilde{\mathbf{X}}]$,

$$[\widetilde{\mathbf{x}}_i]_j = \widetilde{x}_{ij} = \begin{cases} x_{ij} & \text{if } r_{ij} = 1,\\ \mathbb{E}_q(x_{ij}) & \text{if } r_{ij} = 0,\end{cases}$$

and similarly

$$[\widetilde{\mathbf{X}}]_{ij} = \begin{cases} x_{ij} & \text{if } r_{ij} = 1,\\ \widetilde{x}_{ij} & \text{if } r_{ij} = 0.\end{cases}$$

Calculation of the normalising constant for $q(\boldsymbol{\beta})$ is hampered by three things: (a) $\mathbb{E}_q(\mathbf{X})$, (b) $\mathbb{E}_q(\ln(1+\exp(\mathbf{X}\boldsymbol{\beta})))$ and (c) integrating the result with respect to $\boldsymbol{\beta}$. Furthermore we have the problem of finding the normalising constant for the $q(x_{ij})$'s for the missing x_{ij}'s.

If we use the first-order delta method approximation for $q(\boldsymbol{\beta})$ for the expectations with respect to all densities except $q(\boldsymbol{\beta})$ we obtain

$$q(\boldsymbol{\beta}) \overset{\text{approx.}}{\propto} \exp\left[\mathbf{y}^T\widetilde{\mathbf{C}}\boldsymbol{\beta} - \mathbf{1}^Tb(\widetilde{\mathbf{C}}\boldsymbol{\beta}) - \tfrac{1}{2\sigma_\beta^2}\|\boldsymbol{\beta}\|^2\right].$$

We then apply a Laplace approximation. Let $\widetilde{\boldsymbol{\mu}}_{\boldsymbol{\beta}}^{(t)}$ be the current approximate posterior mean for $\boldsymbol{\beta}$. Then the Newton–Raphson updates are of the form

$$\begin{aligned}\widetilde{\boldsymbol{\Sigma}}_{\boldsymbol{\beta}}^{(t+1)} &= \left[\widetilde{\mathbf{C}}^T \text{diag}(b''(\widetilde{\mathbf{C}}\widetilde{\boldsymbol{\mu}}_{\boldsymbol{\beta}}^{(t)}))\widetilde{\mathbf{C}} + \sigma_{\beta}^{-2}\mathbf{I}\right]^{-1},\\ \widetilde{\boldsymbol{\mu}}_{\boldsymbol{\beta}}^{(t+1)} &= \widetilde{\boldsymbol{\mu}}_{\boldsymbol{\beta}}^{(t)} + \widetilde{\boldsymbol{\Sigma}}_{\boldsymbol{\beta}}^{(t+1)} \left[\widetilde{\mathbf{C}}^T \left\{\mathbf{y} - b'(\widetilde{\mathbf{C}}\widetilde{\boldsymbol{\mu}}_{\boldsymbol{\beta}}^{(t)})\right\} - \widetilde{\boldsymbol{\mu}}_{\boldsymbol{\beta}}^{(t)}/\sigma_{\beta}^2\right].\end{aligned}$$

These updates are applied until $\|\widetilde{\boldsymbol{\mu}}_{\boldsymbol{\beta}}^{(t+1)} - \widetilde{\boldsymbol{\mu}}_{\boldsymbol{\beta}}^{(t)}\|_{\infty} < \tau$, where $\tau = 10^{-5}$. Let $\widetilde{\boldsymbol{\mu}}_{\boldsymbol{\beta}}$ and $\widetilde{\boldsymbol{\Sigma}}_{\boldsymbol{\beta}}$ be the converged values upon completion of this process. Then

$$q(\boldsymbol{\beta}) \approx \text{dmvnorm}(\boldsymbol{\beta} \mid \widetilde{\boldsymbol{\mu}}_{\boldsymbol{\beta}}, \widetilde{\boldsymbol{\Sigma}}_{\boldsymbol{\beta}}).$$

For the missing x_{ij}-values we consider a Laplace approximation to approximate $q(x_{ij})$. To this end define

$$\begin{aligned}f_{ij}(x_{ij}) &= -\tfrac{1}{2}\widetilde{\Omega}_{\mu,jj}x_{ij}^2 + d_{ij}x_{ij} - b(o_{ij} + \widetilde{\mu}_{\beta,j}x_{ij}),\\ g_{ij}(x_{ij}) &= -\widetilde{\Omega}_{\mu,jj}x_{ij} + d_{ij} - \widetilde{\mu}_{\beta,j}b'(o_{ij} + \widetilde{\mu}_{\beta,j}x_{ij}) \qquad \text{and}\\ h_{ij}(x_{ij}) &= -\widetilde{\Omega}_{\mu,jj} - \widetilde{\mu}_{\beta,j}^2 b''(o_{ij} + \widetilde{\mu}_{\beta,j}x_{ij}),\end{aligned}$$

where $d_{ij} = (\widetilde{\boldsymbol{\Omega}}_x\widetilde{\boldsymbol{\mu}}_x)_j - \boldsymbol{\Omega}_{x,j,-j}\widetilde{\mathbf{x}}_{i,-j} + y_i\widetilde{\mu}_{\beta,j}$ and $o_{ij} = \widetilde{\mathbf{x}}_{i,-j}^T\widetilde{\boldsymbol{\mu}}_{\boldsymbol{\beta},-j}$. Next, let $\widetilde{\mu}_{x_{ij}}^{(t)}$ and $\widetilde{\sigma}_{x_{ij}}^{2(t)}$ be the current estimates of the posterior mean and variance for x_{ij}. Then the Newton–Raphson updates can be written as

$$\begin{aligned}\widetilde{\sigma}_{x_{ij}}^{2(t)} &= -1/h_{ij}(x_{ij}),\\ \widetilde{\mu}_{x_{ij}}^{(t+1)} &= \widetilde{\mu}_{x_{ij}}^{(t)} + \widetilde{\sigma}_{x_{ij}}^{2(t)}\left[g_{ij}(\widetilde{\mu}_{x_{ij}}^{(t)})\right].\end{aligned}$$

These updates are applied until $\|\widetilde{\mu}_{x_{ij}}^{(t+1)} - \widetilde{\mu}_{x_{ij}}^{(t)}\|_{\infty} < \tau$. If $\widetilde{\mu}_{x_{ij}}$ and $\widetilde{\sigma}_{x_{ij}}^2$ are these values upon convergence, then $q(x_{ij}) \approx \text{dnorm}(x_{ij}|\widetilde{\mu}_{x_{ij}}, \widetilde{\sigma}_{x_{ij}})$.

6.7.1 Pima-Indians diabetes

The Pima-Indians diabetes data set is an immensely popular data set for demonstrating the effectiveness of various pieces of methodology [5]. The data set consists of $n = 768$ samples and $p = 8$ covariates whose aim is to predict a binary outcome indicating whether a subject has diabetes or not. However, most analyses of this data set sidestep the missing values, which is common in the `triceps` and `insulin` covariates, where 29.5% and 48.6% of the samples contain missing data. All other covariates have less than 5% missingness, and so for simplicity we remove a sample that contains missing

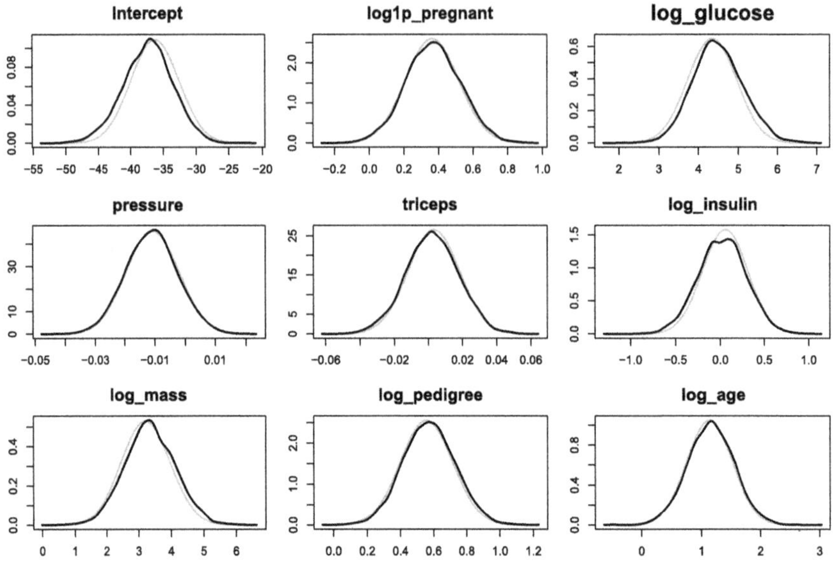

Figure 6.8 Posterior density approximations using MCMC (Black) and VB (Grey) for the regression coefficients.

values in any covariate except `triceps` and `insulin`. We use log transformations for `pregnant`, `glucose`, `insulin`, `mass`, `pedigree` and `age` so that the marginal densities for these variables are more symmetric.

Fig. 6.8 illustrates the posterior density for the regression coefficients whereas Fig. 6.9 illustrates the posterior densities for the variable means. Estimated posterior densities using VB are almost exact except the posterior densities for `triceps` and `insulin`, where the posterior variances are underestimated. Computational times where 7433 seconds for `stan` and 0.5 seconds for our VB approach.

6.8 Conclusion

In this chapter we gave a tutorial like introduction for mean field VB-based approximations for nonstandard semiparametric regression models. We gave several tricks for handling complications when attempting to apply a standard VB approach. Our framework is extremely flexible and is capable of fitting models far beyond the examples we gave here. In all of the real data examples considered in this chapter we achieve reasonable approximations of posterior means for all model parameters and often achieve reasonable approximations of posterior variances. However, all VB methods in this

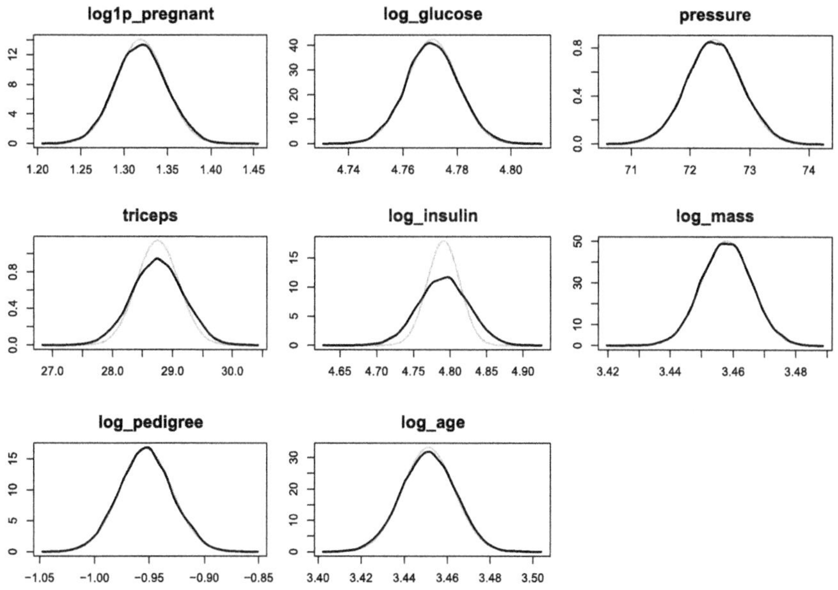

Figure 6.9 Posterior density approximations using MCMC (Black) and VB (Grey) for the predictor means.

chapter are at least 5 times faster than `stan` fits of these models despite `stan` being implemented in `C++`. For this reason we believe that VB can be useful in the context of statistical prediction and exploratory data analysis, and for timely analyses.

Acknowledgements

I would like to thank Sarah Romanes for proofreading and for initial comments on a draft of this chapter.

References

[1] C.M. Bishop, Pattern Recognition and Machine Learning, Springer, New York, 2006.

[2] C. Broyden, The convergence of a class of double-rank minimization algorithms, Journal of the Institute of Mathematics and Its Applications (1970) 76–90.

[3] B. Carpenter, A. Gelman, M. Hoffman, D. Lee, B. Goodrich, M. Betancourt, M. Brubaker, J. Guo, P. Li, A. Riddell, Stan: a probabilistic programming language 76 (2017) 1–32.

[4] R.J. Carroll, D. Ruppert, Transformation and Weighting in Regression, Chapman & Hall, Ltd., London, UK, 1988.

[5] N. Chopin, J. Ridgway, Leave Pima Indians alone: binary regression as a benchmark for Bayesian computation, Statistical Science 32 (2017) 64–87, https://doi.org/10.1214/16-STS581.

[6] R. Cook, S. Weisberg, Residuals and Influence in Regression, Chapman & Hall, 1982.

[7] C.M. Crainiceanu, D. Ruppert, R.J. Carroll, A. Joshi, B. Goodner, Spatially adaptive Bayesian penalized splines with heteroscedastic errors, Journal of Computational and Graphical Statistics 16 (2007) 265–288.

[8] M. Davidian, R.J. Carroll, Variance function estimation, Journal of the American Statistical Association 82 (1987) 1079–1091.

[9] N. Draper, H. Smith, Applied Regression Analysis, third edition, John Wiley & Sons, 1998.

[10] P. Eilers, B. Marx, Flexible smoothing with b-splines and penalties (with discussion), Statistical Science 11 (1996) 89–121.

[11] G. Flandin, W.D. Penny, Bayesian fMRI data analysis with sparse spatial basis function priors, NeuroImage 34 (2007) 1108–1125.

[12] R. Fletcher, A new approach to variable metric algorithms, Computer Journal (1970) 317–322.

[13] A. Gelman, Prior distributions for variance parameters in hierarchical models, Bayesian Analysis 1 (2006) 515–533.

[14] D. Goldfarb, A family of variable metric updates derived by variational means, Mathematics of Computation (1970) 23–26.

[15] P. Green, B. Silverman, Nonparametric Regression and Generalized Linear Models, Chapman & Hall, 1994.

[16] T. Hastie, Pseudosplines, Journal of the Royal Statistical Society, Series B 58 (1996) 379–396.

[17] T. Hastie, R. Tibshirani, Generalized Additive Models, Chapman & Hall, 1990.

[18] M. Hoffman, A. Gelman, The No-U-Turn Sampler: adaptively setting path lengths in Hamiltonian Monte Carlo 15 (2014) 1593–1623.

[19] M.I. Jordan, Graphical models, Statistical Science 19 (2004) 140–155.

[20] D.P. Kingma, M. Welling, Auto-encoding variational Bayes, arXiv e-prints, arXiv:1312.6114, 2013.

[21] D.G. Luenberger, Y. Ye, Linear and Nonlinear Programming, 3rd ed., Springer, New York, 2008.

[22] J. Luts, S. Wang, J.T. Ormerod, M.P. Wand, Semiparametric regression analysis via Infer.NET, Journal of Statistical Software 87 (2018) 1–37.

[23] F.S. Nathoo, A. Babul, A. Moiseev, N. Virji-Babul, M.F. Beg, A variational Bayes spatiotemporal model for electromagnetic brain mapping, Biometrics 70 (2014) 132–143.

[24] S. Neville, J.T. Ormerod, M.P. Wand, Mean field variational Bayes for continuous sparse signal shrinkage: pitfalls and remedies, Electronic Journal of Statistics (2014).

[25] J.T. Ormerod, M.P. Wand, Explaining variational approximations, The American Statistician 64 (2010) 140–153.

[26] M. Plummer, Jags: a program for analysis of Bayesian graphical models using Gibbs sampling, in: Proceedings of the 3rd International Workshop on Distributed Statistical Computing, DSC 2003, 2003.

[27] W.H. Press, S.A. Teukolsky, W.T. Vetterling, B.P. Flannery, Numerical Recipes in C: The Art of Scientific Computing, 3rd ed., Cambridge University Press, New York, NY, USA, 2007.

[28] F.J.R. Ruiz, M.K. Titsias, D.M. Blei, The generalized reparameterization gradient, arXiv e-prints, 2016.
[29] D. Ruppert, M. Wand, R. Carroll, Semiparametric Regression, Cambridge University Press, 2003.
[30] T. Salimans, D.A. Knowles, Fixed-form variational posterior approximation through stochastic linear regression, Bayesian Analysis 8 (2013) 837–882, https://doi.org/10.1214/13-BA858.
[31] D. Shanno, Conditioning of quasi-Newton methods for function minimization, Mathematics of Computation (1970) 647–656.
[32] Y.W. Teh, D. Newman, M. Welling, A collapsed variational Bayesian inference algorithm for latent Dirichlet allocation, in: Advances in Neural Information Processing Systems, vol. 19, MIT Press, 2007, pp. 1353–1360.
[33] A.E. Teschendorff, Y. Wang, N.L. Barbosa-Morais, J.D. Brenton, C. Caldas, A variational Bayesian mixture modelling framework for cluster analysis of gene-expression data, Bioinformatics 21 (2005) 3025–3033.
[34] S. Thurston, M.P. Wand, J. Weincke, Negative binomial additive models, Biometrics 56 (2000) 139–144.
[35] G. Wahba, Spline Models for Observational Data, SIAM, 1990.
[36] M. Wand, J. Ormerod, On semiparametric regression with O'Sullivan penalized splines, Australian & New Zealand Journal of Statistics 50 (2008) 179–198.
[37] M.P. Wand, J.T. Ormerod, S.A. Padoan, R. Frühwirth, Mean field variational Bayes for elaborate distributions, Bayesian Analysis 6 (2011) 847–900.
[38] J. Wiencke, S.W. Thurston, K.T. Kelsey, A. Varkonyi, J.C. Wain, E.J. Mark, D.C. Christiani, Early age at smoking initiation and tobacco carcinogen DNA damage in the lung, Journal of the National Cancer Institute 91 (1999) 614–619.
[39] S. Wood, Thin-plate regression splines, Journal of the Royal Statistical Society (B) 65 (2003) 95–114.
[40] S. Wood, mgcv: mixed GAM computation vehicle with automatic smoothness estimation, R package version 1.8-24 2018.
[41] Y. Zhao, J. Staudenmayer, B. Coull, M. Wand, General design Bayesian generalized linear mixed models, Statistical Science 21 (2006) 35–51.

CHAPTER 7

Scalable Bayesian variable selection regression models for count data

Yinsen Miao[a], Jeong Hwan Kook[a], Yadong Lu[b], Michele Guindani[b], Marina Vannucci[a]

[a]Rice University, Department of Statistics, 6100 Main St, Houston, TX 77005, United States
[b]University of California, Irvine, Department of Statistics, Brent Hall 2241, Irvine, CA 92697, United States

Contents

Chapter Points

- We consider linear regression models for count data, specifically negative binomial regression models and Dirichlet-multinomial regression models. We

Flexible Bayesian Regression Modelling
https://doi.org/10.1016/B978-0-12-815862-3.00015-9

address variable selection via the use of *spike-and-slab* priors on the regression coefficients.

- We develop efficient variational methods for scalability in the number of covariates that are based on augmentation techniques and concrete relaxation methods.
- We provide C/C++ code at https://github.com/marinavannucci/snbvbs for the negative binomial case and Python code at https://github.com/mguindanigroup/vbmultdir for the Dirichlet-multinomial case.

7.1 Introduction

Variable selection, also known as feature selection in the machine learning literature, plays an indispensable role in scientific studies: in cancer research, biomedical scientists seek to find connections between cancer phenotypes and a parsimonious set of genes; in finance, economists look for a small portfolio that can accurately track the performance of stock market indices such as the S&P 500. In many research areas with massive data, finding a subset of representative features that best explain the outcome of interest has become a critical component in any researcher's workflow.

As evidenced by numerous research papers published in either theory or practice, variable selection for linear regression models has been an important topic in the statistical literature for the past several decades. Variable selection methods can be categorised into roughly three groups: criteria-based methods including traditional approaches such as AIC/BIC [6,41], penalised regression methods [45,11,13,55] and Bayesian approaches [28, 15,5]. In this chapter, we focus primarily on Bayesian approaches for variable selection that use *spike-and-slab* priors. An obvious advantage when using these priors is that, in addition to the sparse estimation of the regression coefficients, these methods produce posterior probabilities of inclusion (PPIs) for each covariate. Moreover, Bayesian approaches have the advantages of being able to aggregate multiple submodels from a class of possible ones, based on their corresponding posterior probabilities. This approach is known as Bayesian model averaging and can lead to improved prediction accuracy over single models [17].

Despite the great features offered by *spike-and-slab* priors, computational issues remain a challenge. The posterior distribution for a candidate model usually does not have a closed-form expression, and its inference may be computationally intractable even for a moderate number of predictors. To address the problem, approximate methods that use Markov

Chain Monte Carlo (MCMC) stochastic searches have been extensively used [15,5]. Recently, variational inference methods [7,19,32,50,39] have attracted attention as a faster and more scalable alternative. These methods have also been used for model selection in different applied modelling contexts, particularly in bioinformatics [18] and neuroimaging [30,51].

In this chapter, we focus primarily on regression models for count data, and specifically on negative binomial linear regression models and on Dirichlet-multinomial regression models. In both settings, we formulate a Bayesian hierarchical model with variable selection using *spike-and-slab* priors. For posterior inference, we review standard MCMC methods and also investigate computationally more efficient variational inference approaches that use data augmentation techniques and concrete relaxation methods. We investigate performance of the methods via simulation studies and benchmark data sets.

7.2 Bayesian variable selection via spike-and-slab priors

In ordinary linear regression, a response y_i is modelled as

$$y_i = \beta_0 + \boldsymbol{x}_i^T \boldsymbol{\beta} + \epsilon_i, \qquad \epsilon_i \sim \text{Normal}(0, \sigma^2), \tag{7.1}$$

for $i = 1, \ldots, n$, with $\boldsymbol{x}_i \in \mathbb{R}^p$ being a vector of p known covariates, $\boldsymbol{\beta} = [\beta_1, \ldots, \beta_p]^T$ a vector of regression coefficients and β_0 the baseline or intercept. A Bayesian approach to variable selection in linear regression models formulates the selection problem via hierarchical priors on the unknown coefficients β_k, $k = 1, \ldots, p$. In this chapter we examine one of the most widely used sparsity inducing priors, known as the *spike-and-slab* prior [28]. This prior can be written as

$$\beta_k \mid \gamma_k \sim \gamma_k \text{Normal}\left(0, \sigma_\beta^2\right) + (1 - \gamma_k)\, \delta_0, \qquad k = 1, \ldots, p, \tag{7.2}$$

with γ_k being a latent indicator variable of whether the kth covariate has a nonzero effect on the outcome, δ_0 a point mass distribution at 0 and σ_β^2 the variance of the prior effect size. Typically, independent Bernoulli priors are imposed on the γ_k's, i.e. $\gamma_k \sim \text{Bernoulli}(\pi)$. For reviews on the general topic of Bayesian variable selection for regression models with continuous responses we refer interested readers to [31,12]. Alternatively, shrinkage priors, that do not impose a spike at zero, can be considered, such as the normal-gamma [16], the horseshoe [34] and the LASSO [33] priors.

Recently, nonlocal prior densities have been used in Bayesian hypothesis testing and variable selection, as an attempt to balance the rates of convergence of Bayes factors under the null and alternative hypotheses [22]. The large sample properties of Bayes factors obtained by local alternative priors imply that, as the sample size increases, evidence accumulates much more rapidly in favour of true alternative models than the true null models. Suppose the null hypothesis H_0 is $\beta \in \Theta_0$ and the alternative hypothesis H_1 is $\beta \in \Theta_1$. Here, we define a nonlocal density if $p(\beta \mid H_1) = 0$ for all $\beta \in \Theta_0$ and $p(\beta \mid H_1) > 0$ for all $\beta \in \Theta_1$. In the variable selection settings considered in this chapter, the hypotheses relate to the significance of the coefficients, i.e. H_0: $\beta = 0$ versus H_1: $\beta \neq 0$. Therefore, a nonlocal selection prior is defined as a mixture of a point mass at zero and a continuous nonlocal alternative distribution,

$$\beta_k \mid \gamma_k \sim \gamma_k p\left(\beta_k; \sigma_\beta^2\right) + (1 - \gamma_k)\,\delta_0, \quad k = 1, \ldots, p, \tag{7.3}$$

where $p\left(\beta_k; \sigma_\beta^2\right)$ is a nonlocal density characterising the prior distribution of β_k under the alternative hypothesis. Similarly as in the traditional *spike-and-slab* prior formulation, a nonlocal selection prior models the sparsity explicitly by assigning a positive mass at the origin. However, unlike a flat Gaussian distribution, the density $p\left(\beta_k; \sigma_\beta^2\right)$ does not place a significant amount of probability mass near the null value zero, thus properly reflecting the prior belief that the parameter is away from zero under H_1. In this chapter, we use the product second moment (pMOM) prior [22,42] and assume that the β_k's are independent of each other and are drawn from

$$p(\boldsymbol{\beta}; \sigma_\beta^2) = \prod_{k=1}^{p} \frac{\beta_k^2}{\sigma_\beta^2} \text{Normal}\left(0, \sigma_\beta^2\right). \tag{7.4}$$

7.3 Negative binomial regression models

For $i = 1, \ldots, n$, let now y_i indicate observed counts on an outcome variable. Count data can be modelled via a negative binomial distribution, obtaining the regression model

$$y_i \mid r, \psi_i \sim \text{NB}\left(r, \frac{\exp(\psi_i)}{1 + \exp(\psi_i)}\right), \tag{7.5}$$

with $\psi_i = \beta_0 + \boldsymbol{x}_i^T \boldsymbol{\beta}$ and with r being the overdispersion parameter. Given the law of total expectation and variance, the expectation and variance of

y_i can be calculated as

$$\mathbb{E}\left[y_i \mid \boldsymbol{x}_i\right] = \exp\left(\boldsymbol{x}_i^T \boldsymbol{\beta} + \beta_0 + \log r\right),$$
$$\mathrm{Var}\left[y_i \mid \boldsymbol{x}_i\right] = \mathbb{E}\left[y_i \mid \boldsymbol{x}_i\right] + \frac{1}{r}\mathbb{E}^2\left[y_i \mid \boldsymbol{x}_i\right], \tag{7.6}$$

showing that $\mathrm{Var}\left[y_i \mid \boldsymbol{x}_i\right] > \mathbb{E}\left[y_i \mid \boldsymbol{x}_i\right]$ and thus that the negative binomial model can account for overdispersion. Later on we will introduce auxiliary variables to facilitate the use of data augmentation techniques that allow conjugate inference on the parameters $\boldsymbol{\beta}$ and r. We write the prior model as follows:

$$\begin{aligned}
\beta_k \mid \gamma_k &\sim \gamma_k \mathrm{Normal}\left(0, \sigma_\beta^2\right) + (1 - \gamma_k)\,\delta_0, \\
\gamma_k &\sim \mathrm{Bernoulli}\left(\pi\right), \\
\beta_0 &\sim \mathrm{Normal}\left(0, \sigma_{\beta_0}^2\right), \\
r &\sim \mathrm{Gamma}\left(a_r, b_r\right), \\
\sigma_\beta^2 &\sim \text{Scaled-Inv-}\chi^2\left(\nu_0, \sigma_0^2\right).
\end{aligned} \tag{7.7}$$

Typically, a flat normal prior is imposed on the intercept term β_0, since there is usually no reason to shrink it towards zero. Parameters σ_β^2 and π control the sparsity of the model. Performance of variable selection can be sensitive to these parameter settings. Two popular prior choices for π are the beta distribution $\pi \sim \mathrm{Beta}\left(a_\pi, b_\pi\right)$ and the uniform distribution on the log scale $\log(\pi) \sim \mathrm{Uniform}\left(\pi_{\min}, \pi_{\max}\right)$ [54]. When π is marginalised, the obtained prior distributions on $\boldsymbol{\gamma}$ are a beta binomial distribution and a truncated beta distribution, respectively. We impose a convenient heavy-tail conjugate prior called scaled inverse chi squared distribution on the slab variance parameter σ_β^2, where ν_0 is the degree of freedom for the scale parameter σ_0^2. For stability purpose, it is recommended to use a large ν_0 for sparse models [7].

For posterior inference, with variable selection as the main focus, we are interested in recovering a small subset of covariates with significant association to the outcome. In the proposed Bayesian model, the relative importance of the kth covariate can be assessed by computing its marginal posterior probability of inclusion (PPI) as

$$\mathrm{PPI}\left(k\right) \equiv p\left(\gamma_k = 1 \mid \boldsymbol{y}, \boldsymbol{X}\right) = \frac{\sum_{\boldsymbol{\gamma}_{-k}} p\left(\boldsymbol{\gamma}_{-k}, \gamma_k = 1 \mid \boldsymbol{y}, \boldsymbol{X}\right)}{\sum_{\boldsymbol{\gamma}_{-k}} p\left(\boldsymbol{\gamma} \mid \boldsymbol{y}, \boldsymbol{X}\right)}, \tag{7.8}$$

which involves a sum over 2^p possible models marginalised over the other model parameters. Classical MCMC algorithms can be used to compute this analytically intractable term. Approaches that use data augmentation schemes have proven particularly efficient.

7.3.1 Data augmentation

Here we employ the Pólya-Gamma augmentation approach of Polson et al. [35] to sample $\boldsymbol{\beta}$ and an additional data augmentation scheme to obtain a closed-form, tractable update rule for the overdispersion parameter r, which we adapt from Zhou et al. [53].

A random variable ω following a Pólya-Gamma distribution with parameters $b \in \mathbb{R}_+$, $c \in \mathbb{R}$ is defined as

$$\omega \overset{D}{=} \frac{1}{2\pi^2} \sum_{k=1}^{\infty} \frac{g_k}{\left(k - 1/2\right)^2 + c^2 / \left(4\pi^2\right)}, \tag{7.9}$$

where the $g_k \sim \text{Gamma}\left(b, 1\right)$ are independent gamma random variables and $\overset{D}{=}$ indicates equality in distribution. The main result from Polson et al. [35] is that given a random variable ω with density $\omega \sim \text{PG}\left(b, 0\right)$, $b \in \mathbb{R}_+$, the following integral identity holds for all $a \in \mathbb{R}$:

$$\frac{\exp(\psi)^a}{(1 + \exp(\psi))^b} = 2^{-b} \exp(\kappa \psi)\, \mathbb{E}_\omega \left[\exp\left(-\omega \psi^2/2\right)\right], \tag{7.10}$$

where $\kappa = a - b/2$. Additionally, the conditional distribution $p(\omega \mid \psi)$, arising from treating the above integrand as the unnormalised joint density of (ω, ψ), is

$$p(\omega \mid \psi) = \frac{\exp\left(-\psi^2 \omega/2\right)}{\mathbb{E}_\omega \left[\exp\left(-\psi^2 \omega/2\right)\right]} p\left(\omega \mid b, 0\right), \tag{7.11}$$

which is also in the Pólya-Gamma class, i.e. $\omega \mid \psi \sim \text{PG}(b, \psi)$. For more details regarding the derivation of the result, we refer interested readers to Polson et al. [35]. Comparing Eq. (7.10) with the negative binomial regression likelihood given in Eq. (7.5) we can define $a = y_i$ and $b = y_i + r$ and therefore write out the likelihood function as

$$\mathcal{L}\left(y_i \mid \psi_i, r\right) = \frac{\Gamma\left(y_i + r\right)}{\Gamma\left(y_i + 1\right)\Gamma(r)} \frac{\exp(\psi_i)^{y_i}}{(1 + \exp(\psi_i))^{y_i + r}}, \tag{7.12}$$

where $\Gamma(\cdot)$ is the gamma function. We are ready to appeal to the above Pólya-Gamma augmentation and write the likelihood function of the ith observation conditioned on the augmented variable $\omega_i \sim \text{PG}(y_i + r, 0)$ as

$$\mathcal{L}(y_i \mid \psi_i, r) \propto \exp(\kappa_i \psi_i)\, \mathbb{E}_{\omega_i}\left[\exp\left(-\omega_i \psi_i^2/2\right)\right], \tag{7.13}$$

with $\kappa_i = (y_i - r)/2$ and $[\omega_i \mid \psi_i] \sim \text{PG}(y_i + r, \psi_i)$.

We adopt an additional data augmentation scheme to obtain a closed-form, tractable update rule for the overdispersion parameter r. We note that $y_i \sim \text{NB}(r, p_i)$ can be expressed as a compound Poisson distribution [36]

$$\begin{aligned} y_i &= \sum_{l=1}^{L_i} u_{il} \text{ where } i \in \{1, \ldots, n\} \text{ and } l \in \{1, \ldots, L_i\}, \\ L_i &\sim \text{Poisson}\left(-r \log(1 - p_i)\right), \\ u_{il} &\overset{\text{i.i.d.}}{\sim} \text{Logarithmic}(p_i), \end{aligned} \tag{7.14}$$

where L_i can be interpreted as the number of groups, u_{il} is the number of individuals within the lth group and y_i is the number of total individuals for the ith observation. Therefore, exploiting conjugacy between the Gamma and Poisson distributions, a Gamma(a_r, b_r) prior on r leads to the conditional posterior

$$[r \mid \ldots] \sim \text{Gamma}\left(a_r + \sum_{i=1}^{n} L_i,\, b_r - \sum_{i=1}^{n} \log(1 - p_i)\right). \tag{7.15}$$

The remaining question is how to obtain the conditional posterior of L_i. Zhou et al. [53] show that the probability mass function (PMF) of L_i is the Antoniak equation

$$P(L_i = l_i \mid y_i, r) \overset{\text{def}}{=} f_L(l_i \mid y_i, r) = \left|s(y_i, l_i)\right| \frac{r^{l_i}\Gamma(r)}{\Gamma(r + y_i)}, \tag{7.16}$$

where $0 \leq l_i \leq y_i$ and $s(y_i, l_i)$ is the Stirling number of the first kind [3, 43]. By definition, $|s(0,0)| = 1$, $|s(0, l)| = 0$ for $l > 0$, $|s(y_i, l_i)| = 0$ for $l_i > y_i$, and the other values are given by the recursion as $|s(y_i + 1, l)| = |s(y_i, l-1)| + y_i |s(y_i, l)|$. The Antoniak equation (7.16) can also be interpreted as the probability that y_i samples from a Dirichlet process with concentration parameter r will return l_i distinct groups, which follows a Chinese restaurant table (CRT) distribution. Consider a Chinese restaurant with an infinite number of tables, each with infinite capacity. Given a concentration parameter r, we would like to sit y_i customers in this restaurant using the following rule: a customer w, $w = 1, \ldots, y_i$, will either choose a new empty table (group) with probability $r/(r+w-1)$ or decide to sit at an occupied table otherwise. Hence we can treat the event of creating new tables (groups) as an independent Bernoulli trial and count the number of successful events. The expected mean and variance of table counts, given y_i seated customers, are

$$\begin{aligned}\mathbb{E}[L_i] &= \sum_{w=1}^{y_i} \frac{r}{r+w-1} = r\left(\Psi\left(r+y_i\right) - \Psi(r)\right), \\ \mathrm{Var}[L_i] &= r\left(\Psi\left(r+y_i\right) - \Psi(r)\right) + r^2\left(\Psi'\left(r+y_i\right) - \Psi'(r)\right),\end{aligned} \tag{7.17}$$

where $\Psi(\cdot)$ is the digamma function. Using those analytical moments, we apply the central limit theorem [10] and utilise the asymptotic approximations

$$\begin{aligned}L_i &\asymp \mathrm{Normal}\left(\mathbb{E}[L_i], \mathrm{Var}[L_i]\right), \\ L_i &\asymp \mathrm{Poisson}\left(\mathbb{E}[L_i]\right)\end{aligned} \tag{7.18}$$

to sample L_i when y_i is large.

7.3.2 MCMC algorithm

We integrate out the sparsity prior parameter π. Additionally, to gain further computational speed, in our implementation we use the Pólya-Gamma augmentation to marginalise over β_0 and $\boldsymbol{\beta}_\gamma$ when updating the variable selection indicators $\boldsymbol{\gamma}$ and then perform the remaining updates conditional upon a sufficient estimate of those parameters. A generic iteration of our MCMC therefore consists of two Metropolis–Hasting steps on $\boldsymbol{\gamma}$ and $\tau_\beta = \sigma_\beta^{-2}$ within two Gibbs updates on $\boldsymbol{\omega}$ and r:

- To sample the model selection parameter $\boldsymbol{\gamma}$, we follow the modified add-delete-swap algorithm proposed by [7] which selects the variable at a frequency which is proportional to the likelihood. Specifically, we propose an add move with a probability proportional to $p\left(\boldsymbol{\gamma} \mid \mathbf{X}, \gamma_k = 1, \boldsymbol{\gamma}_{-k}, \boldsymbol{\omega}, \tau_\beta, r\right)$ and a delete move with probability proportional to $p\left(\boldsymbol{\gamma} \mid \mathbf{X}, \gamma_k = 0, \boldsymbol{\gamma}_{-k}, \boldsymbol{\omega}, \tau_\beta, r\right)$. Let us denote the marginal likelihood of model M_γ with the abbreviated notation $\ell(\boldsymbol{\gamma})$ as

$$\ell(\gamma) \equiv p\left(y \mid \mathbf{X}, \gamma, \boldsymbol{\omega}, \tau_\beta, r\right) \propto \frac{\tau_\beta^{\frac{m}{2}}}{\sqrt{\bar{\omega}}} \left|\mathbf{S}_\gamma^{\tau_\beta}\right|^{\frac{1}{2}} \exp\left(\frac{1}{2}\left(SSR_\gamma^{\tau_\beta} + \frac{\bar{\kappa}^2}{\bar{\omega}}\right)\right), \tag{7.19}$$

where $\mathbf{S}_\gamma^{\tau_\beta}$ and $\mathrm{SSR}_\gamma^{\tau_\beta}$ are $\left(\mathbf{X}_\gamma^T \hat{\boldsymbol{\Omega}} \mathbf{X}_\gamma + \tau_\beta \mathbb{I}_m\right)^{-1}$ and $\hat{\boldsymbol{\kappa}}^T \mathbf{X}_\gamma \mathbf{S}_\gamma^{\tau_\beta} \mathbf{X}_\gamma^T \hat{\boldsymbol{\kappa}}$, respectively. We define $\boldsymbol{\Omega} = \mathrm{diag}(\boldsymbol{\omega})$, $\bar{\kappa} = \sum_{i=1}^n \kappa_i$, $\bar{\omega} = \sum_{i=1}^n \omega_i$, $\hat{\boldsymbol{\kappa}} = \boldsymbol{\kappa} - \frac{\bar{\kappa}}{\bar{\omega}} \boldsymbol{\omega}$ and $\hat{\boldsymbol{\Omega}} = \boldsymbol{\Omega} - \frac{\boldsymbol{\omega}\boldsymbol{\omega}^T}{\bar{\omega}}$; $\mathbb{I}_m$ is an identity matrix of dimension $m \times m$ and $\mathrm{SSR}_\gamma^{\tau_\beta}$ is often referred to as the sum of squares due to regression (SSR). We write the acceptance probability for the add and delete move as

$$\mathcal{A}\left(\gamma_k = 0, \hat{\gamma}_k = 1\right) = \min\left\{1, \frac{a_\pi + m}{b_\pi + p - m - 1} \frac{\ell\left(\gamma_k = 1, \boldsymbol{\gamma}_{-k}\right)}{\ell\left(\gamma_k = 0, \boldsymbol{\gamma}_{-k}\right)} \frac{\sum_{j:\gamma_j = 0} \frac{\ell\left(\gamma_j = 1, \boldsymbol{\gamma}_{-j}\right)}{\ell\left(\gamma_j = 0, \boldsymbol{\gamma}_{-j}\right)}}{\sum_{j:\hat{\gamma}_j = 1} \frac{\ell\left(\gamma_j = 0, \hat{\boldsymbol{\gamma}}_{-j}\right)}{\ell\left(\gamma_j = 1, \hat{\boldsymbol{\gamma}}_{-j}\right)}}\right\},$$

$$\mathcal{A}\left(\gamma_k = 1, \hat{\gamma}_k = 0\right) = \min\left\{1, \frac{b_\pi + p - m}{a_\pi + m - 1} \frac{\ell\left(\gamma_k = 0, \boldsymbol{\gamma}_{-k}\right)}{\ell\left(\gamma_k = 1, \boldsymbol{\gamma}_{-k}\right)} \frac{\sum_{j:\gamma_j = 1} \frac{\ell\left(\gamma_j = 0, \boldsymbol{\gamma}_{-j}\right)}{\ell\left(\gamma_j = 1, \boldsymbol{\gamma}_{-j}\right)}}{\sum_{j:\hat{\gamma}_j = 0} \frac{\ell\left(\gamma_j = 1, \hat{\boldsymbol{\gamma}}_{-j}\right)}{\ell\left(\gamma_j = 0, \hat{\boldsymbol{\gamma}}_{-j}\right)}}\right\},$$

where $\boldsymbol{\gamma}_{-k}$ is the set of all indicator variables excluding the kth one. Computations can be made more efficient by using Cholesky decompositions. See [38] for details.

- We perform a Metropolis–Hasting update on the log of the slab precision τ_β,

$$\log \hat{\tau}_\beta = \log \tau_\beta + u, \tag{7.20}$$

where u is a random draw from a $\mathrm{Normal}\left(0, \sigma_\epsilon^2\right)$ and σ_ϵ^2 is the Metropolis–Hasting step size variance. Then we admit this candidate $\hat{\tau}_\beta$ with acceptance probability

$$\mathcal{A}\left(\tau_\beta, \hat{\tau}_\beta\right) = \min\left\{1, \exp\left(\frac{1}{2}\left(SSR_\gamma^{\hat{\tau}_\beta} - SSR_\gamma^{\tau_\beta}\right)\right)\left(\frac{\left|\hat{\tau}_\beta \mathbf{S}_\gamma^{\hat{\tau}_\beta}\right|}{\left|\tau_\beta \mathbf{S}_\gamma^{\tau_\beta}\right|}\right)^{1/2}\right\}. \tag{7.21}$$

- Using the compound Poisson distribution [52] representation of the negative binomial distribution, we show the conditional posterior of r as

$$[r \mid \ldots] \sim \text{Gamma}\left(a_r + \sum_{i=1}^{n} L_i,\, b_r + \sum_{i=1}^{n} \log\left(1 + \exp\left(\psi_i\right)\right)\right), \tag{7.22}$$
$$[L_i \mid \ldots] \sim \text{CRT}\left(y_i, r\right),$$

where CRT is a Chinese restaurant table distribution.
- Polson et al. [35] showed that the posterior of ω_i given the linear term ψ_i and the other remaining parameters follows a Pólya-Gamma distribution. Therefore, the conditional update for each ω_i for $i = 1, \ldots, n$ is given by

$$[\omega_i \mid \ldots] \propto \exp\left(-\omega_i \psi_i^2/2\right) \text{PG}\left(\omega_i; y_i + r, 0\right) \propto \text{PG}\left(y_i + r, \psi_i\right). \tag{7.23}$$

7.3.3 Variational inference algorithm

Unlike MCMC methods, variational inference is based on an optimisation problem [4]. Let us consider the set of parameters $(\boldsymbol{\beta}, \boldsymbol{\gamma})$ and the conditional posterior distribution $f(\boldsymbol{\beta}, \boldsymbol{\gamma})$ given $r, \boldsymbol{\omega}, \pi, \sigma_\beta^2$. The underlying idea of variational inference is to pick a family of distributions $q(\boldsymbol{\beta}, \boldsymbol{\gamma}) \in \mathcal{Q}$, with free variational parameter $\boldsymbol{\theta}$, and then use the gradient descent algorithm on $\boldsymbol{\theta}$ to minimise the Kullback–Leibler (KL) divergence between the variational approximation q and the posterior distribution $f(\boldsymbol{\beta}, \boldsymbol{\gamma})$ as

$$\begin{aligned} q^* &= \arg\min_{q \in \mathrm{Q}} KL\left(q \,\|\, f\right) = \int\int q(\boldsymbol{\beta}, \boldsymbol{\gamma}) \log \frac{q(\boldsymbol{\beta}, \boldsymbol{\gamma})}{f(\boldsymbol{\beta}, \boldsymbol{\gamma})} d\boldsymbol{\beta}\, d\boldsymbol{\gamma} \\ &= \log p\left(\boldsymbol{y} \mid \boldsymbol{X}, \boldsymbol{\omega}, \boldsymbol{\vartheta}, r\right) - \left\{\mathbb{E}^{\mathrm{Q}}\left[\log p\left(\boldsymbol{y}, \boldsymbol{\beta}, \boldsymbol{\gamma} \mid \boldsymbol{X}, \boldsymbol{\omega}, \boldsymbol{\vartheta}, r\right)\right] + \mathbb{H}\left[q(\boldsymbol{\beta}, \boldsymbol{\gamma})\right]\right\} \\ &= \log p\left(\boldsymbol{y} \mid \boldsymbol{X}, \boldsymbol{\omega}, \boldsymbol{\vartheta}, r\right) - \text{ELBO}, \end{aligned} \tag{7.24}$$

with $\boldsymbol{\vartheta}$ being the set of hyperparameters or $\boldsymbol{\vartheta} = \left(\pi, \sigma_\beta^2\right)$ and $\mathbb{H}\left[q(\boldsymbol{\beta}, \boldsymbol{\gamma})\right]$ denoting the entropy of the variational distribution. Given that the conditional marginal likelihood $\log p\left(\boldsymbol{y} \mid \boldsymbol{X}, \boldsymbol{\omega}, \boldsymbol{\vartheta}, r\right)$ does not depend on $(\boldsymbol{\beta}, \boldsymbol{\gamma})$, one can maximise the remaining term on the right-hand side, often referred to as the evidence lower bound (ELBO).

For practical reasons the variational family $\mathcal{Q}$ is chosen to be a set of parametric distributions from the exponential family. In particular, in order to reduce the computational complexity of the optimisation, a common approach is to assume that the latent variables are mutually independent and each is governed by a distinct factor in the variational density. This class of variational family $\mathcal{Q}$ is known as the mean field variational family. In particular, in the negative binomial regression model case introduced in this chapter we assume

$$q(\boldsymbol{\beta}, \boldsymbol{\gamma} \mid \boldsymbol{\theta}) = \prod_{k=1}^{p} q(\beta_k, \gamma_k; \theta_k), \tag{7.25}$$

with

$$q(\beta_k, \gamma_k; \theta_k) = \begin{cases} \alpha_k \text{Normal}(\beta_k \mid \mu_k, s_k^2) & \text{if } \gamma_k = 1, \\ (1-\alpha_k)\,\delta_0(\beta_k) & \text{otherwise} \end{cases} \tag{7.26}$$

and variational parameters $\theta_k = \left(\alpha_k, \mu_k, s_k^2\right)$. This factorised approximation is widely used for variational inference with *spike-and-slab* priors [24,47,7, 51,19]. The closed form of the ELBO, which we denote as $F(\boldsymbol{\vartheta}; \boldsymbol{\theta})$, can be derived as

$$\begin{aligned} F(\boldsymbol{\vartheta}; \boldsymbol{\theta}) &\overset{\text{def}}{=} \text{ELBO} = \log p\left(\boldsymbol{y} \mid \boldsymbol{X}, \boldsymbol{\omega}, \pi, \sigma_\beta^2, r\right) \geq -\frac{1}{2}\log\bar{\omega} + \frac{\bar{\kappa}^2}{2\bar{\omega}} + \hat{\boldsymbol{\kappa}}^T \boldsymbol{X} \boldsymbol{A} \boldsymbol{\mu} \\ &+ \sum_{i=1}^{n} \left\{\log\Gamma\left(y_i + r\right) - \log\Gamma\left(y_i + 1\right) - \log\Gamma(r) - \left(y_i + r\right)\log 2\right\} \\ &- \frac{1}{2}\left\{\sum_{k=1}^{p}\left(\boldsymbol{X}^T\hat{\boldsymbol{\Omega}}\boldsymbol{X}\right)_{kk}\left((\mu_k^2 + s_k^2)\alpha_k - \mu_k^2\alpha_k^2\right) + \boldsymbol{\mu}^T\boldsymbol{A}\left(\boldsymbol{X}^T\hat{\boldsymbol{\Omega}}\boldsymbol{X}\right)\boldsymbol{A}\boldsymbol{\mu}\right\} \\ &+ \sum_{k=1}^{p}\frac{\alpha_k}{2}\left[1 + \log\left(\frac{s_k^2}{\sigma_\beta^2}\right) - \frac{s_k^2 + \mu_k^2}{\sigma_\beta^2}\right] - \sum_{k=1}^{p}\alpha_k\log\left(\frac{\alpha_k}{\pi}\right) \\ &- \sum_{k=1}^{p}(1-\alpha_k)\log\left(\frac{1-\alpha_k}{1-\pi}\right), \end{aligned} \tag{7.27}$$

with $\boldsymbol{A} = \text{diag}\left(\alpha_1, \alpha_2, \ldots, \alpha_p\right)$. By taking partial derivatives of the variational parameters and setting them to zero, we obtain the updating rules for α_k, μ_k and s_k^2, i.e.

$$s_k^2 = \frac{1}{\left(\boldsymbol{X}^T\hat{\boldsymbol{\Omega}}\boldsymbol{X}\right)_{kk} + \tau_\beta}, \tag{7.28}$$

Algorithm 1: VIEM algorithm for negative binomial regression.

initialize: $\left(\mu_k, \alpha_k, s_k^2\right)$ for $k = \{1, \dots, p\}, \hat{\omega}, \hat{\sigma}_\beta^2, \hat{\pi}, \hat{r}$

repeat

  Update the variational parameters via coordinate gradient descent:

  for $k = 1 : p$ **do**

    1. Update s_k^2 according to Eq. (7.28).
    2. Update μ_k according to Eq. (7.29).
    3. Update α_k according to Eq. (7.30).

  end

  Update selection hyperparameters $\hat{\sigma}_\beta^2$ and $\hat{\pi}$ via their MAP estimates.

  Update latent variables $\hat{r}$ and $\hat{\omega}_i$, $i \in \{1, \dots, n\}$ via posterior expectations.

until *ELBO Converges*

Figure 7.1 Variational inference expectation maximisation (VIEM) scheme.

$$\mu_k = s_k^2 \left(\left(\mathbf{X}^T \hat{\boldsymbol{\kappa}}\right)_k - \sum_{i \neq k}^{p} \alpha_i \mu_i \left(\mathbf{X}^T \hat{\boldsymbol{\Omega}} \mathbf{X}\right)_{ik} \right), \tag{7.29}$$

$$\text{Logit}\,(\alpha_k) = \frac{\mu_k^2}{2 s_k^2} + \log\left(\frac{s_k}{\sigma_\beta}\right) + \text{Logit}\,(\pi)\,. \tag{7.30}$$

In order to maximise the ELBO, we devise two variational inference expectation maximisation (VIEM) schemes. The first scheme is described in Fig. 7.1 and comprises a VI-step, an E-step and an M-step. In the VI-step, we use coordinate gradient descent which iteratively updates the variational approximation (7.25). In the E-step, we treat the augmentation variable $\boldsymbol{\omega}$ and overdispersion parameter r as missing latent variables and use the results from Polson et al. [35] and Zhou et al. [53] to update them via the corresponding posterior expected values. In the M-step, we solve for the maximum a posteriori (MAP) estimates of σ_β^2 and π. The posterior of σ_β^2 is a scaled inverse chi squared distribution with mode (i.e. the MAP estimator) given by $\hat{\sigma}_\beta^2 = \left(\sum_{k=1}^{p} \alpha_k(\mu_k^2 + s_k^2) + \nu_0 \sigma_0^2\right) / \left(\tilde{\nu}_0 + 2\right)$. The posterior for π is a beta distribution whose posterior MAP is $\hat{\pi} = \left(\sum_{k=1}^{p} \alpha_k + a_\pi - 1\right) / \left(p + a_\pi + b_\pi - 2\right)$. Furthermore, the posterior for r is a gamma distribution with expectation $\mathbb{E}\,[r] = \tilde{a}_r / \tilde{b}_r$, with $\tilde{a}_r = a_r + \sum_{i=1}^{n} \mathbb{E}\,[L_i]$ and $\tilde{b}_r = b_r + \sum_{i=1}^{n} \log\left(1 + \exp\left(\psi_i\right)\right)$, where each expectation of L_i is given by Eq. (7.17) and the posterior distribution of ω_i is given in Eq. (7.23), with expectation $\mathbb{E}\,[\omega_i] = \left(y_i + \mathbb{E}\,[r]\right) \left\{\frac{\tanh(\psi_i/2)}{2\psi_i}\right\}$. With this scheme, we iterate the three steps until some convergence criterion is met. A commonly used stopping rule is to terminate the algorithm when changes of the ELBO

Algorithm 2: VIEM-IS algorithm for negative binomial regression.

---

initialize: $\left(\mu_k, \alpha_k, s_k^2\right)$, for $k = \{1, \ldots, p\}$, $\hat{\boldsymbol{\omega}}$, $\hat{\boldsymbol{\vartheta}} = \left(\hat{\sigma}_\beta^2, \hat{\pi}\right)$, $\hat{r}$
given : Sample $\boldsymbol{\vartheta}^{(1)}, \ldots, \boldsymbol{\vartheta}^{(ns)}$ from importance distribution $\tilde{p}(\boldsymbol{\vartheta})$
for $s = 1 : ns$ **do**
  repeat
    Update the variational parameters via coordinate gradient descent:
    for $k = 1 : p$ **do**
      1. Update s_k^2 according to Eq. (7.28).
      2. Update μ_k according to Eq. (7.29).
      3. Update α_k according to Eq. (7.30).
    end
    Update the latent variables $\hat{r}$ and $\hat{\omega}_i$ for $i \in \{1, \ldots, n\}$ via their posterior expectation.
  until *ELBO Converges*
  Compute the unnormalised importance weights $w(\boldsymbol{\vartheta})$
  Set $\boldsymbol{\alpha}^{(i)} = \boldsymbol{\alpha}$ and $\boldsymbol{\mu}^{(i)} = \boldsymbol{\mu}$.
end

Compute the normalised importance weights $\hat{w}(\boldsymbol{\vartheta})$.
Compute the weighted average of $\boldsymbol{\alpha}^{(s)}$ and $\boldsymbol{\beta}^{(s)} = \boldsymbol{\alpha}^{(s)} \cdot \boldsymbol{\mu}^{(s)}$ using $\hat{w}(\boldsymbol{\vartheta})$.

Figure 7.2 Variational inference expectation maximisation via importance sampling (VIEM-IS) scheme.

between iterations are less than some prespecified threshold. An alternative criterion is to use the entropy of the selection parameter $\boldsymbol{\gamma}$ defined as

$$H(\boldsymbol{\gamma}) = -\sum_{k=1}^{p} \left\{\alpha_k \log_2(\alpha_k) + (1-\alpha_k)\log_2(1-\alpha_k)\right\}. \tag{7.31}$$

In the second variational scheme, described in Fig. 7.2, we integrate out the parameters in $\boldsymbol{\vartheta}$ via importance sampling [7] and estimate the PPIs, defined as in Eq. (7.8), as

$$\mathrm{PPI}(k) \approx \frac{\sum_{s=1}^{N} p\left(\gamma_k = 1 \mid \mathbf{X}, \boldsymbol{y}, \boldsymbol{\omega}, \boldsymbol{\vartheta}^{(s)}, r\right) w\left(\boldsymbol{\vartheta}^{(s)}\right)}{\sum_{s=1}^{N} w\left(\boldsymbol{\vartheta}^{(s)}\right)}, \tag{7.32}$$

with $w(\boldsymbol{\vartheta})$ being the unnormalised importance sampling weight for $\boldsymbol{\vartheta}$, calculated by substituting the unknown marginal likelihood $p\left(\boldsymbol{y} \mid \mathbf{X}, \boldsymbol{\omega}, \boldsymbol{\vartheta}, r\right)$ with its ELBO. Importance sampling can improve the estimates of the PPIs as it averages over $\boldsymbol{\vartheta}$. Furthermore, since importance samples are independent from each other, one can employ a parallel computing framework such as OpenMP [8] to take advantage of multicore computers.

7.4 Dirichlet-multinomial regression models

The second model for count data that we consider is the Dirichlet-multinomial log-linear regression model. Here, for each observation i, $i = 1, \ldots, n$, we assume multivariate count data and write $\boldsymbol{y}_i = (y_{i1}, \ldots, y_{iJ})$ to indicate the vector of counts on J outcome variables, for $j = 1, \ldots, J$. As in the previous model, we let $\boldsymbol{x}_i$ indicate the vector of measurements on p covariates. We start by modelling the multivariate count data $\boldsymbol{y}_i$ using a multinomial distribution

$$\boldsymbol{y}_i \mid \boldsymbol{\phi}_i \sim \text{Multinomial}\left(y_{i+}, \boldsymbol{\phi}_i\right), \tag{7.33}$$

with $y_{i+} = \sum_{j=1}^{J} y_{ij}$ being the summation of all counts in the vector and where the parameter $\boldsymbol{\phi}_i$ is defined on the J-dimensional simplex

$$\mathcal{S}^{J-1} = \left\{ \left(\phi_{i1}, \ldots, \phi_{iJ}\right) : \phi_{ij} \geq 0, \ \sum_{j=1}^{J} \phi_{ij} = 1 \right\}.$$

We further impose a conjugate Dirichlet prior on $\boldsymbol{\phi}_i$, that is, $\boldsymbol{\phi}_i \sim$ Dirichlet($\boldsymbol{\xi}_i$), where $\boldsymbol{\xi}_i = \left(\xi_{i1}, \ldots, \xi_{iJ}\right)$ indicates a J-dimensional vector of strictly positive parameters. An advantage of our hierarchical formulation is that conjugacy can be exploited to integrate $\boldsymbol{\phi}_i$ out, obtaining the Dirichlet-multinomial model, $\boldsymbol{y}_i \sim \text{DM}(\boldsymbol{\xi}_i)$, with PMF

$$f(\boldsymbol{y}_i|\boldsymbol{\xi}_i) = \binom{y_{i+}}{\boldsymbol{y}_i} \frac{\Gamma(y_{i+}+1)\Gamma(\xi_{i+})}{\Gamma(y_{i+}+\xi_{i+})} \prod_{j=1}^{J} \frac{\Gamma(y_{ij}+\xi_{ij})}{\Gamma(\xi_{ij})\Gamma(y_{ij}+1)}, \tag{7.34}$$

and $\xi_{i+} = \sum_{j}^{J} \xi_{ij}$. First described in [29] as the compound multinomial, the Dirichlet-multinomial model allows more flexibility than the multinomial when encountering overdispersion, as it induces an increase in variance by a factor $\left(y_{i+} + \xi_{i+}\right) / (1 + \xi_{i+})$.

Next, we incorporate the covariates into the modelling via a log-linear regression framework where the Dirichlet-multinomial parameters depend on the available covariates. More specifically, we define $\zeta_{ij} = \log(\xi_{ij})$ and assume

$$\zeta_{ij} = \alpha_j + \sum_{k=1}^{p} \beta_{kj} x_{ik}. \tag{7.35}$$

In this formulation, the intercept term α_j corresponds to the log baseline parameter for outcome j, whereas the regression parameter β_{kj} captures the association between the kth covariate and the jth outcome. Identifying the significant associations is then equivalent to determining the nonzero β_{kj} parameters, a task we can achieve via *spike-and-slab* priors. Here, we use the formulation of [44] and introduce a set of latent binary indicators of the type $\boldsymbol{\gamma}_j = (\gamma_{1j}, \gamma_{2j}, \ldots, \gamma_{pj})$ such that $\gamma_{kj} = 1$ if the kth covariate influences the jth outcome and $\gamma_{kj} = 0$ otherwise, and we write the prior on β_{kj} as

$$\beta_{kj} \mid \gamma_{kj} \sim \gamma_{kj} p\left(\beta_{kj}; \sigma_\beta^2\right) + (1 - \gamma_{kj})\, \delta_0, \tag{7.36}$$

$$\gamma_{kj} \sim \text{Bernoulli}\,(\pi)\,, \tag{7.37}$$

where $p(\beta_{kj}; \sigma_\beta^2)$ is the nonlocal prior and π again controls the sparsity of the model. For the nonlocal prior, we consider the pMOM prior described in (7.4). Finally we assume normal priors on the baseline α_j's, i.e. $\alpha_j \sim \text{Normal}\left(0, \sigma_\alpha^2\right)$, and use large σ_α^2 to encode a diffuse prior on each α_j.

7.4.1 MCMC algorithm

We refer readers to [48] for an MCMC stochastic search method for the Dirichlet-multinomial regression model. Here, instead, we formulate an alternative, scalable variational Bayes algorithm.

7.4.2 Variational inference with reparameterisation

Unlike the negative binomial regression model, the Dirichlet-multinomial regression model does not have any known data augmentation schemes that can be paired with a parametric variational family to exploit conditional conjugacy. This is often the case for Bayesian hierarchical models where the corresponding ELBO objective is a function of intractable expectations with respect to the variational distributions. In such settings, the optimal variational parameters can be found via the gradient descent algorithm and the ELBO can be approximated by Monte Carlo samples from the variational distributions. Reducing the variance of the gradient estimators plays a significant role in improving model accuracy and scalability of these methods. Below we review the generalised reparameterisation (G-REP) gradient method proposed in [40] to obtain a low-variance gradient in the case of continuous latent variables.

7.4.2.1 Reparameterisation of the gradient

Given data x and a continuous latent variable z such that $p(x, z)$ is differentiable with respect to z, a reparameterisation transforms z into a new random variable ϵ defined by an invertible transformation $\epsilon = \mathcal{T}^{-1}(z; \theta)$ and $z = \mathcal{T}(\epsilon; \theta)$, where $\epsilon = \mathcal{T}^{-1}(z; \theta)$ can be considered as a standardisation procedure that makes the distribution of ϵ weakly dependent on z. By change of variable, the reparameterised model can be written as $p(x, \epsilon; \theta) = p(x, \mathcal{T}(\epsilon; \theta)) \times J(\epsilon; \theta)$, where $J(\epsilon; \theta) = |\det \nabla_\epsilon \mathcal{T}(\epsilon; \theta)|$ denotes the determinant of the Jacobian of the transformation. A noticeable property of a valid reparameterisation is the marginal likelihood invariance property

$$p(x) = \int p(x, z)dz = \int p(x, \epsilon)d\epsilon = \int p(x, \mathcal{T}(\epsilon; \theta))J(\epsilon; \theta). \tag{7.38}$$

Thus, while θ enters into the above equation as a new model parameter, the marginal probability $p(x)$ remains unchanged. However, the reparameterised posterior distribution $p(\epsilon|x, \theta)$ is dependent on θ and this dependence of the posterior on θ can be exploited to improve accuracy and computational efficiency [46]. In the variational inference context, we can consider $p(\epsilon|x, \theta)$ to be the first part of the ELBO objective corresponding to the expectation of the log likelihood with respect to the variational distributions parameterised by θ. When updating θ via stochastic gradient descent, one can now take advantage of the information provided from the model likelihood. This will generally lead to a faster convergence of θ and fewer samples of ϵ to estimate a low-variance gradient [40].

7.4.2.2 Concrete relaxation

While G-REP can be used to optimise the variational parameters for the regression coefficients β, this approach cannot be used for the discrete model selection variable γ. Recently, Maddison et al. [26] and Jang et al. [20] have proposed a reparameterisation for discrete random variables using the Concrete distribution, which is a continuous relaxation of discrete random variables. The Concrete distribution is a parametric family of continuous distributions on the simplex with closed-form densities, parameterised by a location $a > 0$ and a temperature $\lambda > 0$. A key feature of this class of distributions is that any discrete distribution can be seen as the discretisation of a Concrete one. For example, the binary model selection random variable $\gamma \sim \text{Bernoulli}(\pi)$ is equivalent to $\gamma \sim \text{BinConcrete}(a, \lambda)$, and γ can be sampled as

$$\gamma = \frac{1}{1 + \exp\left(-\left(\log(a) + L\right)/\lambda\right)}, \qquad L = \frac{u}{1-u}, \tag{7.39}$$

where $u \sim \text{Uniform}(0, 1)$. When λ approaches zero, the concrete distribution $q_{a,\lambda}(\gamma)$ converges to Bernoulli($\pi = \frac{a}{1+a}$). Because the discretisation procedure of the Concrete distribution allows for the optimisation of parameter a via gradient-based methods, we can use this reparameterisation scheme to optimise π with respect to the ELBO.

7.4.2.3 Hard concrete distribution

A drawback of the Binary Concrete distribution is that a realisation from the distribution may not be exactly zero and may be susceptible to the temperature value λ. To resolve this problem, Louizos et al. [25] extended the work of Maddison et al. [26] and Jang et al. [20] and introduced the Hard Concrete Distribution. Let s be a random variable with probability density $q(s) = \text{BinConcrete}(a, \lambda)$ and cumulative density $Q(s)$. After sampling s, we can "stretch" the value to the (c_0, c_1) interval, with $c_0 < 0$ and $c_1 > 1$, and apply a hard-sigmoid

$$s \sim \text{BinConcrete}(a, \lambda), \quad \bar{s} = s(c_1 - c_0) + c_0, \quad z = \min\left(1, \max\left(0, \bar{s}\right)\right). \tag{7.40}$$

This induces a distribution where the mass of $q(\bar{s})$ on the negative domain is "folded" to a delta peak at zero, and mass larger than one is "folded" to a delta peak at one, such that $q(\bar{s})$ is truncated to the $(0, 1)$ range. Then, z is a hard-sigmoid rectification of s with support $\{0, 1\}$, as desired. It can be shown that the probability of z being nonzero can be computed as

$$p(z \neq 0) = Q(\bar{s} \geq 0) = \frac{1}{1 + \exp\left(-\left(\log(a) - \lambda \log\left(-\frac{c_0}{c_1}\right)\right)\right)}. \tag{7.41}$$

With this reparameterisation, we can sample a discrete Bernoulli random variable with the above probability and learn a via gradient descent. For posterior inference, we follow Louizos et al. [25] and use $c_0 = -0.1$, $c_1 = 1.1$, $\lambda = \frac{2}{3}$.

7.4.2.4 Variational inference approximation

Finally, we describe the variational distributions $q(\boldsymbol{\beta}, \boldsymbol{\gamma}) \in \mathcal{Q}$, with free variational parameter $\boldsymbol{\theta}$, for our Dirichlet-multinomial model. For efficient computation, we again use a mean field approximation of the joint posterior of $(\boldsymbol{\beta}, \boldsymbol{\gamma})$ of the type

$$q(\boldsymbol{\beta}, \boldsymbol{\gamma}) = \prod_{k=1}^{p} \prod_{j=1}^{J} q(\beta_{kj}, \gamma_{kj}) = \prod_{k=1}^{p} \prod_{j=1}^{J} q(\beta_{kj} \mid \gamma_{kj})\, q(\gamma_{kj}), \tag{7.42}$$

where $q(\beta_{kj} \mid \gamma_{kj})$ is defined as

$$q(\beta_{kj} \mid \gamma_{kj}; \boldsymbol{\theta}_{kj}) = \begin{cases} \frac{1}{2}\text{Normal}\left(\beta_{kj} \mid \mu_{1kj}, \sigma_{1kj}^2\right) + \frac{1}{2}\text{Normal}\left(\beta_{kj} \mid \mu_{2kj}, \sigma_{2kj}^2\right) & \text{if } \gamma_{kj} = 1, \\ \delta_0 & \text{if } \gamma_{kj} = 0, \end{cases} \tag{7.43}$$

with variational parameter $\boldsymbol{\theta}_{kj} = (\mu_{1kj}, \sigma_{1kj}, \mu_{2kj}, \sigma_{2kj})$. Since the pMOM density has two modes, we propose a mixture of two normal distributions as the variational approximation when $\gamma_{kj} = 1$, while the approximation collapses to a spike at zero when $\gamma_{kj} = 0$. Samples from the above distribution can be obtained via the reparameterisation $u \sim \text{Uniform}(0, 1)$, $\epsilon \sim \text{Normal}(0, 1)$ and

$$\beta_{kj} \mid \gamma_{kj} = \begin{cases} \epsilon\sigma_{1kj}^2 + \mu_{1kj} & \text{if } u < 0.5 \text{ and } \gamma_{kj} = 1, \\ \epsilon\sigma_{2kj}^2 + \mu_{2kj} & \text{if } u \geq 0.5 \text{ and } \gamma_{kj} = 1, \\ 0 & \text{if } \gamma_{kj} = 0. \end{cases} \tag{7.44}$$

For each γ_{kj} we use a Hard Concrete distribution as the approximation, i.e. $q(\gamma_{kj}) \sim \text{HardBinConcrete}(a_{kj}; \lambda = \frac{2}{3}, c_0 = -0.1, c_1 = 1.1)$. Thus we can learn $q_{a_{kj}}(\gamma_{kj} = 1)$ by performing gradient descent on a_{kj}. For the baseline terms $\alpha_j's$, we use MAP estimates, since we are mainly interested in performing variable selection on $\beta_{kj}'s$. In summary, the ELBO objective of the Dirichlet-multinomial model can be written as

$$\begin{aligned} \text{ELBO} &= \mathbb{E}^{Q}\left[\log f(\boldsymbol{Y} \mid \boldsymbol{X}, \boldsymbol{\alpha}, \boldsymbol{\beta}, \boldsymbol{\gamma})\right] - \text{KL}\left(q(\boldsymbol{\beta}, \boldsymbol{\gamma}) \parallel p(\boldsymbol{\beta}, \boldsymbol{\gamma})\right) \\ &= \mathbb{E}^{Q}\left[\log f(\boldsymbol{Y} \mid \boldsymbol{X}, \boldsymbol{\alpha}, \boldsymbol{\beta}, \boldsymbol{\gamma})\right] - \sum_{k=1}^{p} \sum_{j=1}^{J} \text{KL}\left(q(\gamma_{kj}) \parallel p(\gamma_{kj})\right) \\ &\quad - \sum_{k=1}^{p} \sum_{j=1}^{J} q_{\pi}(\gamma_{kj} = 1)\, \text{KL}\left(q_{\boldsymbol{\theta}_{kj}}(\beta_{kj} \mid \gamma_{kj} = 1) \parallel p(\beta_{kj} \mid \gamma_{kj} = 1)\right). \end{aligned} \tag{7.45}$$

Since our prior on each γ_{kj} is Bernoulli(π), the KL term for γ_{kj} is

$$\begin{aligned}&\mathrm{KL}\left(q_{a_{kj}}\left(\gamma_{kj}\right) \parallel p\left(\gamma_{kj}\right)\right)\\ &=q_{a_{kj}}\left(\gamma_{kj}=1\right)\log\left(\frac{q_{a_{kj}}\left(\gamma_{kj}=1\right)}{\pi}\right)+q_{a_{kj}}\left(\gamma_{kj}=0\right)\log\left(\frac{q_{a_{kj}}\left(\gamma_{kj}=0\right)}{1-\pi}\right).\end{aligned}$$

The KL term corresponding to the pMOM prior can be expressed as

$$\begin{aligned}&\mathrm{KL}\left(q_{\boldsymbol{\theta}_{kj}}\left(\beta_{kj} \mid \gamma_{kj}=1\right) \parallel p\left(\beta_{kj} \mid \gamma_{kj}=1\right)\right)\\ &=-\,\mathbb{H}\left(\beta_{kj} \mid \gamma_{kj}=1\right)-\mathbb{E}_{q_{\boldsymbol{\theta}_{kj}}\left(\beta_{kj}\mid\gamma_{kj}=1\right)}\left(\log p\left(\beta_{kj} \mid \gamma_{kj}=1\right)\right),\end{aligned} \tag{7.46}$$

where $\mathbb{H}(\beta_{kj} \mid \gamma_{kj}=1)$ denotes the entropy under $q_{\boldsymbol{\theta}_{kj}}(\beta_{kj} \mid \gamma_{kj}=1)$. Both terms on the right-hand side of (7.46) can be computed using Monte Carlo approximations. Furthermore, to reduce the variance of the gradient, we can express the expectation in (7.46) analytically as

$$\frac{1}{S}\sum_{s=1}^{S}\left[\log\left(\left(\beta_{kj}^{(s)}\right)^2\right)-\frac{\mu_{1kj}^2+\sigma_{1kj}^2}{4\sigma_\beta^2}-\frac{\mu_{2kj}^2+\sigma_{2kj}^2}{4\sigma_\beta^2}-\log\left(\sqrt{2\pi}\right)-\frac{3}{2}\log\left(\sigma_\beta^2\right)\right], \tag{7.47}$$

where S is the number of Monte Carlo samples used in the approximation.

7.4.2.5 Posterior inference using tensorflow

The optimisation procedure to perform posterior inference using the proposed reparameterisation within the variational framework is implemented in TensorFlow [1] and uses the Adam optimiser proposed by Kingma and Ba [23] for gradient optimisation. The actual computation for the gradients is handled using Tensorflow's API for automatic differentiation. In order to reduce the complexity of the optimisation scheme, we standardised the data, both in simulations and real data analyses, and fixed the variance variational parameters $\sigma_{1kj}^2, \sigma_{2kj}^2$ of β_{kj}, for $k=1,\ldots,p$ and $j=1,\ldots,J$, to 1. Given that we are interested in the selection of the relevant variable, these parameters are not the prime interest of our inference and, also, they tend to be underestimated by variational inference schemes. In case it is of interest to learn these parameters, it is advised to perform a log transform $\log(\sigma_{kj}^2)=\tilde{\sigma}_{kj}^2$ so that the parameters remain in the positive domain during gradient updates. More details regarding the implementation can be found at https://github.com/mguindanigroup/vbmultdir.

7.5 Simulation study

In this section, we conduct several simulation studies and compare selection performances among different methods. For comparisons, we calculate accuracy (ACC), precision, recall, the F1 score and the Matthews correlation coefficient (MCC). Given the number of true positives (TPs), false positives (FPs), true negatives (TNs) and false negatives (FNs), the accuracy is calculated as (TP+TN)/(P+N), the precision as (TP)/(TP+FP), the recall as (TP)/(TP+FN), the F1 score as the geometric mean between precision and recall and the Matthews correlation coefficient as

$$\text{MCC} = \frac{\text{TP} \times \text{TN} - \text{FP} \times \text{FN}}{\sqrt{(\text{TP} + \text{FP})(\text{TP} + \text{FN})(\text{TN} + \text{FP})(\text{TN} + \text{FN})}}. \tag{7.48}$$

The Matthews correlation coefficient takes all values of the confusion matrix into account and is generally regarded as a balanced measure that can be used even if the true classes are imbalanced. We further compute and plot the receiving operating characteristic (ROC) curve and the area under the ROC curve (AUC) to show the selection performance of each method using different thresholds on the PPIs.

Negative binomial – small p large n example

We first simulated synthetic data with $n = 100$ samples and $p = 50$ features. The design matrix $\boldsymbol{X}$ was simulated according to a multivariate Normal$(\boldsymbol{\mu}, \boldsymbol{\Sigma})$, where each μ_k, $k = 1, \ldots, p$, was drawn from a Normal$(0, 0.1)$ and where the (l, m)th entry of the covariance matrix was set to be $\boldsymbol{\Sigma}_{lm} = \rho^{|l-m|}$ for $l \neq m$, with $\rho = 0, 0.3, 0.6, 0.9$. We sampled the marginal indicators of inclusion γ_k independently from a Bernoulli(π) with $\pi \in$ Uniform$(0.1, 0.2)$ and the corresponding nonzero β_k uniformly from the intervals $\pm[0.5, 2.0]$. Finally, we sampled the count data from a gamma-Poisson mixture model of the type

$$\begin{aligned} y_i &\sim \text{Poisson}(\lambda_i), \\ \lambda_i &\sim \text{Gamma}(r, 1/\exp(\psi_i)), \\ \psi_i &= (\boldsymbol{x}_i)_\gamma^T \boldsymbol{\beta}_\gamma + \beta_0, \end{aligned} \tag{7.49}$$

where we set $r = 1$ and $\beta_0 = 2$. Integrating λ_i out, y_i follows a negative binomial distribution of the type

$$y_i \sim \text{NB}\left(r, \frac{\exp(\psi_i)}{1 + \exp(\psi_i)}\right) \stackrel{\text{def}}{=} \text{NB}(r, p_i). \tag{7.50}$$

We assessed performances of the Bayesian negative binomial regression model described in this chapter, using MCMC and the variational inference algorithms for posterior inference. We also considered the LASSO method [45] using the glmnet R package [14]. Finally, we considered the *spike-and-slab* prior versus an adaptive shrinkage horseshoe prior [34]. When fitting the Bayesian models to the data, we imposed a flat Gamma$(0.01, 0.01)$ prior on the overdispersion r, a Scaled-Inv- $\chi^2(10, 1)$ on σ_β^2 and an improper uniform prior on the baseline β_0. For the VIEM and MCMC methods, we set the prior expectation of inclusion to be the true value, while for the VIEM-IS we used 30 equally spaced grids on the prior log odds of π from -500.0 to -1.0 as the important samples. Results we report here were obtained by running the MCMC algorithms for 23,000 iterations and discarding the initial 3000 samples as burn-in. We assessed convergence of the MCMC algorithms visually via the trace plots of the number of included variables. For the variational algorithms, we terminated the iterations when the absolute changes of the ELBO was less than 0.0001. We utilised six threads out of a hexacore CPU to conduct parallel computation for the VIEM-IS algorithm.

Table 7.1 reports results for precision, recall, MCC, AUC, F1 score, ACC and computing time in seconds, averaged across 50 replicated data sets, with standard deviations in parentheses, and Fig. 7.3 shows the corresponding ROC curves, for the different values of ρ. When features are independent ($\rho = 0.0$) or weakly correlated ($\rho = 0.3$), we find that the selection performance of the variational methods closely matches that of the sampling-based methods. Fig. 7.3A and 7.3B also illustrate that the ROC curves of VIEM (green dotted line) and VIEM-IS (purple solid line) are close in performance to those of the MCMC-HS (red (dark grey in print version) dashed line) and MCMC-SS (blue dot-dash line). When the correlation coefficient ρ increases, we notice a decrease in performance of the VIEM method. This is because the density landscape of the posterior likelihood becomes multimodal as ρ increases and the expectation maximisation (EM) algorithm is notoriously vulnerable to be trapped in local optima [39]. The VIEM-IS, instead, which utilises different hyperparameters $\boldsymbol{\vartheta}$ and also several variational parameters $\boldsymbol{\theta}$ to solve each EM optimisation independently in parallel, shows more robust performance. When the variables are strongly correlated ($\rho = 0.9$), the fully factorised assumption of the variational approximation in (7.23) becomes invalid and hence the performance of both variational methods becomes inferior to those of the sampling-based methods. Furthermore, as we can see in Table 7.1, the MCC values

Table 7.1 Negative binomial – small p large n example: Performance comparison of variational inference EM *spike-and-slab* (VIEM-SS), variational inference EM *spike-and-slab* with importance sampling on π (VIEM-SS-IS), MCMC *spike-and-slab* (MCMC-SS), MCMC horseshoe (MCMC-HS) and glmnet (LASSO). Accuracy, recall, precision, F1 score and Matthews correlation coefficient (MCC) are shown, averaged over 50 replicated simulated data sets (standard deviation in parentheses).

	MCMS-HS	MCMC-SS	VIEM-SS	VIEM-SS-IS	LASSO
			$\rho = 0.0$		
Precision	0.987 (0.056)	0.966 (0.091)	0.807 (0.215)	0.980 (0.061)	0.184 (0.110)
Recall	0.967 (0.086)	0.959 (0.115)	0.958 (0.095)	0.939 (0.102)	0.997 (0.022)
MCC	0.973 (0.058)	0.956 (0.090)	0.858 (0.163)	0.953 (0.062)	0.300 (0.151)
AUC	0.999 (0.005)	0.976 (0.057)	0.975 (0.044)	0.985 (0.038)	0.209 (0.148)
F1	0.974 (0.057)	0.957 (0.089)	0.862 (0.159)	0.954 (0.061)	0.297 (0.139)
ACC	0.995 (0.011)	0.993 (0.014)	0.969 (0.040)	0.992 (0.010)	0.079 (0.026)
Time (s)	32.270 (1.187)	29.012 (3.559)	0.047 (0.039)	0.325 (0.256)	0.339 (0.091)
			$\rho = 0.3$		
Precision	0.983 (0.067)	0.957 (0.088)	0.751 (0.221)	0.960 (0.084)	0.186 (0.095)
Recall	0.963 (0.087)	0.947 (0.116)	0.957 (0.086)	0.937 (0.102)	0.992 (0.037)
MCC	0.969 (0.071)	0.944 (0.096)	0.818 (0.157)	0.940 (0.069)	0.296 (0.139)
AUC	0.999 (0.004)	0.971 (0.059)	0.975 (0.028)	0.992 (0.018)	0.220 (0.139)
F1	0.971 (0.066)	0.947 (0.092)	0.823 (0.154)	0.942 (0.066)	0.302 (0.122)
ACC	0.994 (0.015)	0.990 (0.017)	0.955 (0.047)	0.990 (0.012)	0.085 (0.031)
Time (s)	32.476 (1.352)	29.754 (4.112)	0.043 (0.033)	0.311 (0.230)	0.350 (0.069)
			$\rho = 0.6$		
Precision	0.964 (0.103)	0.971 (0.083)	0.727 (0.254)	0.971 (0.067)	0.196 (0.116)
Recall	0.964 (0.091)	0.948 (0.108)	0.921 (0.123)	0.905 (0.120)	0.983 (0.076)
MCC	0.957 (0.077)	0.953 (0.087)	0.782 (0.202)	0.928 (0.073)	0.306 (0.154)
AUC	0.998 (0.014)	0.972 (0.055)	0.956 (0.056)	0.977 (0.038)	0.190 (0.143)
F1	0.958 (0.077)	0.955 (0.081)	0.790 (0.196)	0.931 (0.071)	0.312 (0.142)
ACC	0.992 (0.016)	0.991 (0.018)	0.945 (0.060)	0.988 (0.013)	0.085 (0.034)
Time (s)	33.501 (4.543)	29.291 (4.125)	0.048 (0.034)	0.341 (0.233)	0.452 (0.121)
			$\rho = 0.9$		
Precision	0.889 (0.189)	0.887 (0.190)	0.587 (0.280)	0.772 (0.223)	0.234 (0.099)
Recall	0.743 (0.197)	0.705 (0.226)	0.624 (0.218)	0.580 (0.222)	0.901 (0.159)
MCC	0.784 (0.176)	0.766 (0.211)	0.545 (0.247)	0.618 (0.186)	0.342 (0.131)
AUC	0.960 (0.063)	0.848 (0.117)	0.820 (0.123)	0.845 (0.116)	0.192 (0.117)
F1	0.791 (0.167)	0.774 (0.198)	0.591 (0.208)	0.624 (0.187)	0.356 (0.113)
ACC	0.962 (0.037)	0.961 (0.039)	0.910 (0.067)	0.937 (0.043)	0.089 (0.038)
Time (s)	32.456 (1.343)	28.670 (3.468)	0.036 (0.031)	0.269 (0.225)	0.803 (0.160)

of MCMC-HS and MCMC-SS also decrease sharply when ρ increases from 0.6 to 0.9. Therefore, we conclude that sampling methods also suffer to some extent from severe multicollinearity, which is also illustrated in Fig. 7.3D. From a computational point of view, as expected, variational methods (VIEM-SS and VIEM-SS-IS) show a dramatic improvement in speed over the sampling-based methods (MCMC-SS and MCMC-HS). In particular, the variational methods are 100 to 1000 times faster than the sampling methods.

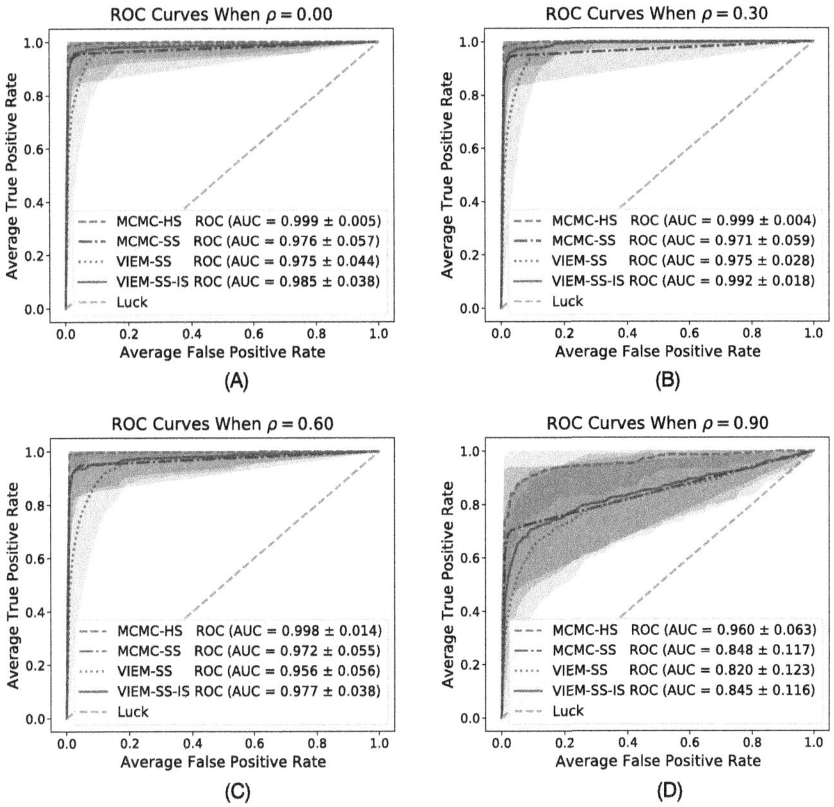

Figure 7.3 Negative binomial – small p large n example: Comparison of selection performance (ROC curves). Variational Inference EM *spike-and-slab* (VIEM-SS), Variational Inference EM *spike-and-slab* with importance sampling on π (VIEM-SS-IS), MCMC with *spike-and-slab* prior (MCMC-SS) and MCMC with horseshoe prior (MCMC-HS). The ROC curves and the corresponding standard deviations are averaged over 50 replicated data sets. (A) $\rho = 0.0$, (B) $\rho = 0.30$, (C) $\rho = 0.6$, (D) $\rho = 0.9$.

Negative binomial – large p small n example

Next, we considered a simulation with $p = 1000$ and $n = 100$, which we obtained from the previous one simply by adding 950 zero coefficients and adding another 950 columns of independent variables $\tilde{\boldsymbol{X}}_{100\times 950} \sim \text{Normal}(\mathbf{0}, \mathbb{I})$ to the design matrix. We used the same hyperparameter configuration as in the previous example. We dropped the MCMC-HS algorithm, since the moment matrix is not full rank when $p \gg n$. Results are reported in Table 7.2 and Fig. 7.4. Both variational methods achieve similar performance as the MCMC-SS method but still are around 15 to 75

Table 7.2 Negative binomial – large p small n example: Performance comparison of variational inference EM *spike-and-slab* (VIEM-SS), variational inference EM *spike-and-slab* with importance sampling on π (VIEM-SS-IS), MCMC *spike-and-slab* (MCMC-SS) and glmnet [14] (LASSO). Values averaged over 50 replicated simulated data sets are shown (standard deviation in the parentheses).

	MCMC-SS	VIEM-SS	VIEM-SS-IS	LASSO
		$\rho = 0.0$		
Precision	0.755 (0.227)	0.460 (0.274)	0.945 (0.103)	0.100 (0.054)
Recall	0.840 (0.320)	0.965 (0.071)	0.925 (0.108)	0.912 (0.199)
MCC	0.799 (0.242)	0.639 (0.205)	0.931 (0.075)	0.275 (0.069)
AUC	0.919 (0.160)	0.977 (0.039)	0.970 (0.047)	0.014 (0.014)
F1	0.817 (0.203)	0.584 (0.240)	0.928 (0.079)	0.168 (0.068)
ACC	0.997 (0.003)	0.988 (0.011)	0.999 (0.001)	0.005 (0.002)
Time (s)	1039.920 (94.772)	14.256 (29.387)	82.463 (177.261)	0.815 (0.109)
		$\rho = 0.3$		
Precision	0.773 (0.221)	0.424 (0.301)	0.814 (0.284)	0.117 (0.046)
Recall	0.842 (0.308)	0.909 (0.132)	0.854 (0.184)	0.921 (0.124)
MCC	0.812 (0.221)	0.588 (0.240)	0.818 (0.227)	0.310 (0.064)
AUC	0.920 (0.154)	0.947 (0.070)	0.928 (0.093)	0.012 (0.012)
F1	0.801 (0.234)	0.534 (0.271)	0.807 (0.242)	0.203 (0.071)
ACC	0.997 (0.003)	0.985 (0.014)	0.996 (0.009)	0.006 (0.002)
Time (s)	1086.613 (163.832)	14.228 (20.609)	74.665 (107.522)	0.782 (0.110)

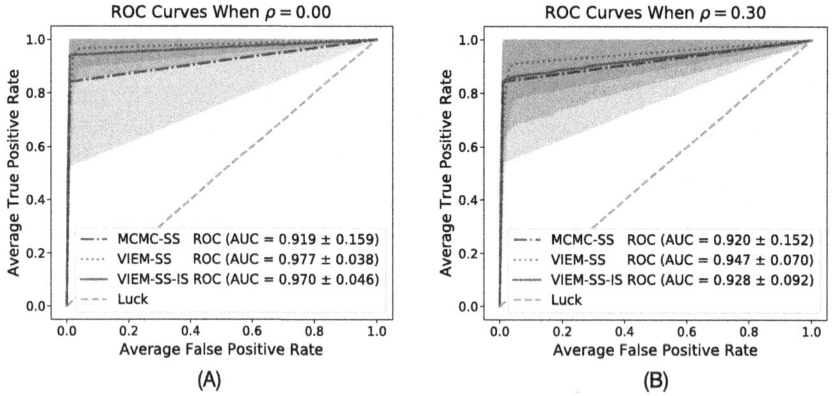

Figure 7.4 Negative binomial – large p small n example: Comparison of selection performance (ROC curves). Variational Inference EM *spike-and-slab* (VIEM-SS), Variational Inference EM *spike-and-slab* with importance sampling on π (VIEM-SS-IS), MCMC with *spike-and-slab* prior (MCMC-SS) and MCMC with horseshoe prior (MCMC-HS). The ROC curves and the corresponding standard deviations are averaged over 50 replicated data sets. (A) $\rho = 0.0$, (B) $\rho = 0.30$.

times faster than the MCMC-SS. For the tuning parameter in the LASSO method, we used the default **cv.glmnet** and we report the results for the parameter with the smallest cross-validation error.

Dirichlet-multinomial example

Finally, we conducted a simulation study to assess performance of the Bayesian Dirichlet-multinomial regression model for multivariate responses. We used the approximate variational method described in this chapter and the MCMC posterior sampling of [48], which employs *spike-and-slab* priors. We also considered the penalised likelihood approach of [9]. We simulated data with $n = 100$, $J = 50$ and $p = 50$. More specifically, for each sample $i = 1, \ldots, n$, we generated a matrix of covariates $\boldsymbol{x}_i \sim \text{Normal}(0, \Sigma)$, where the (l, m)th entry of the covariance matrix was set to be $\Sigma_{lm} = \rho^{|l-m|}$ for $l \neq m$. Here, we set $\rho = 0.4$. The responses were sampled from a Multinomial-Dirichlet regression model of the type

$$\boldsymbol{y}_i \sim \text{Multinomial}(y_{i+}, \boldsymbol{\phi}_i), \tag{7.51}$$

$$\boldsymbol{\phi}_i \sim \text{Dirichlet}(\xi_{i1}, \ldots, \xi_{i50}), \tag{7.52}$$

with $y_{i+} \sim \text{Uniform}(1000, 2000)$ as the observed total count of each sample and where $\boldsymbol{\phi}_i$ denotes the 50×1 vector of multinomial parameters. In order to evaluate the effect of different assumptions about overdispersion in the data, we set the parameters of the Dirichlet prior by letting $\xi_{ij} = \frac{\xi_{ij}}{\xi_i^+} \times \frac{1-r}{r}$, $j = 1, \ldots, 50$, where small values of r lead to more overdispersed data; ξ_{ij} was associated to the covariates through a log link of the type

$$\log(\xi_{ij}) = \alpha_j + \sum_{k=1}^{p} \beta_{kj} x_{ik}, \tag{7.53}$$

with intercept $\alpha_j \sim \text{Uniform}(-2.3, 2.3)$, similarly as in [48] and [9].

Table 7.3 reports the results for precision, recall, MCC, AUC, F1 score, and accuracy, averaged across 50 replicated data sets, with standard deviations in parentheses, and Fig. 7.5 reports the ROC curves. For the Bayesian methods, in each data set relevant associations were selected to ensure a Bayesian false discovery rate (FDR) control of 0.1. Results show that the proposed variational Bayes approach performs comparably with the MCMC approach, although it is characterised by lower recall values. The performance of the penalised Group LASSO appears to degrade with increasing overdispersion.

Table 7.3 Dirichlet-multinomial example: Performance comparisons of variational inference with nonlocal prior (VI), MCMC spike-and-slab (MCMC) and the penalised Group LASSO approach (Group LASSO). The selection performance is evaluated using accuracy, recall, precision, F1 score and Matthews correlation coefficient (MCC), all averaged over 50 replicated simulated data sets (standard deviation in parentheses).

	$r = 0.01$			$r = 0.1$		
	DMBVS	VI	Group LASSO	DMBVS	VI	Group LASSO
Precision	0.99 (0.02)	0.95 (0.06)	0.60 (0.07)	0.98 (0.04)	0.76 (0.11)	0.33 (0.07)
Recall	0.48 (0.10)	0.41 (0.13)	0.81 (0.09)	0.28 (0.14)	0.44 (0.10)	0.63 (0.14)
MCC	0.68 (0.08)	0.61 (0.10)	0.69 (0.07)	0.51 (0.14)	0.57 (0.08)	0.48 (0.10)
AUC	0.99 (0.01)	0.99 (0.01)	0.90 (0.04)	0.94 (0.03)	0.91 (0.05)	0.86 (0.10)
F1	0.64 (0.10)	0.56 (0.13)	0.68 (0.07)	0.42 (0.17)	0.55 (0.09)	0.45 (0.09)
ACC	0.99 (0.001)	0.99 (0.001)	0.99 (0.002)	0.99 (0.001)	0.99 (0.001)	0.98 (0.004)

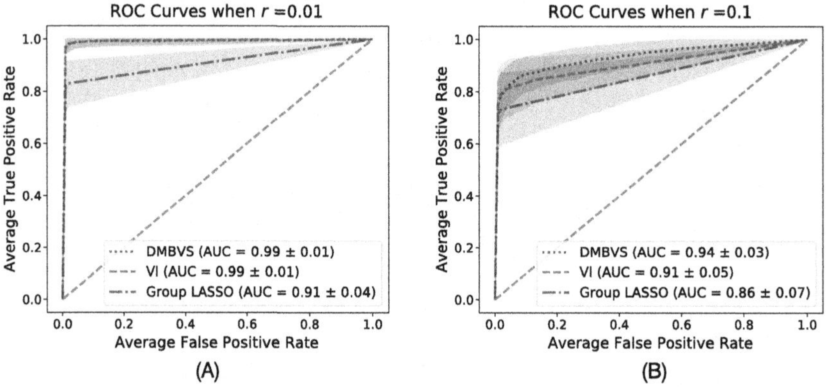

Figure 7.5 Dirichlet-multinomial example: Comparison of selection performance (ROC curves). DMBVS, variational inference (VI) and Group LASSO. The ROC curves and the corresponding standard deviations are averaged over 50 replicated data sets. (A) $r = 0.01$, (B) $r = 0.10$.

7.6 Benchmark applications

Next, we show performances of the methods on some benchmark applications and case study data. In particular, we use the well-known Boston housing data set for an application of the negative binomial model and apply the Dirichlet-multinomial model to a case study data set on microbiome data.

Boston housing data

The Boston housing data set, collected by the U.S. Census Service, can be obtained from the **StatLib** archive at http://lib.stat.cmu.edu/datasets/boston, and has been used extensively to benchmark different algorithms.

The data set consists of 506 observations on 14 variables. Here we use the nonnegative attribute **medv** (median value of owner-occupied home in \$1000) as the outcome and the remaining 13 features as predictors. We preprocessed the data by standardising the predictors to account for the different units of measurement. We also created a larger data set by adding 300 noise random features sampled from a standard Gaussian distribution.

For this data set, we focused in particular on the predictive accuracy of the method and considered prediction results averaged over 100 random splits of the whole data set into training (405 observations, 80%) and validation (101 observations, 20%) sets. To test the goodness-of-fit, we evaluate the widely used metric in GLMs called Pearson residuals on the training set,

$$E = \sum_{i=1}^{n} \left(\frac{y_i - \hat{\mu}_i}{\sqrt{\hat{\mu}_i (1 + \hat{\kappa} \hat{\mu}_i)}} \right)^2,$$

where $\hat{\mu}$ and $\hat{\kappa}$ are the estimated mean and quasidispersion ($\hat{\kappa} = 0$ for Poisson and $\hat{\kappa} = \hat{r}^{-1}$ for the negative binomial regression models). We also compute the root mean squared predictive error (RMSPE) on the testing set. We compared performances of the two variational-based algorithms (VIEM-SS and VIEM-SS-IS), the two sampling-based algorithms (MCMC-HS and MCMC-SS) and the LASSO method. For the Bayesian methods, we used the same hyperparameter setting as in the simulation study and ran 13,000 Gibbs sampling iterations with the initial 3000 samples discarded as burn-in. For the variational algorithms, we terminated them when changes of the ELBO were less than 0.001. For the LASSO method, we again used the default **cv.glmnet** function [14] with cross-validation.

Results are summarised in Table 7.4, where we again observe that the two variational methods achieve similar performance to the MCMC methods, but at a much faster computational speed. In terms of goodness-of-fit measured by Poisson residuals, the LASSO-based Poisson model performs the worst due to its unrealistic equal-dispersion assumption, while the negative binomial model significantly improves the performance when assuming a gamma-distributed multiplicative random effect term r [53]. When looking into the variable selection performances, we notice that all Bayesian methods would choose **lstat** as the only important feature, while LASSO tended to include more covariates in the model (results not shown).

Table 7.4 Boston housing data: Completion times in second, Pearson residuals and RMSPE. Values averaged over 100 random splits of the whole data set into training and validation sets are shown (standard deviations in parentheses).

Methods	Time (s)	Pearson residuals	RMSPE
	Small data set ($p = 13$)		
MCMC-HS	98.280 (13.190)	34.705 (1.518)	6.063 (0.702)
MCMC-SS	68.830 (3.860)	37.670 (3.508)	5.849 (0.807)
VIEM-SS	0.005 (0.002)	38.779 (2.030)	5.730 (0.594)
VIEM-SS-IS	0.036 (0.005)	38.841 (1.885)	5.729 (0.592)
LASSO (1SE)	0.182 (0.026)	356.213 (25.330)	4.413 (0.650)
LASSO (MIN)	0.183 (0.018)	307.235 (17.790)	4.171 (0.576)
	Large data set ($p = 313$)		
MCMC-HS	211.260 (21.350)	37.016 (1.916)	5.862 (0.629)
MCMC-SS	486.810 (77.710)	37.815 (2.538)	5.765 (0.595)
VIEM-SS	0.050 (0.010)	39.035 (1.959)	5.752 (0.635)
VIEM-SS-IS	0.400 (0.030)	38.913 (1.803)	5.728 (0.591)
LASSO (1SE)	3.541 (0.344)	418.373 (31.456)	4.831 (0.622)
LASSO (MIN)	3.561 (0.319)	344.157 (26.746)	4.510 (0.645)

Microbiome data

We apply our variational method with nonlocal prior to a human gut microbiome data set, which has been previously used in [49] to investigate the association of dietary and environmental variables with the gut microbiota. Here, the multivariate outcome $\boldsymbol{y}_i$ represents the vector of counts obtained as the taxonomic abundances of q taxa. More specifically, the data set contains microbiome 16S rDNA sequencing data from a cross-sectional analysis of $n = 98$ healthy volunteers. The original microbiome abundance table contained 3068 operational taxonomic units (OTUs) (excluding the singletons), which were further combined into 127 genera. More specifically, here we follow [9] and consider a subset of 30 relatively common genera that appeared in at least 25 subjects. Diet information was also collected on all subjects, using a food frequency questionnaire and then converting to nutrient intake values, which were summarised in an $n = 98 \times p = 117$ matrix of representative nutrients. We considered the squared root transformed values of taxon abundance, similarly as in [9].

We applied the Dirichlet-multinomial model, with nonlocal priors and variational inference. Our method selected four genera and eight nutrient types, after controlling for a Bayesian FDR of 0.1, corresponding to a PPI of 0.745. Selected associations are visualised in a bipartite graph in Fig. 7.6.

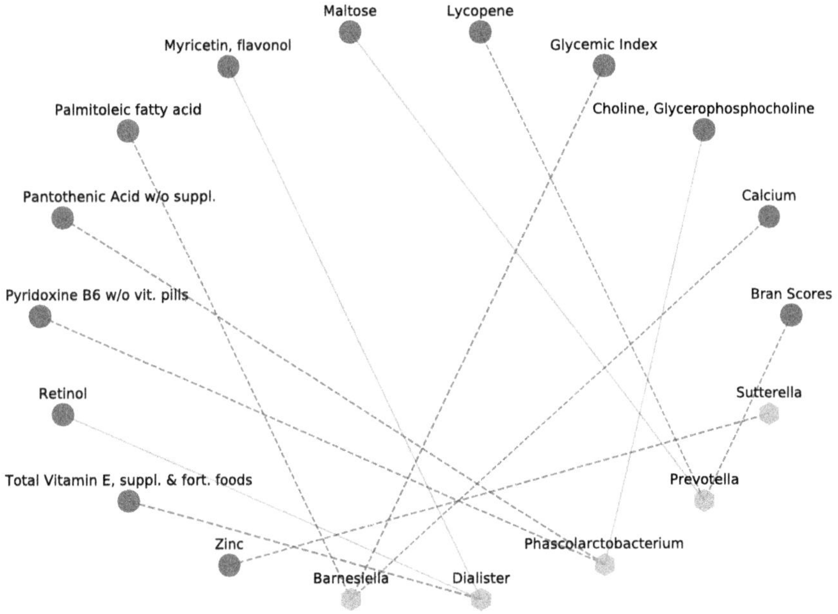

Figure 7.6 Microbiome data: Bipartite graph of selected taxon-covariate associations. *Blue dashed lines*, negative associations; *red solid lines*, positive associations.

Similarly as in [49], *Prevotella* is found to be highly associated with maltose, which is a common disaccharide, indicative of a high-carbohydrate diet. At the same time, *Prevotella* is found to be negatively associated with nutrients typical of a high-fibre diet, a finding which has also been confirmed in the literature (see e.g. [21]). Also, increased *Barnesiella* has been linked to diets rich in gluten, characterised by high glycemic index [27]. The penalised Group LASSO approach selected a larger number of significant associations, involving 12 nutrient types and 10 genera (results not shown).

7.7 Conclusion

We have developed Bayesian variable selection approaches using variational inference for the negative binomial and Dirichlet-multinomial regression models. For the negative binomial model, we have introduced two data augmentation schemes to obtain deterministic update rules for the parameters of interest via variational EM approaches. For the Dirichlet-multinomial model, we have proposed a low-variance stochastic gradient method to optimise the ELBO objective. The variational algorithms we have developed can be applied to other Bayesian regression settings, with variable selection. We have shown on simulated data that the variational schemes have similar selection performance as the sampling-based MCMC methods.

Some of the shortcomings of the variational approach can be explained by the approximating family distributions. While the proposed factorisation in Eq. (7.25) allows for a tractable closed-form computation, the independence assumption can cause the model to underestimate the posterior variance of the latent variables. In situations with correlated explanatory variables, the performance is sensitive to initialisation and can be subject to poor optima. To overcome the problems mentioned above, attempts have been made to specify an expressive variational distribution while maintaining efficient computation [37] and to make posterior inference robust to initialisation by constraining the optimisation path [2].

References

[1] M. Abadi, A. Agarwal, P. Barham, E. Brevdo, Z. Chen, C. Citro, G.S. Corrado, A. Davis, J. Dean, M. Devin, S. Ghemawat, I. Goodfellow, A. Harp, G. Irving, M. Isard, Y. Jia, R. Jozefowicz, L. Kaiser, M. Kudlur, J. Levenberg, D. Mané, R. Monga, S. Moore, D. Murray, C. Olah, M. Schuster, J. Shlens, B. Steiner, I. Sutskever, K. Talwar, P. Tucker, V. Vanhoucke, V. Vasudevan, F. Viégas, O. Vinyals, P. Warden, M. Wattenberg, M. Wicke, Y. Yu, X. Zheng, TensorFlow: large-scale machine learning on heterogeneous systems, Software available from tensorflow.org, 2015.

[2] J. Altosaar, R. Ranganath, D.M. Blei, Proximity variational inference, arXiv preprint, arXiv:1705.08931, 2017.

[3] C.E. Antoniak, Mixtures of Dirichlet processes with applications to Bayesian nonparametric problems, The Annals of Statistics (1974) 1152–1174.

[4] D.M. Blei, A. Kucukelbir, J.D. McAuliffe, Variational inference: a review for Statisticians, Journal of the American Statistical Association 112 (518) (2017) 859–877.

[5] P.J. Brown, M. Vannucci, T. Fearn, Multivariate Bayesian variable selection and prediction, Journal of the Royal Statistical Society: Series B (Statistical Methodology) 60 (3) (1998) 627–641.

[6] K.P. Burnham, D.R. Anderson, Model Selection and Multimodel Inference: A Practical Information-Theoretic Approach, Springer Science & Business Media, 2003.

[7] P. Carbonetto, M. Stephens, et al., Scalable variational inference for Bayesian variable selection in regression, and its accuracy in genetic association studies, Bayesian Analysis 7 (1) (2012) 73–108.

[8] R. Chandra, L. Dagum, D. Kohr, D. Maydan, R. Menon, J. McDonald, Parallel Programming in OpenMP, Morgan Kaufmann, 2001.

[9] J. Chen, H. Li, Variable selection for sparse Dirichlet-multinomial regression with an application to microbiome data analysis, The Annals of Applied Statistics 7 (1) (2013).

[10] R. Durrett, Probability: Theory and Examples, Cambridge University Press, 2010.

[11] J. Fan, R. Li, Variable selection via nonconcave penalized likelihood and its oracle properties, Journal of the American Statistical Association 96 (456) (2001) 1348–1360.
[12] J. Fan, J. Lv, A selective overview of variable selection in high dimensional feature space, Statistica Sinica 20 (1) (2010) 101.
[13] J. Fan, H. Peng, et al., Nonconcave penalized likelihood with a diverging number of parameters, The Annals of Statistics 32 (3) (2004) 928–961.
[14] J. Friedman, T. Hastie, R. Tibshirani, Regularization paths for generalized linear models via coordinate descent, Journal of Statistical Software 33 (1) (2010) 1.
[15] E.I. George, R.E. McCulloch, Approaches for Bayesian variable selection, Statistica Sinica 7 (1997) 339–373.
[16] J.E. Griffin, P.J. Brown, et al., Inference with normal-gamma prior distributions in regression problems, Bayesian Analysis 5 (1) (2010) 171–188.
[17] J.A. Hoeting, D. Madigan, A.E. Raftery, C.T. Volinsky, Bayesian model averaging: a tutorial, Statistical Science (1999) 382–401.
[18] J.C. Huang, Q.D. Morris, B.J. Frey, Bayesian inference of MicroRNA targets from sequence and expression data, Journal of Computational Biology 14 (5) (2007) 550–563.
[19] X. Huang, J. Wang, F. Liang, A variational algorithm for Bayesian variable selection, arXiv preprint, arXiv:1602.07640, 2016.
[20] E. Jang, S. Gu, B. Poole, Categorical reparameterization with Gumbel-Softmax, CoRR, arXiv:1611.01144, 2016.
[21] H.B. Jang, M.-K. Choi, J.H. Kang, S.I. Park, H.-J. Lee, Association of dietary patterns with the fecal microbiota in Korean adolescents, BMC Nutrition 3 (1) (2017) 20.
[22] V.E. Johnson, D. Rossell, On the use of non-local prior densities in Bayesian hypothesis tests, Journal of the Royal Statistical Society: Series B (Statistical Methodology) 72 (2) (2010) 143–170.
[23] D.P. Kingma, J. Ba, Adam: a method for stochastic optimization, arXiv preprint, arXiv: 1412.6980, 2014.
[24] B.A. Logsdon, G.E. Hoffman, J.G. Mezey, A variational Bayes algorithm for fast and accurate multiple locus genome-wide association analysis, BMC Bioinformatics 11 (1) (2010) 58.
[25] C. Louizos, M. Welling, D.P. Kingma, Learning sparse neural networks through l_0 regularization, in: International Conference on Learning Representations, 2018.
[26] C.J. Maddison, A. Mnih, Y.W. Teh, The concrete distribution: a continuous relaxation of discrete random variables, CoRR, arXiv:1611.00712, 2016.
[27] E.V. Marietta, A.M. Gomez, C. Yeoman, A.Y. Tilahun, C.R. Clark, D.H. Luckey, J.A. Murray, B.A. White, Y.C. Kudva, G. Rajagopalan, Low incidence of spontaneous type 1 diabetes in non-obese diabetic mice raised on gluten-free diets is associated with changes in the intestinal microbiome, PLoS ONE 8 (11) (2013) e78687.
[28] T.J. Mitchell, J.J. Beauchamp, Bayesian variable selection in linear regression, Journal of the American Statistical Association 83 (404) (1988) 1023–1032.
[29] J.E. Mosimann, On the compound multinomial distribution, the multivariate β-distribution, and correlations among proportions, Biometrika 49 (1/2) (1962) 65–82.
[30] F. Nathoo, A. Babul, A. Moiseev, N. Virji-Babul, M. Beg, A variational Bayes spatiotemporal model for electromagnetic brain mapping, Biometrics 70 (1) (2014) 132–143.
[31] R.B. O'Hara, M.J. Sillanpää, et al., A review of Bayesian variable selection methods: what, how and which, Bayesian Analysis 4 (1) (2009) 85–117.

[32] J.T. Ormerod, C. You, S. Müller, et al., A variational Bayes approach to variable selection, Electronic Journal of Statistics 11 (2) (2017) 3549–3594.
[33] T. Park, G. Casella, The Bayesian lasso, Journal of the American Statistical Association 103 (482) (2008) 681–686.
[34] N.G. Polson, J.G. Scott, Shrink globally, act locally: sparse Bayesian regularization and prediction, Bayesian Statistics 9 (2010) 501–538.
[35] N.G. Polson, J.G. Scott, J. Windle, Bayesian inference for logistic models using Pólya–Gamma latent variables, Journal of the American Statistical Association 108 (504) (2013) 1339–1349.
[36] M.H. Quenouille, A relation between the logarithmic, Poisson, and negative binomial series, Biometrics 5 (2) (1949) 162–164.
[37] R. Ranganath, D. Tran, D. Blei, Hierarchical variational models, in: International Conference on Machine Learning, 2016, pp. 324–333.
[38] S.J. Roberts, Bayesian Gaussian Processes for Sequential Prediction, Optimisation and Quadrature, PhD thesis, University of Oxford, 2010.
[39] V. Ročková, Particle EM for variable selection, Journal of the American Statistical Association (2018) 1–14.
[40] F.R. Ruiz, M.K. Titsias, D.M. Blei, The generalized reparameterization gradient, in: Advances in Neural Information Processing Systems, 2016, pp. 460–468.
[41] G. Schwarz, et al., Estimating the dimension of a model, The Annals of Statistics 6 (2) (1978) 461–464.
[42] M. Shin, A. Bhattacharya, V.E. Johnson, Scalable Bayesian variable selection using non-local prior densities in ultrahigh-dimensional settings, Statistica Sinica 28 (2) (2018) 1053.
[43] T. Stepleton, Understanding the "Antoniak equation", unpublished manuscript, 2008.
[44] F.C. Stingo, et al., A Bayesian graphical modeling approach to microRNA regulatory network inference, The Annals of Applied Statistics 4 (4) (2010) 2024–2048.
[45] R. Tibshirani, Regression shrinkage and selection via the lasso, Journal of the Royal Statistical Society. Series B (Methodological) (1996) 267–288.
[46] M.K. Titsias, Learning model reparametrizations: implicit variational inference by fitting MCMC distributions, arXiv preprint, arXiv:1708.01529, 2017.
[47] M.K. Titsias, M. Lázaro-Gredilla, Spike and slab variational inference for multi-task and multiple kernel learning, in: Advances in Neural Information Processing Systems, 2011, pp. 2339–2347.
[48] W.D. Wadsworth, R. Argiento, M. Guindani, J. Galloway-Pena, S.A. Shelburne, M. Vannucci, An integrative Bayesian Dirichlet-multinomial regression model for the analysis of taxonomic abundances in microbiome data, BMC Bioinformatics 18 (1) (2017) 94.
[49] G.D. Wu, J. Chen, C. Hoffmann, K. Bittinger, Y.-Y. Chen, S.A. Keilbaugh, M. Bewtra, D. Knights, W.A. Walters, R. Knight, et al., Linking long-term dietary patterns with gut microbial enterotypes, Science 334 (6052) (2011) 105–108.
[50] C.-X. Zhang, S. Xu, J.-S. Zhang, A novel variational Bayesian method for variable selection in logistic regression models, Computational Statistics & Data Analysis (2018).
[51] L. Zhang, M. Guindani, F. Versace, J.M. Engelmann, M. Vannucci, et al., A spatiotemporal nonparametric Bayesian model of multi-subject fMRI data, The Annals of Applied Statistics 10 (2) (2016) 638–666.
[52] M. Zhou, L. Carin, Negative binomial process count and mixture modeling, IEEE Transactions on Pattern Analysis and Machine Intelligence 37 (2) (2015) 307–320.

[53] M. Zhou, L. Li, D. Dunson, L. Carin, Lognormal and gamma mixed negative binomial regression, in: Proceedings of the International Conference on Machine Learning. International Conference on Machine Learning, vol. 2012, NIH Public Access, 2012, p. 1343.
[54] Q. Zhou, Y. Guan, et al., Fast model-fitting of Bayesian variable selection regression using the iterative complex factorization algorithm, Bayesian Analysis (2018).
[55] H. Zou, T. Hastie, Regularization and variable selection via the elastic net, Journal of the Royal Statistical Society: Series B (Statistical Methodology) 67 (2) (2005) 301–320.

CHAPTER 8

Bayesian spectral analysis regression

Taeryon Choi[a], **Peter J. Lenk**[b]
[a]Korea University, Department of Statistics, Seoul, Republic of Korea
[b]University of Michigan, Stephen M. Ross School of Business, Ann Arbor, MI, United States

Contents

8.1 Introduction

The Bayesian analysis of nonparametric regression or, more appropriately, flexible regression is conceptually similar to Bayes [2], who estimates the probability for Bernoulli trials, except in its details, which concerns three issues. First, how should one construct a prior distribution on the space of regression functions? The short answer for this chapter is to use Gaussian processes ([37] and [47]). Second, given that the regression function is infinite-dimensional, how can we possibly estimate it? All methods use some kind of discrete approximation when implementing the algorithm, and we use a finite series approximation of cosine functions. Third, nonparametric regression can be too flexible and overfit the data. Our solution is to use a smoothing prior that dampens high-frequency terms in the spectral representation by shrinking them towards zero.

Gaussian processes have three characteristics that make them an attractive candidate for a probability model on the space of smooth functions. The mean of the Gaussian process is the prior mean of the regression function; the correlation function determines the smoothness of the regression

Flexible Bayesian Regression Modelling
https://doi.org/10.1016/B978-0-12-815862-3.00013-5

function, and the variance controls the trade-off between the prior mean and the sample data. The standard analysis of Gaussian process priors makes heavy use of conditional normal distributions, which can be numerically taxing because they involve inverting $n \times n$ covariance matrices where n is the sample size, and these matrices may be ill conditioned. Moreover, it can be challenging to extend the basic model to include shape constraints and nonnormal likelihoods.

This chapter summarises Bayesian spectral analysis regression (BSAR) ([26] and [28]), which represents the Gaussian process with a finite sum of cosine functions. BSAR offers multiple benefits. First, the spectral representation provides a natural method to describe smoothness. The rate at which the spectral coefficients converge to zero controls the smoothness of the sample paths of the Gaussian process, and smooth functions do not have high-frequency oscillations. BSAR uses a hierarchical smoothing prior that shrinks the spectral coefficients to zero, and the amount of shrinkage increases with the frequency of the coefficient. This specification dampens spurious, high-frequency oscillations, thus resulting in a smooth estimate. Second, the method is fully Bayesian, and the smoothing hyperparameters are estimated by Bayesian inference and not cross-validation. Finally, spectral analysis linearises the Gaussian process, which results in simpler computations and facilitates model extensions, such as shape constraints and nonnormal likelihoods. Lenk and Choi [28] propose a number of shape constraints based on the signs of the first and second derivatives:

- monotonically increasing and decreasing functions with strictly positive or negative first derivatives and unconstrained second derivatives;
- monotonically increasing and decreasing functions that are also convex or concave with different combinations of strictly positive or negative first and second derivatives;
- U-shaped or inverted U-shaped functions where the first derivative changes signs at the minimum or maximum and the second derivative is unconstrained; and
- S-shaped functions with first derivatives that are strictly positive or negative and the second derivative changes signs at single point.

These classes of functions are not mutually exclusive. Shape constraints can greatly improve inference because uncharacteristic behaviour in the data, such as decreasing measurements when the regression function should be increasing, is treated as measurement error or noise and not signal.

The chapter has the following organisation. The next section reviews the literature about smoothing priors. Section 8.3 presents BSAR. Section 8.4 extends BSAR to include shape constraints by modelling the first or second derivatives of the regression function with squared, Gaussian processes. Section 8.5 presents nonnormal extensions to the model in a generalised linear model framework and mixture of Dirichlet processes (MDP). Section 8.6 provides several examples using the `bsamGP` library in R [19], available at http://cran.r-project.org/package=bsamGP.

8.2 Smooth operators

Nonparametric or flexible regression differs qualitatively from standard, parametric models because the danger of overfitting the data is real and present. Overfitting occurs when the model has a remarkably good fit to the data, which is usually a good outcome with parametric models; however, its prediction on test data performs poorly because the model mistakes noise for signal in the training data and has spurious 'wiggles' in its attempt to hit each observation. To protect against overfitting, flexible regression imposes side constraints on the estimator that penalises rough estimates. These penalty terms often reflect the analyst's subjective opinion about the smoothness of the function, and we term them 'smoothing priors'.

The first Bayesian analysis for flexible regression is presented in the brilliant paper by Whittaker [52]. The paper considers equally spaced, discrete data, such as the number of female annuitants $\{y_i\}$ at different age classes in years $\{x_i\}$. The likelihood assumes that each age class x_i has a unique parameter μ_i, which is the conditional of mean of Y_i given x_i or $Y_i = \mu_i + \epsilon_i$, where $\{\epsilon_i\}$ is a random sample from a normal distribution with mean zero. Whittaker's model has as many parameters as data points! If one would use ordinary least squares (OLS) or maximum likelihood (ML) methods, the estimated $\{\mu_i\}$ would be identical to the observed $\{y_i\}$, and the error variance would be zero.

Whittaker's insight was that neighbouring classes x_i should have similar values for μ_i and that 'irregularities' are due to sampling error. He goes on to define 'smooth': 'We may make the somewhat vague word "smooth" more precise to mean that the third differences are to be very small'. First differences model the local slope of the function; second differences model local curvature, and third differences model the local rate of change in the curvature. Whittaker's smoothing prior anticipates few peaks and valleys in the regression function since the rate of change of the curvature is believed to be small. By this means, the small changes in neighbouring values of $\{y_i\}$

are considered to be from sampling variation, and the corresponding $\{\mu_i\}$ jointly shrink towards the values of their respective neighbours.

Whittaker uses the third difference criterion to construct a normally distributed smoothing prior for $\{\mu_i\}$, and performs the Bayesian analysis given the prior variance, which determines the fidelity to the data and the amount of shrinkage to the smoothing prior. A small prior variance forces the estimated μ_i to be closer to the estimates of its neighbours μ_{i-1} and μ_{i+1}, while large prior variance relaxes the smoothing constraint, and the estimated μ_i will be closer to y_i. The paper would be thoroughly modern if only it included cross-validation ([43], [48], [5] and [7]) to pick the prior variance instead of picking a value that works reasonably well by trial and error. Whittaker's model assumes discrete, evenly spaced values for $\{x_i\}$ and fails to make the jump to continuity. However, we could easily imagine using a large number of bins to approximate a continuous function or replacing the differences with derivatives.

Whittaker [52] marks a change in mindset. One way to think about statistical models, admittedly an uncommon position, is that they smooth the data to separate signal from noise. For instance, the empirical distribution function F_n completely describes a sample of observations, but that is equivalent to saying the model for the data is the data. The ML estimation of the density function is Dirac-delta functions at the observations, which has maximum roughness: spikes that reach infinity at the observations and zero elsewhere. This is the extreme case of Good [13]'s concern about zero counts for multinomial data when estimating probabilities. If the analyst believes that the data are from a parametric family with density $f(\bullet|\theta)$, then the log likelihood smooths the empirical CDF F_n:

$$L(\theta) = n \int \log[f(y|\theta)]dF_n(y) = \sum_{i=1}^{n} \log[f(y_i|\theta)].$$

After computing the ML estimation $\hat{\theta}$, we usually discard the rough F_n for the much smoother $f(y|\hat{\theta})$ in reports and subsequent analysis. A side benefit is data compression: storing the name of the parametric family, $\hat{\theta}$, n and other sufficient statistics requires substantially less memory than storing the empirical distribution or the raw data. Similarly, linear and parametric nonlinear regression smooths the scatter plot by assuming a simple functional form between the dependent variables and independent variables.

In most of our parametric models, the likelihood function provides the structure to smooth the data. A downside occurs when the assumed likelihood inadequately describes the phenomenon under consideration. These modelling errors persist regardless of the amount of sample data. In fact, evidence of model inadequacy tends to grow with sample size in most applications, in which case the analyst needs to go back to the raw data and construct better models.

In contrast, Whittaker's regression function is maximally flexible: each observation y_i has its unique conditional mean μ_i, and the likelihood does not impose any constraint on the regression function. The ML estimation for μ_i is y_i, and we overfit the data. If a cell x_i is empty, then the ML estimation for that cell is undefined. Whittaker does not force a functional form in the likelihood to achieve smoothing. Instead, he uses a smoothing prior to constrain the estimates of μ_i. It shifts the model's development from specifying likelihood functions to developing prior distributions to express subjective beliefs about smoothness.

An upside to this approach is that the likelihood eventually dominates the prior distribution, and the analyst will eventually discover the truth with enough data. A downside is that different prior specifications can lead to different conclusions for a given data set. The data alone are silent about the form of smoothing. Given a criterion for smoothness, such as third differences are small, the data are informative about the amount of smoothness as defined by the variance parameter in Whittaker's smoothing prior. However, the choice of third differences over second or fourth differences is a subjective decision, and a different analyst is free to make a different choice. Whittaker picks third differences because actuaries often use first and second differences in further analyses. By limiting the size of third differences, his prior dampens irregularities in first and second differences. Thus, Whittaker's choice of third differences is motivated both by the theoretical considerations about the behaviour of functions with small third differences and by practical considerations about how the estimates are used in subsequent analyses.

Whittle [53] recognised the problem of different definitions of smoothness: 'The difficulty in constructing smoothing formulae is to express quantitatively the type of smoothness that one expects of the curve one is estimating'. He introduces the stochastic process view where the targeted function is a realisation from a population of curves. This provides a prior distribution for the ordinates $f(x)$ of the curve. Moreover, he advocates that smoothness can be expressed as the correlation among neighbouring ordinates. In particular, the correlation of $f(x+\delta)$ and $f(x)$ should approach one as δ goes to zero. This theme is continued in [54] for density estimation.

Kimeldorf and Wahba [21] build on Whittle's idea that the true function is a realisation of a stochastic process to show the connection between Bayesian estimation using stochastic processes and smoothing splines. They note that 'a choice of smoothing criterion L is equivalent to a prior probability measure for a random function'. In fact, Grace Wahba's influential work on splines assumes that the target function belongs to a Sobolev space where the norm is defined by integrated squares of the derivatives [47]. This approach leads to polynomial splines as the solution to the minimisation problem

$$\sum_{i=1}^{n}[y_i - f(x_i)]^2 + \lambda \int [f^{(m)}(x)]^2 dx,$$

where $f^{(m)}$ is the mth derivative of f. This objective function penalises sums-of-squares errors for rough f. The roughness penalty is the continuous version of Whittaker's smoothing prior when m is three.

There is also a large body of literature on flexible regression methods outside of the Bayesian tradition, which is aptly described in the following books: Simonoff [42] develops non-Bayesian smoothing models; Efromovich [6] uses orthogonal basis functions; Eubank [9], Gu [15], Ruppert et al. [41] and Wang [51] discuss spline models; Härdel [16], Wand and Jones [49], Fan and Gijbels [10] and Loader [31] present kernel regression; and Vidakovic [46] and Nason [35] discuss wavelet methods for statistical modelling. Many modern machine learning and AI methods use smoothing priors to 'regularise' estimation of flexible regression models [18] even if data scientists are not aware of their Bayesian roots from the predigital age.

The next section presents the spectral analysis of regression functions by imposing a smoothing prior on the spectral coefficients of a Gaussian process. In signal processing and time series analysis, the researcher has the choice of analysing the data either in the time domain or the frequency domain. In regression analysis, 'time domain' broadly means the independent x-variable. Analysis in the time domain focuses on how the signal or regression function f changes with x. The analysis in the references of this section and most of the work on flexible regression stays in the time domain, and smoothing priors constrain how rapidly the function changes by limiting the size of higher-order derivatives (see e.g. [22] and references therein for further historical perspectives and their use in time series data analysis). Analysis in the frequency domain represents the signal or regression function as a series of basis functions, usually sines and/or cosine functions in a

Fourier series. The frequency domain analysis studies the behaviour of the basis coefficients as a function of the frequency. Instead of directly imposing smoothing conditions on the function in the time domain, the next section imposes a smoothing prior in the frequency domain.

8.3 Bayesian spectral analysis regression

Our semiparametric regression model includes a parametric component and one or more unknown functions f_k, which depend on the scalars x_k, i.e.

$$Y_i = \boldsymbol{w}_i^\intercal \boldsymbol{\beta} + \sum_{k=1}^{K} f_k(x_{i,k}) + \epsilon_i \text{ for } i = 1, \ldots, n.$$

The parametric model has $(p+1)$-dimensional vectors of covariates $\boldsymbol{w}_i$ and coefficients $\boldsymbol{\beta}$. The Y-intercept β_0 is included in $\boldsymbol{\beta}$. The error terms $\{\epsilon_i\}$ are a random sample from a normal distribution, $N(0, \sigma^2)$. Without loss of generality, we assume that $0 \le x_{i,k} \le 1$; otherwise, they can be transformed to the unit interval. We identify the model by assuming that the f_k integrate to zero.

In this section, $f_k = Z_k$, where Z_k is a second-order Gaussian process prior. We drop the subscript k to simplify the presentation. The Gaussian process Z has mean function $E[Z(x)] = \mu(x)$ and covariance function $Cov[Z(x), Z(u)] = \nu(x, u)$. Further, the marginal distribution of Z at a finite set of n points $\{x_j\}$ is a multivariate normal distribution with mean vector $[\mu(x_1), \ldots, \mu(x_n)]^\intercal$ and covariance matrix $[\nu(x_i, x_j)]_{i,j=1}^n$. The mean function μ is the prior mean of f. We will assume that the mean functions are zero, i.e. $\mu(x) = 0$. This prior assumption is equivalent to saying that X does not have an effect on Y, and we bias the results towards the null hypothesis of no effect. If our beliefs of the prior mean are different, then we could add μ to the model without greatly complicating the analysis.

BSAR expresses the Gaussian process as an infinite series expansion with the Karhunen–Loève representation, i.e.

$$Z(x) = \sum_{j=0}^{\infty} \theta_j \varphi_j(x),$$

where $\{\varphi_j\}$ forms an orthonormal basis on $[0, 1]$:

$$\int_0^1 \phi_i(x)\phi_j(x)dx = \begin{cases} 1 & \text{if } i = j, \\ 0 & \text{if } i \neq j. \end{cases}$$

Using orthonormal basis functions greatly facilitates estimation by reducing multicollinearity in the design matrix. The spectral coefficients $\{\theta_j\}$ are

$$\theta_j = \int_0^1 Z(x)\bar{\varphi}_j(x)dx,$$

where $\bar{\varphi}_j$ is the complex complement of φ_j if it is a complex function. The distribution of the spectral coefficients is derived from the Gaussian process Z. The spectral coefficients are mutually independent because the basis functions are orthogonal, and they have normal distributions because Z is Gaussian. The means of the spectral coefficients are zero because μ is zero, and their variances v_j^2 are

$$v_j^2 = \int_0^1 \int_0^1 v(s, t)\varphi_j(s)\bar{\varphi}_j(t)ds\, dt.$$

The covariance function becomes

$$v(s, t) = \sum_{j=0}^{\infty} v_j^2 \varphi_j(s)\bar{\varphi}_j(t),$$

provided $\sum_{j=0}^{\infty} v_j^2 < \infty$. Thus, in principle, if one has a preferred covariance function for the Gaussian process, then he or she can derive the variance of the spectral coefficients. Conversely, the specification of the spectral coefficients' variances implies a covariance function for the Gaussian process.

Our choice of orthonormal system is the cosine basis on $[0, 1]$, so we have

$$\varphi_0(x) = 1 \text{ and } \varphi_j(x) = \sqrt{2}\cos(\pi j x) \text{ for } j \geq 1.$$

Kreider et al. [23] show that the cosine basis is complete for the space of piecewise continuous functions. Note that in the usual Fourier analysis, the basis functions are sines and cosines; however, this basis forces the end points to be equal, $f(0) = f(1)$, while the cosine basis does not. The frequency of the cosine functions is $j/2$ and the wavelength is $2/j$. If the support of f is not the unit interval, then the problem can be transformed to the unit interval by using a cumulative distribution function Q with density q, i.e. $\varphi_0(x) = \sqrt{q(x)}$ and $\varphi_j(x) = \sqrt{2q(x)}\cos[\pi j Q(x)]$. For unrestricted f, θ_0 is confounded with the Y-intercept β_0, and we will drop it from the representation for f; thus, f will satisfy the mean centering condition since φ_j is orthogonal to the constant function.

The cosine basis has a natural ordering based on their frequencies $j/2$: high-frequency cosines have many peaks and valleys. If the spectral coefficients decay at rate $o(j^m)$ for some $m > 1$, then the f is m times differentiable almost everywhere [20]. Consequently, variances of the spectral coefficients control the rate of decay of the coefficients in probability and the smoothness of the sample paths of the Gaussian process. We use the exponential smoothing prior ([24], [25] and [27] for density estimation and [26] and [3] for regression). We have

$$v_j^2 = \sigma^2 \tau^2 \exp(-\gamma j),$$

where τ and γ are positive parameters. We include σ^2 in the specification to make the model scale-invariant: if the dependent variable is multiplied by a constant, then the prior distribution does not change. Then τ can be interpreted as a signal-to-noise ratio, and its range is usually between 1 and 10. In the exponential smoother, τ controls the trade-off between the likelihood function and the prior, while γ controls the smoothness of the function by forcing high-frequency coefficients to shrink more to zero. The amount of shrinkage is greater for larger γ. The implied covariance for the Gaussian process is nonstationary and has a saddle shape. The covariance when $\gamma = 0.5$ and $\sigma = \tau = 1$ is plotted in Fig. 8.1. Lenk [26] and Lenk and Choi [28] also consider a geometric smoother where the variance decreases $o(j^\gamma)$, i.e. $v_j^2 = \sigma^2 \tau^2 \exp[-\gamma \log(j)]$, but we will not present it here.

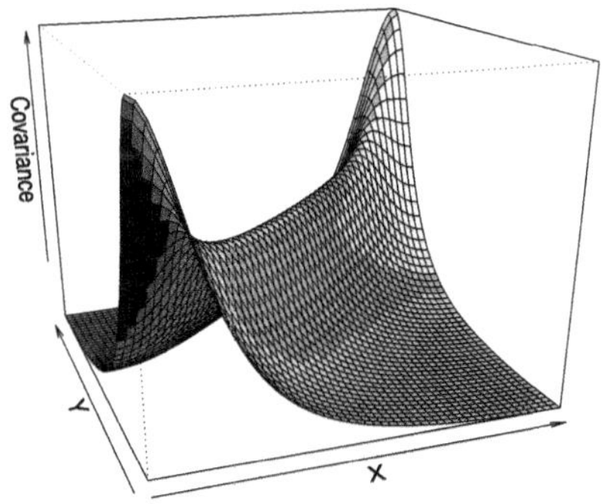

Figure 8.1 Exponential Smoothing Covariance with $\sigma = 1, \tau = 1, \gamma = 0.5$.

We cannot use an infinite Fourier series when implementing the model and truncate the series at J, i.e.

$$Z_J(x) = \sum_{j=0}^{J} \theta_j \varphi_j(x).$$

We will assume that the user picks a J that is sufficiently large so that the error in the approximation is small relative to the noise in the data. The mean integrated square error (MISE) between Z and Z_J decreases exponentially in J:

$$\text{MISE}(J) = \sigma^2 \tau^2 \frac{\exp[-(J+1)\gamma]}{1 - \exp(-\gamma)}.$$

Our estimation strategy is to use large J and let the exponential smoothing prior shrink the high-frequency spectral coefficients to zero instead of the alternative strategy of picking the best J for truncation.

It is interesting to note the relationship of the smoothing priors in the time domain and frequency domain. The time domain (behaviour of f as a function of x) penalty function has an analogue in the frequency domain (behaviour of the spectral coefficient). In spline smoothing the penalised sums-of-squares error objective function of order m is

$$\sum_{i=1}^{n} [y_i - f(x_i)]^2 + \lambda \int [f^{(m)}(x)]^2 dx,$$

and the goal is to find the f to minimise the penalised sums-of-squares error, as also discussed in Section 8.2. If we convert the problem to the frequency domain, the penalty term becomes

$$\begin{aligned} \int [f^{(m)}(x) dx]^2 &= \sum_{j,k=1}^{\infty} \theta_j \theta_k \int \phi_j^{(m)}(x) \phi_k^{(m)}(x) dx \\ &= \sum_{j=1}^{\infty} d_{j,j} \theta_j^2, \text{ and } d_{j,j} = \int \left[\phi_j^{(m)}(x)\right]^2 dx, \end{aligned}$$

assuming that we can interchange the integral and derivatives of order m. The second line follows because the mth derivatives of cosines are either sines or cosines, which are also orthogonal. For cosine basis functions, $d_{j,j}$ is of order j^{2m}, so θ_j needs to converge to zero at a faster rate, i.e. $\theta_j = o(j^m)$. The exponential smoother does not use $d_{j,j}$, but assumes their variance declines exponentially fast. Then the joint density is

$$\log p[y,\theta|\boldsymbol{\beta},\sigma^2,\tau^2,\gamma] \propto -\frac{1}{2\sigma^2}\left\{\sum_{i=1}^{n}[y_i-\boldsymbol{w}_i^{\intercal}\boldsymbol{\beta}-f(x_i)]^2+\frac{1}{\tau^2}\sum_{j=1}^{J}\frac{\theta_j^2}{\exp(-\gamma j)}\right\},$$

where we included the parametric term to be consistent with our original model and only have one function f. The expression in curly brackets is a penalised sums-of-squares error criterion, and the Bayesian maximum a posteriori estimator corresponds to the penalised sums-of-squares error estimator with $\lambda = 1/\tau^2$. However, the exponential smoothing penalty term is different from those in the regularisation literature.

Before completing the model by specifying the hierarchical prior distribution for τ and γ, we give a simple example that illustrates overfitting with OLS and the benefit of using the exponential smoothing prior. The true function has nonzero values for the first five θ_j (including the intercept at $j = 0$) and is zero afterward. Their true values are given in Table 8.1.

There are 21 observations where the x-values are equally spaced from 0 to 1, and the error standard deviation is 1.5. The OLS estimator using the correct model, $J = 4$, works very well and successfully recovers the true parameters. When $J = 20$ the OLS estimator does a reasonable job of estimating the coefficients for frequencies 0 to 4, which is due to the use of an orthonormal basis. However, it incorrectly estimates higher-frequency parameters, which results in overfitting. The data, true function and estimated function are plotted in Fig. 8.2. Panel A shows that OLS is spot-on when the true J is known. Panel B shows that $J = 20$ overfits the data, and the estimated function almost perfectly hits the observations. The estimated error standard deviation is almost zero.

The reader may wonder if LASSO ([44] and [45]) would be a reasonable alternative since it is easily applied for $p >> n$ problems. LASSO penalises the sums-of-squares error, i.e.

$$\text{SSE LASSO} = \sum_{i=1}^{n}\left[y_i - \sum_{j=1}^{J}\theta_j\phi_j(x_i)\right]^2 + \frac{1}{\tau^2}\sum_{j=1}^{J}|\theta_j|,$$

which is equivalent to using a double exponential or Laplace prior ([40], [34] and [39]). We use $\lambda = 1/\tau^2$ to keep the notation consistent with the smoothing prior. If the OLS estimate of a coefficient is sufficiently close to zero, its LASSO estimator will be forced to zero. We set $\tau = 0.25$ so that the estimated error standard deviation is close to the true value. Larger values of τ result in rougher estimates, and smaller values provide smoother estimates

Table 8.1 Estimated parameters for OLS, LASSO and exponential smoothing.

Frequency	True	OLS ($J = 4$)	OLS ($J = 20$)	LASSO ($J = 20$)	Exponential ($J = 20$)
0	10.0	9.786	9.697	9.376	9.790
1	−4.0	−3.832	−3.870	−3.454	−3.809
2	−2.0	−1.910	−2.036	−1.523	−1.847
3	1.0	0.996	0.959	0.575	0.837
4	0.5	0.339	0.214	0.000	0.141
5	0	0	0.478	0.093	0.044
6	0	0	0.406	0.118	0.007
7	0	0	−0.195	0.000	0.000
8	0	0	−0.746	−0.234	0.000
9	0	0	−0.096	0.000	0.000
10	0	0	0.180	0.000	0.000
11	0	0	−0.169	0.000	0.000
12	0	0	0.279	0.000	0.000
13	0	0	−0.171	0.000	0.000
14	0	0	0.615	0.327	0.000
15	0	0	0.467	0.084	0.000
16	0	0	0.405	0.117	0.000
17	0	0	−0.328	0.000	0.000
18	0	0	0.341	0.053	0.000
19	0	0	0.463	0.078	0.000
20	0	0	0.085	0.000	0.000
σ	1.5	1.571	5.14E−06	1.458	1.577
τ				0.250	10
γ					2

that overestimate the true function when $x < 0.4$ and underestimate the true function when $x > 0.4$. Panel C of Fig. 8.2 shows that LASSO is more smooth than Panel B; however, it does not perform very well. It has trouble with spectral analysis because it treats all spectral coefficients equally, while we anticipate that higher-frequency coefficients should have more shrinkage.

For this example, we implemented the exponential smoother by penalising the sums-of-squares error with the normal prior on the coefficients, i.e.

$$\text{SSE exponential smoother} = \sum_{i=1}^{n}\left[y_i - \sum_{j=1}^{J}\theta_j\phi_j(x_i)\right]^2 + \frac{1}{\tau^2}\sum_{j=1}^{J}\exp(\gamma j)\theta_j^2.$$

Once again, we picked τ and γ so that the estimated error standard deviation was close to the true values. The estimated spectral coefficients aggressively shrink the higher-frequency ones to zero, and Panel D shows that it recovers the true regression curve almost as well as OLS with $J = 4$, which uses knowledge about the true model.

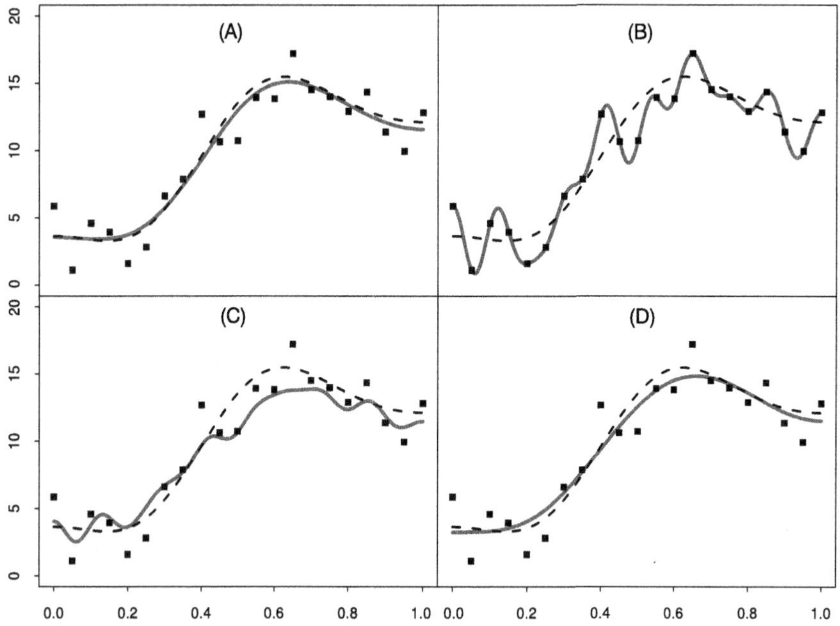

Figure 8.2 Smoothing Examples. *Dashed line*, true function; *dots*, data; *solid line*, the estimator. (A) OLS $J = 4$, (B) OLS $J = 20$, (C) LASSO $J = 20$, (D) Exponential Smoother $J = 20$.

Fitting the functions by trial and error of the smoothing parameters is less than desirable. We complete our Bayesian model with the following hierarchical prior specifications:

$$\begin{aligned}
\boldsymbol{\beta}|\sigma &\sim \mathrm{N}(\boldsymbol{m}_{0,\beta}, \sigma^2 \boldsymbol{V}_{0,\beta}), \text{ the normal distribution,}\\
\sigma^2 &\sim \mathrm{IG}\left(\frac{r_{0,\sigma}}{2}, \frac{s_{0,\sigma}}{2}\right), \text{ the inverse Gamma distribution,}\\
\theta_j|\sigma,\tau,\gamma &\sim \mathrm{N}(0, \sigma^2\tau^2\exp[-j\gamma]) \text{ for } j \geq 1,\\
\tau^2 &\sim \mathrm{IG}\left(\frac{r_{0,\tau}}{2}, \frac{s_{0,\tau}}{2}\right), \text{ the inverse Gamma distribution,}
\end{aligned}$$

$$\gamma \sim \text{Exp}(w_0), \text{ the exponential distribution.}$$

We call this the 'T-smoother' because integrating out τ gives the spectral coefficients a multivariate T distribution. Lenk [26] gives the fully Bayesian estimation of the model using Markov chain Monte Carlo (MCMC).

8.4 Shape constraints

Often the analyst has strong prior beliefs about the general shape of the unknown functions. For example, pressure increases with temperature; the age of a fossil increases with the ratio of carbon-12 to carbon-14; and people burn more calories with more strenuous exercise. This additional information can greatly improve fitting the function. If one knows that the relationship is increasing, then wiggles in the unconstrained estimate are due to noise. Monotonic regression will smooth over the wiggles and increase estimation accuracy if the assumption is correct.

Bayesian models express these a priori shape constraints in the prior distribution of the unknown function. There have been recent developments on Bayesian shape constraints for semiparametric models, in particular, using Gaussian process priors (see e.g. [30], [12], [50] and [28]). This section reviews the BSAR models with shape constraints from [28]. The modelling approach forces the signs of the first and second derivatives to be positive or negative:

1. The sign of the first derivative is positive (negative) for increasing (decreasing) functions.
2. In addition to the condition on the first derivatives in (1), the sign of the second derivative is positive (negative) for convex (concave) functions that are also monotone.
3. The sign of the first derivative flips from negative (positive) to positive (negative) at a point for U-shaped (inverted U-shaped) functions.
4. In addition to the condition on the first derivatives in (1), the sign of the second derivative flips from positive (negative) to negative (positive) at a point for increasing S-shaped (rotated increasing S-shaped) or decreasing S-shaped (rotated decreasing S-shaped).

Section 8.4.1 gives the details for the models where the signs of the first and second derivatives remain constant, and Section 8.4.2 presents the models when their signs flip at one point. Lenk and Choi [28] give the MCMC algorithms, which are not presented here.

8.4.1 Monotonic functions

The main idea is to model the derivatives of the function f as squares of a Gaussian process Z, i.e.

$$f^{(q)}(x) = \delta Z^2(x) \text{ for } \delta = 1 \text{ or } -1 \text{ and } q = 1 \text{ or } 2,$$

where δ and q are given by the user. When q is 1, f is monotonically nondecreasing if δ is 1 and monotonically nonincreasing if δ is -1, i.e.

$$f(x) = \delta\left[\int_0^x Z^2(s)ds - \int_0^1 \int_0^x Z^2(s)ds\, dx\right].$$

We include the last term so that f will integrate to zero, which is an identification condition that allows us to estimate the intercept. When q is 2, f is a nondecreasing and convex function when $\delta = 1$ and a nonincreasing and concave function when $\delta = -1$, i.e.

$$f(x) = \delta\left[\int_0^x \int_0^s Z^2(t)dt\, ds - \int_0^1 \int_0^x \int_0^s Z^2(t)dt\, ds\, dx\right] + \alpha(x - 0.5),$$

where the second term and α are constants of integration and make f satisfy the mean centering condition. To ensure monotonicity, $\delta\alpha \geq 0$. The first and second derivatives have the same sign in this model. We can reverse their signs by reversing the range of x in the integrals to produce functions where the first and second derivatives have opposite signs. The model for nondecreasing and concave functions ($\delta = 1$) or nonincreasing and convex functions ($\delta = -1$) is

$$f(x) = -\delta\left[\int_0^{1-x} \int_0^s Z^2(t)dt\, ds - \int_0^1 \int_0^{1-x} \int_0^s Z^2(t)dt\, ds\, dx\right] + \alpha(x - 0.5),$$

where $\delta\alpha \geq 0$.

Recall that BSAR in Section 8.3 for unconstrained functions dropped the constant function since the intercept is included in the parametric model. Since we are squaring Z, we can identify θ_0 up to its sign, so we include it in the spectral representation of Z. Also, BSAR uses scale-invariant priors for the spectral coefficients. Since Z is squared, the scale-invariant prior becomes

$$\begin{aligned}
\theta_0|\sigma &\sim N(0, \sigma v_{\theta_0}^2)I(\theta_0 \geq 0), \text{ the truncated normal distribution,} \\
\theta_j|\sigma, \tau, \gamma &\sim N(0, \sigma\tau^2 \exp[-j\gamma]).
\end{aligned}$$

8.4.2 S- and U-shaped functions

In this subsection we assume that $f^{(q)}$ for $q=1$ or 2 has a unique root at $x=\omega$ and the sign of the derivative flips at ω, i.e.

$$\delta f^{(q)}(x) > 0,\ 0 < x < \omega,\ \delta f^{(q)}(\omega) = 0 \text{ and } \delta f^{(q)}(x) < 0,\ \omega < x < 1$$

for $\delta = -1$ or 1. We use an auxiliary function, h, which we call the 'squish' function, to make the sign of the derivatives flip at ω; h is a decreasing logistic function between 1 and -1 and is zero at ω. The model for f is

$$\begin{aligned} f^{(q)}(x) &= \delta Z^2(x)h(x) \text{ for } \delta = 1 \text{ or } -1 \text{ and } q = 1 \text{ or } 2, \\ h(x) &= \frac{1-\exp[\psi(x-\omega)]}{1+\exp[\psi(x-\omega)]} \text{ for } \psi > 0 \text{ and } 0 < \omega < 1, \end{aligned}$$

where ω is a unique zero of h, and the slope ψ controls the steepness of h at ω. As ψ goes to infinity, $h=1$ before ω and $h=-1$ after ω, and f will be discontinuous at ω. We treat ω and ψ as unknown parameters. Their prior distributions are truncated normal, so

$$\begin{aligned} \omega &\sim N\left(\mu_{0,\omega}, \sigma^2_{0,\omega}\right) I(0 < \omega < 1), \\ \psi &\sim N\left(\mu_{0,\psi}, \sigma^2_{0,\psi}\right) I(0 < \psi). \end{aligned}$$

When $q=1$, ω is the maximum for inverted U-shaped functions ($\delta = 1$) or the minimum for U-shaped functions ($\delta = -1$). The model for f is

$$f(x) = \delta\left[\int_0^x Z^2(s)h(s)ds - \int_0^1 \int_0^x Z^2(t)h(t)dtds\right].$$

The second term is the constant of integration and satisfies the mean centering constraint for f.

When $q=2$, ω is the inflection point of f, and the model for f is

$$f(x) = \delta \int_0^x \int_0^s Z^2(t)h(t)dt + c_1 x + c_2,$$

where c_1 and c_2 are constants of integration. We select c_2 to satisfy the mean centering constraint. S-shaped functions require a second condition on the first derivative to ensure monotonicity of f, which imposes a condition on c_1. We consider four cases that are specified by a combination of δ and a second indicator ζ: increasing and convex-to-concave

$(\delta = 1, \zeta = 1)$, decreasing and concave-to-convex $(\delta = -1, \zeta = 1)$, increasing and concave-to-convex $(\delta = 1, \zeta = -1)$ and decreasing and convex-to-concave $(\delta = -1, \zeta = -1)$. The model for f is

$$\begin{aligned} f(x) &= \delta\zeta\left[\int_0^x \int_0^s Z^2(t)h(t)dt\,ds - \int_0^1 \int_0^x \int_0^s Z^2(t)h(t)dt\,ds\,dx\right] \\ &\quad + (\alpha - \delta\xi)(x - 0.5), \\ \xi &= \min\left[0, \min_{x\in[0,1]} \zeta \int_0^x Z^2(s)h(s)ds\right], \end{aligned}$$

where $\delta\alpha > 0$.

8.5 Nonnormal distributions

This section considers situations where the likelihood function is not derived from normal distributions. The first extension is generalised linear models (GLMs) ([14], [36], [33] and [17]) where the likelihood function is from the exponential family and depends on the linear model through the link function g, i.e.

$$g(\mu_i) = \boldsymbol{w}_i^\top \boldsymbol{\beta} + \sum_{k=1}^{K} f_k(x_{i,k}),$$

where μ_i is the conditional mean of Y_i or some other, natural parameter. See [19] for the implementation of this extension with the `gbsar` function in the R package `bsamGP`. The exponential family of distribution includes most of the standard distributions such as the normal, binomial, geometric, hypergeometric, negative binomial, Poisson, exponential and Gamma, but not the uniform.

A different approach is to use an MDP model [8] for the error terms in the additive model, i.e.

$$\begin{aligned} \epsilon_i &\sim \int N\left(\epsilon_i|\mu, \sigma^2\right) dG(\mu, \sigma^2), \\ G(\mu, \sigma^2) &\sim DP(M, G_0), \\ G_0(\mu, \sigma^2) &\sim N\left(\mu|\mu_0, \kappa\sigma^2\right) IG\left(\sigma^2|\frac{r_0}{2}, \frac{s_0}{2}\right). \end{aligned}$$

The mixture distribution G has a Dirichlet process prior $DP(M, G_0)$ with prior scale parameter M and prior mean or centering distribution G_0. To keep the model conditionally conjugate, we assume that the centering distribution is the product of a normal distribution for the mean and an inverted Gamma (IG) distribution for the variance. Often, we assume that μ is zero, and then MDP is a scale mixture and G and G_0 only depend on the variance σ^2. The model is also implemented by the `bsardpm` function in the R package `bsamGP` with the 'no-gaps' algorithm of [32].

8.6 R library bsamGP

This section presents three examples using the R Library `bsamGP`. See [19] for more details about options and further citations. The first example explores the relationship between iPhone sales and internet searches to determine if searches are a leading indicator of sales. Apple provides information about a new iPhone version before the release date. After the release date, paid technology writers review the phone, and customers post reviews on social media. The hypothesis is that potential customers will search for information about the new version before making a purchase decision. If so, there should be a spike in searches preceding the sales spike due to a new release. The dependent variable is quarterly iPhone sales in millions of dollars as reported by Statista.[1] The independent variable that measures internet search intensity is provided by Google Trends where the keyword is 'iPhone' and is measured relative to the search category Internet and Telecommunications. Google Trends is measured monthly, and we summed the monthly figures in each quarter to convert them to quarterly figures.

Revenue and Google Trends are plotted versus time in panel A of Fig. 8.3. Panel B lags Google Trends by two quarters. The vertical reference lines are the quarter in which new versions were released, which occurred about once every four quarters. The original iPhone was released in 2007Q3. The sales trajectory follows an S-shaped curve with spikes and valleys that are influenced by new releases. The S-shaped curve is common for new products, which is based on a contagion differential equation ([1] and [29]). Initial sales are low as innovators, who tend to be more adventurous, passionate about the category or wealthier than the general consumer, try the iPhone. Their word-of-mouth and media reports 'infect' early adopters, and sales start to take off. Sales continue to accelerate from 2010 to 2012 as the early majority buy the phone. Sales continue to grow, but at a decreasing rate of change, after 2012 as the late majority enter the market. Sales may eventually asymptote as the market matures.

[1] https://www.statista.com/stats/iphone%20sales.

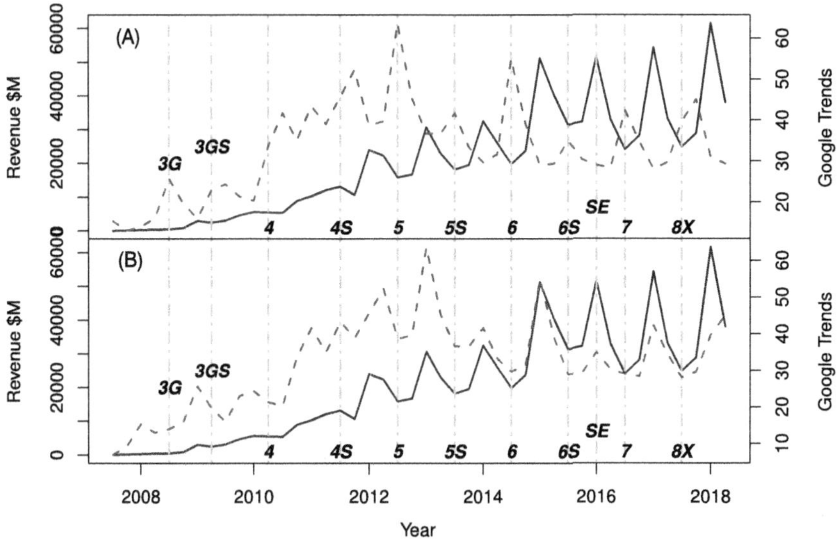

Figure 8.3 iPhone Revenue and Google Trends versus time. *Solid blue line*, revenue; *dotted red line*, Google Trends. (A) No Lag, (B) Lag 2.

The Bass model [1] derives an S-shaped curve for cumulative adopters assuming a fixed population of potential customers, while quarterly revenue appears to have an S-shaped curve because the sales figures include first-time adopters and repeat purchases. Repurchases add an interesting dynamic. Loyal customers often plan upgrades relative to release dates of new versions after factoring in the condition and performance of their existing iPhone. Additionally, many of the purchases before 2007 were tied to a fixed-term contract with a telecommunications service provider. A common practice was to purchase an iPhone with a two-year contract. After two years, Apple would have released one or two upgrades, and the customer's current iPhone seems not so great: degraded battery life, slower performance, dimmer screen, inferior camera, lack of memory and physical damage. The customer may then time the update of their next purchase after the contract period and the release of the new version. Sales tend to slump before the release as customers anticipate the release, and then pick up in the following quarters after the release, often peaking two quarters after the release.

One exception is the SE, which provides the exception that proves the rule. The SE, a budget iPhone, was launched between the highly successful 6S and 7 and was sold concurrently with both. It combined the design of the older 5S with upgraded components from 6S. The SE had a 4-inch screen, while the 6S and 7 had larger screens. More than likely, few iPhone 5, 6 and 6S owners downgraded to the SE. Apple hoped that the SE would attract price-sensitive customers. The sales data have a peak during the quarter of the SE release, while most of the other versions have a valley during their release quarter. The SE's peak is mostly due to sale of the 6S, which was released two quarters earlier. Two quarters after its release, SE sales slump when they normally should be peaking. The slump probably corresponds to the trough during the release of the iPhone 7.

Google Trends for 'iPhone' grow from a very low level in 2007Q3 to a peak during the iPhone 5 release. They then decline to a steady state, with peaks around release dates as consumers search for information about the new product. Panel B lags Google Trends by two quarters in an attempt to align the peaks in Google Trends with the peaks in iPhone sales. Searches seem to peak at the time of release of a new version, while sales tend to peak two quarters hence. The level and size of the search peaks increase until 2014 and then seem to be stabler after 2014. This pattern may indicate that iPhone is maturing and that improvements since 2014 are incremental instead of revolutionary.

Next, we fit various BSAR models with and without shape constraints for Google Trends lag 2. We also use time as a covariate, where time is a sequential variable that counts the number of quarters. Our model is

$$\text{Revenue} = \beta_0 + f_1(\text{Trends}) + f_2(\text{Time}) + \epsilon_i.$$

We fit a series of models where f_1 is unconstrained, increasing, increasing concave (diminishing rate of change), increasing convex (increasing rate of change) and increasing S, and f_2 is always an increasing S curve. We fit the models with the `bsar` function from the `bsarmGP` library in R. First, we initialise parameters for the algorithm:

```
nbasis = 20
prior  = list(beta_m0 = numeric(1), beta_v0 = diag(1000, 1),
                   w0 = 2, tau2_m0 = 1, tau2_v0 = 100,
                   sigma2_m0 = 1, sigma2_v0 = 1000)
mcmc   = list(nblow = 50000, nskip = 10, smcmc = 5000, ndisp=50000)
```

where

1. '`nbasis`' is the number of basis functions;

2. '`prior`' is a list of prior parameters, where the prior means and variances are indicated by `m0` and `v0`;
3. '`mcmc`' gives the iterations for the MCMC; '`nblow`' is the initial number of iterations that are used in the burn-in period; '`smcmc`' is the number of iterations that are saved and used in the analysis; '`nskip`' is the number of iterations between saved iterations; and '`ndisp`' is the number of iterations displayed in the trace plots.

The call to `bsar` is

```
fout   = bsar(y ~ fs(Google_Trend_Lag2) + fs(Time),
            shape = c('Free','IncreasingS'),
            xmin=c(7,1), xmax=c(64,44),
            nbasis = nbasis, mcmc = mcmc, prior = prior)
```

where '`fs`' is a placeholder for the BSAR function. Its shape is given in '`shape=`'. The function for Google Trend lag 2 is unconstrained ('`Free`'), and the function for Time is increasing S. The minimum value for Google Trends is 7, and its maximum is 65. Likewise, Time ranges from 1 to 44. The output can be viewed with `plot(fout)` and `summary(fout)`. `fitted(fout,HDP=TRUE)` computes the posterior means of the functions and 95% HPD intervals.

```
plot(fout)
print(summary(fout))
fit  = fitted(fout,HPD=TRUE)
plot(fit,ggplot2=TRUE)
```

Table 8.2 gives the fit statistics for the different models. The maximum log integrated likelihood or LIL [11] favours the increasing concave model for Google Trends. This confirms that internet searches are predictive of sales, and they also have a diminishing impact.

Table 8.2 Fit statistics for different functional forms for Google Trends.

Model for Trends	LIL	Newton–Raftery	R squared
Free	−528.540	−456.772	0.862
Increasing	−509.351	−449.207	0.880
Increasing concave	−504.336	−454.933	0.834
Increasing convex	−506.177	−452.915	0.852
Increasing S	−518.363	−457.047	0.853

Selected functions from the model are plotted in Fig. 8.4. The estimated increasing S function for Time did not change much for the different models, so we only plot the one that corresponds to the increasing concave function for Google Trends in panel D. The free function for Google Trends is plotted in Panel A, while the shape constraints increasing and increasing concave are plotted in panels B and C. The shape-constrained functions are smoother than the free function and also have narrower HPD intervals. Even though the free function is more flexible and has one parameter less, θ_0, the log iterated likelihood, favours the shape constraints because of the increased estimation accuracy. Panel D confirms that the iPhone is a maturing product and is past its inflection point ω, which is estimated to be Time $= 23.5$ or between 2012Q3 and 2012Q4.

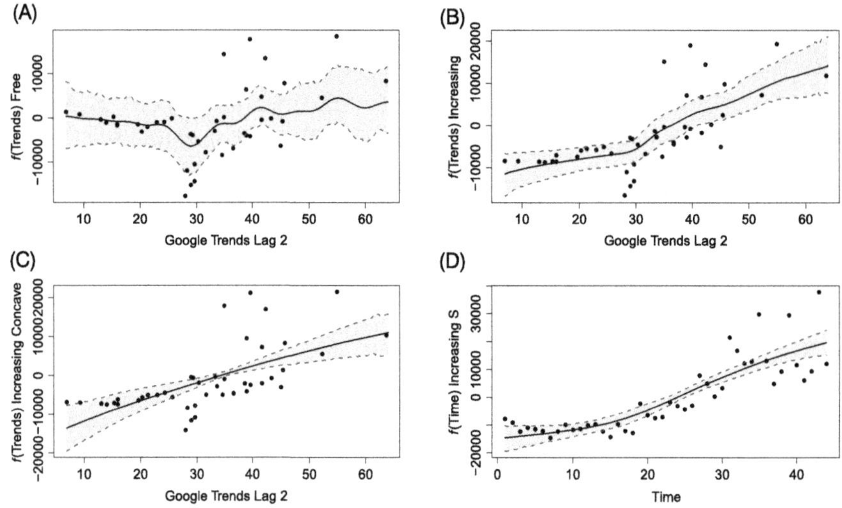

Figure 8.4 iPhone Revenue. (A) Free function for Google Trends lag 2. (B) Increasing function for Google Trends lag 2. (C) Increasing concave function for Google Trends lag 2. (D) Increasing S Function for time when Google Trends lag 2 has an increasing concave function. *Dots*, parametric residuals; *solid lines*, posterior mean of *f*; *dashed lines*, 95% HPD intervals.

Our next example asks the question, 'When is the solar radiance in Ann Arbor, Michigan maximum?' To estimate the maximum, we fit an inverted U-shaped function. The data are from the National Renewable Energy Laboratory's National Solar Radiation Data Base,[2] which reports hourly readings throughout the day. Our dependent variable is the daily maximum of extraterrestrial radiation on a horizontal surface or ETR, which is measured in Watthours per square meter. We used 5 years of data, from 2006 to

[2] https://rredc.nrel.gov/solar/old_data/nsrdb/.

2010, to capture year-to-year variation due to cloud cover, solar flares and other factors. The maximum daily ETR ranged from 581 to 1260. The ETR on the same day from year-to-year was surprisingly consistent. The maximum of the daily standard deviations of ERT over the 5 years was only 2.28, and the percent error of the 5-yearly reading on one day from their average only ranged from −0.38% to 0.41%.

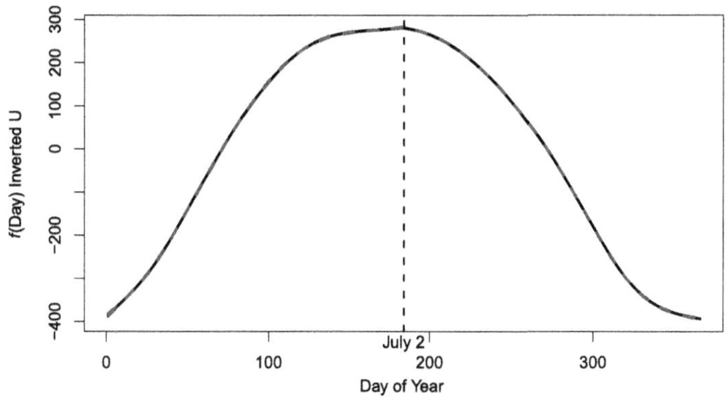

Figure 8.5 Maximum daily solar radiation in Ann Arbor, Michigan. *Black line*, the posterior mean of the inverted U function; *red (grey in print version) dashed lines*, the 95% HPD intervals.

The `bsar` command for the inverted U shape is

```
fout = bsar(y ~ fs(x), shape = c('InvertedU'),  xmin=1, xmax=366,
                                nbasis = nbasis, mcmc = mcmc, prior = prior)
```

where `y` is the daily maximum of ERT and `x` is the day of year. The maximum day of year is 366 due to leap years. The estimated, inverted U function is plotted in Fig. 8.5. Because the year-to-year variation in ETR is small, the width of the 95% HPD intervals is the same as the lines in the plot. The day with the maximum, expected ETR is July 2, which is the posterior mean of ω in the inverted U model. The summer solstice, which is between June 20 and June 22, precedes the maximum solar radiation by about 10 days.

The last example illustrates modelling nonnormal random error with MDP. The data are from the Consumer Expenditures Diary Survey[3] that is conducted by the U.S. Department of Labor, Bureau of Labor Statistics.

[3] https://www.bls.gov/cex/.

The example uses data from the 2012Q1 survey. We focus on monthly grocery expenditures, excluding alcohol. We hypothesise that grocery expenditures should increase with income and family size: wealthier families buy premium items, and larger families have more people to feed. The relationship with age of the head of household is less certain. Young households probably burn more calories than older households, but younger households may take more meals outside of the house, thus reducing grocery bills. Middle age households tend to have larger family sizes and hit maximum spending when children are teenagers.

Empirical data analysis indicated log transformations for grocery expenditures and family income. OLS estimation confirms that grocery expenditures increase with income and family size. Also, the OLS estimate of a quadratic model in age has a significant coefficient for age squared. However, the OLS residuals were not normally distributed, even after the log transformation.

Next, we use MDP to model the nonnormal error distribution. Initialising the algorithm's parameters is done in a similar fashion to the previous examples, with the addition of adding prior parameters for the MDP.

```
nbasis  = 30                  # Number of basis
prior   =       list(beta_m0 = numeric(3), beta_v0 = diag(1000, 3),
                        w0 = 2, tau2_m0 = 1, tau2_v0 = 100,
                        sigma2_m0 = 1, sigma2_v0 = 1000)
prior   =       append(prior,
                        list(kappa_r0=1, kappa_s0=1,tmass_a=2,
                             tmass_b=4))
mcmc    =       list(nblow = 50000, nskip = 10, smcmc = 5000)
```

The estimation is performed with `bsardpm`:

```
fout            =       bsardpm(GroceryLog ~ Size + IncomeLog +
                                fs(Age),
                                shape = c('InvertedU'), xmin=c(19),
                                xmax=c(87),
                                nbasis = nbasis, location=FALSE,
                                mcmc = mcmc, prior = prior)
```

The model's output is processed as follows:

```
print(summary(fout))
fit = fitted(fout,HPD=TRUE)
plot(fit,ggplot2=TRUE)
```

The estimated model is

$$\log \text{grocery} = 1.587 + 0.092(\text{family size}) + 0.067(\log \text{income}) + f(\text{age}).$$

The inverted U function for age is plotted in Panel A of Fig. 8.6. The maximum expenditure occurs when the head of household is 55.35 years old, which is the posterior mean of ω. The posterior mean of ψ is 100.31, which makes the squish function h steep at ω and results in the apparent kink at 55.35. The density for the random error from the MDP is plotted in Panel B. It has longer tails than a normal distribution.

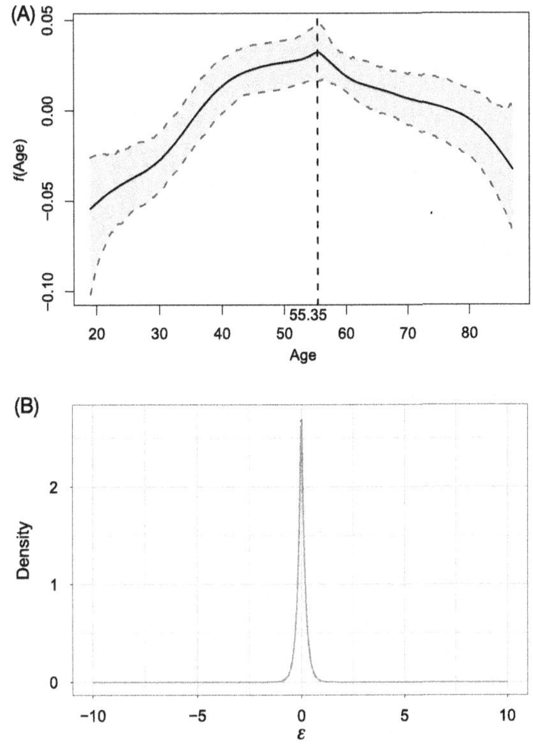

Figure 8.6 Food expenditure. (A) Inverted U for age. (B) Density for random error. *Solid lines*, posterior mean of *f*; *dashed lines*, 95% HPD intervals.

8.7 Conclusion

The Bayesian analysis of flexible regression functions using smoothing priors has a long history. Gaussian process priors provide a natural model for flexible functions. The mean is the prior mean; the variances control the trade-off between the data and the prior mean; and the correlations determine the smoothness of the sample paths. This chapter reviews the spectral analysis of Gaussian processes. Spectral analysis projects the Gaussian process onto a lower-dimensional, linear space by a finite series of cosine functions. Smooth functions do not have high-frequency oscillations, so we a priori expect the high-frequency coefficients to be close to zero. A hierarchical prior on the spectral coefficients expresses these beliefs. It shrinks the coefficients to zero with greater shrinkage for higher-frequency coefficients. BSAR estimates the hyperparameters that control the amount of shrinkage in a fully Bayesian model without recourse to cross-validation.

BSAR also simplifies the computations by linearising the Gaussian process, which enables extensions to shape constraints and nonnormal likelihoods. Shape constraints can improve estimation accuracy because the shape constraint helps to separate signal from noise in the data. BSAR provides a flexible modelling approach that allows for numerous extensions. Further details and developments of BSAR can also be found in [26] and [28] for general methods, theory and computations, in [19] for a software application in R, in [3] and [4] for model selection consistency and in [38] for fast variational approximation.

Acknowledgements

Research of Taeryon Choi was supported by the Basic Science Research Program through the National Research Foundation of Korea (NRF) funded by the Ministry of Education (NRF-2019R1A2C1010018).

References

[1] F.M. Bass, A new product growth model for consumer durables, Management Science 15 (1969) 215–227.
[2] T. Bayes, An essay in solving a problem in the doctrine of chances, Philosophical Transactions of the Royal Society of London 53 (1763) 370–418.
[3] T. Choi, J. Lee, A. Roy, A note on the Bayes factor in a semiparametric regression model, Journal of Multivariate Analysis 100 (6) (2009) 1316–1327.
[4] T. Choi, J. Rousseau, A note on Bayes factor consistency in partial linear models, Journal of Statistical Planning and Inference 166 (2015) 158–170.
[5] P. Craven, G. Wahba, Smoothing noisy data with spline functions, Numerische Mathematik 31 (4) (1979) 377–403.
[6] S. Efromovich, Nonparametric Curve Estimation: Methods, Theory, and Applications, Springer Series in Statistics, Springer-Verlag, New York, 1991.
[7] B. Efron, Estimating the error rate of a prediction rule: improvement on cross-validation, Journal of the American Statistical Association 78 (382) (1983) 316–331.

[8] M.D. Escobar, M. West, Bayesian density estimation and inference using mixtures, Journal of the American Statistical Association 90 (430) (1995) 577–588.
[9] R.L. Eubank, Nonparametric Regression and Spline Smoothing, second edition, Statistics: Textbooks and Monographs, vol. 157, Marcel Dekker, New York and Basel, 1999.
[10] J. Fan, I. Gijbels, Local Polynomial Modelling and Its Applications, Monographs on Statistics and Applied Probability, vol. 66, Chapman and Hall, New York, 1996.
[11] A.E. Gelfand, D.K. Dey, Bayesian model choice: asymptotics and exact calculations, Journal of the Royal Statistical Society. Series B 56 (3) (1994) 501–514.
[12] S. Golchi, D.R. Bingham, H. Chipman, D.A. Campbell, Monotone emulation of computer experiments, SIAM/ASA Journal on Uncertainty Quantification 3 (1) (2015) 370–392.
[13] I.J. Good, The Estimation of Probabilities, MIT Press, Cambridge, MA, 1965.
[14] P.J. Green, B.W. Silverman, Nonparametric Regression and Generalized Linear Models: A Roughness Penalty Approach, Monographs on Statistics and Applied Probability, vol. 58, Chapman & Hall/CRC, Boca Raton, London, New York, Washington D. C., 1994.
[15] C. Gu, Smoothing Spline ANOVA Models, Springer Series in Statistics, Springer-Verlag, New York, 2002.
[16] W. Härdel, Applied Non-parametric Regression, Econometric Society Monographs, vol. 19, Cambridge University Press, Cambridge, 1990.
[17] T. Hastie, R. Tibshirani, Generalized Additive Models, Monographs on Statistics and Applied Probability, vol. 43, Chapman and Hall Ltd., London, 1990.
[18] T. Hastie, R. Tibshirani, J. Friedman, The Elements of Statistical Learning: Data Mining, Inference, and Prediction, second edition, Springer Science + Business Media, New York, NY, 2009.
[19] S. Jo, T. Choi, B. Park, P.J. Lenk, bsamGP: an R package for Bayesian spectral analysis models using Gaussian process priors, Journal of Statistical Software 90 (10) (2019) 1–41, https://doi.org/10.18637/jss.v090.i10.
[20] Y. Katznelson, An Introduction to Harmonic Analysis, third edition, Cambridge University Press, Cambridge, United Kingdom, 2004.
[21] G. Kimeldorf, G. Wahba, A correspondence between Bayesian estimation on Gaussian processes and smoothing by splines, Annals of Mathematical Statistics 41 (2) (1970) 495–502.
[22] G. Kitagawa, W. Gersch, Smoothness Priors Analysis of Time Series, Lecture Notes in Statistics, vol. 116, Springer-Verlag, New York, 1996.
[23] D.L. Kreider, R.G. Kuller, D.R. Ostberg, F.W. Perkins, An Introduction to Linear Analysis, Addison-Wesley, Boston, MA, 1966.
[24] P.J. Lenk, Towards a practicable Bayesian nonparametric density estimator, Biometrika 78 (3) (1991) 531–543.
[25] P.J. Lenk, A Bayesian nonparametric density estimator, Journal of Nonparametric Statistics 3 (1) (1993) 53–69.
[26] P.J. Lenk, Bayesian inference for semiparametric regression using a Fourier representation, Journal of the Royal Statistical Society. Series B 61 (4) (1999) 863–879.
[27] P.J. Lenk, Bayesian semiparametric density estimation and model verification using a logistic-Gaussian process, Journal of Computational and Graphical Statistics 12 (3) (2003) 548–565.

[28] P.J. Lenk, T. Choi, Bayesian analysis of shape-restricted functions using Gaussian process priors, Statistica Sinica 27 (2017) 43–69.
[29] P.J. Lenk, A.G. Rao, New models from old: forecasting product adoption by hierarchical Bayes procedures, Marketing Science 9 (1) (1990) 42–53.
[30] L. Lin, D.B. Dunson, Bayesian monotone regression using Gaussian process projection, Biometrika 101 (2) (2014) 303–317.
[31] C. Loader, Local Regression and Likelihood, Statistics and Computing, Springer-Verlag, New York, 1999.
[32] S.N. MacEachern, P. Müller, Estimating mixture of Dirichlet process models, Journal of Computational and Graphical Statistics (1998) 223–238.
[33] P. McCullagh, J.A. Nelder, Generalized Linear Models, second edition, Chapman & Hall, London, Great Britain, 1989.
[34] A.F.S. Mitchell, A note on the posterior moments of a normal mean with double-exponential prior, Journal of the Royal Statistical Society. Series B 56 (4) (1994) 605–610.
[35] G. Nason, Wavelet Methods in Statistics With R, Use R!, Springer Science + Business Media, New York, 2008.
[36] J.A. Nelder, R.W.M. Wedderburn, Generalized linear models, Journal of the Royal Statistical Society, Series A 135 (3) (1972) 370–384.
[37] A. O'Hagan, Curve fitting and optimal design for prediction, Journal of the Royal Statistical Society. Series B 40 (1) (1978) 1–42.
[38] V.M.H. Ong, D.K. Mensah, D.J. Nott, S. Jo, B. Park, T. Choi, A variational Bayes approach to a semiparametric regression using Gaussian process priors, Electronic Journal of Statistics 11 (2) (2017) 4258–4296.
[39] T. Park, G. Casella, The Bayesian lasso, Journal of the American Statistical Association 103 (482) (2008) 681–686.
[40] L.R. Pericchi, A.F.M. Smith, Exact and approximate posterior moments for a normal location parameter, Journal of the Royal Statistical Society. Series B 54 (3) (1992) 793–804.
[41] D. Ruppert, M.P. Wand, R.J. Carroll, Semiparametric Regression, Cambridge Series in Statistical and Probabilistic Mathematics, vol. 12, Cambridge University Press, Cambridge, 2003.
[42] J.S. Simonoff, Smoothing Methods in Statistics, Springer Series in Statistics, Springer-Verlag, New York, 1996.
[43] M. Stone, Cross-validation and multinomial prediction, Biometrika 61 (3) (1974) 509–515.
[44] R. Tibshirani, Regression shrinkage and selection via the lasso, Journal of the Royal Statistical Society. Series B 58 (1) (1996) 267–288.
[45] R. Tibshirani, Regression shrinkage and selection via the LASSO: a retrospective, Journal of the Royal Statistical Society. Series B 73 (2) (2011) 273–282.
[46] B. Vidakovic, Statistical Modeling by Wavelets, Wiley Series in Probability and Statistics: Applied Probability and Statistics, John Wiley & Sons, Inc., New York, 1999, A Wiley-Interscience Publication.
[47] G. Wahba, Spline Models for Observational Data, vol. 90, Siam, Philadelphia, Pennsylvania, 1990.
[48] G. Wahba, S. Wold, A completely automatic French curve: fitting spline functions by cross validation, Communications in Statistics 4 (1) (1975) 1–17.

[49] M.P. Wand, M.C. Jones, Kernel Smoothing, Monographs on Statistics and Applied Probability, vol. 60, Chapman & Hall/CRC, Boca Raton, London, New York, Washington D. C., 1995.
[50] X. Wang, J.O. Berger, Estimating shape constrained functions using Gaussian processes, SIAM/ASA Journal on Uncertainty Quantification 4 (1) (2016) 1–25.
[51] Y. Wang, Smoothing Splines: Methods and Applications, Monographs on Statistics and Applied Probability, vol. 121, Chapman & Hall/CRC, Boca Raton, London, New York, 2011.
[52] E.T. Whittaker, On a new method of graduation, Proceedings of the Edinburgh Mathematical Society 41 (1923) 63–75.
[53] P. Whittle, Curve and periodogram smoothing, Journal of the Royal Statistical Society, Series B 19 (1) (1957) 38–63.
[54] P. Whittle, On the smoothing of probability density functions, Journal of the Royal Statistical Society, Series B 20 (2) (1958) 334–343.

CHAPTER 9

Flexible regression modelling under shape constraints

Andrew A. Manderson[a], **Kevin Murray**[b], **Berwin A. Turlach**[a]
[a]The University of Western Australia, Department of Mathematics and Statistics, 35 Stirling Highway, Crawley, WA 6009, Australia
[b]The University of Western Australia, School of Population and Global Health, 35 Stirling Highway, Crawley, WA 6009, Australia

Contents

Flexible Bayesian Regression Modelling
https://doi.org/10.1016/B978-0-12-815862-3.00014-7

9.1 Introduction

In this chapter we address regression problems of the form $\boldsymbol{Y} = \boldsymbol{X}\boldsymbol{\beta} + \boldsymbol{\varepsilon}$, where $\boldsymbol{\beta}$ is subject to constraints that are easy to check, but difficult to mathematically enumerate or structurally incorporate. The example of interest in this chapter is the requirement for the fitted regression line $\boldsymbol{X}\boldsymbol{\beta}$ to be monotonic, however similar derivative-based constraints such as convexity could be substituted, as well as other computationally inexpensive to check constraints. We will focus specifically on monotonic polynomials, where the $\boldsymbol{X}$ matrix is a polynomial basis, but the techniques we employ can be readily adapted to other design matrices and regression problems. For example, when $\boldsymbol{X}$ contains a B-spline basis, and we require the fitted spline to be monotonic or convex.

The requirement for the fitted polynomial to be monotonic is difficult to mathematically enumerate. It typically requires adopting a highly nonlinear parameterisation, such as that of Elphinstone [2], Hawkins [7] or Murray et al. [11,12], which can prove computationally challenging (Manderson et al. [10] discuss some of the computational challenges of one of these parameterisations in a Bayesian framework). An alternative method for estimating monotonic polynomials, based on a particular form of coordinate descent titled *penalised constrained orthogonal least squares*, is presented in Bon et al. [1]; however, the methodology therein does not readily admit a Bayesian approach. In this chapter, we will make use of the ease with which one can check if a polynomial is monotonic, in order to incorporate our monotonicity requirement into our prior distribution. When combined with techniques to orthonormalise the design matrix, this allows us to quickly sample the posterior distribution of the monotonic polynomial, and we can readily extend this formulation to enable coherent polynomial degree selection.

This chapter begins by discussing the QR decomposition, and how regression problems such as monotonic polynomial regression and covariate selection necessitate its use. We then demonstrate how to incorporate the monotonicity constraint into the prior distribution, and we develop a Markov chain Monte Carlo (MCMC) sampler for a simple example. We will demonstrate an implementation of the Metropolis-adjusted Langevin algorithm (MALA), as many regression problems have readily available gradient information. The focus will then shift to variable selection, where we will specify a family of possible models and use the reversible jump Markov chain Monte Carlo (RJMCMC) algorithm in order to select the appropriate-degree monotonic polynomial, for a variety of data sets.

9.2 Orthonormal design matrices

Working directly with design matrices with highly correlated columns can prove numerically challenging for many sampling algorithms and approximating methodologies. For polynomial design matrices of degree q, the correlated nature of the columns of the $n \times (q+1)$ design matrix $\boldsymbol{X}$ induces a correlated posterior for the $(q+1) \times 1$ vector $\boldsymbol{\beta}$. This is particularly apparent when the columns of $\boldsymbol{X}$ are the typical monomial basis of degree q, i.e. $\boldsymbol{X} = [\mathbf{1}, \boldsymbol{x}, \boldsymbol{x}^2, \ldots, \boldsymbol{x}^q]$, but is common to many regression problems. To avoid working directly with $\boldsymbol{X}$ and $\boldsymbol{\beta}$, consider an *orthonormal* basis, i.e.

$$\boldsymbol{Y} = \boldsymbol{Q}\boldsymbol{\gamma} + \boldsymbol{\varepsilon},$$

where $\boldsymbol{X} = \boldsymbol{QR}$ and $\boldsymbol{\beta} = \boldsymbol{R}^{-1}\boldsymbol{\gamma}$. The construction of $\boldsymbol{Q}$ is such that the columns of $\boldsymbol{Q}$ are orthonormal to each other, i.e. the dot product of any two columns is zero, and each column has unit magnitude. The $\boldsymbol{R}$ matrix is an upper triangular matrix, and its inverse is used to transform the new regression parameters $\boldsymbol{\gamma}$ back to the regression parameters on the original space $\boldsymbol{\beta}$. This decomposition of the $\boldsymbol{X}$ matrix is called the QR decomposition, and it is commonly used in Bayesian modelling to improve MCMC performance. By formulating our regression problem in terms of an orthonormal design matrix, we are able to fit the same regression model by sampling the considerably less correlated posterior distribution of $\boldsymbol{\gamma}$. Orthogonalisation steps have been employed in regression settings, particularly polynomial regression, for some time; see Wong [18], Forsythe [5] and Emerson [3] for examples. Orthonormality is also invaluable when we allow the size of $\boldsymbol{\gamma}$ to vary (see Mallick [8] for another example) as the values of the other coefficients of $\boldsymbol{\gamma}$ change minimally when a coefficient is added/removed. We will elaborate on this in Section 9.4.

In order to construct the $\boldsymbol{Q}$ and $\boldsymbol{R}^{-1}$ matrices, we make use of the iterative routine of Thisted [15], which is specific for polynomial design matrices and avoids directly computing the high-degree polynomial terms. Alternatively, there is the `qr()` function found in base `R` which is also numerically stable, with the minor caveat being that one has to remember to centre the columns of the design matrix before calling `qr()` for optimal performance. Our implementation of [15] is available as part of our `R` package `rjmonopoly`, which is available at https://github.com/hhau/rjmonopoly. We will demonstrate this package's primary purpose in Section 9.4 of this chapter.

9.3 Monotonic polynomial model

We will first consider a straightforward regression problem, where we wish to fit a monotonic polynomial of degree q to a data set. The aim is to illustrate some useful model estimation techniques, specifically the aforementioned QR decomposition technique and the MALA proposal mechanism for the regression coefficients.

9.3.1 Model specification and estimation

Consider the $n \times 1$ vector of observations $\boldsymbol{Y}$, which we wish to model via a monotonic polynomial of degree q. Using the QR decomposition, we can construct an $n \times (q+1)$ orthonormal polynomial design matrix $\mathbf{Q}$, with a corresponding $(q+1) \times 1$ vector of regression coefficients $\boldsymbol{\gamma}$. Assuming a Gaussian distribution for the noise results in the following likelihood:

$$\boldsymbol{Y} \sim \mathrm{N}\left(\mathbf{Q}\boldsymbol{\gamma}, \sigma_Y^2 I_n\right). \tag{9.1}$$

We incorporate our requirement for the fitted polynomial to be monotonic via the prior distribution for $\boldsymbol{\gamma}$. Specifically, we represent the requirement for the fitted regression line $\mathbf{Q}\boldsymbol{\gamma}$ to be monotonic via an indicator function, which is 1 if $\mathbf{Q}\boldsymbol{\gamma}$ is monotonic in the (possibly) compact interval of interest: $\left[a, b\right] \subset \mathbb{R}$. This divides the posterior distribution for $\boldsymbol{\gamma}$ into feasible and infeasible regions, and we denote the feasible region by $\Omega(a, b)$. Combining this prior with a weakly informative normal prior for $\boldsymbol{\gamma}$ results in a truncated normal distribution, which we write as

$$\boldsymbol{\gamma} \sim \mathrm{N}\left(\mathbf{0}_{q+1}, 10^2 I_{q+1}\right) \cdot \mathbb{I}\{\boldsymbol{\gamma} \in \Omega(a, b)\}. \tag{9.2}$$

The independent $\mathrm{N}(0, 10^2)$ priors for each component of $\boldsymbol{\gamma}$ are weakly informative due to the orthonormal nature of $\mathbf{Q}$, as long as the observations $\boldsymbol{Y}$ are standardised. Similarly, we consider the positive half-normal $\mathrm{N}_+(0, 1^2)$ prior for σ_Y^2 weakly informative, for standardised $\boldsymbol{Y}$, and use it in our model. This results in the log posterior being proportional to the following expression:

$$\log\left(\Pr(\boldsymbol{\gamma}, \sigma_Y^2 \mid \boldsymbol{Y})\right) \propto \Bigg(-\frac{n}{2}\log\left(\sigma_Y^2\right) - \frac{1}{2\sigma_Y^2}\left(\boldsymbol{Y} - \mathbf{Q}\boldsymbol{\gamma}\right)^{\top}\left(\boldsymbol{Y} - \mathbf{Q}\boldsymbol{\gamma}\right) \\ - \frac{1}{2 \cdot 10^2}\boldsymbol{\gamma}^{\top}\boldsymbol{\gamma} + \log(\mathbb{I}\{\boldsymbol{\gamma} \in \Omega(a, b)\}) - \frac{1}{2}\left(\sigma_Y^2\right)^2\Bigg). \tag{9.3}$$

It is preferable to compute the posterior on the log scale, as this computation is numerically more stable. Note that $\log(\mathbb{I}\{\boldsymbol{\gamma} \in \Omega(a, b)\})$ is negative infinity when the fitted values of $\boldsymbol{\gamma}$ result in a nonmonotonic regression curve. The generic forms of (9.2) and (9.3) permit any indicator style constraint, e.g. convexity constraints.

9.3.2 Posterior simulation

We now detail an MCMC sampling scheme to sample from the log posterior in (9.3). In doing so we will illustrate how one can leverage the gradient of log posterior to accelerate the process of locating the bulk of the posterior mass, and some of the disadvantages of using the gradient to do so in the presence of constraints. Specifically, we are going to implement a Metropolis-adjusted Langevin proposal for $\boldsymbol{\gamma}$ and a separate random walk proposal for $\log(\sigma_\gamma^2)$.

Our motivations for doing so are two-fold. Firstly, the gradients of the posterior distribution are relatively easy to calculate and compute, which is ideal for demonstrating how one implements MALA. Secondly, finding suitable initial values for the monotonic polynomial coefficients, without actually fitting the monotonic polynomial, can be challenging. We use MALA to move the Markov chain towards the posterior distribution more rapidly, reducing the impact of our initial values, which are typically linear polynomials, on the posterior samples. Using MALA in the constrained environment does have its drawbacks, primarily that if the posterior is truncated by the constraint in a region of high probability, the gradient will push the proposal towards the infeasible region. This behaviour can be undesirable, and a possible solution may be to randomise the sign of the gradient term in the MALA update, although we do not explore this here.

Notationally, in this section the current state of the Markov chain is denoted $\theta^{[t]}$, and the proposed state is denoted θ^*.

9.3.2.1 Proposal mechanisms and acceptance probabilities

Proposal for $\boldsymbol{\gamma}$

The Metropolis-adjusted Langevin proposal for $\boldsymbol{\gamma}$ is specified as

$$\boldsymbol{\gamma}^* = \boldsymbol{\gamma}^{[t]} + \boldsymbol{d}^{[t]} + \varepsilon_\gamma \boldsymbol{z}^{[t]}, \tag{9.4}$$

where $\boldsymbol{d}^{[t]}$ is the *drift* term such that

$$\boldsymbol{d}^{[t]} = \left(\frac{\varepsilon_\gamma^2}{2}\right) \frac{\partial \log\left(\Pr(\boldsymbol{\gamma}, \sigma_\gamma^2 \mid \boldsymbol{Y})\right)}{\partial \boldsymbol{\gamma}}\bigg|_{\boldsymbol{\gamma}=\boldsymbol{\gamma}^{[t]}}, \tag{9.5}$$

where $\boldsymbol{z}^{[t]}$ is a draw from the $(q+1)$-dimensional standard normal random variable, and the step size parameter ε_γ is a user-tuned parameter. We have chosen to update all components of $\boldsymbol{\gamma}$ at once as there is some theoretical justification (see Neal et al. [13]) supporting this. This seems to offset some of the decrease in acceptance rate, due to the increased number of proposals in the infeasible region in this higher-dimensional space.

The log proposal probability for $\boldsymbol{\gamma}$, required for the acceptance probability calculation, is then proportional to

$$\log\left(\Pr(\boldsymbol{\gamma}^* \mid \boldsymbol{\gamma}^{[t]})\right) \propto -\frac{1}{2\sigma_\gamma^2}(\boldsymbol{\gamma}^* - \boldsymbol{\gamma}^{[t]} - \boldsymbol{d}^{[t]})^\top(\boldsymbol{\gamma}^* - \boldsymbol{\gamma}^{[t]} - \boldsymbol{d}^{[t]}). \tag{9.6}$$

The drift term requires us to compute the derivative of the log posterior with respect to $\boldsymbol{\gamma}$, and the result of this computation is

$$\frac{\partial}{\partial \boldsymbol{\gamma}} \log\left(\Pr(\boldsymbol{\gamma}, \sigma_\gamma^2 \mid \boldsymbol{Y})\right) \propto -\frac{1}{\sigma_\gamma}\left(\boldsymbol{\gamma}^\top \mathbf{Q} - \boldsymbol{\gamma}^\top\right) - \frac{1}{10^2}\boldsymbol{\gamma}^\top. \tag{9.7}$$

Although this quantity is a row vector, we use the column vector version of it when calculating the new proposal for $\boldsymbol{\gamma}$.

Proposal for σ_γ^2

We use a log-normal random walk proposal for σ_γ^2, i.e.

$$\left(\sigma_\gamma^2\right)^* \sim \text{Log-normal}\left(\log\left((\sigma_\gamma^2)^{[t]}\right), \varepsilon_\sigma^2\right), \tag{9.8}$$

as it seems to perform well in the upcoming example and it allows us to demonstrate the use of two distinct proposal mechanisms at once. The innovation variance for this proposal, ε_σ^2, is another user-tuned parameter. The log probability of this proposal, required for the acceptance probability calculation, is

$$\log\left(\Pr((\sigma_\gamma^2)^* \mid (\sigma_\gamma^2)^{[t]}\right) \propto -\log((\sigma_\gamma^2)^*) - \frac{1}{2\varepsilon_\sigma^2}\left(\log((\sigma_\gamma^2)^*) - \log((\sigma_\gamma^2)^{[t]})\right)^2. \tag{9.9}$$

Acceptance probability

For the $\boldsymbol{\gamma}$ proposals the log acceptance probability is

$$
\begin{aligned}
\log(\alpha_{\boldsymbol{\gamma}}(\boldsymbol{\gamma}^*, \boldsymbol{\gamma}^{[t]})) = \\
&\log\left(\Pr(\boldsymbol{\gamma}^*, (\sigma_y^2)^{[t]} \mid \mathbf{Y})\right) - \log\left(\Pr(\boldsymbol{\gamma}^{[t]}, (\sigma_y^2)^{[t]} \mid \mathbf{Y})\right) \\
&+ \log\left(\Pr(\boldsymbol{\gamma}^{[t]} \mid \boldsymbol{\gamma}^*)\right) - \log\left(\Pr(\boldsymbol{\gamma}^* \mid \boldsymbol{\gamma}^{[t]})\right), \quad (9.10)
\end{aligned}
$$

and for the σ_y^2 proposals the log acceptance probability is

$$
\begin{aligned}
\log(\alpha_{\sigma}((\sigma_y^2)^*, (\sigma_y^2)^{[t]})) = \\
&\log\left(\Pr(\boldsymbol{\gamma}^{[t+1]}, (\sigma_y^2)^* \mid \mathbf{Y})\right) - \log\left(\Pr(\boldsymbol{\gamma}^{[t+1]}, (\sigma_y^2)^{[t]} \mid \mathbf{Y})\right) \\
&+ \log\left(\Pr((\sigma_y^2)^{[t]} \mid (\sigma_y^2)^*)\right) - \log\left(\Pr((\sigma_y^2)^* \mid (\sigma_y^2)^{[t]})\right). \quad (9.11)
\end{aligned}
$$

Strictly, (9.10) and (9.11) are taken to be the minimum of themselves and 1, in order to ensure they remain probabilities.

9.3.2.2 Summary

A summary of the MALA scheme detailed in this section is presented in Algorithm 1.

9.3.3 Implementation details

We provide below a discussion about the actual implementation in `R`, to illustrate a few computational techniques for MCMC that we believe are noteworthy.

Implementing the monotonicity constraint and calculating the log posterior

The monotonic indicator component of the prior, discussed in Section 9.2, has a notable implementation. Specifically, the monotonic indicator works by converting the $\boldsymbol{\gamma}$ coefficients back to $\boldsymbol{\beta}$ coefficients and checks the monotonicity of this set of coefficients using the `ismonotone` function from the `MonoPoly` package. This function works by calculating the roots of the derivative of the $\boldsymbol{\beta}$ polynomial, then checks to see if there are any real roots and, if so, checks what the multiplicity of these real roots is. If there are no real roots, or if all real roots have even multiplicity, then the polynomial is monotonic on the interval of interest.

As this constraint is part of the prior, it is natural to check if the constraint is satisfied when calculating the log posterior. The code that per-

Input : $\mathbf{Y}, \mathbf{Q}, \boldsymbol{\gamma}^{[0]}, (\sigma_\gamma^2)^{[0]}, \varepsilon_\gamma, \varepsilon_\sigma$
for $t \leftarrow 0$ **to** $N_{MCMC} - 1$ **do**
    Propose γ^* by (9.4) and (9.5);
    Compute $\alpha_\gamma(\boldsymbol{\gamma}^*, \boldsymbol{\gamma}^{[t]})$ by (9.10);
    Simulate $u_1 \sim \text{Unif}(0, 1)$;
    if $u_1 < \alpha_\gamma(\boldsymbol{\gamma}^*, \boldsymbol{\gamma}^{[t]})$ **then**
        $\boldsymbol{\gamma}^{[t+1]} \leftarrow \gamma^*$;
    else
        $\boldsymbol{\gamma}^{[t+1]} \leftarrow \gamma^{[t]}$;
    end
    Propose $(\sigma_\gamma^2)^*$ by (9.8);
    Compute $\alpha_\sigma((\sigma_\gamma^2)^*, (\sigma_\gamma^2)^{[t]})$ by (9.11) using $\boldsymbol{\gamma}^{[t+1]}$;
    Simulate $u_2 \sim \text{Unif}(0, 1)$;
    if $u_2 < \alpha_\sigma((\sigma_\gamma^2)^*, (\sigma_\gamma^2)^{[t]})$ **then**
        $(\boldsymbol{\sigma}_\gamma^2)^{[t+1]} \leftarrow (\sigma_\gamma^2)^*$;
    else
        $(\boldsymbol{\sigma}_\gamma^2)^{[t+1]} \leftarrow (\sigma_\gamma^2)^{[t]}$;
    end
end

Algorithm 1: Summary of the MALA sampler.

forms this calculation is shown in Fig. 9.1 and includes some other simple numerical techniques. In general, it is preferable to calculate $\boldsymbol{x}^\top \boldsymbol{x}$ as $\sum_i x_i^2$, as this is faster than transposing $\boldsymbol{x}$ and performing the matrix multiplication, and it is also faster than calling `crossprod()` in any form (at least in our testing). We have also dropped all multiplicative constants in the posterior, which are additive constants in the log posterior, as they are unnecessary.

General MCMC scheme

The high-level MCMC scheme can be implemented using the for loop specified in Fig. 9.2, where each of the functions either generates proposals for the model parameters or calculates the acceptance probabilities detailed in (9.10) and (9.11). This permits the code to be broken down into smaller, more manageable functions. We generally prefer to begin implementing an MCMC scheme by writing down the key iterative routine, such as the one detailed in Fig. 9.2. This kind of top-down implementation can assist in deciding where certain quantities can be calculated, and in this specific

```
log_post <- function(y_vec, q_mat, r_inv_mat, gamma_vec,
 variance, gamma_prior_variance)  {

  beta <- r_inv_mat %*% gamma_vec
  if (!MonoPoly::ismonotone(beta, a = -1, b = 1, EPS = 1e-10)) {
    return(-Inf)
  }

  mu <- q_mat %*% gamma_vec
  likelihood_temp_1 <- y_vec - mu
  likelihood_temp_2 <- sum(likelihood_temp_1^2)

  n <- length(y_vec)

  log_post <- - (n * 0.5) * log(variance) -
    (0.5 / variance) * (likelihood_temp_2)  -
    (0.5 / gamma_prior_variance) * (sum(gamma_vec^2)) -
     0.5 * (variance)^2

  return(log_post)

}
```

Figure 9.1 The R function that calculates the log posterior, which includes checking to see if the monotonicity constraint is satisfied on the interval $[-1, 1]$.

example it illustrates the use of a Metropolis-within-Gibbs style updating scheme.

9.3.4 A simulated data example

We focus now on a simple regression example, in which we have $n = 50$ data points simulated from the polynomial $p(x) = 1 + 2x - 1.5x^2 + 0.4x^3$ with $X \sim \mathrm{U}[-1, 1]$, which then has $\mathrm{N}(0, 0.3^2)$ noise added to it. In our particular realisation of this data set, the unconstrained fit is not monotonic, despite the true polynomial being so. We fit a monotonic polynomial of degree $q = 3$ to the data, and present the posterior mean estimate of this polynomial, and the 95% posterior prediction interval, in Fig. 9.3. The unconstrained polynomial fit has a decreasing section around $x \in [0.7, 1]$, arising purely due to noise, which the monotonic fit does not have.

The posterior distribution of $\boldsymbol{\gamma}$, which is plotted in a pairwise manner in Fig. 9.4, displays substantial correlation between γ_2 and γ_3. This is despite the use of the QR decomposition, and is attributable to the trun-

```
for (ii in 2:(n_iterations + 1)) {
  gamma_current <- gamma_samples[ii - 1,]
  variance_current <- variance_samples[ii - 1]

  # generate gamma via MALA update
  gamma_prop <- generate_gamma_proposal(
    y, q_mat, gamma_current, variance_current,
    gamma_prior_variance, eps_gamma_step
  )

  # calculate acceptance probability, accept new value for gamma
  log_gamma_accept <- calculate_log_gamma_acceptance_pr(
     y, q_mat, r_inv_mat, gamma_current, gamma_prop,
     variance_current, gamma_prior_variance,
     eps_gamma_step
  )

  if (runif(1) < exp(log_gamma_accept)) {
    gamma_samples[ii, ] <- gamma_prop
  } else {
    gamma_samples[ii, ] <- gamma_current
  }

  # generate variance via RW on log scale
  variance_prop <- generate_variance_proposal(
    variance_current, eps_variance_step
  )

  # calculate acceptance probability, accept new value for variance
  log_variance_accept <- calculate_log_variance_acceptance_pr(
    y, q_mat, r_inv_mat, gamma_current, variance_current,
    variance_prop, gamma_prior_variance,
    eps_variance_step
  )

  #
  if (runif(1) < exp(log_variance_accept)) {
    variance_samples[ii] <- variance_prop
  } else {
    variance_samples[ii] <- variance_current
  }

}
```

Figure 9.2 Main iterative routine for the Metropolis-within-Gibbs MCMC loop, where γ is updated via MALA and σ_y^2 is updated according to a log random walk.

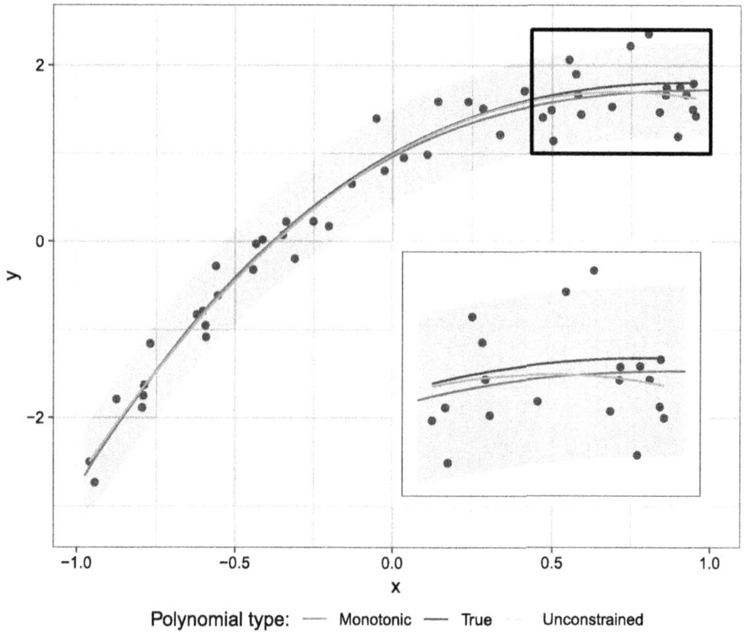

Figure 9.3 The true polynomial, unconstrained least squares polynomial fit and the posterior mean and 95% posterior predictive interval of the monotonic polynomial for the simulated data set. The inset panel highlights how monotonic data generating processes can produce data sets with nonmonotonic unconstrained estimates.

cation of the parameter space by the monotonicity constraint. Posterior distributions with substantial correlation can take longer to approximate with Metropolis–Hastings MCMC schemes, as the effective sample size per second of computation time can be quite low. Indeed, in this simple example it takes several hundred thousand iterations, which takes a few minutes of computation, to accrue a minimum of 500 effective samples for each parameter.

9.4 Covariate selection

As we are using polynomial design matrices, covariate selection is akin to selecting the appropriate polynomial degree for the data set of interest. In order to select the appropriate polynomial degree, we specify a family of possible models, i.e. a set of possible polynomial degrees for the data set, and estimate the posterior probabilities of each model. We will demonstrate

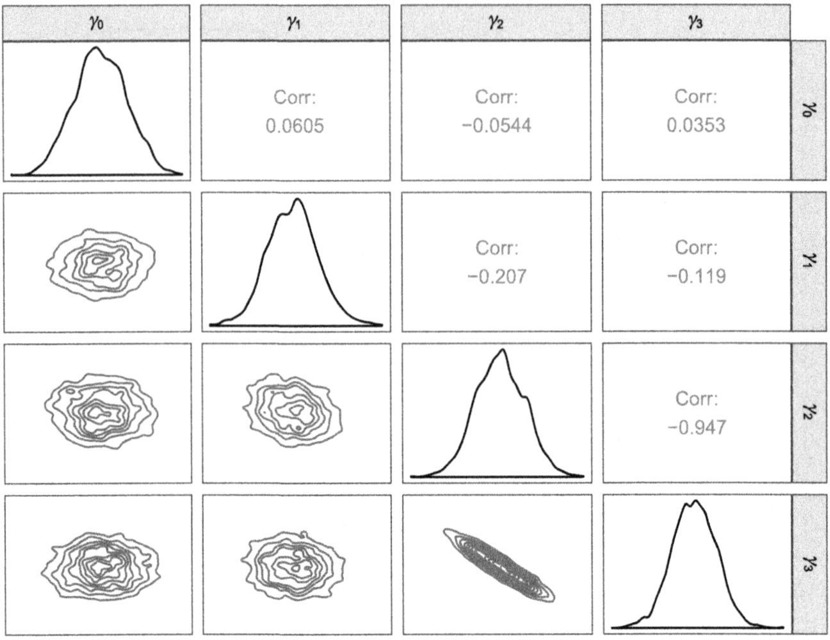

Figure 9.4 Pairwise posterior density estimates and correlations for the elements of γ. Of note is the correlation between γ_2 and γ_3 despite the use of the QR decomposition and covariate centring.

this on a variety of simulated data sets, as well as the Berkeley growth data set [16] in the `fda` [14] package for `R`.

Simulating from the posterior distribution of a family of possible models is made possible by the RJMCMC sampling algorithm [6]. The RJMCMC algorithm allows for the dimension of the parameter space to change between each iteration of the MCMC sampler. In the polynomial context this means the degree of polynomial can change between MCMC samples. The RJMCMC algorithm enables the selection of an appropriate model, as it will naturally produce more MCMC samples from the model with greatest posterior probability. The Bayesian specification of the family of allowable models also ensures contextual knowledge is made explicit in the form of the prior distribution over said model space. Our implementation of a reversible jump sampler for monotonic polynomials is available at https://github.com/hhau/rjmonopoly.

Notationally, in this section, the Markov chain is assumed to be at time point t and in the polynomial model of degree $q^{[t]}$. The proposed values for the following time point are indicated by an asterisk $(\boldsymbol{\theta}^*, q^*)$, and a prime symbol is used to indicate if the proposal exists in a different dimension to that of the previous value $(\boldsymbol{\theta}^{*'}, q^{*'})$. That is to say that $\boldsymbol{\theta}^{*'}$ has a higher/lower number of elements than $\boldsymbol{\theta}^{[t]}$, and $q^{*'} \neq q^{[t]}$. Note that $\boldsymbol{\theta}$ is a generic parameter vector that is assumed to contain all the parameters in that model, excluding the degree of the current and proposed models.

9.4.1 Model specification

Before implementing an RJMCMC sampling scheme, we must explicitly define the set of models under consideration. In our case, the set of models of interest are the monotonic polynomials of degree $q_{\min}$ to $q_{\max}$, and this section discusses the likelihood, priors, and corresponding posterior expression for these models.

9.4.1.1 Likelihood expression

As we are fundamentally performing only univariate polynomial regression, the likelihood term is relatively simple, and we can express it in terms of the orthonormal design matrix. We write the distributional statement for a given polynomial degree as

$$\boldsymbol{Y} \sim \mathrm{N}\left(\mathbf{Q}\boldsymbol{\gamma}, \sigma_y^2 \mathcal{I}_q\right) \tag{9.12}$$

and the likelihood as

$$\begin{aligned}\Pr\left(\boldsymbol{Y} \mid \boldsymbol{\theta}, q\right) &= \Pr\left(\boldsymbol{Y} \mid q, \boldsymbol{\gamma}, \sigma_y^2\right) \\ &= \left(\sqrt{2\pi\sigma_y^2}\right)^{-n/2} \exp\left\{-\frac{1}{2\sigma_y^2}\left(\boldsymbol{Y} - \mathbf{Q}\boldsymbol{\gamma}\right)^{\mathrm{T}}\left(\boldsymbol{Y} - \mathbf{Q}\boldsymbol{\gamma}\right)\right\}. \end{aligned} \tag{9.13}$$

Note that we include q in the likelihood term, as the number of columns of $\mathbf{Q}$ and the size of $\boldsymbol{\gamma}$ depend on it.

9.4.1.2 Prior specification

Regression coefficient prior

The prior for the regression parameters and the noise of the data are the same as in Section 9.3. We again use the product of a weakly informative normal prior with a monotonic indicator function as the prior for $\boldsymbol{\gamma}$, i.e.

$$\boldsymbol{\gamma} \sim \mathrm{N}\left(\mathbf{0}_{q+1}, 10^2 I_{q+1}\right) \cdot \mathbb{I}\{\boldsymbol{\gamma} \in \Omega(a, b)\}. \tag{9.14}$$

Of course, this is not strictly the same prior as in (9.2), as the number of elements in $\mathbf{0}_{q+1}$ and I_{q+1} can vary across models.

Variance prior

We again use an $\mathrm{N}_{+}(0, 1^2)$ prior on the variance σ_y^2, which is weakly informative as long as the data are rescaled. Explicitly,

$$\sigma_y^2 \sim \mathrm{N}_{+}(0, 1^2). \tag{9.15}$$

Polynomial degree prior

As the polynomial degree is a parameter of interest, it too must have a prior distribution. As we limit the support of q to be the inclusive set of integers between $q_{\min}$ and $q_{\max}$, our prior must also be defined on this support. In practice we do this by generating a prior that appropriately represents our knowledge on $\{0, \ldots, q_{\max}\}$ and then remove the terms corresponding to degrees less than $d_{\min}$. A flat prior over the set of permissible polynomial degrees can be used, although this is typically inappropriate as one usually has some idea of how much flexibility the regression curve requires. As such, the `rjmonopoly` implementation allows for a binomial prior option, where the probability parameter η of said binomial distribution is used as a control parameter, which allows us to express our knowledge about the prior likelihood of higher/lower polynomial degrees. Explicitly,

$$q \sim \mathrm{Bin}_{[q_{\min}, q_{\max}]}(q_{\max}, \eta), \tag{9.16}$$

where $\mathrm{Bin}_{[q_{\min}, q_{\max}]}$ indicates a truncated binomial distribution over the set of positive integers $\{q_{\min}, \ldots, q_{\max}\}$. Normalising this prior distribution is unnecessary, as the normalising constants drop out in the acceptance probability calculation. Note that the `rjmonopoly` implementation currently assumes that $q_{\max} - q_{\min} \geq 2$.

9.4.1.3 Posterior expression

Combining the likelihood with the prior distributions gives us the proportional posterior, i.e.

$$\Pr(q, \boldsymbol{\gamma}, \sigma_y^2, \mid \mathbf{Y}) \propto \left(2\pi\sigma_y^2\right)^{-n/2} \exp\left\{-\frac{1}{2\sigma_y^2}\left(\mathbf{Y} - \mathbf{Q}\boldsymbol{\gamma}\right)^{\top}\left(\mathbf{Y} - \mathbf{Q}\boldsymbol{\gamma}\right)\right\} \cdot \exp\left\{-\frac{1}{2 \cdot 100^2}\boldsymbol{\gamma}^{\top}\boldsymbol{\gamma}\right\} \cdot \mathbb{I}\{\boldsymbol{\gamma} \in \Omega(a, b)\} \tag{9.17}$$

$$\cdot \exp\left\{-\frac{1}{2}\left(\sigma_{\gamma}^{2}\right)^{2}\right\}$$
$$\cdot \binom{q_{\max}}{q} (\eta)^{q} (1-\eta)^{q_{\max}-q},$$

where $\boldsymbol{\gamma} \subset \mathbb{R}^{q+1}$, $\sigma_{\gamma}^{2} \subset \mathbb{R}^{+}$ and $q \in \{q_{\min}, \ldots, q_{\max}\}$.

9.4.2 Sampling from the posterior distribution

Given the complete specification of our family of models, we can start to implement an RJMCMC scheme to sample from the posterior distribution of interest. We will specify appropriate proposal distributions for each of the parameters of interest, and discuss the acceptance probability calculation.

9.4.2.1 Dimension proposal

We specify upper and lower bounds for the proposal distribution of the degree of the polynomial, based on the prior values for $q_{\min}$ and $q_{\max}$. This is to ensure that the Markov chain in polynomial-degree space is neither initialised in an inadmissible region (according to the prior), nor proposes polynomial degrees with zero prior mass. For example, we should never propose polynomials of degree smaller than $q_{\min}$. The existence of a $q_{\max}$ also allows for straightforward generation of initial values, which will be discussed in Section 9.4.2.2.

When the Markov chain is in either the maximum or the minimum dimension space, the proposal for q^* is a discrete uniform distribution on that current dimension and the dimension immediately lower or higher than it, respectively. When not in the maximum or minimum dimension states, the proposal is a discrete uniform distribution on its current dimension and the dimensions immediately above and below it. This distribution is best explained by the code used to generate proposals from it, which is shown in Fig. 9.5. This simple proposal distribution admits a straightforward term to the proposal ratio in the acceptance probability expression. It is 1 if the previous degree and proposed degree are not $q_{\max}$ or $q_{\min}$, and it is $\frac{3}{2}$ or $\frac{2}{3}$ if either the proposed or previous degree are.

9.4.2.2 Regression coefficient proposal

As discussed in Section 9.2, we define our models in terms of the orthogonal regression coefficients $\boldsymbol{\gamma}$. This is advantageous as all the coefficients are orthogonal to each other, and as such a random walk with diagonal covariance matrix can be used to produce acceptable proposals. In the monomial

```
dimProposer <- function(q_current, q_min, q_max) {
  if (q_current < q_min | q_current > q_max) {
   stop("current dimension is outside of allowed bounds")
  }

  if (q_current == q_min) {
    res <- sample(x = c(q_current, q_current + 1), size = 1)

  } else if (q_current == q_max) {
    res <- sample(x = c(q_current, q_current - 1), size = 1)

  } else {
    res <- sample(x = c(q_current - 1, q_current, q_current + 1),
                  size = 1)
  }

  return(res)
}
```

Figure 9.5 The R code that proposes a new polynomial degree.

space this would not be true, as the covariance structure for all $\boldsymbol{\beta}$ coefficients is hard to determine, and the probable values of $\boldsymbol{\beta}$ would also change considerably each time the degree of the polynomial changed.

When the proposed dimension is the same as that of the previous dimension, generating the proposal for the regression coefficients is straightforward:

$$\boldsymbol{\gamma}^* \sim \mathrm{N}\left(\boldsymbol{\gamma}^{[t]}, \sigma^2_{\gamma,\text{innov}} \mathcal{I}_{q^{[t]}+1}\right), \tag{9.18}$$

where $\sigma^2_{\gamma,\text{innov}}$ is the innovation variance associated with the proposal distribution of $\boldsymbol{\gamma}$, and $\mathcal{I}_{q+1}$ is the $(q+1) \times (q+1)$ identity matrix.

When the proposed dimension does not match the current dimension, things are more difficult. Consider a proposed dimension one greater than the previous dimension, $q^{*'} = q^{[t]} + 1$. We could use a random walk proposal for the first $q^{[t]} + 1$ components of $\boldsymbol{\gamma}^{*'}$; however, the $((q)^{*'} + 1)$th component does not exist in $\boldsymbol{\gamma}^{[t]}$. As such we need a different proposal distribution for this specific coefficient. It would be preferable to use a random walk with mean equal to the value of the last time we were in the $q^{*'}$ space, i.e.

$$\gamma^{*'}_{q^{*'}} \sim \mathrm{N}\left(\gamma^{[s]}_{q^{*'}}, \sigma^2_{\gamma,\text{innov}}\right),$$

where s is the time point where the chain was last in state $q^{*'}$. However, as this depends upon a time point prior to $t-1$ it constructs a sampling scheme that is no longer Markovian, and as such breaks the detailed balance required for the Metropolis–Hastings algorithm. As a result, we use an independent proposal for $\gamma^{*'}_{q^{*'}+1}$, with a very particular mean to ensure it proposes in the right region of the parameter space. To obtain this mean we first fit a polynomial of degree $q_{\max}$ using either [10] or the `R` package `MonoPoly` by [17]. The estimates for $\boldsymbol{\beta}$ are then converted to their corresponding orthonormal coefficients $\boldsymbol{\gamma}$ for use as means of independent proposal distributions. Mathematically,

$$\boldsymbol{\gamma}^{*'} \sim \mathrm{N}\left(\left[\boldsymbol{\gamma}^{[t]}, \mu_{\gamma,q^{*'}+1}\right]^{\top}, \sigma^2_{\gamma,\text{innov}} \mathcal{I}_{q^{*'}+1}\right), \tag{9.19}$$

where $\mu_{\gamma,q^{*'}+1}$ includes the $(q^{*'}+1)$th component of the aforementioned initial $q_{\max}$ fit. There is an acceptance probability implication of this choice, as the independently proposed term no longer cancels in the ratio of proposal distributions. This will be discussed in more detail in Section 9.4.3.

9.4.2.3 *Variance proposal*

We use a log-normal random walk to propose values for $(\sigma^2)^*$, i.e.

$$(\sigma^2_\gamma)^* \sim \mathrm{Log-normal}\left(\mathrm{Log}((\sigma^2_\gamma)^{[t]}), \sigma^2_{\sigma^2,\text{innov}}\right), \tag{9.20}$$

as we need the value of σ^2_γ to remain positive.

9.4.3 Acceptance probability

The generic form of the acceptance probability is a combination of the standard Metropolis–Hastings algorithm and the necessary reversible jump terms, presented in [4]. Note that $\mathrm{Q}(\cdot)$ here represents the proposal distribution for the quantity enclosed within it. We use $\alpha^*(\cdot)$ to denote the acceptance quantity prior to the application of the $\min\{1,\cdot\}$ operation, after which we denote the produced acceptance probability with $\alpha(\cdot)$. This general form can be written as

$$\begin{aligned}\alpha^*\left(\left(q^{*'},\boldsymbol{\theta}^{*'}\right),\left(q^{[t]},\boldsymbol{\theta}^{[t]}\right)\right) &= \frac{\mathrm{L}(\boldsymbol{\theta}^{*'}\mid \boldsymbol{Y})}{\mathrm{L}(\boldsymbol{\theta}^{[t]}\mid \boldsymbol{Y})}\cdot\frac{\mathrm{Pr}(\boldsymbol{\theta}^{*'})}{\mathrm{Pr}(\boldsymbol{\theta}^{[t]})}\cdot\frac{\mathrm{Q}(\boldsymbol{\theta}^{[t]}\mid\boldsymbol{\theta}^{*'})}{\mathrm{Q}(\boldsymbol{\theta}^{*'}\mid\boldsymbol{\theta}^{[t]})}\cdot\\ &\quad\frac{\mathrm{Q}(q^{*'}\to q^{[t]})}{\mathrm{Q}(q^{[t]}\to q^{*'})}\cdot\frac{1}{\mathrm{Q}_{q^{[t]}\to q^{*'}}(u)}\cdot\left|\frac{\partial g_{q^{[t]}\to q^{*'}}(\boldsymbol{\theta}^*_{1:q^{[t]}},u)}{\partial(\boldsymbol{\theta}^*_{1:q^{[t]}},u)}\right|,\end{aligned} \tag{9.21}$$

$$\alpha\left(\left(q^{*'},\boldsymbol{\theta}^{*'}\right),\left(q^{[t]},\boldsymbol{\theta}^{[t]}\right)\right)=\min\left\{1,\alpha^{*}\left(\left(q^{*'},\boldsymbol{\theta}^{*'}\right),\left(q^{[t]},\boldsymbol{\theta}^{[t]}\right)\right)\right\}, \tag{9.22}$$

the terms of which we will now elaborate on.

Consider the previous state of the Markov chain $(q^{[t]}, \boldsymbol{\theta}^{[t]})$ with a proposed degree and state of $(q^{*'}, \boldsymbol{\theta}^{*'})$, where $q^{*'} = q^{[t]} + 1$, in line with our proposal distribution for q^*. Such a proposal would contain a proposed value for the $(q^{*'} + 1)$th coefficient of $\boldsymbol{\gamma}$, which we can think of as the extra random realisation needed to make the number of random objects *match* the proposed dimension. This realisation is denoted u in the acceptance probability. In this manner, u contributes to the acceptance probability not only in the Metropolis–Hastings proposal term, the third term in (9.21), but also in the $Q_{q^{[t]}\to q^{*'}}(u)$ term. We also require a specific definition for the function that maps the combination of the previous state and u to the proposed state, i.e.

$$g_{q^{[t]}\to q^{*'}}(\boldsymbol{\theta}^{[t]}, u)=\begin{bmatrix}\boldsymbol{\theta}^{[t]}\\ 0\end{bmatrix}+\begin{bmatrix}\mathbf{0}\\ u\end{bmatrix}. \tag{9.23}$$

It is for this reason the sixth and final term in the acceptance probability is written as a function of the first $q^{[t]}$ components of our proposal *and* the component corresponding to u.

The remaining terms fall out naturally now, as the term which concerns the dimension proposal is typically 1, and it only differs when we either are in or propose to be in $q_{\max}$ or $q_{\min}$. The parameter proposal term (third term) contains the log-normal σ^2 proposal and the independent proposal for u. The prior term and likelihood term are evaluated with respect to the distributions discussed in previous sections. For implementation details, please see the package source available at https://github.com/hhau/rjmonopoly.

The above strictly only considers moves where $q^{*'} = q^{[t]}+1$ and $q^{*'} = q^{[t]}$. Moves from $q^{[t]}$ to $q^{*'} = q^{[t]} - 1$ are accepted with probability, i.e.

$$\alpha\left(\left(q^{*'},\boldsymbol{\theta}^{*'}\right),\left(q^{[t]},\boldsymbol{\theta}^{[t]}\right)\right)=\min\left\{1,\alpha^{*}\left(\left(q^{[t]},\boldsymbol{\theta}^{[t]}\right),\left(q^{*'},\boldsymbol{\theta}^{*'}\right)\right)^{-1}\right\}, \tag{9.24}$$

noting the swap in the order of the arguments to $\alpha^*(\cdot)$. Calculating the acceptance probability in this manner is a very explicit use of the detailed balance assumption, as it tells us that the probability of moving from q to $q-1$ is the same as the inverse of the move from $q-1$ to q, i.e. $\Pr(q \to q-1) =$

$\Pr(q-1 \to q)^{-1}$. However, we must again consider the monotonicity constraint, as nonmonotonic proposals will have $\alpha^*(\cdot) = 0$, which would lead to $\alpha(\cdot) = 1$, unless we check our monotonicity indicator after the inversion.

9.4.3.1 Summary

A summary of the RJMCMC scheme detailed in this section is presented in Algorithm 2.

Input : $\mathbf{Y}, \mathbf{Q}, q^{[0]}, \boldsymbol{\gamma}^{[0]}, (\sigma_\gamma^2)^{[0]}, \sigma^2_{\gamma,\text{innov}}, \sigma^2_{\sigma^2,\text{innov}}$
for $t \leftarrow 0$ **to** $N_{MCMC} - 1$ **do**
  Propose q^* according to Section 9.4.2.1;
  Propose $\boldsymbol{\gamma}^{*'}$ using q^* by (9.19);
  Propose $(\sigma_\gamma^2)^*$ by (9.20);
  Compute $\alpha\left(\left(q^{*'}, \boldsymbol{\theta}^{*'}\right), \left(q^{[t]}, \boldsymbol{\theta}^{[t]}\right)\right)$ via (9.21) and (9.22);
  Simulate $u \sim \text{Unif}(0, 1)$;
  if $u_1 <$ **then**
    $q^{[t+1]}, \boldsymbol{\gamma}^{[t+1]}, (\sigma_\gamma^2)^{[t+1]} \leftarrow q^*, \boldsymbol{\gamma}^{*'}, (\sigma_\gamma^2)^*$;
  else
    $q^{[t+1]}, \boldsymbol{\gamma}^{[t+1]}, (\sigma_\gamma^2)^{[t+1]} \leftarrow q^{[t]}, \boldsymbol{\gamma}^{[t]}, (\sigma_\gamma^2)^{[t]}$;
  end
end

Algorithm 2: Summary of the RJMCMC sampler.

9.4.4 Simulated data examples

This section contains several simulated data exercises, which are performed to test the model and implementation to ensure that known quantities can be appropriately estimated. It also explores the relationship between the posterior distribution of the polynomial degree and data size and variance. It should be noted that polynomials have few defining features as their degree increases. Either the number of turning/inflection points increases, or the duration at which the polynomial appears 'flat' increases. As we are concerned with monotonicity, polynomials with turning points inside the region of interest are inappropriate objects of study. Instead we focus on cases with large 'flat' regions, such as in Example 9.4.4.1, or with a distinct number of inflection points, such as in Example 9.4.4.2.

9.4.4.1 The relationship between noise and estimated degree

We quantify the relationship between the quantity of noise added to the true data generating process and the estimated polynomial degree. This exercise is performed with 1000 x-values between 0 and 1 and uses the polynomial $\mathrm{p}(x) = 2 + (2x - 1)^{11} + 1.5x$ with a varying amount of noise added. The motivation for the additional linear term is to move the true polynomial sufficiently far away from the boundary of monotonic space, in order to avoid the numerical inefficiencies induced by high posterior correlation and high rejection rates due to the proximity of the posterior to the boundary of allowable coefficient values.

Fig. 9.6 shows that as we decrease the magnitude of the added noise, the polynomial degree increases towards the true polynomial degree. This is to be expected, as adding noise sufficiently blurs the location of the start and end of the 'flat' sections of the true polynomial, and as such it can be appropriately modelled by a lower-degree polynomial. We also see the posterior distribution appropriately favours odd-degree polynomials, particularly in Fig. 9.6D, where degree 9 and 7 are preferable to degree 8. This is again unsurprising given the fundamentally different asymptotic behaviour in even- and odd-degree polynomials, and the manner in which that affects the polynomial's ability to fit the data.

When fitting regression models to comparatively noise-free data, such as in Figs 9.6G and 9.6H, the choice of tuning parameters, specifically the innovation variances, becomes paramount. This is because the minimal noise added to the data manifests itself not only as a relative certainty of a small estimate for σ_y^2, but also in the relatively precise nature in which we know $\boldsymbol{\gamma}$. As such, we need to considerably reduce the innovation variance for $\boldsymbol{\gamma}$, and not just the innovation variance for σ_y^2, as one might intuitively expect.

We can compare the polynomial-degree estimates above to the estimates obtained using the 'm out of n' bootstrap methodology presented in [12]. This bootstrap approach proceeds by drawing m samples (with replacement) from the n observations, fitting all permissible polynomial degrees to the sampled data, and using the nonsampled data as a predictive validation set. This constitutes one iteration of the bootstrap, and in each iteration the polynomial degree with the lowest prediction error is selected. The result, presented in Fig. 9.7, was produced using 100 iterations for each value of m. Reassuringly, the results from this are broadly similar to those of the reversible jump sampler. There are minor differences for a given level of

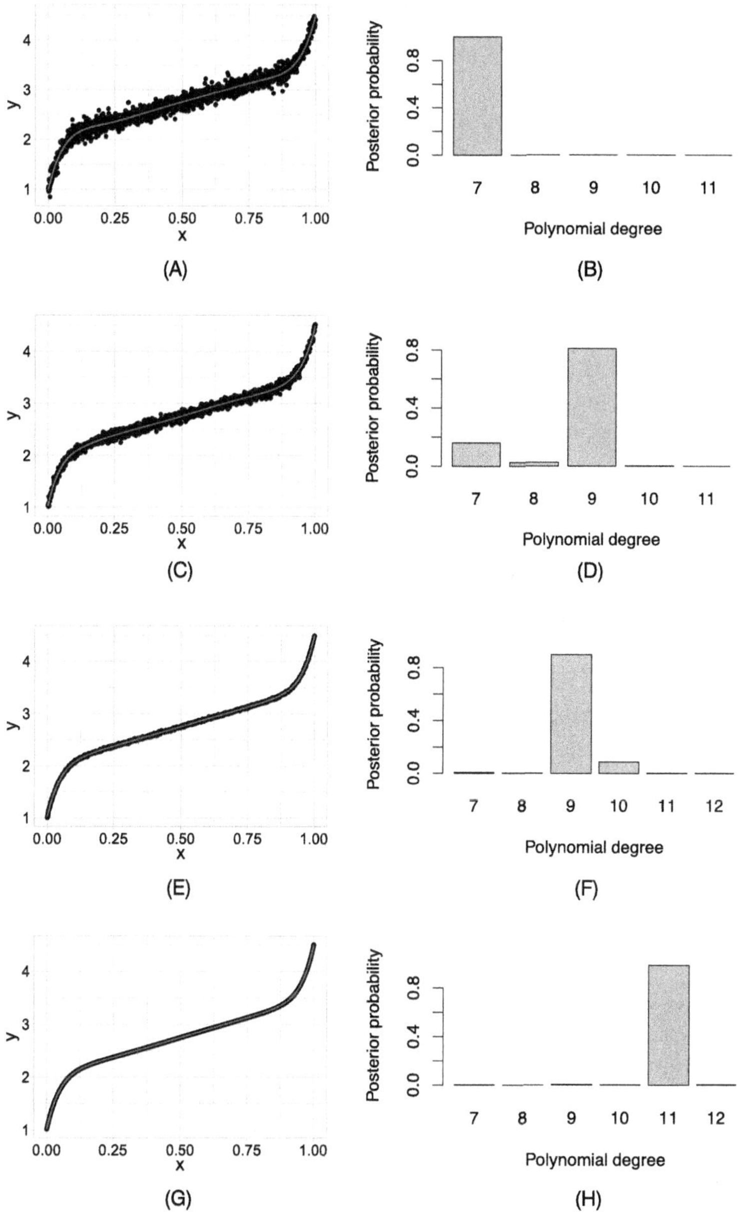

Figure 9.6 Simulation results using the reversible jump sampler, where the true polynomial is $p(x) = 2 + (2x - 1)^{11} + 1.5x$, with $N(0, \sigma^2)$ noise. (A) Fit for $\sigma = 0.1$, (B) Degree posterior distribution for $\sigma = 0.1$, (C) Fit for $\sigma = 0.05$, (D) Degree posterior distribution for $\sigma = 0.05$, (E) Fit for $\sigma = 0.01$, (F) Degree posterior distribution for $\sigma = 0.01$, (G) Fit for $\sigma = 0.0001$, (H) Degree posterior distribution for $\sigma = 0.0001$.

noise, where the '*m* out of *n*' bootstrap appears to favour slightly higher-degree polynomials. For example, in Fig. 9.7C, the bootstrap suggests a polynomial of at least degree 10, whereas the comparable reversible jump result in Fig. 9.6F is very good for degree 9. This may be due to the difference in parameterisations, as the bootstrap methodology makes use of the parameterisation discussed in [12]. However, this is a very minor difference, as one would not expect the posterior distribution to perfectly match the sampling distribution induced by a mean squared error-based prediction metric. The only considerable difference in the two methodologies is in the run-time, where the reversible jump sampler has an advantage in this scenario. Each of the images in Fig. 9.7 took approximately 10 minutes to generate, using 100 bootstrap iterations for each *m*. Each row in Fig. 9.6 was produced in approximately 20 seconds on the same hardware using the reversible jump sampler, using a chain length of 50,000. This is not surprising, as the bootstrap has to fit all possible polynomial degrees at each iteration, whereas the reversible jump sampler only ends up sampling degrees according to the posterior distribution of the polynomial degree. As such, it can avoid fitting high-degree polynomials in data sets where they are not required.

9.4.4.2 The relationship between the number of data points and estimated degree

To explore this relationship, we assume the underlying polynomial is the following:

$$\mathrm{p}(x) = 12 + \frac{1}{500}\left(-225.24x^3 + 89.48x^4 - 13.72x^5 + 0.93x^6 - 0.02x^7\right), \tag{9.25}$$

which subsequently has normally distributed noise, with zero mean and standard deviation 0.5, added to it. We generate values for x that range between 0 and 12. As opposed to having a large 'flat' section like the previous example, this monotonic polynomial has a specific number of inflection points. The method with which we derive the polynomial in (9.25) is of note and consists of the following steps. We begin by specifying the second derivative of the polynomial via its roots, i.e.

$$\mathrm{p}''(x) = (-x)(x - 2.4)(x - 5.7)(x - 8.9)(x - 11.1),$$

which we then expand into a monomial basis form, i.e.

$$\mathrm{p}''(x) = -1351.45x + 1073.80x^2 - 274.47x^3 + 28.1x^4 - x^5.$$

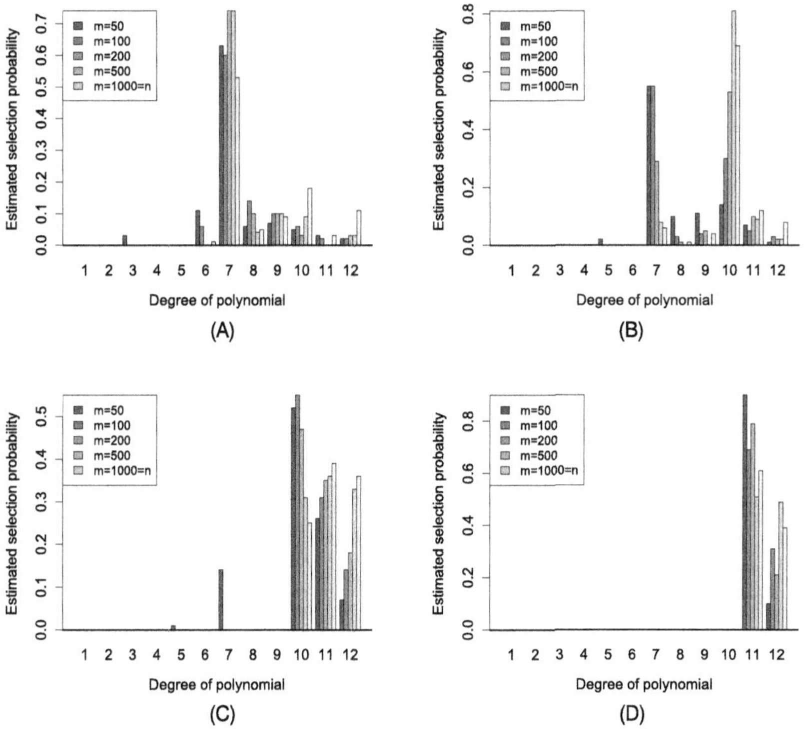

Figure 9.7 Simulation results using the '*m* out of *n*' bootstrap methodology, where the true polynomial is $p(x) = 2 + (2x - 1)^{11} + 1.5x$, with $N(0, \sigma^2)$ noise. (A) Probability of degree selection for $\sigma = 0.1$, (B) Probability of degree selection for $\sigma = 0.05$, (C) Probability of degree selection for $\sigma = 0.01$, (D) Probability of degree selection for $\sigma = 0.0001$.

Then we integrate twice to arrive at the following final monomial basis coefficients:

$$
\begin{aligned}
p'(x) &= -675.72x^2 + 357.93x^3 - 68.18x^4 + 5.62x^4 - 1.67x^6, \\
p(x) &= -225.24x^3 + 89.48x^4 - 13.72x^5 + 0.93x^6 - 0.02x^7.
\end{aligned}
$$

Finally, the polynomial was rescaled and shifted for use as a comparative model in the dental application detailed in [12], which also has the added benefit of rendering the region of interest on a more natural scale.

Repeated X-values

We consider an example with a fixed number of possible x-values, with either 3 or 9 measurements at each of the 13 distinct integer values. The posterior of the polynomial degree and the fit using the posterior mode are displayed in Fig. 9.8. The trend is as expected, in that our ability to estimate the appropriate degree, and our corresponding certainty of said estimate, increases as the number of data points per x-value increases. Fig. 9.8D is a good example of typical sampler behaviour in the presence of a comparatively 'flat' posterior for the polynomial degree, and it is reassuring to see the sampler is capable of exploring a wide variety of possible polynomial degrees under fixed values for the tuning parameters.

Unique X-values

We now consider the same number of data points as in the previous example, but distributed across unique x-values instead. Fig. 9.9 contains the corresponding output, and the pattern is unsurprisingly similar. Of interest in this exercise is the apparent bimodality of the posterior distribution for the polynomial degree visible in Fig. 9.9D. This demonstrates the sampler's ability to move between modes. If such behaviour is observed in a real-world scenario, the sampler should be run for considerably longer, in order to ensure the posterior modes have the appropriate number of samples drawn from them.

9.4.5 Child growth data

In this chapter we have entirely focused on data sets consisting of one individual, that is, one set of $(\boldsymbol{X}, \boldsymbol{Y})$'s. However, in a hierarchical modelling setting, the data set of interest typically consists of a number of individuals. The manner in which we should apply our method for model selection to such a data set is not obvious. We could naively combine all individuals to form one large pair of $(\boldsymbol{X}, \boldsymbol{Y})$'s; however, this typically results in the selection of a polynomial degree that is too low, as it is fundamentally incorrect to combine subject-specific measures in this manner. Instead we can rely on the speed of our implementation, and the functional nature of our `R` package, to quickly estimate the appropriate degree for each individual, which can then be used to select the appropriate degree for hierarchical models, such as in [1] and Chapter 3 of [9].

We include the following section, which consists of descriptions around code snippets, to demonstrate the relative ease with which we can switch from single individuals to whole data sets. It also serves as an illustrative example of the `rjmonopoly` package for potential future users. The fact that the code is available in an `R` package makes this task considerably easier,

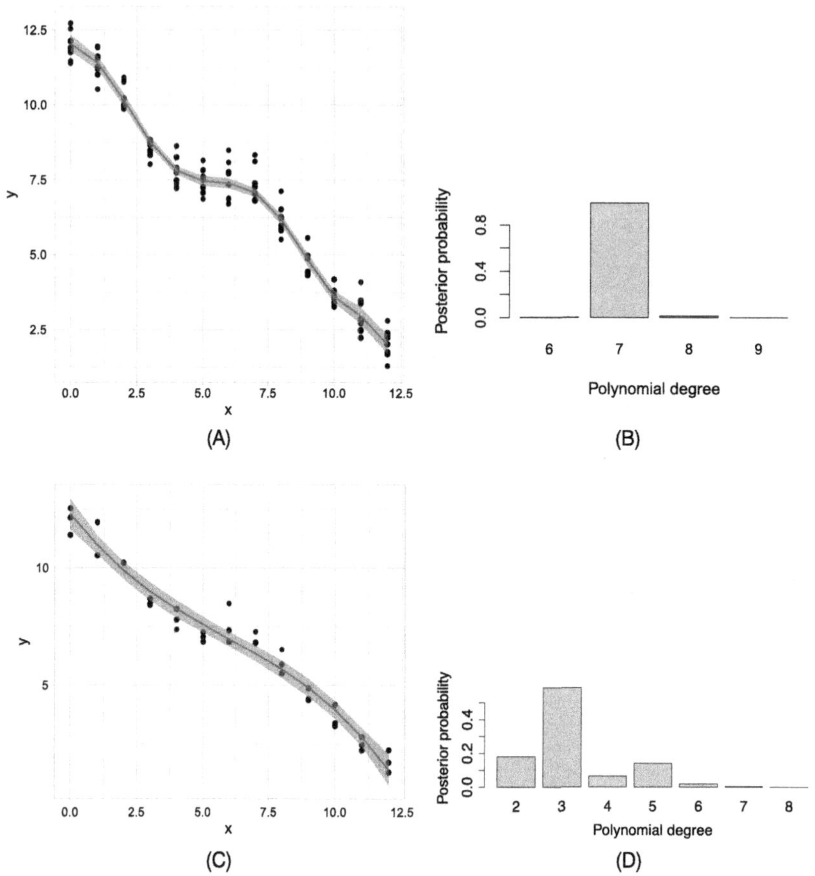

Figure 9.8 Simulation results for a varying number of data points per *nonunique* x-value for the polynomial $p(x) = 12 + \frac{1}{500}\left(-225.24x^3 + 89.48x^4 - 13.72x^5 + 0.93x^6 - 0.02x^7\right)$. (A) Fit for 9 points per x-value, (B) Degree posterior distribution for 9 points per x-value, (C) Fit for 3 points per x-value, (D) Degree posterior distribution (for initial 750,000 posterior samples) for 3 points per x-value.

and we only have to be familiar with the `apply` family of functions within base `R`. Consider the following snippet:

```
library(rjmonopoly); library(fda)
library(ggplot2); library(gridExtra); library(knitr)

func_applicator <- function(y, x = growth$age, ...) {
```

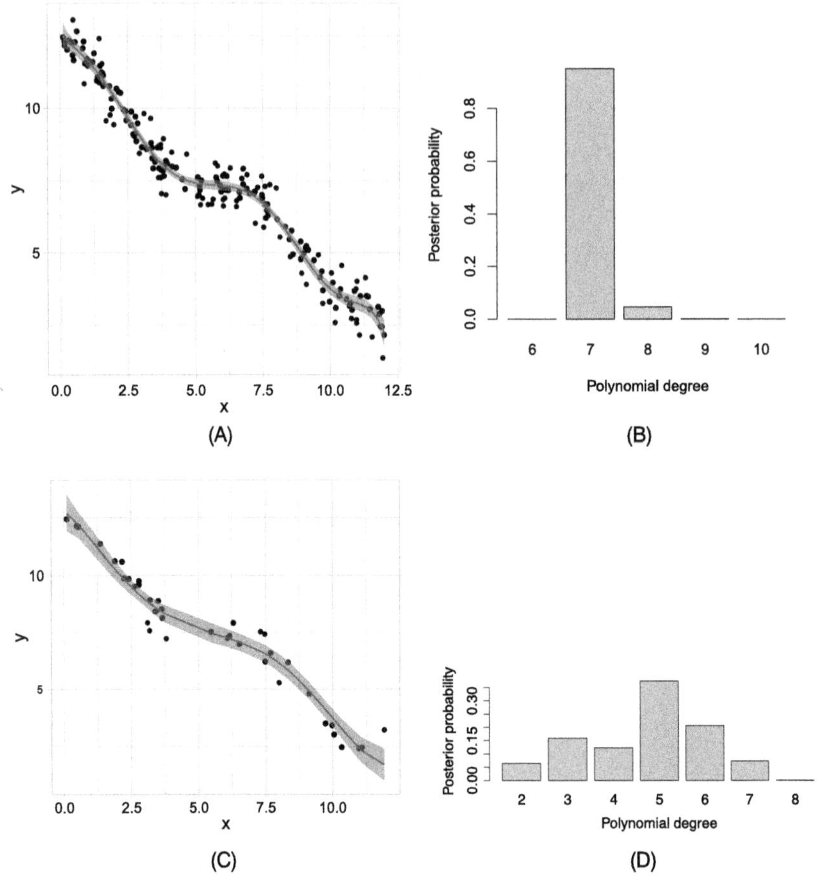

Figure 9.9 Simulation results for a varying number of data points per *unique* x-value for $p(x) = 12 + \frac{1}{500}\left(-225.24x^3 + 89.48x^4 - 13.72x^5 + 0.93x^6 - 0.02x^7\right)$. (A) Fit for 195 unique x-values, (B) Degree posterior distribution for 195 unique x-values, (C) Fit for 39 unique x-values, (D) Degree posterior distribution (for initial 250,000 samples) for 39 unique x-values.

```
res <- rjmonopoly::rjmonopoly(x = x, y = y,
         d_min = 5, d_max = 12, # tuning params
         prior_prob = 0.5,
         starting_var_val = 5e-5,
         control = list(
           innov_sd_var = 0.001,
           innov_sd_beta = 0.001
```

```
            )
          )
    return(res)
}

y_mat <- growth$hgtm
res_list <- apply(y_mat, 2, function(X) func_applicator(y = X))
```

Here, we have applied our RJMCMC sampler to every male individual in the `growth` data set of the `fda` package [14]. We can then quickly perform inference at the level of the whole data set. Note that we have adjusted some of the sampler's tuning parameters in order to produce samples with acceptable diagnostics, including, but not limited to, traceplots and minimum effective sample sizes. In the following snippet, we thin the output and inspect the fitted curves for every individual[1]:

```
res_list <- lapply(res_list, function(X) {
    rjmonopoly::thin(X, thin_period = 50, warm_up = 500)
  })

fit_plots <- lapply(res_list, rjmonopoly::plotFit)
gridExtra::marrangeGrob(fit_plots, ncol = 4, nrow = 10)
```

We can also quickly inspect the polynomial-degree posterior for each individual:

```
lapply(res_list, function(x) {
  rjmonopoly::plotDegreePost(x, only = "barplot")
})
```

Although this is not always ideal, as 39 barplots might be somewhat visually overwhelming, it does enable the quick visual identification of any individuals in our data set whose degree posterior is distinct. Alternatively, we could take one step back and consider the empirical distribution of the degree selected for each individual. Here, we use the 99% quantile of each individual's polynomial-degree posterior as our selection rule, so that we

[1] The plots produced from the following snippets are not presented here, as fixed width and height noninteractive conglomerates of subplots are not ideal for the printed format.

do not unnecessarily restrict the flexibility of any models we may choose to fit subsequently:

```
selected_degrees <- unlist(lapply(res_list, function(X) {
  quantile(X$d_samples, 0.99)
}))
knitr::kable(as.data.frame(table(selected_degrees)))
```

Table 9.1 The selected polynomial degrees from all males in the *growth* data set of the `fda` package.

Selected degree	Frequency	Probability
6	1	0.03
7	4	0.10
8	26	0.67
9	8	0.21

The output of Table 9.1 would lead us to select a degree of 9 for our hierarchical model in Chapter 3 of [9], or the model detailed in [1], as a substantial number of individuals in the data set have a selected degree of 9, and we lose some model flexibility to the hierarchical structure.

9.5 Conclusion

In this chapter we have demonstrated methods to perform shape-constrained regression and covariate selection, specifically in the context of monotonic polynomials. In doing so, we have highlighted some computational techniques for MCMC, which increase the effectiveness of our methodology. These techniques include (i) using the QR decomposition of the design matrix, (ii) proposing possible values for the regression coefficients using MALA and (iii) using RJMCMC for the purposes of covariate selection in the presence of shape constraints. These techniques are demonstrated on a number of simulated and real data sets, and the results could be further used to inform modelling decisions in larger, hierarchical models.

References

[1] J.J. Bon, K. Murray, B.A. Turlach, Fitting monotone polynomials in mixed effects models, Statistics and Computing 29 (1) (2019) 79–98, https://doi.org/10.1007/s11222-017-9797-8.

[2] C.D. Elphinstone, A target distribution model for non-parametric density estimation, Communications in Statistics - Theory and Methods 12 (2) (1983) 161–198, https://doi.org/10.1080/03610928308828450.
[3] P.L. Emerson, Numerical construction of orthogonal polynomials from a general recurrence formula, Biometrics 24 (3) (1968) 695–701, http://www.jstor.org/stable/2528328.
[4] Y. Fan, S.A. Sisson, Reversible jump MCMC, in: S. Brooks, A. Gelman, G. Jones, X. Meng (Eds.), Handbook of Markov Chain Monte Carlo, Chapman & Hall/CRC Handbooks of Modern Statistical Methods, CRC Press, 2011, pp. 67–91, chapter 3.
[5] G. Forsythe, Generation and use of orthogonal polynomials for data-fitting with a digital computer, Journal of the Society for Industrial and Applied Mathematics 5 (2) (1957) 74–88, https://doi.org/10.1137/0105007.
[6] P.J. Green, Reversible jump Markov chain Monte Carlo computation and Bayesian model determination, Biometrika 82 (4) (1995) 711–732, https://doi.org/10.1093/biomet/82.4.711.
[7] D.M. Hawkins, Fitting monotonic polynomials to data, Computational Statistics 9 (3) (1994) 233–247.
[8] B.K. Mallick, Bayesian curve estimation by polynomial of random order, Journal of Statistical Planning and Inference 70 (1) (1998) 91–109, https://doi.org/10.1016/S0378-3758(97)00179-1.
[9] A. Manderson, Methodology for Bayesian Monotonic Polynomials, Master's thesis, The University of Western Australia, 2018.
[10] A.A. Manderson, E. Cripps, K. Murray, B.A. Turlach, Monotone polynomials using BUGS and Stan, Australian & New Zealand Journal of Statistics 59 (4) (2017) 353–370, https://doi.org/10.1111/anzs.12207.
[11] K. Murray, S. Müller, B.A. Turlach, Revisiting fitting monotone polynomials to data, Computational Statistics 28 (5) (2013) 1989–2005, https://doi.org/10.1007/s00180-012-0390-5.
[12] K. Murray, S. Müller, B.A. Turlach, Fast and flexible methods for monotone polynomial fitting, Journal of Statistical Computation and Simulation 86 (15) (2016) 2946–2966, https://doi.org/10.1080/00949655.2016.1139582.
[13] P. Neal, G. Roberts, Optimal scaling for partially updating MCMC algorithms, The Annals of Applied Probability 16 (2) (2006) 475–515, https://doi.org/10.1214/105051605000000791.
[14] J.O. Ramsay, H. Wickham, S. Graves, G. Hooker, fda: functional data analysis, R package version 2.4.4, https://CRAN.R-project.org/package=fda, 2014.
[15] R.A. Thisted, Elements of Statistical Computing: Numerical Computation, Taylor & Francis, 1988.
[16] R. Tuddenham, M. Snyder, Physical Growth of California Boys and Girls From Birth to Eighteen Years, Publications in child development, University of California Press, 1954.
[17] B.A. Turlach, K. Murray, MonoPoly: functions to fit monotone polynomials, R package version 0.3-8, http://cloud.r-project.org/package=MonoPoly, 2016.
[18] Y.K. Wong, An application of orthogonalization process to the theory of least squares, The Annals of Mathematical Statistics 6 (2) (1935) 53–75, http://www.jstor.org/stable/2957660.

Index

D

W